LEARNING RESOURCES CTR/NEW ENGLAND TECH.
GEN   D231.P64 1987
Politics and culture in ea

3 0147 0001 1760 9

D 231 .P64 1987

Politics and culture in
early modern Europe

DATE DUE

DEMCO 38-297

NEW ENGLAND INS
OF TECHNOLOGY
LEARNING RESOURCES CENTER

S0-BAQ-547

POLITICS AND CULTURE IN
EARLY MODERN EUROPE

H. G. KOENIGSBERGER

Photos by Guy E. Wells

NEW ENGLAND INSTITUTE
OF TECHNOLOGY
LEARNING RESOURCES CENTER

POLITICS AND CULTURE IN EARLY MODERN EUROPE

Essays in Honor of
H. G. Koenigsberger

Edited by

PHYLLIS MACK

Rutgers University

and

MARGARET C. JACOB

Eugene Lang College, New York
New School for Social Research

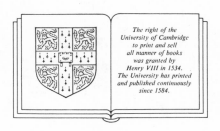

The right of the
University of Cambridge
to print and sell
all manner of books
was granted by
Henry VIII in 1534.
The University has printed
and published continuously
since 1584.

CAMBRIDGE UNIVERSITY PRESS

Cambridge

London   New York   New Rochelle

Melbourne   Sydney

NEW ENGLAND INSTITUTE
OF TECHNOLOGY
LEARNING RESOURCES CENTER

13580241

Published by the Press Syndicate of the University of Cambridge,
The Pitt Building, Trumpington Street, Cambridge CB2 IRP
32 East 57th Street, New York, NY 10022, USA
10 Stamford Road, Oakleigh, Melbourne 3166, Australia

© Cambridge University Press, 1987

First published 1987

Printed in Great Britain by the University Press, Cambridge

British Library cataloguing in publication data
Politics and culture in early modern Europe:
essays in honor of H. G. Koenigsberger.
1. Europe–Politics and government
2. Europe–Civilization
I. Koenigsberger, H. G. II. Mack, Phyllis
III. Jacob, Margaret C.
320.94   JN7

Library of Congress cataloguing in publication data
Politics and culture in early modern Europe.
Bibliography of the writings of Helmut Georg
Koenigsberger.
1. Europe–Politics and government–1492–1648.
3. Europe–Civilization. 3. Koenigsberger,
H. G. (Helmut Georg) I. Mack, Phyllis. II. Jacob,
Margaret C., 1943–   . III. Koenigsberger,
H. G. (Helmut Georg)
D231.P64 1987   940.2   86–11763

ISBN 0 521 30197 1

UP

CONTENTS

Introduction   *page* 1

The court of the Spanish Habsburgs: a peculiar institution?
J. H. ELLIOTT   5

The magnificent Lorenzo de' Medici: between myth and
history
MELISSA MERIAM BULLARD   25

Political rhetoric and poetic meaning in Renaissance culture:
Clément Marot and the Field of Cloth of Gold
PHYLLIS MACK   59

The unlikely Machiavellian: William of Orange and the
princely virtues
GUY WELLS   85

The Estates of Brabant to the end of the fifteenth century: the
make-up of the assembly
EMILE LOUSSE   95

Presents and pensions: a methodological search and the case
study of Count Nils Bielke's prosecution for treason in
connection with gratifications from France
RAGNHILD HATTON   101

Between Bruni and Machiavelli: history, law and historicism in
Poggio Bracciolini
FREDERICK KRANTZ   119

Constitutional discourse in France, 1527–1549
SARAH HANLEY   153

Contents

Lieuwe van Aitzema: a soured but knowing eye
HERBERT H. ROWEN
169

John Calvin's contribution to representative government
ROBERT M. KINGDON
183

Luther and the humanists
A. G. DICKENS
199

Scholars and ecclesiastical history in the Early Modern period:
the influence of Ferdinando Ughelli
DENYS HAY
215

'By an Orphean charm': science and the two cultures in
seventeenth-century England
JAMES R. JACOB
231

The crisis of the European mind: Hazard revisited
MARGARET C. JACOB
251

Isaac Beeckman and music
D. P. WALKER
273

Decadence, shift, cultural changes and the universality of
Leonardo da Vinci
DOROTHY KOENIGSBERGER
285

Bibliography of the writings of
HELMUT GEORG KOENIGSBERGER
305

Index
309

INTRODUCTION

The subject of these essays is politics and culture in early modern
Europe; themes long regarded as central to the historiography of the
period. As separate and distinct areas of human experience and as the
interaction of ideas and values with the necessities of power and interest,
politics and culture have occupied the scholarly attention of H. G.
Koenigsberger for the last thirty or more years. His interests and
expertise have ranged, in geographical terms, from Sicily and Spain to
Germany, France and The Netherlands. In cultural terms, he has
excelled at analyzing figures as diverse as Machiavelli and Monteverdi,
themes as disparate as artistic inspiration and political corruption – all
of which has been both inspiring and somewhat daunting to his students.
The contributors to this volume pay tribute to Helli Koenigsberger's
interests, and to their remarkable yield, by taking up themes that
resonated through his lectures and seminars as well as in his published
writings. As his former students, most of us know that spoken legacy
intimately; for those among us who are peers there have been the many
hours of conversation and reading that have enabled us to share, and to
attempt to emulate, the subtlety and enthusiasm which continue to
inform his work.

In his writings, in his teaching, and in his professional activities (in
particular, his service as President of the International Commission for
the History of Representative and Parliamentary Institutions), Helli
Koenigsberger has conveyed a particularly dynamic way of thinking
about the relation of politics and culture. Not only has he made the
machinations of political actors come alive; perhaps more important, he
has alerted us to the less obvious, but more profound connections
between political behavior and cultural values. He has written on the
mutual impact of culture – in particular religion, art and music – and
changes in the structure and operation of the early modern state, giving
special attention to the phase of the decline of state power and the power

of religious groups, and the impact of that decline on contemporary attitudes and systems of belief; on scientific advances, political thinking and aesthetic judgements. It has become almost common-place for social and cultural historians to attempt to link cultural artifacts and customs with underlying trends in political and economic development, relating popular festivals or artistic genres to the circumstances of power and patronage; few historians have tackled the problem of analyzing the actual nature and quality of artistic creativity, as Koenigsberger has done so ingeniously in his articles on mannerism and music in the courts of sixteenth- and seventeenth-century Europe.

Others of Koenigsberger's books and articles have dealt with what might be called the anatomy of political behaviour: the organization of revolutionary parties, the informal mechanisms of political patronage, and the varied rationales for the exercise of power, from theology to doctrines of reason of state. In these works he has shown himself to be a master of synthesis. In discussing the evolution of revolutionary parties in France and The Netherlands, he focused on the parallel development of political attitudes and behaviour in the disparate religious ideologies of the French Catholic League and Protestants of the Low Countries. In his forthcoming work on the States General of The Netherlands in the fifteenth and sixteenth centuries, he will consider the problem of Dutch and Belgian historiography in relation to representative institutions and the growth of absolute monarchy in Europe as a whole.

In this volume we have sought to be both general and specific. Helli Koenigsberger is a master of close, archival work, a presenter of new evidence with which to fashion new historical insights. Yet he never feared generalization; and here too we are prepared to address problems of cultural shifts, declines and crises. Several of these essays deal directly with the theme of political behavior and with the relationship of culture to the character and scope of political authority. J. H. Elliott writes on the Spanish court of the sixteenth and seventeenth centuries, and on the use of theatre and court ceremonial as elements in the construction of the mythology of kingship. Melissa Bullard discusses Lorenzo de' Medici as both political actor and cultural icon. Phyllis Mack interprets the poetry of the courtier Clément Marot in relation to the political persona of king Francis I of France. Guy Wells writes on William of Orange as an embodiment of Machiavellian *virtu*, while the Belgian scholar Emile Lousse focuses on the Estates of Brabant. Finally, Ragnhild Hatton dissects the machinations of bribery and corruption in relations between the courts of Sweden and France during the reign of Louis XIV – based, to quote her original letter outlining her paper, on 'exceptionally rich and unique material (I found the cypher key to documents which had defeated me for twenty years)'.

Other writers take political thinking as their central theme: Frederick Krantz writes on the development of the humanist juridical thought of Poggio Bracciolini; Sarah Hanley, on the *lit de justice* assembly in sixteenth-century France and the political and rhetorical debate which surrounded it; Herbert Rowen, on a little-known, highly astute chronicler of the seventeenth-century political order, the Dutch diplomat Lieuwe van Aitzema.

The relationship between political activity and the broader cultural developments of the time forms the basis for contributions in the areas of religion, science, literature and music. Robert Kingdon discusses the religious and political evolution of Calvin's Geneva, while the scholarship and values of Martin Luther and the Counter Reformation and of the historian Ferdinando Ughelli are presented by A. G. Dickens and Denys Hay, respectively. James Jacob investigates the origins of modern science and the impact of scientific thought on the widening gulf between elite and popular culture in seventeenth-century England, while Margaret Jacob re-assesses that moment in early modern Europe when the new elite culture emerged as triumphant – what Hazard once called 'the crisis of the European consciousness.'

What emerges from a juxtaposition of these figures is an overriding concern with intellectual unity: a worldview which would both encompass and reconcile the values of the politician or scholar with those of the spiritual idealist. D. P. Walker's (sadly posthumous) account of Isaac Beeckman's musical theory relates church music to contemporary ideas about architecture, colors, memory and expectation, and the effects of ancient music, while Dorothy Koenigsberger reconstructs the mental universe of Leonardo da Vinci, focussing on Leonardo's attempt to achieve intellectual unity through experiments in art, natural science and geometry. In these and several other essays, we see thinkers and political actors searching for a synthesis which would render their scholarship, or art, or expertise, compatible with their larger cosmological or religious interests. Even the most overtly political of these major cultural figures, as Robert Kingdon's discussion of Calvin demonstrates, bent their political will to the service of an extraordinary spiritual idealism.

To lavish praise on a modest man is to risk exposing his shyness. Helli Koenigsberger taught on both sides of the Atlantic, lived in profoundly different cultures and excelled among the historians of his generation, while always remaining a generous, unassuming, immensely charming human being whose social and intellectual companionship is a source of great pleasure for all who have experienced it. He and Dorothy have stimulated and entertained (and civilized) two generations of graduate students while maintaining a profound interest in music, opera and the arts. We wish there were more music and art history for him in these pages; we wish we could say how much we cherish him and his historical achievements without causing him embarrassment. Perhaps the best we can do is ask him to enjoy this volume as much as it gives us pleasure in presenting it.

PHYLLIS MACK*
Rutgers University

MARGARET C. JACOB*
October, 1985   *New School for Social Research, Eugene Lang College*

*We wish to thank Margaret van Sant at the Institute for Advanced Study, Princeton, for her kind assistance. The Institute housed this project in its final stages. J. H. Elliott offered thoughtful encouragement throughout, and Dorothy Koenigsberger proved to be a superb co-conspirator as did Robert Oresko. Secretarial assistance was also provided by Claire Potter and Barbara Baillet at Eugene Lang College and Kali Krauss at Rutgers University.

The court of the Spanish Habsburgs: a peculiar institution?

J. H. ELLIOTT

According to Lord Herbert of Cherbury – but can his story really be true? – Philip II of Spain once saw fit to rebuke one of his ambassadors for neglecting some piece of business in Italy because of a disagreement with the French ambassador over a point of honour. How, he asked his ambassador, had he "left a business of importance for a ceremony?" The ambassador boldly replied to his master *como por una ceremonia? Vuessa Majesta misma no es sino una ceremonia.* "How, for a ceremony? Your Majesty's self is but a ceremony."[1]

The elaborately ceremonious character of Spanish court life was notorious among Europeans of the late sixteenth centuries. But if they laughed, they also imitated. Charles I of England, deeply impressed by his experiences on his visit to Madrid as Prince of Wales in 1623, introduced a decorum into the ceremonial of the English court which bid fair to outdo that of the Spaniards.[2] Yet in spite of the pervasive influence of Spanish manners and ceremonial in Early Modern Europe, all too little is known about the character and organization of the court of the Spanish Habsburgs, and the ways in which it developed.[3] From

[1] *The Autobiography of Edward, Lord Herbert of Cherbury*, ed. Sidney L. Lee (London, 1886), pp. 205–6. I have left Lord Herbert's unorthodox rendering of Spanish uncorrected.

[2] Peter W. Thomas, 'Charles I of England', in A. G. Dickens (ed), *The Courts of Europe* (London, 1977), p. 193.

[3] There is much material of interest in Dalmiro de la Valgoma y Díaz-Varela, *Norma y ceremonia de las reinas de la Casa de Austria* (Madrid, 1958), and Antonio Rodríguez Villa, *Etiquetas de la Casa de Austria* (Madrid, 1913) provides a useful description of various court functions and offices, but no general survey is available covering the history of the Spanish court during the two centuries of Habsburg rule. Ludwig Pfandl, 'Philipp II und die Einführung des burgundischen Hofzeremoniells in Spanien', *Historisches Jahrbuch*, LVIII (1938), pp. 1–33, ranges wider than its title, and makes some suggestive points. The most extensive literature on the Spanish court during this period belongs to the reign of Philip IV, for which see J. H. Elliott, 'Philip IV of Spain', in Dickens, *The Courts of Europe*, ch. 8, and the bibliography there given, together with Jonathan Brown and J. H. Elliott, *A Palace for a King. The Buen Retiro and the Court of Philip IV* (New Haven and London, 1980). In the piece which follows

5

Saint-Simon to Norbert Elias[4] it is the court of Louis XIV of France that
has been taken as the archetype of courtly society in the age of
absolutism. This is partly because Versailles became the model for so
many of the courts of eighteenth-century Europe, and partly because the
Spanish court by comparison is poorly documented and has elicited
relatively little study.

Yet, as interest in the history of European courts revives, it is their
variety that impresses, at least as much as their uniformity.[5] Courts
differed markedly in character, not only from country to country, but
also from one reign to the next, undergoing changes over time far more
drastic than could ever be anticipated from the glacial and apparently
immobile surface imposed by ceremonial and etiquette. This should
hardly be a matter for surprise. Institutions, as Helmut Koenigsberger
has shown us in his writings, can adapt to new needs while preserving
the carapace of old forms, and their reaction (or the lack of it) to new
challenges and requirements is likely at any given moment to be dictated
by the play of personality on organization, in response to political, social
and economic forces, and to the movement of ideas. The princely court,
for all its regulated protocol and archaic ceremonial, can hardly be an
exception to this rule of institutional history.

Certain general characteristics of the Early Modern European court
can be identified from the model constructed by Norbert Elias on the
basis of Versailles. Everything possible, for instance, was done by means
both of ceremonial and household organization to preserve the sacred
character of kingship through the maintenance of *distance*.[6] The monarch, as God's representative on earth, was placed at the centre of a
universe carefully designed to duplicate the harmonious ordering of the
heavens.

The Spanish court in this respect had little to learn and much to teach.
The king was presented as a figure at once remote and yet the centre of
universal attention – a presentation that became especially artful in the
seventeenth century as mastery was achieved over the illusionistic

I have sought to give a picture of the character and development of the court over a
longer period, offering an interpretative synthesis on the basis of contemporary
descriptions and such work as has been published on the Spanish and other European
courts in recent years. Some of the points here presented were first made at a conference
held at Duke University in April 1981 on 'Arts, letters and ceremonial at the court of
the Spanish Habsburgs'.

[4] Norbert Elias, *Die höfische Gesellschaft* (Neuwied and Berlin, 1969). I cite here from
the English translation by Edmund Jephcott, *The Court Society* (New York, 1984).
[5] Dickens, *The Courts of Europe*, gives a good idea of this variety, and is likely to be the
starting point for the study of European courts for many years to come.
[6] For the importance of distance, see Elias, *The Court Society*, p. 118.

devices of the theatre. When plays were performed in the palace of the Alcázar in Madrid, the king was seated some ten or twelve feet from the back wall, at the exact point at which the perspective design of the stage set could be appreciated to the full. On either side of the room were standing ranks of courtiers, with their eyes fixed on the king and queen as much as on the play. For in a sense the king and queen *were* the play. Theatrical contrivance could be brilliantly used to underline the point, as when the curtain was raised on one occasion to reveal on centre stage a throne beneath the canopy of which were two portraits – of the king and queen. The monarchs in effect looked on themselves, as in a mirror, while the audience gazed in admiration at this double image of majesty, the original and the likeness.[7]

Setting, ceremonial, household organization, all served to emphasize the unique and remote splendour of a godlike king. 'It cannot be denied', wrote Alonso Núñez de Castro in the seventeenth century, 'that palaces which are sumptuous in the beauty of their buildings and the richness of their furnishings, are an adornment that makes majesty plausible, as also is the accompaniment of guards, servants and confidants who perform those respectful ceremonies with which princes, as human deities, ought to be venerated.'[8] We still know far too little about the composition and functioning of the Spanish court,[9] but it was well endowed with the guards and servants deemed necessary to minister to the needs of a deified monarch. As in other European courts, there were three principal functionaries responsible for attending to the king's material wants: the *mayordomo mayor*, or Lord High Steward, in charge of his feeding and housing; the Grand Chamberlain (*camarero mayor*), or, as the office fell into abeyance, the *sumiller de corps*, or Groom of the Stole, to organize his personal service; and the Master of the Horse (*caballerizo mayor*), to attend to his stables and transportation. Each of these palace officials had his own extensive staff.

An idea of the scale of the enterprise can be gained from a list of the household servants of the king and queen, drawn up in 1623 in the early years of Philip IV.[10] Excluding the three hundred members of the royal guards, and the 167 officials and servants employed for the king's

[7] See J. E. Varey, 'The Audience and the Play at Court Spectacles: the role of the King', *Bulletin of Hispanic Studies*, LXI (1984), pp. 399–406.
[8] Alonso Núñez de Castro, *Libro histórico político, sólo Madrid es corte*, 3rd edn (Madrid, 1675), p. 192.
[9] Mr. R. G. Trewinnard is preparing a Ph.D. thesis for the University of Wales on 'The Household of the Spanish Habsburgs, 1606–65: Structure, Cost and Personnel', which should provide us with much new information.
[10] B(ritish) L(ibrary), Add(itional) Ms.36,466, fos.247–259v., *Relación de todos los criados que ay en la casa real del rey de España este año de 1623 años.*

sporting and hunting activities, there were around 350 principal servants in the household of the king. These included 12 *mayordomos*, 18 gentlemen of the household on active duty, another 25 who had formerly served or enjoyed the right of entry, 47 gentlemen to wait on the royal table, and 10 valets or *ayudas de cámara*. In addition there was an ecclesiastical establishment under the direction of the Archbishop of Santiago as *capillán mayor*. In it were to be found the royal confessor, 10 royal preachers, some lesser clerics and a chapel master in charge of the choristers and of 63 musicians (instrumentalists and vocalists). The queen's household, for its part, included 8 *mayordomos*, 10 dames of honour, 18 ladies in waiting, 12 *meninas* – all daughters of noblemen – and 20 principal ladies as *ayudas de cámara*, 'not to mention the ladies' servants and the menial servants, of whom there are large numbers.' The total number of household officials and service staff on the court books in 1623 was around 1700.[11]

That the figure at the centre of these ministrations was of more than human character was indicated by some of the ancient rituals that were still attached to his personal service. An observer noted as late as 1655 the survival of the Castilian custom by which no one could ride a horse once it had been ridden by the king. When the Duke of Medina de las Torres sent Philip IV a splendid horse as a present, the king returned it with the words *sería lástima* – it would be a pity if he were to mount it and so prevent such a noble steed from ever being ridden again.[12]

But if the court was the residence of a quasi-divine monarch, it was also the centre of political and administrative power – a point emphasized by the layout of the royal palace of the Alcázar in Madrid, with its royal apartments on the first floor, and the council chambers and secretarial offices on the floor below. The uneasy combination of personal and bureaucratic kingship so characteristic of Early Modern European societies was reflected in Madrid in the decision of the two greatest seventeenth-century ministers, the Duke of Lerma and the Count-Duke of Olivares, to combine their governmental duties with the household offices of Groom of the Stole and Master of the Horse, which guaranteed them close proximity to the king both inside and outside the palace. The Groom of the Stole – *sumiller de corps* – was assured of access on all occasions by virtue of his duties. He had general supervision of the king's chamber and of his dining arrangements, and combined this with specific

[11] Gil González de Avila, *Teatro de las grandezas de la villa de Madrid* (Madrid, 1623), p. 333. Sixty-six years earlier, in 1557, the Venetian ambassador, Federico Badoero, reported that Philip II had 1500 officials in his household service (*Relazioni di ambasciatori veneti al senato*, vol. VIII, *Spagna* [1497–1598], Turin, 1981, p. 150).

[12] 'Voyage d'Antoine Brunel en Espagne (1655)', *Revue Hispanique*, XXX (1914), p. 213.

personal services. As practised in the seventeenth century, these duties involved passing him his shirt, towel and clothes when he rose each morning, handing him his goblet at lunch and dinner when he ate alone, and being in attendance at all royal audiences. He supervised the making of the king's bed, and lighted the way to the royal bedchamber at night. He was also expected to sleep in a portable bed in the royal apartment, unless – as presumably happened with Lerma and Olivares – the king dispensed him from this obligation and appointed a substitute.[13]

It was, however, not only political and administrative power that radiated outwards from the apartments of the king. The Early Modern court served also as an 'exemplary centre,'[14] at once national and international in its range. The rivalry of European princes was inevitably reflected in the competitive display of their courts. But it hardly seems an accident that it was the lesser rulers who needed to be the innovators in matters of display – the fifteenth-century dukes of Burgundy in ceremonial display, the sixteenth-century Medici in the art of court spectacle. It was only by a compensatory effort of this kind that they could hope to hold their own in a world of great powers. But the great powers in turn would follow at their own pace and convenience, conferring their own prestige on practices first developed in the lesser courts. This happened with Burgundian ceremonial, introduced by Ferdinand at the court of Vienna with his court orders of 1527 and 1537,[15] and subsequently imposed by his brother, the Emperor Charles V, on the household of the heir to the throne of Castile in 1548. The resulting Habsburg–Burgundian style, once established in Vienna and Madrid, enjoyed a European preeminence sustained by Habsburg political hegemony. It was this style which would inspire Charles I's reforms at the English court, where the ceremonial introduced by Edward IV 'after the manner of Burgundy'[16] had become tarnished with the passage of time, and dismally failed to conform to the exacting standards of Madrid.

At the national level, the court as exemplary centre had a vital part to

13 Royal Library, Copenhagen. Ny.kgl.S.no.190, *Etiquetas de la real cámara de SMC el señor Rey Don Felipe Quarto* (11 August 1646), fo.7v. See also Yves Bottineau, 'Aspects de la cour d'Espagne au XVIIe siècle: l'étiquette de la chambre du roi', *Bulletin Hispanique*, LXXIV (1972) pp. 138–57, for these duties. Edward Hyde, Lord Clarendon, who was in Madrid in 1649, uses Groom of the Stole as the English equivalent of *sumiller de corps* (*The History of the Rebellion and Civil Wars in England*, ed. W.D. Macray, 5 vols. (Oxford, 1888), v, p. 93).
14 The expression is borrowed from Clifford Geertz, *Negara. The Theatre State in Nineteenth-Century Bali* (Princeton, 1980), p. 13.
15 Hubert Ch. Ehalt, *Ausdrucksformen absolutischer Herrschaft. Der Wiener Hof im 17 und 18 Jahrhundert* (Munich, 1980), p. 35.
16 Cited by Neville Williams, 'The Tudors', in Dickens, *The Courts of Europe*, p. 148.

play in the 'civilizing process'. Court etiquette, with its fine hierarchical gradations and its exact delimitation of functions, proved – whether in London, Paris or Madrid – to be an important device for inculcating social discipline. When the Admiral of Castile in a fit of pique took from his neck the chain from which hung his golden key of office and handed it back to Philip IV during the royal visit to Barcelona in 1626, the king spoke witheringly of 'this poor, badly educated, *caballero*', and had him placed under arrest and banished to his estates.[17] Education in politeness, education in taste, education to service – the court as exemplary centre was potentially equipped to provide all three.

Like any other European court of the period, therefore, the Spanish court performed at least three major functions. It protected and sustained the sacred character of kingship. It served as a centre of political and administrative power. And it constituted an exemplary centre for foreigners and nationals alike. But inevitably it had its own distinctive way of performing these functions; and how and why it developed its own distinctive approaches still needs to be systematically explored.

If we take our stand in the middle years of the seventeenth century, two features of Spanish court life immediately seize the attention. The first is the highly religious character of Spanish kingship in its public manifestations. The bulk of the monarch's public appearances were motivated by religious occasions – the celebration of mass at one or other of Madrid's many churches and convents, and attendance at *autos de fe*. While this reflects the extreme piety of individual monarchs, it also testifies to a particular conception of kingship, in which the relationship of the king to his God is regarded as more than usually close. As the officially styled *rey católico*, and the recipient of a divine favour which had made him the greatest monarch in the world, the king of Spain had a special obligation to uphold with particular fervour the ceremonies of the church and the purity of the faith.

Commentators, however, seem to have felt a continuing need to emphasize the piety – *piedad* – of the monarch. This was partly for domestic reasons, in a society which saw itself under constant threat from the forces of Protestantism, Judaism and Islam. But their concern also had an international dimension, particularly in the light of the king of Spain's perennial rivalry with the Most Christian king of France. In this context, it is significant that the king of Spain, unlike the king of

---

[17] Instituto de Valencia de Don Juan, Madrid. Envío 109 (91). Statement by Philip IV on the behaviour of the Admiral of Castile.

France, was not endowed with healing powers.[18] Nor did he benefit, like the French monarch, from the public sanction of a coronation ceremony – a deficiency which gave Cornelius Jansen a certain amount of trouble when he wrote his *Mars Gallicus* in defence of Spanish policy on the outbreak of war between France and Spain in 1635.[19] This made it all the more necessary to underline the king of Spain's uniquely Catholic credentials.

> How many times [wrote Claudio Clemente of Philip IV] have we seen Your Majesty in solemn processions, on foot and bare-headed beneath a burning sun, surrounded by an innumerable multitude of every order and estate and moving through a cloud of dust to accompany the holy sacrament long distances... We have seen Your Majesty in the most ordinary dress go on foot in Holy Week to visit many temples through streets covered with mud and with rain pouring from the skies, and returning home soaked to the skin... We have seen Your Majesty enter the house of a sick person and not continue his journey until the sacrament has been returned to its temple...[20]

These highly public displays of devotion, however, were performed by a monarch who otherwise was rarely seen. For the outstanding feature of Spanish court life, at least in the eyes of seventeenth-century foreign observers, was the invisibility, and indeed the sheer inaccessibility, of the king. The Venetian ambassador describes Philip III as spending a large part of his year 'in solitude, with very little court'.[21] The Maréchal de Gramont, visiting the court of Philip IV in 1659, observes that even the grandees saw the king only when they accompanied him to mass, and again in the evening when plays were performed; 'and the only time they speak to him is in audience, when business compels them to request one'.[22] Gramont's description makes clear how different were the spatial relationships between king and court in France and Spain. In Spain, the king was approached through a succession of rooms, each one more exclusive of access than the one before. Even in the eighteenth century after the advent of the Bourbons, Saint-Simon noticed how bare these rooms in the Alcázar looked – primarily because they contained no chairs. In the suite of rooms leading to the king's private apartments

[18] Marc Bloch, *Les rois thaumaturges* (Paris, 1961), p. 155.
[19] French trans., *Le Mars François* (1637), Bk.I, ch.IX. For the abandonment of the coronation ceremony in medieval Castile, see Teófilo F. Ruiz, 'Une royauté sans sacre: la monarchie castillane du bas moyen âge', *Annales*, XXXIX (1984), pp. 429–53.
[20] Claudio Clemente, *El machiavelismo degollado por la christiana sabdiuría de España y de Austria* (Alcalá, 1637), pp. 120–1.
[21] Simeone Contarini (1604) in *Relazioni di ambasciatori veneti*, vol. IX, *Spagna* [1602–1631] (Turin, 1978), p. 288.
[22] *Mémoires de Maréchal de Gramont*, in A. Petitot and L. J. N. Monmerqué, *Collection des mémoires relatifs à l'histoire de France*, 77 vols. (Paris, 1820–9), LVII, p. 78

there were only two, both of them folding chairs, one for the use of the *mayordomo mayor* and the other for that of the *sumiller de corps*.[23]

Lesser dignitaries were received in one or other of the outer rooms, and the right of entry to the holy of holies, the king's study or *aposento*, was restricted to the papal nuncio, the President of the Council of Castile, cardinals, viceroys, and those fortunate individuals who had been accorded special royal permission.[24] Tucked away beyond the *aposento* was the royal bedchamber. The only members of the court allowed access to it were gentlemen of the chamber on active duty. According to Gramont, these posts of gentlemen of the chamber were the only court offices coveted by the grandees 'because, serving the king at table, and dressing and undressing him, they enjoy during their week of service the privilege of seeing his Majesty, a privilege from which all the others are excluded'.[25]

This highly private bedchamber ritual contrasts strikingly with the publicity attending the *lever* and *coucher* of the king of France – events of such importance at the French court that, when Versailles came to be built, the royal bedroom occupied the central position on the first floor, and was the focal point of the palace.[26] A similar contrast was to be found in the dining arrangements. Apart from a few special occasions, by the seventeenth century the king of Spain dined alone, except for the twenty or so officials who waited upon him, carrying and removing plates with the ritual precision required of a corps de ballet. The meal was taken in complete silence, and on the rare occasions when the queen dined with the king, she had her own separate service and no words were exchanged.[27] The king of France, on the other hand, dined in public. So, too, did Charles I of England and Henrietta Maria.[28] At the Imperial court in Vienna the practice was closer to that of Madrid, although the meals seem a little less bleak. The Emperor Ferdinand II 'did ordinarily dine in his Antechamber, but most commonly sup with the Empresse... When his Imperial Majesty sits at table with the Empresse... then there is most exquisite musicke; otherwise there is no musicke at dinner, unless it be on festivals and holydaies.'[29]

The punctiliousness of the etiquette surrounding the largely invisible king of Spain, and the extreme formality of Spanish court ceremonial,

[23] *Mémoires de Saint-Simon*, ed. A. de Boislisle (Paris, 1879–1930), XXXIX, p. 409.
[24] Pfandl, 'Philipp II und die Einführung des burgundischen Hofzeremoniells', p. 14.
[25] *Mémoires*, p. 81.
[26] Elias, *The Court Society*, p. 82.
[27] Pfandl, 'Philipp II', pp. 21–2.
[28] Thomas, 'Charles I', in Dickens, *The Courts of Europe*, p. 194.
[29] *The Particular State of the Government of the Emperor Ferdinand the Second, as it was at his decease in the year 1636* (London, 1637), fos.67–67v.

never ceased to surprise and impress seventeenth-century visitors to Madrid. Marshal Gramont on his embassy of 1659 tells us 'there was an air of grandeur and majesty which I have seen nowhere else.'[30] But reservations are also expressed. Antoine de Brunel, visiting the Spanish court in 1655, keeps his admiration within bounds:

no prince lives like the king of Spain; all his actions and all his occupations are always the same, and move with such regularity that, day by day, he knows exactly what he will do for the whole of his life. One could say that there is some law which obliges him never to miss what he is accustomed to. So the weeks, the months, the years and the divisions of the day bring no change in his pattern of life, and never allow him to see anything new.[31]

Coming from the subject of a king of whom Saint-Simon would later write that 'with an almanac and a watch one could tell, three hundred leagues away, what he was doing',[32] the words possess a certain piquancy. Is it possible that punctuality reached Paris by way of Madrid?

Not surprisingly, the frozen ritual of Spanish court etiquette was also reflected in the deportment of the king. Foreign observers were struck by his impassivity. Philip IV was described by François Bertaut in 1659 as a 'statue'.[33] The pattern of a royal audience was always the same. Those admitted to the king's presence would invariably find him *arrimado a un bufete* – standing at a console table – as they entered the audience chamber. He would raise his hat as they came in, and then stand motionless throughout the audience. The studiously non-comittal remark that closed the audience at least indicated that the statue talked.

We have here, then, a monarch who seems to be little more than a marionette, concealed for much of the time from public view, but occasionally brought on stage to be put through a series of carefully modulated ritual movements before a hushed and reverential audience. Does this indicate, as has been suggested, the triumph of oligarchy over personal kingship? In the France of Louis XIV, where the king lived out his life beneath the public gaze, the nobles were grouped round a highly visible monarch to enhance his prestige. In the Spain of Philip III and IV and Carlos II, court ceremonial was used to isolate the sovereign and confine him to the company of a few privileged aristocrats.[34] But is it the French style of public kingship or the Spanish style of private kingship that stands in need of explanation?

[30] *Mémoires*, p. 51.
[31] 'Voyage d'Antoine Brunel', p. 144.
[32] Cited Elias, *The Court Society*, p. 131.
[33] François Bertaut, 'Journal du Voyage d'Espagne (1659)', *Revue Hispanique*, XLVII (1919), p. 35.
[34] Bottineau, 'Aspects de la cour d'Espagne', pp. 152–3.

Any attempt to explain the developments of distinctive court styles in terms of the relationship of king to aristocracy (important as this may have been in determining the final configuration) can easily overlook an element common to all institutional history, and nicely described by Norbert Elias in relation to royal courts as 'a ghostly *perpetuum mobile* that continued to operate regardless of any direct use-values, being impelled, as by an inexhaustible motor, by the competition for status and power of the people enmeshed in it...and by their need for a clearly graded scale of prestige'.[35] The classic instance of the operation of this 'ghostly *perpetuum mobile*' at the Spanish court is the celebrated story told by Bassompierre of Philip III contracting his fatal fever from the heat of a brazier which had been placed too close to him, and which the Duke of Alba, as gentleman of the chamber, was unwilling to move without orders from the *sumiller de corps*, the Duke of Uceda, who happened to be out of the palace at the time.[36]

Although the story does not seem to figure in any Spanish source, Bassompierre claims to have heard it from another gentleman of the chamber, the Marquis of Povar, and it does not look inherently implausible. It became popular in the seventeenth century as an example of the absurdity of Spanish court etiquette, but a parallel is to be found in an incident at the French court in the following century, when Marie Antoinette's chemise was passed ceremoniously from hand to hand, while the queen herself stood naked and shivering as the proprieties of rank were observed among her ladies in waiting.[37] Both instances, whether apocryphal or not, exemplify the tendency of court ceremonial to develop a machine-like momentum, crushing in its course those sacrosanct royal figures it had been specifically designed to protect.

In the absence of a personality strong enough to mould an institution to his will, the institution itself takes command. But in the history of the Spanish court, three personalities – Charles V, Philip II, and the Count-Duke of Olivares – proved strong enough either to arrest the 'ghostly *perpetuum mobile*' or to master it to suit their own designs. Above all, it is to that virtuoso of political stagecraft, Charles V, that we must turn for the decisions which set the pattern of life for his successors on the Spanish throne. Heir to the Burgundian traditions which had surrounded him during the first years of his life, no man was more acutely aware of the way in which symbols could be deployed and manipulated for political effect. When Philip II asked the aged Duke of Alba in 1579 for

[35] Elias, *The Court Society*, pp. 86–7.
[36] *Journal de ma vie. Mémoires du Maréchal de Bassompierre*, ed. Marquis de Chantérac, II (Paris, 1873), pp. 240–1.
[37] Elias, *The Court Society*, p. 86.

a written account of the royal household and its ceremonial, the duke confirmed that this was something he had frequently discussed with the Emperor, 'the man who was best informed about such matters'.[38]

The Emperor's hand was everywhere to be found in the ceremonial arrangements used in Spain to ensure the royal preeminence. In the matter, for instance, of the exclusive right of grandees to go covered in the royal presence, Alba recalled, in response to Philip's request, that the question did not arise under the Catholic Kings 'because all kinds of people went covered. Going bare-headed in Castile was introduced only after His Imperial Majesty came here'. By regulating the wearing of hats in the royal presence, the Emperor at once distanced himself from his subjects, introduced a hierarchical gradation at court, and created a coveted privilege which would increase the dependence of the high nobility on the monarch.

There is no direct evidence as to why Charles entrusted a reluctant Duke of Alba in January 1548 with the task of imposing the Burgundian style on the household of Prince Philip.[39] The political circumstances of the moment, however, provide a clue to the Emperor's intentions. In the aftermath of his victory at Mühlberg, he could begin to make the necessary dispositions for the future of his dominions. Central to his strategy was the retention of the link between Spain and the Burgundian inheritance of the Netherlands. With this in mind he planned a visit by his son, as the rightful heir to the inheritance, to his northern realms, and it was obviously important that Philip should come to the Netherlands surrounded by the correct Burgundian trappings. There may have been rumblings of dissent in Castile over 'thus discrediting the Castilian style, which on grounds of antiquity alone ought to have been preserved',[40] but Brussels was worth a *sumiller de corps*.

If, as Charles hoped, Philip might yet succeed to the Empire itself, the fact that the Burgundian style was already in use in his own household and at his brother's court in Vienna further strengthened the case for its adoption at the court of Castile. To judge from a report later drawn up

[38] BL Add.Ms.28,361, fos. 11–12, Duke of Alba to Mateo Vázquez, 15 Nov. 1579. I am indebted to Dr David Lagomarsino for this reference, and for his general advice on points of etiquette. I am also grateful to him for making available to me a copy of Jean Sigonney's report on ceremonial in the Emperor's household, discussed below.

[39] Alba's reluctance is reported by his seventeenth-century biographer, Ossorio, who had access to papers now lost. See P. Antonio Ossorio SJ, *Vida y hazañas de Don Fernando Alvarez de Toledo, Duque de Alba*, ed. José López de Toro (Madrid, 1945), pp. 163–5. See also William S. Maltby, *Alba. A Biography of Fernando Alvarez de Toledo, Third Duke of Alba, 1507–1582* (Berkeley, Los Angeles, London, 1983), pp. 66–7.

[40] Prudencio de Sandoval, *Historia de la vida y hechos del Emperador Carlos V* (Barcelona, 1625), II, p. 588.

for Philip by Jean Sigonney, the Comptroller of Charles' household,[41] the new-old style which he imposed on his son's household in 1548 was the one that his own household had followed for many years. It is open to question, however, how far this style was authentically Burgundian. Sigonney himself clearly had his doubts. The preface to his account of the Emperor's household arrangements suggests that Burgundian household organization first lost something of its pristine grandeur when the Habsburg Maximilian married Mary of Burgundy in 1477 and brought to the marriage his own German household. Still more was lost when Maximilian's son, Philip the Fair, married Joanna of Spain. When Maximilian gave his grandson Charles a household of his own at the age of ten, it was – so Sigonney had heard – very different in style from the household of the old Dukes of Burgundy, and not much of this now survived, except for the dining arrangements, which themselves were falling into desuetude.

Sigonney remembered that the Emperor was once questioned about the oblivion into which so many of the Burgundian practices had fallen. His answer was highly characteristic. Just as the Dukes of Burgundy 'had taken the liberty to live in their own way, he wanted a similar freedom in not having to imitate them in things he did not like'.[42] If Charles now denied his son this same freedom, it was presumably because he thought that the new style of ceremonial and household organization would enhance the prestige of his son in his dealings both with his own subjects and with his fellow-princes.

Philip, as the dutiful son of his father, seems to have accommodated himself to the Emperor's wishes, although the household organization that prevailed in his reign gives every sign of maintaining a highly syncretic character. No doubt the old forms and practices had a way of reasserting themselves. Ceremonial in the royal chapel of the Alcázar, for example, had been brought into line with the 'usage of Burgundy' in 1546. But in 1586 it was subjected to a new and definitive reform, in accordance with 'the usage of Castile and Burgundy.' This proved in practice to be a blending of Aragonese, Castilian, Burgundian and Flemish styles with those of the papal court.[43]

The ceremonial designed for the court of Spain by Charles V was well calculated to make kingship at once impressive and remote. The effect

[41] Biblioteca Nacional, Madrid. Ms.1080, *Relación de la forma de servir que se tenía en la casa del Emperador don Carlos nuestro señor ... el año de 1545 y se avia tenido algunos años antes.*

[42] Fo.4.

[43] Véronique Gérard, 'Los sitios de devoción en el Alcázar de Madrid: capilla y oratorios', *Archivo Español de Arte*, LVII (1983), pp. 275–84.

of Philip II's adoption and adaptation of that ceremonial was to make it impressive but withdrawn. Charles, with his peripatetic court, combined grandeur with a high degree of visibility. Philip, in settling his court and government in Madrid in 1561,[44] reduced the degree of visibility by withdrawing himself geographically to a central location in Castile. But the process of withdrawal was more than merely geographical. Philip also engaged in what might be described as a psychological withdrawal, as he moulded Spanish kingship to the forms of his own temperament and style of life. The muted style of the court under Philip II, underlined by the gravity of the king's deportment and the sobriety of his dress, found an appropriate embodiment in that mausoleum of monarchy, the Escorial.

The effect of Philip's decision to pursue an essentially reclusive form of life, more appropriate to a monk than a monarch, was to deprive him of some of the political advantages conventionally attributed to the sixteenth-century court – the prestige, for example, associated with public display, and the opportunities for occupying the high nobility in harmless court employment. It is not surprising that the nobility of Castile found little temptation to linger in so lugubrious a court. But there were compensating political advantages to be gained from sheer royal remoteness. The awe, amounting to terror, of those who found themselves in his presence makes it clear that private kingship, no less than public, could be used to powerful political effect in the hands of a master.

But Philip II's style of kingship was a highly personal one, not easily transmitted to his heirs, even though – in its religiosity and its dedication to paper work – it was consistently held up as the model that they were expected to follow. Where Philip II moulded the form of the court to suit the character of his kingship, Philip III, lacking all character to his kingship, allowed himself to be enveloped by the forms. During the first two decades of the seventeenth century, the court may be said to have imposed itself on the king.

The manner of Philip III's life, indeed, suggests a rather pathetic attempt to escape from its clutches. Whenever possible, Philip was on the move, but – in contrast to his grandfather – this was peripatetism without purpose. He was for ever travelling from one country residence to another – the Pardo, the Escorial, Aranjuez – or escaping into the countryside to indulge his passion for hunting, which afforded him some relief from the constraints of ceremonial and the tedious obligations of

---

[44] For a useful reappraisal of Philip's decision, see Juan Ignacio Gutiérrez Nieto, 'En torno al problema del establecimiento de la capitalidad de la monarquía hispánica en Madrid', *Revista de Occidente*, 27–8, extraordinario VIII (1983), pp. 52–65.

government.[45] It was only in his exemplary display of public devotion that he sustained and reinforced a central tradition of Spanish kingship.

Yet it was in the reign of this unpromising monarch that Spain acquired a genuine court life, even if Philip's own active contribution was confined to little more than court festivities. Sir Charles Cornwallis, reporting from the court at Valladolid in 1605, describes him as taking part in the equestrian sport of the *juego de cañas* – 'a thing not formerly seen in this kingdom, and done on purpose (as to us it was delivered) to honour our Nation'.[46] The new vigour of court life reflected the appearance of a new and young king, and one with a growing family of infantes and infantas – itself a striking novelty in Habsburg Spain. It also reflected the capture of the crown by a faction of the aristocracy, as the Duke of Lerma assumed power as the king's favourite and principal minister, and appointed his relatives and dependents to court and government office.

It was natural that a heavily indebted aristocracy should descend on the court, now that power and patronage were in the hands of one of its own. The process accelerated after the court's return to Madrid in 1606 from its unhappy five-year sojourn in Valladolid. Henceforth the definitive capital of a world-wide empire, Madrid became the magnet of the nobility, whose acquisition or construction of town houses brought it into daily contact with those who had some formal attachment to the court, either as palace functionaries, or as ministers, royal secretaries and officials.

Professor Koenigsberger has pointed to the conjunction of court and great metropolis as a major formative influence on seventeenth-century European cultural developments – in the visual arts, drama and music – because it gave birth to a 'dual patronage and audience, courtly and urban'.[47] The existence of a wealthy and leisured elite in the Madrid of Philip III augured well for this conjunction. By the time of Philip's death in 1621, Madrid, with its 150,000 inhabitants, possessed most of the ingredients of what we have come to regard as standard court life in Early Modern Europe, with, however, one significant exception. The Spanish court remained in large degree a court without a king. With Philip absent at Aranjuez or away at one of his hunting lodges, the court

[45] Pietro Gritti (1619): 'He spends a large part of the year in his country retreats, constantly engaged in hunting.' *Relazioni di ambasciatori veneti*, IX, p. 527.
[46] Ralph Winwood, *Memorials of Affairs of State in the Reigns of Queen Elizabeth and King James I* (1725), vol. II, p. 73 (Sir Charles Cornwallis to the Lords of the Council, 31 May 1605).
[47] 'Republics and Courts in Italian and European Culture in the Sixteenth and Seventeenth Centuries', *Past and Present*, no.83 (1979), pp. 33–56. See p. 45.

lacked a real master of ceremonies. The houses of leading aristocrats like the Dukes of Sessa or Osuna served as centres of patronage, but social and literary life lacked a single focal point. It was the accession of Philip IV in 1621, and the rise of new favourite, the Count of Olivares, that supplied the missing centre.

The twenty-two years of the Olivares regime, from 1621 to 1643, are the climacteric years of the court of the Spanish Habsburgs, and they also mark a critical moment in the history of the court as a European institution. Olivares, bringing with him from Seville the expansive notions of patronage of the Andalusian aristocracy, perceived the possibilities of the court as an instrument of policy in a way that they had not previously been perceived in Habsburg Spain. He was helped in this by the tendency of his generation to view public life in terms of the theatre. Kings and ministers, courtiers and generals, were all seen as playing a part in the great theatre of the world. But, as Richelieu was to find with Louis XIII, a sense of theatre was not in itself sufficient if the leading actor was not prepared to enter fully into his part. In the young Philip IV, Olivares was fortunate in having first-class material to hand. Philip was intelligent enough to learn his lines, but also docile enough to take direction; he had bodily grace and an innate sense of dignity; he combined a mastery of horsemanship and open air sports with a taste for cultural and theatrical activities, and a highly discerning eye for works of art; and he possessed the punctiliousness that was essential for anyone who had to live his life according to strict laws of protocol.

Olivares' grooming of Philip IV for his star role – or, more accurately, his planetary part as the original Sun King, the *rey planeta*[48] – was a conscious act of policy, designed to restore the authority of kingship in a society in which, as he saw it, the political balance had in recent years tilted dangerously in favour of the grandee houses of Castile. The court appointments made by the Duke of Lerma had in effect made Philip III the prisoner of a grandee faction. It was one of the ironies of the Olivares regime that the only way to break the monopoly of this faction was to fill court posts with members of another – his own. The dominance of the Sandovals was therefore duly replaced in the 1620s and 1630s by that of the rival families of the Guzmáns, the Haros and the Zúñigas. But the intent, at least in Olivares' view of the world, was not to capture but to rescue kingship. In his celebrated secret memorandum of 1624, destined only for the eyes of the king, he refers admiringly to Philip II's policy of keeping the grandees dependent on the crown by sending them on

---

[48] For this grooming process, see Brown and Elliott, *A Palace for a King*, pp. 40–9.

embassies and employing them on ceremonial duties which would force them to dig deeply into their pockets.[49]

Although the details still escape us, there can be no doubting the intention of Olivares, patiently seconded and pursued by Philip IV, to make the court at once the focus and the regulator of aristocratic life in Spain. Alonso Carrillo in 1657 describes the court of Philip IV as 'a school of silence, punctiliousness and reverence.'[50] Philip showed himself over the years to be an exacting schoolmaster. He revised the details of court etiquette and the household arrangements in 1624 and again in the late 1640s, set the most punctilious standards for himself, and – as his scathing reference to the Admiral of Castile as 'this poor, badly educated *caballero*' indicates – was not willing to tolerate breaches of propriety.

Yet for all the efforts of king and minister to raise the standards of politeness and courtly etiquette, the court never quite became the school of virtue which Olivares had envisaged. With growing frustration he contemplated the insubordination, riotous behaviour and general aimlessness of the younger generation of nobles who frittered away their days on the fringes of the court. 'I see the Monarchy being lost because the young are not being properly brought up.'[51]

A programme of rigorous training was needed, that would produce a generation of nobles dedicated to the service of the crown in peace and war alike. The king himself, with his mastery of the equestrian arts and his intensive programme of self-education, offered an admirable example for the younger nobles to copy,[52] but they proved singularly reluctant to follow their sovereign's lead. The jousts and tourneys so lavishly staged at the new palace of the Buen Retiro notably failed to produce a more martial generation; nor were the young nobles willing to attend the new court college for the nobility, the Colegio Imperial.[53]

In the mid-1630s, as an alternative solution, Olivares proposed the creation in different parts of Spain of a number of academies, two of them at court.[54] But lack of money, and perhaps also of enthusiasm, made his scheme a dead letter. Later, in 1639, he drew up new instructions for the education of the court pages, who came under his charge as

[49] John H. Elliott and José F. de la Peña, *Memoriales y cartas del Conde Duque de Olivares*, 2 vols. (Madrid, 1978–80), I, doc.IV, pp. 54–5.
[50] Alonso Carrillo, *Origen de la dignidad de grande de Castilla* (Madrid, 1657), fo.12.
[51] Elliott and de la Peña, *Memoriales y cartas*, II, doc. XI, p. 76.
[52] *Ibid.*, doc.XIIa, p. 81 (Olivares to President of Council of Castile, 18 Sept. 1632).
[53] See José Simón-Díaz, *Historia del Colegio Imperial*, 2 vols. (Madrid, 1952–9), I, and Richard L. Kagan, *Students and Society in Early Modern Spain* (Baltimore and London, 1974), pp. 38–9.
[54] See Elliott and de la Peña, *Memoriales y cartas*, II, doc.XIIc.

Master of the Horse.[55] These provide a vivid insight into his ideal of the courtier and the way he should be trained. The pages were to 'profess such good and exemplary customs as to make it impossible to differentiate them from members of the most strict religious orders'. They were to be given no home leave ('the source of all the evils of youth'), and every hour of the day was to be scrupulously filled. They must learn to read 'perfectly' books written in Spanish, Portuguese, 'Lemosina' (Catalan) and French, and to 'write very well our language, Italian, and French if possible'. They were to know Latin 'preeminently well', and read historians and poets 'and at least understand them'. Instruction was to be given in cosmography, geography and navigation, and pupils were to acquire sufficient mathematics to master the art of fortification. Open air training would be provided in military pursuits, and the young men were to become masters of horsemanship, dancing and fencing.

According to the Jesuit Jean-Charles della Faille, who instructed the twenty-one pages in the art of fortification, the young men enjoyed their classes;[56] but in general there is an archaizing, medieval character to this vision of an exemplary school for pages designed, in Olivares' words, to be a 'mirror for the nobility of Castile'. Perhaps the days of palace schools were passed. The lack of appeal of his educational schemes to the nobility for whom they were intended suggests the limitations of court culture by the seventeenth century as an instrument for moral improvement and ethical reform.

But other, less didactic, aspects of the Count-Duke's policy for the court enjoyed more success. In particular, he succeeded in making it a centre of cultural patronage and a showcase for the arts, acting on the principle that it was letters as well as arms that made a monarch great.[57] In a town which already boasted munificent patrons, Philip IV was to become the greatest patron of them all, giving a new impetus to patronage and picture collecting at court and among the high nobility. A roll-call of the great collectors of the middle decades of the century – the Counts of Monterrey and Leganés, Don Luis de Haro, the Admiral of Castile – suggests something of the impact of the royal example.[58]

[55] Real Academia de la Historia, Madrid. Salazar K-8, fos.361–7. *Instrucción para la casa de los pajes*, 30 April 1639.
[56] Omer Van de Vyver S.I., 'Lettres de J.-Ch. della Faille S.I., cosmographe du roi à Madrid, a M.-F. Van Langren, cosmographe du roi a Bruxelles, 1634–1645', *Archivum Historicum Societatis Iesu*, XLVI (1977), pp. 145, 148, 149 (letters of 10 April, 18 May and 8 July 1639).
[57] For Philip IV's insistence on the importance of letters as well as arms, see Brown and Elliott, *A Palace for a King*, p. 42.
[58] *Ibid.*, p. 115; and see J. H. Elliott, 'Art and Decline in Seventeenth-Century Spain',

No one was more aware than Olivares of the important political dividends to be derived from the patronage of artists and men of letters – a patronage that Philip IV exercised on an impressive scale. According to a recent estimate, 223 writers held positions in the personal service of the king and his family during the reign of Philip IV. This compares with sixty-six in the reign of Philip II and seventy-six in that of Philip III.[59] In their books and plays these men would sing the praises of the Planet King, and project to the world the brilliant image of Spanish kingship which the regime of Olivares was seeking to promote. The same theme was developed in the visual arts, especially in the celebrated Hall of Realms in the palace of the Buen Retiro, for which Velázquez and his fellow artists executed a series of paintings designed to glorify the dynasty and commemorate the victories of a triumphant Philip IV.[60]

But, as at the contemporaneous court of Charles I of England,[61] the degree of system in the politics of court culture under Philip IV can be overstated. Although Olivares possessed a general programme for the king and the court, there is a marked element of improvisation in its execution. The haphazard planning of the royal pleasure palace of the Buen Retiro in the 1630s[62] was characteristic of the way in which the programme was managed. Part of the explanation is to be found in the exigencies of the crown's finances, which made systematic planning difficult; part, also, in what the eighteenth-century Scottish historian, Robert Watson, nicely described as the 'sublime but irregular genius' of the Count-Duke himself.[63] But modern historiography, in its search for hidden symbols and meanings, is all too prone to forget that the prime purpose of court culture was to divert and entertain. The Spanish court, like the other courts of seventeenth-century Europe, was more often speaking to itself than speaking to the world.

Yet even the ways in which it spoke to itself could not fail to project a certain image, and Olivares, with his superb sense of theatre, always had a sharp eye for the possibilities. He even turned bad weather to

in *Bartolomé Esteban Murillo* (Catalogue of the Exhibition at the Royal Academy of Arts, London, 1983), pp. 40–51.
[59] José Simón Díaz, 'Los escritores-criados en la época de los Austrias', *Revista Universidad Complutense* (1981), pp. 169–78. It should be noted that 95 of these were court chaplains or preachers. These number 124 in the reign of Carlos II, out of a grand total of 190.
[60] See Brown and Elliott, *A Palace for a King*, ch.6.
[61] See Malcolm Smuts, 'The Political Failure of Stuart Cultural Patronage', in Guy Fitch Lytle and Stephen Orgel (eds.), *Patronage in the Renaissance* (Princeton, 1981), ch. 6.
[62] See Brown and Elliott, *A Palace for a King*, ch. 3.
[63] *The History of the Reign of Philip the Third, King of Spain* (London, 1783), p. 422.

account, as in the inaugural ceremonies of 1633 for the Buen Retiro, when glass panels adorned with red velvet and damask were placed over the balcony to protect Philip from the rain, making him look, at least to one observer, like a holy relic in a reliquary.[64] Here was the king as God on earth, to be reverenced and adored. We have only to move forward fifty years, to Philip's nephew and son-in-law, Louis XIV, to see the themes that made their appearance in the Spain of Olivares marshalled into a more coherent programme for the glorification of another, and greater, Sun King. By then the court of Madrid was eclipsed by the courts both of Versailles and Vienna. Carlos II, the prisoner of oligarchy, and sheltered behind the barrier of court protocol which his father had elaborated with such meticulous attention to detail, was incapable of sustaining the role expected of a king of Spain in the theatre of the world. Quevedo once wrote that for an idle king 'palaces are the sepulchres of a living death'.[65] The palace in Madrid never resembled a sepulchre more closely than in those last tragic decades of the seventeenth century.

Anyone surveying the century and a half of Spanish court history since the imposition of Burgundian ceremonial on the household of Prince Philip in 1548 is likely to be impressed on the one hand by the continuity of forms, traditions and themes, and on the other by the way in which strong personalities could impose themselves on these traditional forms and turn them to advantage. Two different and not entirely compatible strains were to be found in the style of life which Charles V selected for the court of his son. One of these was the isolation of the king as a remote figure, visible for most of the time to only a privileged few. Royal privacy, used to great political effect by Philip II, degenerated into royal obscurity in the reigns of his son, Philip III, and his great-grandson, Carlos II. The other strand in the legacy of Charles V was the use of political imagery and court ceremonial and festivities around the person of the monarch to project the glories of the dynasty. Olivares grasped the possibilities inherent in this aspect of the Emperor's legacy, and developed them with skill to create a public image of Philip IV as Felipe el Grande, the Planet King whose brilliance illuminated the earth.

Yet splendour at court was a double-edged weapon, as the regime of Olivares discovered to its cost. The court of the Spanish Habsburgs may have been unique among the courts of Early Modern Europe in the degree of tension that prevailed between the claims of reclusive and

[64] Brown and Elliott, *A Palace for a King*, p. 68.
[65] 'Política de Dios y gobierno de Cristo', in Francisco de Quevedo, *Obras completas*, ed. Felicidad Buendía, 6th edn., 2 vols. (Madrid (1966–7), I, p. 627 (ch.XIII).

J. H. ELLIOTT

public kingship. It was possible to combine them to powerful effect, but the balance was not easily achieved. 'One can sin through excess', wrote Núñez de Castro, 'as well as through deficiency. Pomp and circumstance are fitting, but they must be controlled by reason, moderated according to the season, and regulated by prudence ... Expenditure should produce decorum, not ostentation; veneration and not vainglory.'[66] The elaborate court ceremonial of the Spanish Habsburgs could be used at once to protect and project the person of the king. But if the balance was wrong, if the king was either too ostentatiously presented or became too remote, not much remained to shield him from the devastating perception that 'Your Majesty's self is but a ceremony'.

[66] *Libro histórico político, sólo Madrid es corte*, pp. 192–3.

The magnificent Lorenzo de' Medici; between myth and history

MELISSA MERIAM BULLARD

We make certain historical figures into cultural heroes and grant them an afterlife ofttimes richer and filled with more rewards and recognition than their actual chronological lives. Lorenzo de' Medici is one of them. Mention his name, and vivid and striking images of the golden age of Florence and the Renaissance spring to mind. Lorenzo the Magnificent plays a double role for us. He is that historical person who lived in fifteenth-century Florence, and at the same time, he is a symbol of his age. As with many a figure from the past, historians can study his thought and actions through contemporary records, through his own copious correspondence and other primary sources, but those historical documents are hardly adequate sources for an analysis of his larger symbolic role.

Historical myths present special difficulties for the historian, first of all because it is not clear exactly what they are. They exist somewhere between myth and history. Like myth they are expressions of collective belief, but not disembodied belief devoid of connections to established fact. Rather they acquire significance precisely because they are beliefs about the past. The subjects of historical myths, men like Lorenzo de' Medici or George Washington, are the curious stepchildren of history because they combine elements of both myth and historical reality. They are similar to the ancient Greek demigods or Roman emperors who people believed were half-mortal, half-divine, neither entirely one nor the other. One common characteristic of historical myths is that they often attribute global significance to otherwise normal events, such as for example the rifle shot on a Concord, Massachusetts green, which, because of the American Revolution that followed, became the 'shot heard round the world'. A second characteristic is that they often include pseudo-historical material, usually in the form of stories or anecdotes which illustrate fundamental aspects of the myth. The famous anecdote recounted by Parson Weems in his biography of

25

George Washington that as a boy the President could not tell a lie about the cherry tree he had chopped down illustrates Washington's fundamental honesty.[1] In the case of Lorenzo de' Medici, the apocryphal school for young artists he established in his garden illustrates his great interest in and patronage of Renaissance culture.[2]

What precisely are the origins of these historical myths? Are they the product of a person's fame and reputation during his lifetime? Are they the deliberate, propagandistic fabrications of self-interested groups which then find a wider audience? Or do historical myths contain a transcendent quality that reaches beyond specific circumstances and intentions by striking a concordant note deep within the collective memory of a culture? Until recently historians have confronted historical myths iconoclastically, treating them as impostors posing as reality, which should be exposed and shattered in the greater interests of revealing historical truth.[3] However, we need not dismiss historical myths as antithetical to reality in order to investigate them. Rather we can more profitably study them if we regard them as standing in a close and friendly proximity to historical reality in so far as they comprise the evolving process of human belief about history. This is perhaps the only way, case by case, in which we can hope to learn more about the mysterious process by which figures like Lorenzo de' Medici become mythologized and are awarded the transcendent qualities that transform them into symbols of their age.

Since historical myths do not lend themselves to investigation using traditional historical sources, we do not know precisely how they come into being, or why some figures from the past become mythologized and

[1] Mason L. Weems, *The Life of Washington*, ed. Marcus Cunliffe (Cambridge, Mass., 1962), p. 12.
[2] André Chastel, 'Vasari et la légende Médicéenne: "L'École du Jardin de Saint Marc"', *Studi Vasariani* (Florence, 1952), pp. 159–67. See also E. Barfucci, *Lorenzo de' Medici e la società artistica del suo tempo* (Florence, 1957), pp. 181–217, who called the school 'The apotheosis of Lorenzo's patronage', p. 216.
[3] Delio Cantimori makes this implicit assumption in his criticism of the uncritical idolatry present in William Roscoe's late eighteenth-century biography of Lorenzo in his remarks before the 1955 meeting of the International Congress of Historical Sciences in Rome, *Relazioni del X Congresso Internazionale di Scienze Storiche*, IV (Florence, 1955), p. 127 and cited in Ernst Gombrich, 'Renaissance and Golden Age', *Journal of the Warburg and Courtauld Institutes*, XXIV (1961), p. 306. Discussion at the Congress prompted the international sponsorship of the first critical edition of Lorenzo's letters, the preparation of which is still in progress. Since 1955 several monographs have appeared which treat myth in the Renaissance as a proper subject from a variety of perspectives, mostly notably, H. Levin, *The Myth of the Golden Age in the Renaissance* (Bloomington, Ind., 1969); Donald Weinstein, *Savonarola and Florence: Prophecy and Patriotism in the Renaissance* (Princeton, N.J., 1979); Giovanni Cipriani, *Il mito etrusco nel rinascimento fiorentino* (Florence, 1980); and Edward Muir, *Civic Ritual in Renaissance Venice* (Princeton, N.J., 1981).

others not. We can be sure, however, that someone like Lorenzo de' Medici did not become the subject of historical myth by accident. The symbolic association between Lorenzo and the Renaissance that we know today is a post-Enlightenment development subsequent to elaborations by Voltaire and others of the idea of the Italian Renaissance as a special epoch of glorious intellectual and cultural achievement and of the Medici in particular as its exemplary patrons.[4] The modern identification of Lorenzo with the Renaissance draws primarily upon posthumous, sixteenth-century sources, the histories by Niccolò Valori, Guicciardini, Machiavelli and Vasari, in which the Medici myth was first codified. Lorenzo was singled out then for his remarkable genius as a statesman and peace-maker of Italy, his magnanimity as cultivator of the arts, and his grandeur as head of his family's regime in Florence. The early sixteenty-century historians who first wrote about his life and gave his biography historical interpretation established the outlines of a magnificent portrait that would be copied and embellished in literature and art in the centuries to come. Twentieth-century historians who first became interested in historical views of the Medici as part of the phenomenon of the Renaissance and its place in the development of European historiography, have focussed almost exclusively on this sixteenth-century phase of the Medici myth and its subsequent modern developments.[5] The codification of the myth in the sixteenth century, however, was only an intermediate stage in a much larger myth-making process that had been underway while Lorenzo was still alive. The focus

[4] Wallace K. Ferguson, *The Renaissance in Historical Thought. Five Centuries of Interpretation* (Cambridge, Mass., 1948), pp. 78–94. Monsignor A. Fabroni shared this view in the first modern biography of Lorenzo, *Laurentii Medicis Magnifici vita* (Pisa, 1784). It was popularized subsequently by William Roscoe in his widely read *Life of Lorenzo de' Medici Called the Magnificent* (London, 1796) to which citations here are from the fifth edition in 1806.

[5] Felix Gilbert, 'Bernardo Rucellai and the Orti Oricellari: a Study on the Origin of Modern Political Thought', *Journal of the Warburg and Courtauld Institutes*, XII (1949), pp. 101–31 and reprinted in *History. Choice and Commitment* (Cambridge, Mass, 1977), pp. 215–46; *idem*, 'Guicciardini, Machiavelli, Valori on Lorenzo Magnifico', *Renaissance News*, XI (1958), pp. 107–14; *idem*, *Machiavelli and Guicciardini, Politics and History in Sixteenth-Century Florence* (Princeton, N. J., 1965), pp. 105–22; John R. Hale, *England and the Italian Renaissance* (London, 1954), passim; *idem*, 'Cosimo and Lorenzo dei Medici: Their Reputation in England from the Sixteenth to the Nineteenth-Century', *English Miscellany*, VIII (1957), pp. 179–94; André Chastel, *Art et humanisme à Florence au temps de Laurent le Magnifique* (Paris, 1959); Ernst Gombrich, 'Renaissance and Golden Age', pp. 306–9; and most recently Nicolai Rubinstein, 'The Formation of the Posthumous Image of Lorenzo de' Medici', in Edward Chaney and Neil Ritchie (ed.), *Oxford, China and Italy. Writings in Honour of Sir Harold Acton on his Eightieth Birthday* (London, 1984), pp. 94–106 in which is referenced yet another forthcoming article on this topic by E. Gusberti entitled 'Un mito del Cinquecento: Lorenzo il Magnifico' for the *Bullettino dell'Istituto storico italiano per il Medio Evo*.

of the following discussion is upon the entire process of myth formation
and especially upon its critical developments during Lorenzo's lifetime.

Three principal catalytic elements contributed to the myth-making
process already in the fifteenth century. In the first place dozens of
humanists and friends had been singing Lorenzo's praises from the time
of his birth. Most of them did not do so for the sake of posterity, but
fixed their gaze firmly on their own terrestrial patronage requests. But
the language of epideictic rhetoric which they used lent a powerful idiom
of eulogy and glorification to Lorenzo's virtues and deeds which would
long outlast them. The second crucial contemporary factor was Lorenzo's own exercise of a guiding hand in the myth-making process by
consciously promoting an image of his own magnificence. To be sure,
his image-making had immediate political ends, but this image, like the
humanists' praise, survived him and projected itself through the
centuries. The third contributing element to the Medici myth was the
love of the Florentine people and the respect of admirers from all over
Italy and abroad which concretized those images and praise and thus
awarded him a special, elevated place in history. No one of these factors
by itself can adequately explain the development of Lorenzo the
Magnificent's historical myth. The myth arose from the complex
interaction over time of all of them. At its very heart, then, the historical
myth of Lorenzo is best understood not as a static, codified product of
belief which, like a literary piece, can be analyzed structurally or
thematically. Rather it is a dynamic and fluid process that involves the
continued interaction between the historical reality of Lorenzo's life and
the leavening of belief about the nature and significance of that reality,
whether in the minds of sixteenth-century Florentines, some of whom
remembered Lorenzo and wrote about him; of eighteenth-century
Londoners who had read William Roscoe's popular biography; or of
twentieth-century university students who have just emerged from a
lecture on the Renaissance.[6] Our interest in Lorenzo the Magnificent is

[6] For a general definition of myth, I found helpful Ben Halpern's article on the
distinction between myth and ideology using the writings of Sorel and Mannheim in
which the origin of myth is defined as existing somewhere between non-rational drives
and rational communication, as 'an area where beliefs arise and social consensus is
established', '"Myth" and "Ideology" in Modern Usage', *History and Theory*, 1
(1961), p. 143. Historical myths, however, cannot profitably be studied in the abstract
or in an historical vacuum. For this reason the currently popular theories of myth
formulated by modern anthropologists are only of limited use here. Clifford Geertz
sees myth, like art, language, and ritual, as a product of culture, one of the systems
of significant symbols which provide 'models of emotion' and 'public images of
sentiment', *The Interpretation of Culture* (New York, 1973), pp. 48, 82. His concern,
however, is for the social function of myth as providing 'charters for social institutions
and rationalizations of social privilege' (p. 88), not for its process of development. Nor

with the process of myth, and our emphasis lies on contemporary fifteenth-century contributions to his myth more than on its modern product. But in order to identify more clearly how the process gave shape to the myth, we must begin with that product and work backward through the sixteenth century.

LORENZO AND MYTHS OF THE RENAISSANCE

The special historical significance attributed to Lorenzo the Magnificent today cannot be understood apart from other widely held beliefs about the Renaissance which Lorenzo is thought to personify. Ernst Gombrich pointed out the connection between what he appropriately labeled the 'Medici myth' and a more encompassing myth of the Renaissance as golden age, which, he wrote, 'makes the Medici in general, and Lorenzo in particular, directly responsible for a magic efflorescence of the human spirit, the Renaissance'.[7] Filling out the sizeable dimensions of Lorenzo's modern role as symbol of the Renaissance constitutes part of the mythopoeic process, and certain aspects of his character and many of his deeds became exaggerated over time.[8] In keeping with Lorenzo's Augustan role as evoker of the golden age, his patronage of the arts and learning has been specially emphasized. Even though it has been demonstrated that claims for Medici patronage have been greatly exaggerated, and that, notably, the famous school Lorenzo supposedly

does myth, when viewed as a dynamic process unfolding over time, lend itself to the sort of static structural analysis applied to texts. Claude Lévi-Strauss recognized the double nature of myth, its being both historical and ahistorical, but his approach dictates that those elements stand in opposition to one another, rather than in synchronic harmony as argued here. See for example, his 'The Structural Study of Myth' in Thomas A. Sebeok (ed.), *Myth: a Symposium* (Bloomington, Ind., 1955), pp. 81–106. What the semioticist Umberto Eco has to say about 'open works' and the creative role of the interpreter's interaction with a text would come closest in the field of literary criticism to my approach to historical myths as involving active, constant belief. See his *The Role of the Reader. Explorations in the Semiotics of Texts* (Bloomington, Ind., 1979), especially pp. 3–40 and 107–24 ('The Myth of Superman'). Eco's allowance for the role of the reader is an elaboration in modern terminology from the point of view of the reader of the Classical rhetorical rule in the introduction or *exordium* in which the orator should stimulate the interest and sympathy of his addressee by taking account of the latter's character and disposition towards the case to be discussed, as explained, for example, in Quintillian's *Institutio Oratoria*, IV: I. The emphasis here on the role of the believer in the myth-making process is particularly appropriate to the Renaissance since Classical theories of persuasion, especially Cicero's and Quintillian's, helped shape so much of Renaissance culture, and consequently Renaissance myths.

[7] Gombrich, 'Renaissance and Golden Age', p. 306.
[8] A modern parallel exists in the mythicization of public figures by the mass media which often involves making their public characters conform to an ideal image. See the discussion by Andrew Greeley, 'Myths, Symbols and Rituals in the Modern World', *The Critic*, xx, no. 3 (Dec.–Jan. 1961–2), pp. 18–25.

founded for young artists to study the antique sculptures in his garden at S. Marco was a later Vasari invention aimed at encouraging Duke Cosimo I's patronage of the arts, that belief still persists down to the present day.[9] The other mainstay of the Medici myth, which is likewise associated with the Vergilian metaphor of a golden age, is that the Medici ushered in an era of peace in Italy lasting as long as Lorenzo was alive. That war did break out not long after his death confirmed to many that he had been solely responsible for the peace of Italy. Lorenzo's general wisdom and peacemindedness were praised by contemporaries, but over the centuries the significance of his diplomatic feats has grown to include links to the development of the modern state system and the 'concert of Europe' idea.[10] No matter that the publication of his correspondence now reveals that he never articulated a concept of balance of power diplomacy, or that the idea of the peace of Italy, so tightly bound with his name, turns out to be commonplace in the diplomatic writings of his day.[11]

Another general myth about the Renaissance which has found specific focus in Lorenzo concerns the idea of the universal man. Here his historiographical portrait broadens beyond patronage and diplomacy to include his literary endeavors, his business activities, even his physical prowess. Samples of Lorenzo's writings and poetry are regularly represented in Renaissance anthologies even though literary scholars admit

[9] Gombrich, 'The Early Medici as Patrons of Art', in E. F. Jacob (ed.) *Italian Renaissance Studies* (London, 1960), pp. 304–11; Chastel, 'Vasari et la Légende Médicéenne', pp. 159–67. The balance of opinion is now beginning to tip back in the other direction towards a greater appreciation at least of Lorenzo's architectural patronage. See Caroline Elam, 'Lorenzo de' Medici and the Urban Development of Renaissance Florence', *Art History*, I (1978), pp. 43–66.

[10] L. von Ranke, *History of the Latin and Teutonic Nations from 1494–1514*, trans. Philip A. Ashworth (London, 1887), pp. 37–40; R. Palmarocchi, *La politica italiana di Lorenzo de' Medici* (Florence, 1933), pp. 229–46, 273–83; E. W. Nelson, 'Origins of Modern Balance of Power Diplomacy', *Medievalia and Humanistica*, I (1943), pp. 124–42.

[11] To date four volumes of the letters have appeared, and research is underway up through 1488. Lorenzo de' Medici, *Lettere*, ed. R. Fubini and N. Rubinstein (Florence, 1977–81), I–IV. The first discussions of a general peace in Italy occurred in 1486 in the aftermath of the Barons' War when Milan, Venice, Florence, the papacy, and Naples all talked about the possibility of a general league, but the idea never advanced beyond tentative discussions. Lorenzo seems to have had little faith in a general league, preferring to secure Florence's traditional alliance with Milan and Naples first. His discussion of the idea must be placed within the context of his other purposes, namely to discourage the pope's separate negotiations with Venice and to promote his own private alliance with Innocent. Lorenzo's thinking on these matters is contained in his correspondence during December 1486 with Piero Alamanni, Florentine ambassador to Milan, Archivo Segreto Vaticano (ASV), Mss. Patetta, 1739, fos. 1–8. In the early sixteenth century Bernardo Rucellai introduced the term balance of power into political literature, and Guicciardini attributed it to Lorenzo, Gilbert, *History. Choice and Commitment*, pp. 216, 506–7.

much of it is modeled on Petrarch or is pedantically Neoplatonic, implying that if taken by itself apart from Lorenzo's authorship, it might not receive such reverential treatment.[12] Lorenzo was also an international banker, and even though the Medici firm nearly went bankrupt during his lifetime, his activity in the financial affairs of his day constitutes an important facet of his posthumous image.[13] Aspects of his personal life complete the portrait of Lorenzo the Magnificent as the well-rounded Renaissance individual. He is renowned for his hospitality in the Medici palace on the Via Larga where he hosted heads of state in elegance and carefully understated luxury. His banquets and entertainments were famous for their lavish inventiveness. In addition, he was a lively gamesman and tournament champion.[14] The charming story used to illustrate the special affinity between Lorenzo, the quasi-chivalric hero, and his steed concerns his favorite racehorse Morello who was reportedly so attached to his master that if Lorenzo did not come every day to feed him, the horse would lie down despondently and refuse to eat.[15] Since Lorenzo's name was linked to at least three aristocratic beauties, he even acquired a certain renown for his sexual appetite, but at the same time enjoyed a reputation as a loving and devoted father to his seven children.[16]

To Lorenzo's association with the myth of the Renaissance as golden age and to the myth of the universal man must be added his identification with the special destiny of Florence. Savonarola had linked his prophecies to the myth of Florence,[17] but an earlier identification of the destiny of the city with that of her most prominent citizen most certainly

[12] A. Rochon, *La jeunesse de Laurent de Médicis (1449–1478)* (Paris, 1963), pp. 148–59; 475–543; F. De Sanctis, *Storia della letteratura italiana* (Mondadori: Milan, 1956), pp. 367–9.
[13] N. Machiavelli, *History of Florence*, Eng. Trans. (New York, 1960), p. 405; Raymond de Roover, *The Rise and Decline of the Medici Bank 1397–1494* (New York, 1966), pp. 221–4; 358–75. In his classic biography William Roscoe, himself a Liverpool banker and businessman and connoisseur of the arts, placed special emphasis on the mercantile origins of the Medici and their instrumental role in the revival of the arts, *Life of Lorenzo de' Medici*, I, 13–18, 179–84.
[14] His tournaments were the talk of Italy. See the letters in J. Ross, *Lives of the Early Medici as Told in Their Correspondence* (London, 1910), pp. 124, 126, 160. Duke Galeazzo Maria Sforza's visit in 1471 has become the subject of an anecdote, recounted first by Niccolò Valori and elaborated by Roscoe to emphasize Lorenzo's patronage. According to the story, the duke was so impressed by the fine collections of art and antiques at the Medici palace that he commented that all his own gold and silver were as nothing in comparison. Niccolò Valori, *Vita del Magnifico Lorenzo de' Medici il Vecchio*, Ital. trans., published as an unpaginated preface to the *Diario* of Biagio Buonaccorsi (Florence, 1568); Roscoe, *Life of Lorenzo de' Medici*, I, pp. 185–7.
[15] The story was first recounted by Valori, *Vita*, p. 38 (my pagination) and as recently as 1974 in Hugh Ross Williamson, *Lorenzo the Magnificent* (New York, 1974), p. 224.
[16] N. Machiavelli, *History of Florence*, p. 407; Rochon, *La jeunesse*, pp. 88–99, 239–50.
[17] Weinstein, *Savonarola and Florence*, p. 132–84.

occurred with Lorenzo at the time of the Pazzi Conspiracy. Like the myth of the divine twins or the stories of Cain and Abel and Romulus and Remus, Lorenzo was the brother who survived to carry on the destiny of his people. The symbolic significance of the plot to assassinate him and his brother Giuliano was not lost either on contemporaries or on succeeding generations. The assassination was to take place at the high point of the mass on the holiest day of the year, Easter Sunday, in the ritual center of the city, the cathedral. That Lorenzo barely escaped with his life made his and Florence's salvation all the more dramatic.[18] In the face of defeat in the ensuing war against the papacy and Naples, Lorenzo decided to go to Naples and throw himself at the mercy of King Ferrante and sue for peace. That this feat met with success thereby restoring peace and saving Florence from a dishonorable defeat made him all the more easily identified with the fortunes of the city. The medal struck to commemorate his escape and his brother's murder depicts Lorenzo as *salus publicus*, salvation of the people, and Giuliano as *luctus publicus*, grief of the people.[19]

By now the facts of Lorenzo's life are thoroughly impregnated with elements of myth, making his posthumous image larger than life. Many of the stories and anecdotes which have become a part of Lorenzo's mythicized biography are apocryphal, or exaggerations at best, and cannot be borne out by historical research. But what is interesting about the mythic aura surrounding Lorenzo is not so much that the importance of his deeds should have become puffed up over time, but rather how the mythopoeic process was set into motion and achieved literary form so rapidly. It is noteworthy that most of the marvelous stories attached to Lorenzo's life were already recounted within a generation of his death and had quickly found written expression in a number of histories and biographies dating from the early sixteenth century.

[18] Poliziano's contemporary account of the Pazzi Conspiracy is filled with identifications of Lorenzo with 'the public safety', 'the well-being of the whole Florentine Republic', and 'the hope and power of the people', *Coniurationis commentarium* published in Roscoe, *Life of Lorenzo de' Medici*, III, app. XXI, pp. 125–43 and in English translation by E. Welles in B. Kohl and R. Witt, *The Earthy Republic. Italian Humanists on Government and Society* (Philadelphia, 1978), *pp.* 305–22.

[19] The design of the medal has been attributed to Giovanni di Bertoldo, K. Langedijk, *The Portraits of the Medici*, 3 vols. (Florence, 1981–3), I, 27 and II, 1168. On a later medal by Niccolò Fiorentino, the reverse shows Florence sitting under the shade of a laurel tree, signifying Lorenzo, with the inscription *tutela patrie*, guardian of the country, *ibid.*, I, 30.

The magnificent Lorenzo de' Medici

THE CRISIS OF ITALY

The most widely supported explanation for the rapid idealization of Lorenzo which occurred in the generation after his death relates to the changing political situation in Florence at that time. Felix Gilbert has argued persuasively that the small but influential group of Florentine historians and political thinkers who attended the discussions in the *Orti Oricellari* sponsored by Bernardo Rucellai and his sons over the first two decades of the sixteenth century made a concerted, conscious effort to transform Lorenzo into an ideal leader and Laurentian Florence into an ideal age.[20] According to Gilbert their idealization of Lorenzo was not the result of a search for historical accuracy but rather a deliberate fabricating of an historical myth.[21] The myth was born out of their discontent with the changes in the government after Lorenzo's death and their attempts to press for reform. Rucellai and the conservative members of the *Orti* gatherings sought an aristocratic regime for Florence in which the Medici would be *primi inter pares*, maintaining order and stability but without either kowtowing to the will of the masses or assuming too much independent control over the city. In their desire to cast a new image of Lorenzo, the Rucellai group reversed earlier opinion which had assessed Lorenzo's management of the Florentine state negatively. Leaving aside for the moment the question of contemporary opinion while Lorenzo was still alive, which had hardly solidified and was by no means uniformly critical, if the Rucellai group, meeting ten to twenty years after his death, was set upon revising a negative opinion of Lorenzo, it was the one Savonarola and his followers had been putting forth in the mid 1490s. In his sermons Savonarola had made scarcely veiled allusions to Lorenzo as the tyrant personified.[22] Such allusions accorded with Savonarola's republican views and his support of the more republican Great Council he had helped to introduce, which government, together with its chief proponent, Rucellai and the aristocrats meeting in the *Orti* heartily despised.

[20] Gilbert, *History. Choice and Commitment*, pp. 234–8. 1501 is the earliest mention in Piero Parenti's *Istorie fiorentine* of widespread nostalgia for the way things had been in Lorenzo's day, in J. Schnitzer, *Quellen und Forschungen zur Geschichte Savonarolas* (Munich, 1904), IV, p. 299.

[21] Gilbert, *Machiavelli and Guicciardini*, p. 109.

[22] According to Bartolomeo Cerretani, Savonarola's apocalyptic sermons began right after Lorenzo's death, *Storia fiorentina*, in Schnitzer, *Quellen und Forschungen*, III, pp. 6–7, but his vicious attacks on the Medici government did not commence until his return to Florence in November 1494 at the height of the crisis preceding Piero de' Medici's flight and Charles VIII's entrance into Florence. They culminated in his treatise on the Florentine government, the *Tratto circa il reggimento e governo della città di Firenze* written shortly before his death.

33

Politics undeniably played a determining role in shaping the main outlines of Lorenzo's idealized portrait in the early sixteenth century. This can be seen in the way images of him were periodically altered by highlighting now one, now another aspect of his character, depending upon which was appropriate comment on the successive changes in government. In the years before 1512 during the republican government of the Great Council, the aristocratic critics of the regime emphasized three themes, the peace and stability Florence had enjoyed under Lorenzo, the special favor he had bestowed on the arts and learning, together with the honor he had shown leading citizens such as themselves, all features of past times noticeably neglected by the then present republican regime.[23] In the period following the Medici's return from exile in 1512 when Lorenzo's grandson became too high-handed for their tastes, critics clad The Magnifico in republican garb and emphasized how he had been ever respectful of the city's *vita civile* and had always consulted leading citizens publicly on important matters.[24] The successive appropriations of different facets of Lorenzo's character continued through the period of the Medici dukes. The new Medici, not direct descendants of Lorenzo's line, adopted the historical Medici of the fifteenth century, and Lorenzo in particular, as their symbolic property. Together with their court iconographers such as Vasari, the later Medici used family history to enhance their own dynasticism. The cycles of decorations in the Palazzo Vecchio and the Pitti Palace depicting Lorenzo consistently show him to be the learned patron of culture and

[23] Examples from the writings of Pietro Crinto, Giovanni Corsi, and Bernardo Rucellai can be found in Gilbert, *History. Choice and Commitment*, pp. 505–6.

[24] 'For he had demonstrated such quality up to now that he has filled with good hopes all this city, and it seems that everybody finds in him happy recollection of his grandfather; because His Magnificence is attentive to business, liberal and pleasant in audience, slow and weighty in his answers. The method of his conversing differs so much from that of the others that no pride is seen in it...He makes himself, in short, both loved and revered, rather than feared...The management of his house is so arranged that, though we see there much splendor and liberality, nonetheless he does not abandon the life of a citizen', English translation in Allan Gilbert (ed.), *The Letters of Machiavelli* (New York, 1961), pp. 138–9. Lodovico Alamanni in his *Discorso sopra il fermare lo stato di Firenze nella devozione de' Medici* likewise advised a return to the civilian ways of 'Lorenzo il vecchio', praising 'his use of the customs and habits of a citizen, his conducting the affairs of government in the *palazzo* and his coming into the piazza everyday and giving audiences readily, such that to the citizens he seemed more of a brother than a superior, and for this they loved him and were all the more content and faithful', published as an appendix to R. von Albertini, *Das florentinische Staatsbewusstsein im Übergang von der Republik zum Prinzipat* (Bern, 1955), p. 369. The revisionism that had occurred over a generation is clearly reflected in Guicciardini's writings from the early appraisal of Lorenzo in his *History of Florence*, to his post-1512 eulogy published in *Scritti politici e Ricordi*, ed. R. Palmarocchi (Bari, 1933), pp. 223–8. See Gilbert, 'Guicciardini, Machiavelli', pp. 107–9 and Rubinstein, 'The Formation', pp. 97–102.

the wise statesman who was arbiter of Italy. Absent is any reference to Lorenzo's respect for Florence's republican ways, no longer an appropriate theme in a city ruled by Medici dukes.[25]

The changing portrait of Lorenzo in the early sixteenth century involved, however, more than the conscious manipulation of an historical person for limited political and ideological purposes on the part of the *Orti Oricellari* group or the Medici family. Had this been the case, the resurrected image of Lorenzo probably would not have survived beyond the period of its political usefulness once the principate had been instituted or have passed beyond local dynasticism within the Medici family. The images of Lorenzo arose from a deeper psychological level of mythic consciousness.[26] To that generation of Florentines in the early sixteenth century, the memory of Lorenzo struck a much deeper resonance of response which included but reached beyond their immediate reaction to the political upheavals in their city. The sixteenth-century images of Lorenzo must also be understood against the broader background of the crisis of the whole period of the Italian wars which profoundly affected contemporary psycho-historical consciousness. The Italian wars, which began with Charles VIII's invasion in 1494 and lasted some forty years, saw repeated invasions of the Italian peninsula by French and Spanish armies. During that time the peace of Italy crumbled from within and without, and one after another the Italian states lost their independence to the more powerful European monarchies. For Rucellai, Machiavelli, Guicciardini, and other of their contemporaries, the peace of Italy had died with Lorenzo de' Medici, and they drew a direct causal link between his death and the onslaught of the invasions. In his *De bello italico* Rucellai had been the first to articulate a connection between Charles VIII's coming and the disintegration of the diplomatic course Lorenzo had set during his lifetime, and Machiavelli implicitly accepted the same new periodization of history when he chose the death of Lorenzo as the ending point for his *History of Florence*.[27]

The events of 1494 were especially pressing in Florentine minds because the invasion of Charles coincided with the exile of Piero de'

---

[25] Remarkably few contemporary portraits were made of Lorenzo compared to the number of idealized posthumous ones. For the artistic representations of Lorenzo and their reflections of his changing image, see K. Langedijk, *The Portraits*, especially I, 26–68; II, 1138–67 and Rubinstein, 'The Formation', pp. 102–5.

[26] This accords with Halpern's distinction between myth and ideology in '"Myth" and "Ideology"', pp. 129–49.

[27] Rucellai, *De bello italico* (London, 1733); Machiavelli, *History of Florence*. On Rucellai's contribution, see Gilbert, *History. Choice and Commitment*, pp. 211–46; *idem, Machiavelli and Guicciardini*, pp. 112–13.

Medici and the revolution that brought the government by the Great Council into the city. But once the dust had settled on the political debates in Florence, once aristocratic constitutional reform had failed and the Medici principate was firmly ensconced with its Spanish backers in the 1530s, still the death of Lorenzo and Charles VIII's invasion remained the critical dividing line in Florentine history. Conjunction of those two events did not fade away from the Florentine historical consciousness. In his masterful *History of Italy*,[28] written between 1537 and 1540, long after the Italian Wars were over, when his perspective on the crisis had clarified with the passage of time, Guicciardini perceived a sharp break in history between his own sorrowful times and the previous golden era of independence and relative peace in Italy while Lorenzo was still alive. Guicciardini perhaps more than any other of his contemporary historians realized the significance of the crisis for all of Italy, not just Florence, and consequently his portrait of Lorenzo, the departed peacemaker whom he characterized as the fulcrum (*bilancia*) of Italy, looms even larger in the *History* than it had in his earlier works dealing specifically with Florence.[29] In the *History* Guicciardini did not evaluate Lorenzo's policies in their own pre-invasion context, but retrospectively across the barrier of the invasions. The impact of the crisis of the sixteenth century itself had helped produce the myth of Lorenzo as Italian peace-maker, which theme was repeated again and again in subsequent historical and biographical sketches of him and in the historical paintings adorning the Palazzo Vecchio and the Pitti Palace.

THE TRADITION OF PRAISE

The crisis of Italy had sparked in Guicciardini and many of his contemporaries a heightened awareness of history. They had to understand the tragedy of their own times, and they sought explanation by reinterpreting the recent past and Lorenzo's role in shaping it. Consequently, Lorenzo's life was given literary form very rapidly. Rucellai's *De bello italico* and Guicciardini's *Storie fiorentine* both contained early

---

[28] *History of Italy*, trans. Sidney Alexander (London, 1969).

[29] Guicciardini begins his *History* with a description of the peace and prosperity in Italy in 1490, credit for which he attributes to Lorenzo and his balance of power policy. For Guicciardini the tranquility of Italy ended abruptly with Lorenzo's death. 'His death was indeed most untimely for the rest of Italy, not only because efforts toward the continuation of the common security were carried on by hands other than his, but also because he had been the means of moderating, and practically a bridle, in the disagreements and suspicions which very often developed for diverse reasons between Ferdinand and Lodovico Sforza, princes of almost equal power and ambition', *ibid.*, p. 9.

historical appreciations, but it was not until Niccolò Valori wrote a substantial biography of the Magnifico that the significance of his life could be considered as a whole and stories of his youth used to prefigure the achievements of his maturity. Valori's biography was probably written soon after Leo X's election in 1513, although he claimed to have composed it shortly after Lorenzo's death.[30] Valori's family had had close ties to the Medici, and the biography included personal family recollections combined with elegiac *exempla* cloaked in Neoplatonic overtones, the latter probably the legacy of Marsilio Ficino, whom for many years the Valori had supported and the publication of whose works they had helped finance.[31] The biography contains nearly all of the marvelous anecdotes about Lorenzo which were to be repeated over and over again, the stories about his horse, the remarkable events surrounding the famous trip to Naples, illustrations of his erudition and practical wisdom, his passion for collecting, his entertainments, patronage and diplomatic skill. It even includes an extensive description of the series of extraordinary portents that prefigured or accompanied Lorenzo's death, calling to mind ancient models such as Suetonius' life of Caesar.

Valori projected a mythic aura around Lorenzo's life and classed him among the 'miracles of nature'.[32] According to Valori the course of Lorenzo's life was accompanied by a series of signs from the heavens, and he gave every indication of special election while still young. His wise counsel was noted at an uncommonly early age as well as his cleverness, when he saved his father from an assassination attempt by outwitting the assassins.[33] The Pazzi Conspiracy and war with Sixtus IV were, according to Valori, acts of God so that Lorenzo could prove himself in adversity.[34] Divine intervention saved him from a series of

[30] Recent attempts to date the manuscript place it after 1512 when many Florentines, like Machiavelli, who had participated in the Soderini government, were trying to ingratiate themselves anew with the Medici. Valori was himself in prison for complicity in an anti-Medicean plot and would have had every interest in trying to win Medici favor. The polished version of his biography was in fact dedicated and presented to Leo X around 1517. Mario Martelli argues that the Italian version Niccolò's son Filippo prepared and dedicated to another of Lorenzo's children, Leo's sister, Lucrezia Salviati, was based on a lost, earlier Latin version. see his 'Le due redazioni della Laurentii Medicei Vita di Niccolò Valori', *La bibliofilia*, LXVI (1964), pp. 235–63. The dating of the Latin composition is discussed by Gilbert, 'Guicciardini, Machiavelli', pp. 112–13 and Rubinstein, 'The Formation', p. 98 note.
[31] Valori places special emphasis on how Lorenzo had thoroughly absorbed the intricacies of Plato's philosophy under Ficino's guidance and had become convinced that without knowledge of Plato it was impossible either to be a good citizen or to understand Christian doctrine, *Vita*, p. 8.   [32] *Ibid.*, p. 2.   [33] *Ibid.*, p. 6.
[34] 'I believe that without a doubt it happened by the command and will of God Almighty alone, so that in adversity he (Lorenzo) could better demonstrate his *virtù* and prudence', *ibid.*, p. 14.

other assassination plots, and all would-be assassins, Valori notes, justly
suffered violent deaths themselves.[35] It was only natural that all men
should love Lorenzo when animals like his racehorse, inspired by natural
intelligence, not reason, showed him a special, natural affection.[36] Under
the guidance of Lorenzo's wisdom, Florence and her citizenry flourished
in peace and prosperity and gained great fame. According to the
biography, Lorenzo's last words were like 'divine oracles', and his death
which had been accompanied by such awesome portents was greeted by
a great public outburst of grief, grief for the loss of so great a leader and
for the common misery of Italy.[37] In Valori's biography Lorenzo had
achieved the status of a demigod or a Florentine saint. These overtones
of sanctity were not lost upon the contemporary satirist, Giovanni di
Domenico Mazzuoli known as *lo Stradino Fiorentino*, whose humorous
note penned in his copy of the Italian version of Valori's biography to
the effect that this was 'the life of the Magnificent, or rather of *Saint
Lorenzo de' Medici*' (italics mine), had a ring of truth to it.[38]

Valori's *Vita* belongs to the tradition of lives of illustrious men, a
favorite Renaissance topos revived from Antiquity, which served to
provide moral *exempla* from both recent and ancient history.[39] In the
dedicatory preface to Leo X, Valori remembers that when the pope made
his celebrated entrance to Florence in 1515, he had wept in front of the
effigy of his father, and compares the event to Alexander's visit to the
grave of Achilles and Caesar's to the grave of Alexander. This then

[35] *Ibid.*, p. 47.   [36] *Ibid.*, pp. 38-9.   [37] *Ibid.*, pp. 50-2.
[38] 'La Vita del Magnifico, anzi Santo Lorenzo de' Medici', published in Martelli, 'Le
due redazioni', p. 239.
[39] Numerous collections of biographies and painted portraits of famous persons survive
from the fifteenth and sixteenth centuries. Vespasiano da Bisticco, Bartolomeo Fazio,
Aeneas Sylvius Piccolomini, Giovanni Caroli, and Paolo Cortesi, to name a few, all
wrote anthologies of historical lives. See Jacob Burckhardt's classical appreciation of
the importance of biography and the elevation of classical virtues in the Renaissance
in *The Civilization of the Renaissance*, trans. S. Middlemore, 2 vols. (New York, 1958),
I, pp. 148-61; II, pp. 324-33. On Giovanni Caroli's less known *Vitae fratrum*, lives
of famous Dominicans each prefaced with a dedicatory epistle to one of the author's
friends, see Salvatore I. Camporeale, 'Giovanni Caroli e le "Vitae fratrum S. M.
Novellae". Umanesimo e crisi religiosa (1460-1480)', *Memorie Domenicane*, new series,
XII (1981), pp. 141-267. Federigo da Montefeltro had decorated his *studiolo* with
portraits of famous men; Bernardo Rucellai placed busts of emperors, philosophers
and poets from Antiquity along the paths of his garden, Gilbert, *History. Choice
and Commitment*, p. 229. In the sixteenth century Ottaviano de' Medici made a
portrait collection of leading members of the Medici family, and Paolo Giovio, who
later wrote a series of lives of famous men including Lorenzo, had also wanted to
furnish a room as a 'temple of virtue' with portrait busts of famous persons,
Langedijk, *The Portraits*, I, pp. 65-8. Giorgio Vasari's *Lives of the Artists* and his
portrait of Lorenzo painted for Cosimo I in which he portrays Lorenzo as a model of
virtue which has overcome vice, belong to this tradition of the lives of illustrious men
serving as moral *exempla*.

became the ostensible reason for making Leo a gift of the *Vita*, and Valori felt that Leo would find there his own image in his father and that of his father in himself,[40] an idea reminiscent of Ficino's recognition of the spirit of Cosimo present in Lorenzo a generation earlier.[41] Valori's biography was well known to contemporaries. It seems to have been the major source for Guicciardini's portrait sketch of Lorenzo written between his *Storie fiorentine* and his *History of Italy* and of Machiavelli's sketch in his *History of Florence*.[42] Both the Latin and the Italian versions of the biography enjoyed repeated publications beginning in 1568 and continuing on in the eighteenth and nineteenth centuries.[43] Together with Machiavelli's, Guicciardini's and Vasari's writings, the *Vita* of Valori became the standard source for Lorenzo's life.

Eulogies of Lorenzo, of course, did not originate in the sixteenth century, but have their roots back in the fifteenth century in the humanist praise of him and other members of the Medici family. The culture of the Renaissance was steeped in classical rhetorical models and informed by ancient handbooks on rhetoric and oratory. The style of epideictic rhetoric itself encouraged lavish praise often in the form of metaphors replete with cosmic and mythological themes employed to illustrate and enhance the virtues of the person being praised.[44] In Poliziano's letters and verse, for example, Lorenzo became the 'man destined for the very summits';[45] 'Etruria's chief';[46] and 'the toast of every muse and nymph'.[47]

[40] The text of the preface is published in M. Martelli, 'Le due redazioni', pp. 238–40.
[41] See note 50.
[42] Gilbert, 'Guicciardini, Machiavelli', pp. 110–14.
[43] In 1567 Valori's grandson Bacio presented a manuscript copy of the Italian *Vita* with a dedication to Cosimo I, and like his grandfather and father before him, hoped thereby to win Medici favor, in Martelli, 'Le due redazioni', pp. 240–1. The following year the Italian version was published, the Latin version in 1749, a French translation in 1761, and subsequently in 1847. The 1568 Italian *Vita* was most recently reprinted in 1973.
[44] On epideictic rhetoric in the Renaissance, see O. B. Hardison, Jr., *The Enduring Monument: A Study of the Idea of Praise in Renaissance Literary Theory and Practice* (Chapel Hill, 1962), especially chapt. 2, pp. 26–42. For specific applications, see Alison M. Brown, 'The Humanist Portrait of Cosimo de' Medici, *Pater Patriae*', *Journal of the Warburg and Courtauld Institutes* XXIV (1961), pp. 186–221; John W. O'Malley, *Praise and Blame in Renaissance Rome. Rhetoric, Doctrine and Reform in the Sacred Orators of the Papal Court, c. 1450–1521* (Durham, N.C., 1979); John M. McManamon, 'The Ideal Renaissance Pope: Funeral Oratory from the Papal Court,' *Archivum Historiae Pontificiae*, XIV (1976), pp. 9–70, and his unpublished doctoral dissertation '"*Ut crescat laudata virtus*": Funeral Oratory and the Culture of Italian Humanism' (Univ. of North Carolina, Ph.D. Thesis, 1984).
[45] 'Vir ad omnia summa natus', Angelus Politianus Iacobo Antiquario, *Opera Omnia*, ed. Ida Maïer, 3 vols. (Turin, 1970), I, p. 49.
[46] '*Laurens Etruriae caput*', *ibid.*, II, p. 260.
[47] '*Laurus omnium celebris/ Musarum choris/ Nympharum choris*', *ibid.*, II, p. 275.

This kind of eulogy was part of a tradition of praise of the Medici family that had been bestowed on his grandfather Cosimo and father Piero before him.[48] Many of the same images such as father and savior of the country, patron and protector of the people, promoter of culture and beneficent Maecenas that had been used with them were also attributed to Lorenzo. Sometimes humanist praise was no more than well-aimed flattery designed to win favor or a position for its author.[49] In other instances, praise was used for the sincere purpose of evoking virtue. Marsilio Ficino was a great master of edificatory praise. In his letters and dedications he constantly held up to Lorenzo the example of Cosimo so that the younger Medici might learn to model his life according to the virtuous example of his grandfather. But Ficino's language was no less extravagant, and sometimes more so, than that of other eulogizers. He compared Lorenzo to the Phoenix rising and to the light in the rays of the sun.[50] Lorenzo was the one who would bring illumination to the Latin people and glory to the Florentine republic,[51] for he was the 'savior of his country'.[52] Much of this kind of epideictic writing of the second half of the fifteenth century showed strong Neoplatonic influence. This is evident not only in its reliance upon metaphor and poetic imagery but in the natural focus it found in the person of the 'prince' who symbolized the collective virtues of the people. The identification between Lorenzo and Florence flowed easily from such an idiom, illustrated in Poliziano's famous lines,

> And you, Lorenzo, high born, under whose shadow
> Florence reposes happily in peace
> fearing neither winds nor threatening sky[53]

For Lippo Brandolini in the *De laudibus Laurentii Medicis* not only was Lorenzo the sole cause of the peace and prosperity enjoyed by Florence, but the Laurentian golden era surpassed even that of Augustus.[54]

[48] A. Brown, 'The Humanist Portrait', pp. 186–221.
[49] For example, the humanist Benedetto Colucci da Pistoia in his quest for various patronage appointments addressed flowery letters to Lorenzo, his protector, benefactor and Maecenas, whom he compared in one instance to the Apostle Peter himself, letter of 17 Jan. 1480 quoted in Rochon, *La jeunesse*, p. 315.
[50] 'Agnosco nunc in isto adolescente penitus, agnosco totum illum senem [Cosimo], phoenicem video in phoenice, in radio lumen', Marsilius Ficinus Nicolao Micheloctio, *Opera Omnia*, 2 vols. (Basel, 1561, reprinted Turin, 1962), I, p. 652.
[51] 'Lumen ad revelationem, Gentium Latinarum, et Florentiae Reipublicae gloriam', *ibid.*, p. 652.
[52] 'Patronum eundem habemus ambo Magnanimum Laurentium, quem habet et patria servatorem', Marsilius Ficinus Bartholomeo Scala, in P. O. Kristeller, *Supplementum Ficinianum*, 2 vols. (Florence, 1937), I, p. 60.
[53] 'Et tu, ben nato Laur, sotto il cui velo/ Fiorenza lieta in pace si riposa/ Né teme i venti, o 'l minacciar del cielo', *Stanze*, bk. I, st. 4, ll. 1–3, *Opera*, III, p. 6.
[54] Published in Roscoe, *Life of Lorenzo de' Medici*, III, app. L, pp. 272–86.

The very language of praise used by the humanists contributed considerably to the mythopoeic process, for it regularly employed mythicizing metaphors – comparisons with gods, heroes, and illustrious rulers of antiquity – which helped create for posterity a naturally lionized image of Lorenzo.[55] Niccolò Valori drew heavily upon this rhetorical language in his biography of Lorenzo as did Machiavelli and Guicciardini in their portrait sketches. Humanist history was closely allied with rhetoric and had as its purpose providing examples from the past of virtue in action.[56] Historical events could carry symbolic messages, such as did the Pazzi Conspiracy which for Valori became a divinely ordained test of Lorenzo's virtue, or the portents accompanying his death which signaled the departure of a great hero from this life. In the Renaissance, eulogy was a vital component of history, and little attempt was made to distinguish between them, which perhaps explains why Renaissance humanists, the greatest practitioners of both those arts, were such superb myth-makers.

The pervasiveness of the language of praise in the humanist culture of the fifteenth century raises the question to what extent Lorenzo was himself a passive recipient of the extravagant images being cast of him and to what extent he contributed to the process of making his own myth. Lorenzo had been weaned on humanist eulogy. His tutor Gentile Becchi, his secretary Bartolomeo Scala, and Marsilio Ficino never ceased urging him to follow in his grandfather Cosimo's footsteps,[57] and he seems to have genuinely desired to do so. His correspondence with Ficino indicates how fully he had absorbed this and other Neoplatonic teachings regarding ennobling the self through exercising the will, imitating edifying models, and experiencing the elevating powers of platonic love.[58] His desire to cultivate his own magnificence was sincere, and his *Altercazione* and other poetry pulses with a tension and a longing to better himself and lift himself towards union with the Divine.[59]

55 In the cycle of frescoes done for the Medici villa at Poggio a Caiano in the early sixteenth century, episodes from ancient history were used as parallels to Lorenzo's and Cosimo's lives, Langedijk, *The Portraits*, I, pp. 60–3.

56 Nancy S. Struever, *The Language of History in the Renaissance. Rhetoric and Historical Consciousness in Florentine Humanism* (Princeton, N.J., 1970), *passim*.

57 For examples, see A. Brown, 'The Humanist Portrait', pp. 199–212. Bartolomeo Scala, who lived for many years in the Medici palace, collected a codex of writings in praise of Cosimo and presented it to Lorenzo. See Brown's *Bartolomeo Scala, 1430-1497, Chancellor of Florence. The Humanist as Bureaucrat* (Princeton, N.J., 1979), pp. 269–70.

58 There are six extant letters of Lorenzo to Ficino, all from 1474. They reveal Lorenzo's devotion to the philosopher expressed in terms of Neoplatonic ideals of love and friendship; *Lettere*, I, pp. 496–507; II, pp. 35–9. See also P. O. Kristeller, 'Lorenzo de' Medici platonico', *Studies in Renaissance Thought and Letters* (Rome, 1956), pp. 213–19.

59 *L'Altercazione*, ed Emilio Bigi in *Scritti Scelti di Lorenzo de' Medici* (Turin, 1965),

The happy correspondence between the Neoplatonic values of his day and Lorenzo's own attempts to fashion himself accordingly constitutes one of the most important sources of the Medici myth, for contemporaries and especially later generations alike could more easily convince themselves that Lorenzo embodied those very ideals that the fifteenth-century Florentine Renaissance epitomized. For later historians, inheritors of the rhetorical tradition of writing history, Lorenzo became the historical *exemplum* of magnificence *par excellence*.

LORENZO'S IMAGE-MAKING

Was eulogy itself a more powerful conduit of the myth than the force of events during Lorenzo's lifetime? The language of Renaissance praise certainly shaped the literary form which the myth assumed and facilitated its rapid expansion during the time of crisis in the sixteenth century and its survival into later centuries. The fact remains, however, that Lorenzo's fame was more than literary conceit. It was also a fact of life. Both in Italy and abroad he was already widely recognized as a man of heroic proportions. His correspondence shows that popes and princes held him in the highest regard and sought his counsel and mediation on a wide range of political and personal matters.[60] When the King of France wanted to extract a favor from the pope, he wrote to Lorenzo, and when the pope wanted help in settling a dispute in the Papal States, he, too, asked for Lorenzo.[61] Medici accepted these requests precisely because

pp. 51–88, especially chs. II–V, in which Lorenzo has Ficino give a whole poetical discourse on platonic love to which Lorenzo's response, in ch. V, 11. 1–3, is that his heart was so filled by the sweetness of Ficino's words that he felt himself drawn toward that highest Good. '*Era il mio cor sì di dolcezza pieno/ che udendo mi pareva esser tirato/ al Ben che le parole sue dicièno.*' (p. 74). Many of his other poems reflect similar themes, such as the one in which he urges his slumbering genius awake to seek not terrestial, but heavenly things. '*Dèstati, pigro ingegno, da quel sonno.../ Pensa alla dignità del tu intelletto/ Non dato per seguir cosa mortale/ ma perché avessi il cielo per suo obietto*' (p. 102). On the Renaissance idea of self-fashioning in literature, see Thomas Greene, 'The Flexibility of the Self in Renaissance Literature', in Peter Demetz, Thomas Greene, and Lowry Nelson, Jr. (eds.), *The Disciplines of Criticism. Essays in Literary Theory, Interpretation, and History* (New Haven and London, 1968), pp. 241–64, and, more recently, Stephen Greenblatt's application of the idea to English Renaissance writers in his *Renaissance Self-Fashioning* (Chicago and London, 1980). Strangely, neither author considers the rhetorical basis for the concept nor the considerable support for it to be found in Ficino's writings or in the poetry of Lorenzo.

[60] Lorenzo's willingness to extend easy credit through the Medici bank helped solidify his personal relationships with foreign potentates and must be appreciated as an important underpinning to his reputation abroad. On the politics of high finance in the Renaissance, see my *Filippo Strozzi and the Medici. Favor and Finance in Sixteenth-Century Florence and Rome* (Cambridge, 1980).

[61] In 1487 when the king of France asked his help in securing an ecclesiastical

they helped enhance his reputation as a power broker. The vastness of his correspondence itself indicates what a vigorous role he played in the affairs of his time. He devoted several hours a day to dictating letters, and the nearly two thousand of his letters which have survived represent only a fraction of the total.[62] The other side of his correspondence is even more impressive. Probably twenty thousand letters sent to him from all parts of the known world remain in the archives today.

If Lorenzo was fast becoming famous in his own time, information in his correspondence suggests that it was precisely because he consciously sought fame and reputation. He had an intelligent grasp of both the limits and the possibilities inherent in his situation and the ability to make the most of the possibilities. He actively cultivated an image of his own magnificence, culture, wealth, and power and understood clearly how he might use his reputation to gain political advantage. He seems to have wanted to be the arbiter of Italy and rarely refused an opportunity to involve himself in all manner of political and diplomatic negotiations inside and especially outside of Florence. He traded on his quick intelligence, wide-ranging humanist education, and on the fame of Florence to project an image of power and importance well beyond what his or his city's actual position in Italy merited. A contemporary, the Milanese ambassador Sacramoro Sacramori, marveled at Lorenzo's astuteness and ability to 'hoist his sails high at the right moment' and 'to reap the most benefit from a favorable wind'.[63] The Ferrarese ambassador made a similar keen observation that Lorenzo's reputation within Florence depended upon the esteem with which he was regarded by the potentates of Italy and foreign rulers. 'Without their esteem, he would not be so highly regarded at home'.[64]

In Lorenzo's day, long before high-pressure public relations campaigns

appointment, Lorenzo instructed his ambassador in Rome to expedite the matter with the pope so that the King would know he had been responsible, and thereby bring him great honor ('et non solamente desidero la expeditione sua presta et bene, ma che intenda in qualche destro modo che per opera mia sia suto servito costì, la qual cosa reputerò assai per trovarmi a grandissimo mio honore et commodità, perché così è la speranza di quel Signore, el quale è di tanta auctorità et potrà voltarmi tucte o la maggiore parte di quelle expeditioni di là'), Lorenzo de' Medici to Giovanni Lanfredini, Florence, 17 Aug. 1487, Archivio di Stato, Florence (ASF), MAP, LVII, 91. That same summer Lorenzo agreed to arrange a crucial settlement between the condottiere Boccolino Guzzone of Osimo and the pope.

[62] Pier Giorgio Ricci and Nicolai Rubinstein, *Censimento delle lettere di Lorenzo di Piero de' Medici* (Florence, 1964).

[63] 'Astuto e de gran vedere è ello; ma troppo si reputa et troppo alza le vele per bonaza', and 'molto alza le sue vele quando gli pare havere vento prospero', Archivio di Stato, Milan (ASMi), SPE Fir. 183, cited in Brown, *Bartolomeo Scala*, p. 61n.

[64] A. Cappelli, 'Lettere di Lorenzo de' Medici detto il Magnifico conservate nell'Archivio Palatino di Modena', in *Atti e memorie della R. Deputazione di Storia patria per le provincie modonesi e parmensi*, I (1863), p. 165.

and mass political propaganda, cultivating a public image was a novel art whose possibilities he was quick to grasp, for a public image could make a powerful impact in an age when statecraft and diplomacy were highly personalized and political control rested mainly in the hands of powerful princes and rulers. Lorenzo was one of the earliest devotees and most skilled practitioners of the new art. He had already put into practice what Machiavelli was to recommend a generation later in *The Prince*, namely that in political affairs, what you seem to be in the eyes of others is far more important than what you actually are.[65] By mastering the techniques of projecting a powerful public image, Lorenzo greatly assisted in making his own myth, even though his immediate purposes were more limited in scope. His motivation for enhancing his image was both personal and political, personal, in so far as it accorded with his absorption of the humanist culture with its emphasis on self-enhancement and self-fashioning discussed earlier; political, in so far as it became the basis of his power within the Florentine state and the chief instrument of his diplomacy. As the ambassador from Ferrara had noted, his position in Florence and his reputation abroad were interrelated. And both depended upon the image he projected, which image was very complex, often shifting, depending upon which face he showed at any given moment.

Florence was still nominally a republic, and the Medici's position in the city was a bit self-contradictory. The Milanese ambassador reported that Lorenzo had commanded the city in all but name, that he was in fact like a *signore a bachetta*.[66] But Lorenzo, like his grandfather and father before him, prudently maintained an artful balance between the exercise of power and maintaining the appearance of being only the foremost citizen in a republic, not its prince. To this end he was careful to be seen consulting other citizens and he paid lip service to the *Signoria*'s and the Ten's conduct of foreign affairs.[67] Given the unofficial, unconstitutional nature of his rule, appearances were that much more important, and it is not surprising that the foreign ambassadors, who had frequent occasion to observe and comment on his ways, were sometimes puzzled but nonetheless impressed by his abilities. Lorenzo never in fact became that *signore a bachetta* the Milanese would have preferred to deal with, for the job of keeping up appearances involved considerable restraint upon his freedom of action, especially in the early years, and

[65] *The Prince*, ch. XVIII (Modern Library edn., New York, 1950), p. 65; also repeated in the *Discourses*, book I, ch. XXV, p. 182.
[66] ASMi, SPE Fir, 283, cited in Brown, *Bartolomeo Scala*, p. 69n.
[67] N. Rubinstein, 'Lorenzo de' Medici: The Formation of His Statecraft', *Proceedings of the British Academy*, LXIII (1977), pp. 76–81.

his political position in Florence in the end depended heavily upon the willing cooperation of the supporters of his regime.

But he knew how to use those restraints to political advantage. When it served his purpose Lorenzo could always hide behind Florence's republican institutions and disclaim responsibility for the actions of the Florentine government. At the same time he could exercise a guiding control. What has been aptly labeled his 'double-diplomacy'[68] is reflected in the fact that two sets of diplomatic correspondence were maintained, his own private letters and the official letters of the *Signoria* and the Ten. Florentine ambassadors, all hand-picked men, usually Lorenzo's close friends, such as Piero Alamanni and Giovanni Lanfredini, sent back two reports, one a more detailed account to Lorenzo in which all the significant public and private matters were actually discussed, and the other, official reports to the Florentine government which were usually bland and formularistic. Lorenzo sometimes had to remind his ambassadors to keep up the ruse.[69]

The Janus-like face he presented to the world and his assiduous attention to appearances may have had their origins in an astute assessment on his part that, in reality, Florence's political position in Italy was that of a secondary power vis-à-vis the other major Italian states. His elaborate performances were perhaps partly attempts to compensate for the relative weakness of Florence. The balance of power diplomacy for which he later became so famous, is best understood as a diplomacy of expediency arising from need. The Milanese state of the Sforza to the north and the Kingdom of Naples to the south were both more powerful than Florence, and since the Peace of Lodi in 1454 a hinge-point of Florentine policy had been to act as a buffer between the Italian 'super powers'. The relative weakness of the Florentine state became all too clear in 1478 when that alliance was broken in the aftermath of the dispute over Imola and Città di Castello which fuelled the Pazzi Conspiracy and the subsequent war with Sixtus IV allied with Naples against Florence. Experience showed Venice could not be counted on for help other than for promises, and the Neapolitan ambassador was doing all he could in Milan to prise a wavering Lodovico Sforza away from the Florentines.[70] Florentine territory was very vulnerable to attack along her long, difficult-to-defend borders, and the Florentines had to be vigilant against Neapolitan encroachments from

---

[68] *Ibid.*, pp. 88–90.

[69] Lorenzo cautioned Piero Alamanni, 'When you write to the Eight, never mention writing to me about anything important', Lorenzo to Piero Alamanni, 26 Apr. 1487, ASV, Mss. Patetta, 1739, f. 31v.

[70] Lorenzo de' Medici, *Lettere*, III, pp. 133–6; IV, pp. 213, 391.

the sea to the west and from Sienese territory to the south as well as against the forces that had pushed out of the Papal States to the south and east and had advanced into Florentine territory as far as the Mugello.[71] Nor was it easy for Lorenzo to persuade the Florentines with their stubborn merchant mentality to pay for expensive mercenary armies and fight a protracted war when the Florentine economy, dependent upon commerce and investments in Rome and other major European markets, needed peace to prosper. Because of these limitations inherent in Florence's geographical, economic and military position, Lorenzo was virtually helpless to pursue any other diplomatic course than a conservative one designed to maintain the *status quo*.[72] This situation required all of his image-making and diplomatic skills. In the absence of a dependable military or political base of operations, he had one tool within reach, statesmanship. He worked assiduously to involve himself in all manner of diplomatic maneuvers in order to enhance his image and that of the Florentine state as indispensable arbiter of Italy and by that means to increase the respect and regard of other potentates and avoid conflict. In 1487, for example, when he agreed to mediate a settlement between the pope and the rebellious condottiere Boccolino Guzzone of Osimo, he was not only willing to contribute financially to a settlement but to offer Boccolino a commission and refuge in Florence. When Boccolino's nephew, held prisoner in Rome, was not released in accordance with the terms of the agreement, Lorenzo complained bitterly to Giovanni Lanfredini, the ambassador in Rome, about this insult to his honor. He was adamant that his credibility be maintained 'so that others will continue to place their trust in me'.[73]

Because Lorenzo's political and diplomatic strategy was so personal and because his personal image was so closely interwined with that of Florence, it is almost impossible to distinguish between the public and the private benefit produced by his actions. A few contemporary critics could complain about his conduct unbefitting a Florentine citizen such as his open dynasticism in arranging marriage alliances for his eldest son Piero with the powerful Orsini house and for his daughter Maddalena to Franceschetto Cibo, son of Innocent VIII. These marriages had the

[71] *Ibid.*, III, pp. 48, 76; IV, pp. 393–4.
[72] These hard-won lessons from the Pazzi War stayed with Lorenzo and cropped up in his later correspondence. 'I do not have the means to defend myself that His Excellency [Lodovico Sforza] has. I do not want to have to risk my life and other things again like before.' Lorenzo to P. Alamanni, 6 Oct. 1487, BAV, Mss. Patetta, 1739, f. 63; 'The truth is that because we are nearer to the King [of Naples] and less powerful than [Milan],...we have to be more cautious.' *Idem.*, 18 Dec. 1487, ibid, f. 74.
[73] 'Delibero per quanto posso conservarmi la fede et dare materia ad altri di fidarsi di me. Stimo questa cosa quanto alcuna altra che potessi achadermi', 10 Aug. 1487, ASF, MAP LVII, 84.

calculated effect of securing alliances with the pope and with Roberto Orsini, one of the most powerful condottieri in the late fifteenth century, for himself but also for Florence. Largely as a result of Lorenzo's personal rapprochement with Innocent, Florentine bankers in Rome began to play a more prominent role in the financial affairs of the papacy and to regain ground that they had lost as a result of the Pazzi War with Sixtus IV.[74] Personal aggrandizement, or statecraft, or both?

Lorenzo utilized two basic techniques to enhance his image: he mastered the art of the well-chosen gesture, and he traded upon Florence's growing reputation as the center of the new style of Renaissance art and culture and humanist learning, which reputation he in turn bolstered considerably. His correspondence is filled with examples of his astute performances. In 1479 when he embarked upon his famous trip to Naples to sue for peace, his position in Florence was shaky. The long and costly war was going badly for Florence. Sixtus' clever propaganda calling for Lorenzo's expulsion, designed to drive a wedge between Lorenzo and the Florentines with the claim that his only quarrel was with the Medici and not with Florence, was having an effect on the war-weary citizens.[75] In the letter Lorenzo wrote to the *Signoria* explaining the reasons for his trip, he cast himself in the role of the sacrificial lamb, the selfless citizen ready to risk his life for the greater cause of bringing peace to the *patria*:

I have chosen to expose myself to some degree of danger rather than to allow the city to suffer longer under its present trials... Since I am the one whom our enemies are pursuing primarily, by putting myself into their hands, I might be the means of bringing peace back to our city... Perhaps God wills that this war which began with the blood of my brother and of myself, should be ended by my means.[76]

---

[74] An increase is evident from the *Introitus* and *Exitus* accounts of the Apostolic Chamber in the Vatican, ASV, IE, vols. 511–22 for the period 1484–92. On Innocent's finances, see my 'Farming Spiritual Revenues: Innocent VIII's *Appalto* of 1486', *Renaissance Studies in Honor of Craig Hugh Smyth* (Florence, 1985), pp. 238–51.

[75] 'La bocce è ita che questa querra è fatta a me proprio', *Lettere*, III, p. 169. See also *ibid.*, p. 111, and N. Rubinstein, *The Government of Florence Under the Medici 1434 to 1494* (Oxford, 1966), pp. 195–7. In the stinging language of his bull of excommunication against Lorenzo and his adherents, Sixtus called him 'son of iniquity and pupil of perdition'; published in Roscoe, *Life of Lorenzo de' Medici*, III, app. XXVI, pp. 156–66. As the war dragged on into late 1479, some anti-Medici handbills were found, and the people began to agitate for peace, *Lettere*, IV, p. 398, and Rubinstein, 'Lorenzo de' Medici', p. 91n. Rinuccini's treatise *Dialogus de libertate* (1479), published in *Atti e Memorie dell'Accademia Toscana di Scienze e Lettere La Colombaria*, XXII, new series VIII (1957), pp. 270–303, which repeats Sixtus's charge of tyranny against Lorenzo, reflects this discontent. The negative image of Lorenzo as tyrant of Florence resurfaced again, even more vividly, during the Savonarolian period.

[76] *Lettere*, IV, pp. 265–9. The official letter elaborates the sentiments he had expressed

Lorenzo's mission to Naples was in fact well-prepared in advance through private channels and the actual personal risk was minimal. The duke of Calabria had sent his galleys up from Naples to escort Lorenzo with all the honors due someone on an important state visit, and his reception in Naples was equally genial.[77] Nonetheless Lorenzo did not lose this opportunity to portray his actions in the most favorable light possible. The letter was read aloud in public, and his noble words moved people to tears, winning him anew the admiration and support of the citizens who saw in him a patriotic martyr.[78] Though he had embarked on the trip as a private citizen, the Ten soon sent him a full mandate to negotiate a peace settlement for the republic, thus reaffirming the inextricable link between Lorenzo's personal interests and those of Florence.[79]

On another occasion Lorenzo even used his poetic abilities to good advantage. His reputation as the author of love poems probably explains why in 1487 a smitten Lodovico Sforza, regent of Milan, twice pleaded for Lorenzo's advice about the new love which had turned his life upside down. Lorenzo's reply was truly elegant in style and filled with references to Petrarchan sonnets and thoughtful reflections on the joys and pains of falling in love.[80] The letter was undoubtedly designed to gratify Lodovico, and with it Lorenzo recommended himself as a sensitive and cultured person to whom the Milanese ruler could turn for advice even on such delicate personal questions.

How Lorenzo used the commune's reputation is a more complex matter. In the area of art he actively sought to become a connoisseur and arbiter of taste.[81] He judged competitions and recommended many of the leading Florentine artists for commissions abroad. He sent Antonio da Pollaiuolo off to Rome preceded by a letter calling him 'the premier artist of this city in the common opinion of all'.[82] Whether or not other artists

to the *Signoria* in the summer of 1478; *ibid.*, III, p. 286; and in several private letters written just prior to his departure, *ibid.*, IV, pp. 259–72.
[77] *Ibid.*, IV, pp. 250–1.
[78] *Ibid.*, IV, pp. 265, 273–4.
[79] The document, composed by Bartolomeo Scala, assured Lorenzo that the Florentines would approve whatever he negotiated; *ibid.*, IV, pp. 269–70, and A. Brown, *Bartolomeo Scala*, pp. 91–3.
[80] The exchange of letters was through Piero Alamanni, the ambassador. 'His excellency has insisted that I write you and tell you he has newly fallen in love and that in the space of a few days he seems truly to have become a different man...[The experience] is a restorative and aid for all his disturbances, and he recommends you try the same remedy. He is caught up in sonnets and similar things.' ASF, MAP L, 31, 8 Mar. 1487. Lorenzo's reply of 11 Mar. 1487 is published in *Scritti Scelti*, pp. 658–9.
[81] Gombrich, 'The Early Medici', pp. 307–11, and Chastel, *L'Art et Humanisme*, pp. 14–17.
[82] Quoted in Langedijk, *The Portraits*, I, p. 31.

such as Verrocchio, Botticelli and Ghirlandaio who accepted commissions in Venice and Rome did so at Lorenzo's specific recommendation is of no importance. The effect was the same. Florentine art was in great demand, and Lorenzo basked in the reflected glory. Cardinal Carafa, who had hired Filippino Lippi to work in one of the chapels in S. Maria Sopra Minerva in Rome, reported to a friend that because the painter had been sent by the Magnificent Lorenzo, 'he would not have exchanged him for all the painters of ancient Greece'.[83] Lorenzo also kept a watchful eye on those he recommended to make sure they did not discredit him. His agent at the Medici bank in Rome was instructed to keep tabs on Lippi, and he reported:

I understand what you say about Filippino the painter. I was very diplomatic with him the other day and am content that he will do what he promised me and work diligently and economically in such a way that I am sure the Cardinal will remain obliged to you and content with him. I will keep after him and remind him as I see fit.[84]

The fact that Lorenzo commissioned few works of art himself would seem to indicate that he was less interested in patronizing art and artists than in seeing how Florentine art and Florentine artists might be used as ambassadors of Florentine culture abroad.

At home Lorenzo devoted himself to his expensive and private collections of gems, antiques, and rare manuscripts. But they, too, served to attract attention. Scholars and notables travelled great distances to admire them. In 1474 Christian, king of Denmark and Sweden, stopped in Florence to examine a rare Greek manuscript that had been brought from Constantinople.[85] A tour of the collections in the Medici palace formed a regular part of Medici entertainments for special visitors, even mercenary captains. In 1481 when the *condottiere* Costanzo Sforza, signor of Pesaro, made his entry into Florence to receive command of the Florentine forces, the Ferrarese ambassador reported that he toured the city, 'visiting churches and the palace of Lorenzo, who showed him his books, jewels and statues'.[86] A perhaps more appreciative

[83] ASF, MAP XLVI, 556, and in Alfred Scharf, *Filippino Lippi* (Vienna, 1935), doc. IX, p. 89.
[84] '*Vegho quello mi dite di Filippino dipintore. Io li parlai destramente a questi di passati per modo che resto contento et vego che gli oserva quello mi promise di lavorare solecitamente et non ispendere [?] per modo che io sono certo che il Cardinale resterà obrighato a voi et chontento di lui. Non resteró di tenerlo dipresso et recordarli quello che mi paria di bisognio*', N. Tornabuoni to Lorenzo, Rome, 7 May 1490, ASF, MAP, XXVI, 544.
[85] Roscoe, *Life of Lorenzo de' Medici*, I, pp. 213–14. In a letter of 1491, Poliziano pointed out how Lorenzo stood to gain greater reputation than anyone in recent times from his collecting manuscripts for his library and from the favor he showed to intellectuals. *Ibid*, III, app. LII, p. 289. Poliziano himself was, of course, an interested party.
[86] Cappelli, *Atti e memorie*, p. 256.

visitor was the famous Venetian humanist Ermolao Barbaro on his way to Rome in 1490 as legate. He was treated to dinner with the most noted humanists of Florence as guests, Pico della Mirandola, Marsilio Ficino, Angelo Poliziano, and Bernardo Rucellai, followed by the guided tour led by Piero de' Medici, since on this occasion his father was at the baths taking a cure.

> After we had dined, I gave him a complete tour of the house, the medals, vases and cameos, in fact, everything including the garden in which he took great pleasure, although I do not believe he knows much about sculpture. He also liked the ancient medals and the information they contained. Everyone marvelled at the number of such excellent items etc.[87]

Florence had gained a wide reputation as a city of culture and learning, and Lorenzo devoted considerable effort to building up the Florentine *Studio*.[88] Cristoforo Landino and Angelo Poliziano were among the prize lecturers there. Lorenzo also had the best professors brought in from outside at very high salaries to lend prestige to the institution. The most famous physician, Pierleone of Spoleto, who was also Lorenzo's private doctor, received a stipend of one thousand florins, but this was topped by the noted jurist Bartolomeo Sozzini of Siena whose salary was so far above scale that it was determined by Lorenzo personally.[89] Students came from as far away as Portugal, Spain, and France to study at the university, and many a young Florentine product of the *Studio*, among them Francesco Guicciardini, the future historian, and Francesco Soderini, the future cardinal, carried a humanist education along with eloquent style and speech into public office or into the personal service of princes and prelates all over Italy and abroad. Education and culture became a trademark of Florence, and all the Florentine ambassadors whom Lorenzo hand-picked for the city were well-educated and learned men. They commanded great personal respect which reflected favorably on Lorenzo and on Florence. In 1488 Piero Alamanni the ambassador to Milan was even knighted by the duke.[90] Bernardo Rucellai, famous today for the seminars he held in his garden to which he invited Machiavelli and other young and promising humanists, was Lorenzo's brother-in-law and his ambassador to Milan and Naples. Perhaps the

---

[87] 10 May 1490, ASF, MAP XLII, 59.

[88] A Verde, *Lo Studio Fiorentino 1473–1503. Richerche e documenti*, 3 vols. (Florence and Pistoia, 1973–77), III, xxv; Rochon, *La Jeunesse*, pp. 304, 337; M. Martelli, *Studi laurenziani* (Florence, 1965), p. 187; Gene Brucker, 'A Civic Debate on Florentine Higher Education (1460)', *Renaissance Quarterly*, XXXIV, no. 4 (1981), pp. 525–6.

[89] Verde, *Lo Studio*, II, pp. 100–3, 554–5. Then, as now, professors of rhetoric received much less. Poliziano was paid a top salary of 450 florins, and Landino 300 florins: *ibid*, pp. 26–8, 174–5.

[90] Stephano de Castrocaro to Lorenzo, Milan, 2 Feb. 1489, ASF, MAP, L, 27.

best demonstration of how thoroughly Lorenzo had mastered the art of gesture and had understood the political importance of projecting a good image abroad can be found in the famous letter of advice he sent to his young fourteen-year-old son Giovanni who had just been made cardinal and was on his way to Rome to establish his residence:

It is necessary now for you to become a good churchman. You must love the honor and estate of the Holy Church and Apostolic See more than anything in the world, and you must put these considerations before all else. But even with this reservation, you will not lack opportunity to help the city of Florence and our family...You are the youngest cardinal in the College and in the whole history of the church. Therefore, when you have to make agreements with the others you should be the most solicitous and the most humble...Keep to the side of moderation in your display, and I would rather you maintained an elegant, well-ordered and clean household and stable, than a rich and pompous one...Jewels and silk do not become a person of your bearing. You are much better off gracing yourself with a few antiques and beautiful books and with maintaining a learned and well-trained staff rather than a large retinue.[91]

Tournaments and public festivals provided another vehicle for carefully orchestrated display of Medici magnificence and form an important aspect of Lorenzo's cultural politics. His public gestures, movements and manner of dress attracted attention automatically.[92] Who could help but comment on his wedding banquet for 400 guests, each course of which was announced by a fanfare of trumpets, or the jewel encrusted outfits he and Giuliano wore for their tournaments, Lorenzo's emblazoned with his own golden-age motto *le temps revient* embroidered in pearls, his shield sporting a huge Medici diamond and his cap a feather of gold?[93] The tournament of 1469 was the talk of Italy, and the

[91] The letter is printed in Roscoe, *Life of Lorenzo de' Medici*, III, app. LXVI, pp. 336–44, in Bigi (ed.), *Scritti scelti*, pp. 671–75, and an English translation in Ross, *Lives*, pp. 332–5.

[92] A recent comprehensive study of the ritual significance of Lorenzo's public displays is R. Trexler's *Public Life in Renaissance Florence* (New York, 1980), especially pp. 412–62. Trexler argues that Lorenzo had an iconic role as the charismatic centre of Florence 'with no previous parallel in Florentine history, except for religious images like [the Madonna of] Impruneta', p. 433. On Lorenzo's special significance in Florentine confraternal life, see R. Hatfield, 'The Compagnia de' Magi', *Journal of The Warburg and Courtauld Institutes*, XXXIII (1970), pp. 107–61, especially pp. 135–44, and R. Weissman, *Ritual Brotherhood in Renaissance Florence* (New York, 1982), pp. 169–72.

[93] The tournament and the wedding are described in documents in Ross, *The Lives*, pp. 123–6, 129–34. The Medici paid particular attention to their dress for public occasions. In 1489, when Piero de' Medici went to Milan for the wedding of the Duke, he dazzled the whole Milanese court with his outfit emblazoned with the *broncone*, a Medici insignia, and people came to admire it the next day. ASF, MAP, L, 27.

brothers' feats were soon immortalized in the poetry of Pulci and Poliziano.[94] Foreign visitors liked to be in Florence for the celebrations on the feast day of S. Giovanni, patron saint of the city. Eleanor of Aragon, Ferrante's daughter, on her wedding trip to Ferrara, stopped in Florence for S. Giovanni. She was so well entertained by the Medici that Ferrante wrote in thanks that the hospitality shown Eleanor increased his own affection for Lorenzo,[95] which affection later served Medici well on his personal mission to the King in 1479.

PUBLIC VALIDATION

Lorenzo could not single-handedly have created his own myth. There were other active participants, among them the humanists, who as we have seen, were the interpreters of his image, dressing it up in the language of praise and embellishing it with their intimate knowledge of the classical repertory of mythic images and rhetorical devices. Humanist panegyric together with Lorenzo's own efforts to create a public image helped mold contemporary perceptions of him and those we have inherited through the centuries. But the myth-making process involved more than just the deliberate fabrications of the small number of Medici propagandists whether in the fifteenth, or posthumously in the sixteenth century. It also involved the participation of a wider public to whom their messages were directed. The voice of the people in pre-modern Europe is notoriously difficult to detect; however, it seems clear that the Florentine citizenry accepted the images Lorenzo projected and generally supported him, or at least let him know on the occasions it did not. Apart from the outbursts of a few noisy opponents of the regime and the paeans of its many friends and supporters among the aristocracy, few letters or diaries of modest citizens like the druggist Luca Landucci and Bartolomeo Masi, a coppersmith, have survived to give written testimony to wider public opinion.[96] We must rely heavily on indirect evidence, much of it to be inferred from Lorenzo's actions themselves, which were not only his attempts to shape or influence public perceptions of him, but also more widely his reactions to the larger climate of public opinion in which he moved. The magnificent display and the festivities

[94] For letters from Rome and Naples reporting the gossip, see Ross, *The Lives*, pp. 123–6, 160. Pulci composed *La Giostra di Lorenzo de' Medici* and Poliziano his *Stanze per la giostra* in honor of Giuliano.
[95] Cited in C. Ady, *Lorenzo de' Medici and Renaissance Italy* (New York, 1962), p. 60.
[96] Luca Landucci, *A Florentine Diary from 1450–1516*, trans. A. Jervis (London, 1927); *Ricordanze di Bartolomeo Masi calderaio fiorentino, dal 1478 al 1526*, ed. G. Corazzini (Florence, 1906). On the elusiveness of the people and their culture, see Peter Burke, *Popular Culture in Early Modern Europe* (New York, 1978), pp. 64–87.

staged by the Medici *in piazza* were *public* events which involved the citizenry as eager spectators.[97] Without this public face, Medici gesturing might have become the sort of private palace ritual played out by Louis XIV and his nobles at Versailles. But in the same way those French nobles at Versailles by their very presence accepted the rules of the court game, so too, the Florentines by participating in Medici-sponsored events gave their tacit consent to the role he attempted to play in the life of the city.

Recently historians have focussed their attention on the *reggimento*, the group of those friends and members of the Medici regime, and on the extent to which the Medici depended upon their support.[98] More fundamentally, however, Lorenzo's position in Florence rested upon a broader base, not so much of active support in a political sense, but of general acquiescence on the part of the citizenry. Though passive most of the time, the *popolo fiorentino* did on occasion erupt in anger such as following the Pazzi Conspiracy. The Pazzi had been counting upon being able to arouse the people against the Medici, but their invocations of *popolo* and *libertà* were met with countercries of *Palle*, for the Medici. Mob violence directed against the rotting remains of the Pazzi conspirators and fear that the mob would similarly attack Cardinal Riario, implicated in the plot and under house arrest in the Palazzo Vecchio, were all indicators of a strong pro-Medici undercurrent among the Florentine people.[99] The wax votive statues of Lorenzo that friends erected in several churches as objects for public devotion and expressions of thanksgiving for Lorenzo's safety, one clothed in the very suit he had worn the day of the attempt and positioned next to a crucifix with miraculous powers,[100] demonstrate how fully Lorenzo had come to embody the collective Florentine experience.

Lorenzo seems to have been very sensitive and reactive to Florentine public opinion.[101] It was the major factor behind his decision to make

[97] At Lorenzo's wedding, many of the gifts as well as quantities of food and wine were distributed to the Florentines; Ross, *The Lives*, pp. 129–32.

[98] N. Rubinstein, *The Government, passim.*; Dale Kent, *The Rise of the Medici. Faction in Florence, 1426–1434* (Oxford, 1978), and *idem*, 'The Florentine Reggimento', *Renaissance Quarterly*, XXVIII (1975), pp. 575–638.

[99] Poliziano, *Coniurationis commentarium*, in Roscoe, *Life of Lorenzo de' Medici*, III, app., XXI, pp. 135–42; Lorenzo de' Medici, *Lettere*, IV, p. 275; Landucci, *A Florentine Diary*, pp. 16–19.

[100] The votive images are described by Vasari in his life of Verrocchio, *Opere*, ed. G. Milanesi (Florence, 1878), III, pp. 373–4, and quoted in Langedijk, *The Portraits*, I, pp. 27–8. Although Lorenzo was probably not as much of a Florentine religious icon as Trexler would have us believe, he certainly emerged from the crisis of the Pazzi Conspiracy having achieved a symbolic identification with the city that neither his father nor grandfather had had.

[101] According to the Milanese ambassador Sacramoro, following his father's death

the trip to Naples in 1479. Once the Florentine people began to blame him personally for the war with the pope, he reasoned that only his departure would clarify for them that he was not the sole cause of Sixtus' angry agressions. The trip to Naples had the effect of consolidating support behind him, and upon his return he was able to institute reforms to strengthen his hand in the government almost without opposition.[102]

Healthy respect for public sentiment would also explain why on another occasion, eight years later, he was so anxious to press for the expensive campaign against Sarzana, a strategically located fortress between Florentine and Genoese territory which Florence had lost to the Genoese during the Pazzi War and which had become since then a sore spot in Florentine civic pride and a point of Lorenzo's personal honor. Despite the lack of promised allied support, Lorenzo had the Florentine forces launch the attack, and went personally to Pisa to direct the final operations.[103] Valori understood the great symbolic value for the Florentines of the taking of Sarzana when he wrote in his biography that it seemed to many as though Lorenzo had personally brought victory with him.[104] And of course, the celebrations for S. Giovanni several days later must have been particularly jubilant.

Lorenzo's death, on 8 April 1492, like the Pazzi Conspiracy, provided the occasion for a great outpouring of public sentiment. Dressed in mourning, nobles and modest citizens alike came to the church of S. Lorenzo to pay their last respects. Bartolomeo Dei, who was there, said 'it was touching to see such manifest signs of sadness and of sorrow'.[105]

Lorenzo was careful to conduct himself in a manner pleasing to the people, and he observed that 'most Florentines were behind him' ('gli animi dei più sono per lui'). If there was any danger to his position, Sacramoro judged it would come not from the people but from the principal citizens; dispatches of 15 Dec. 1469 and 3 Jan. 1470, in G. Soranzo, 'Lorenzo Magnifico alla morte del padre e il suo primo balzo verso la Signoria', *Archivio Storico Italiano*, CXI (1953), p. 50. Trexler argues that the Medici courted popular favor as evidenced by their support of certain plebeian confraternities; *Public Life*, pp. 412–15.

[102] Rubinstein, *The Government*, pp. 197–203.
[103] 'We hold this matter [of Sarzana] as dear as anything ever before. I have even come here myself specially, and it is of considerable personal honor.' Lorenzo to P. Alamanni, Serzanello, 21 June 1487, ASV, Mss. Patetta, 1739, f. 41.
[104] *Vita*, p. 35. Lorenzo himself was clearly aware of the symbolic importance of his presence, for he had written to his secretary from Pisa on 6 June that he was anxious to come home but did not want to upset the Florentines by leaving, which might have an adverse effect on the campaign either in fact or in people's opinions, ('Io desiderei fra due o tre dì partirmi di qui, ma non vorrei che costì dispiacessi o che in facto o in opinione la impresa peggiorassi di conditione'), Biblioteca Nazionale, Florence, Carte Ginori Conti, 29. 129. III.
[105] His letter to his uncle, the chronicler Benedetto Dei, dated April 14, is published in Ludovico Frati, 'La Morte di Lorenzo de' Medici e il Suicidio de Pier Leoni', *A.S.I.*, ser. 5, vol. IV (1889), pp. 255–60, and translated in Ross, *The Lives*, p. 341–4. For Dei, Lorenzo's death was 'the great and bitter sorrow of the whole city; and with every

The *Signoria* published an unusual official obituary praising Lorenzo's virtues and services to the city, and letters and representations of condolences began to pour in to the *Signoria* and to the family from all over Italy, all of them striking a common note of sadness and a heightened recognition of Lorenzo's remarkable accomplishments, 'not just for Florence, but for all Italy'.[106] Ferrante of Naples is reported to have made the prophetic statement: 'This man has lived long enough for his own immortal fame, but not for Italy. God grant that now he is dead men may not attempt that which they dared not do while he was alive.'[107]

According to Valori and Guicciardini, Lorenzo's death was accompanied by miraculous portents. A comet appeared, wolves were heard howling, and in the church of S. Maria Novella a crazed woman screamed that a bull with horns of fire was burning the city. Caged lions set upon one another killing the most beautiful of their number. And just a few days before Lorenzo died, a great bolt of lightning struck the lantern atop the cupola of the cathedral, knocking out several huge blocks of marble which crashed down in the direction of the Medici palace. Valori claimed he witnessed some of the portents himself and heard of others from reputable sources, among them Marsilio Ficino, who together with several others, had seen giant shadows in the garden and heard eerie screams at the time of Lorenzo's death.[108] Ficino's Neoplatonic interpretation of the portents was that these disturbances of the natural order were verifications of the death of a truly illustrious person as had frequently happened in history when great men died.[109]

These accounts of the portents were not just rhetorical fictions designed to enhance the importance of their subject. Other evidence indicates that the portents were widely believed in and commented upon, which again indicates how deeply Lorenzo dwelt within the collective consciousness of Florentines of all levels of society. Poliziano mentions them in his famous letter describing Lorenzo's death written shortly afterwards.[110] The druggist Landucci records them in his diary, and Johannis Burckard at the papal court in Rome judged them to be so

reason, for no doubt we have lost the splendor not only of Tuscany but of all Italy', p. 341.

[106] On the obituary, see Rubinstein, 'The Formation', p. 94. The letters of condolence are in ASF, Signori, Otto, Dieci, Legazioni e Commissarie, Missive, Responsive, 77, fos. 261–7. So many ambassadors came to pay their respects that the *Signoria* had to contribute 5,700 *lire* in *quattrini* to cover their expenses; ASF, Monte Comune, 1517, f. 74s.

[107] Trans. Ross, *The Lives*, p. 343; also in Valori, *Vita*, p. 52.

[108] *Ibid.*, pp. 51–2; Guicciardini, *History of Florence*, p. 70.

[109] See his letter to Cardinal Giovanni de' Medici, 15 April 1492, *Opera*, I, pt. 2, p. 930.

[110] *Opera*, I, p. 50.

significant as to recount them in great detail in his *Liber notarum*.[111] The events were interpreted again and again from the pulpits of the major Florentine churches in a rising tide of apocalyptic awareness.[112]

The myth-making process had long been underway during Lorenzo's lifetime at least partially under his control, but his death noticeably intensified it. A great and talented man, sung by poets, who had captured the imagination and esteem of a whole generation had been carried away by an untimely death. With his death the posthumous elaboration of the myth could begin, first in little ways as stories about his death and his life were recounted, and then as their significance became clearer with the passage of time, anecdotal material was added to make their meaning that much more evident. Landucci, for example, has Lorenzo himself validating the portents. In the diary it says when Lorenzo was told about the lightning striking the cupola, he exclaimed, 'Alas! I shall die, because they [the stones] fell towards my house'.[113] It was not long before Savonarola and others began to 'remember' how the Dominican friar had previously predicted Lorenzo's death in one of his prophetic utterances.[114]

Piero de' Medici lacked the charisma of his father and failed to fill Lorenzo's symbolic role in Florence. The Florentines' disillusionment with him led ultimately to his expulsion in 1494. Cut adrift from the guiding image of a Medici leader, they looked first to Charles VIII, whom Savonarola heralded as a divine agent sent to restore the city's lost liberties, and then to Savonarola himself as the symbolic leader of their city.[115] The early stages of Lorenzo's posthumous career as lived out in the mytho-historical imaginations of the Florentines were as rocky as the course of these events. As Savonarola began to fill the void left by Lorenzo, he and his followers sought to validate their new positions by drawing out the dark or negative side of Lorenzo's character as tyrant of Florence. The old charges that Sixtus IV had used against him back

---

[111] Landucci, *A Florentine Diary*, pp. 52–4; Johannis Burkard, *Liber Notarum*, *R.I.S.*, XXXII: I, pp. 347–8. The source of his account is probably Ficino, who had also written about Lorenzo's death to Francesco Valori, ambassador in Rome. Machiavelli devoted an entire chapter in the *Discourses* to portents, among which those accompanying Lorenzo's death figure prominently; book I, ch. 56, pp. 257–8.

[112] Weinstein, *Savonarola and Florence*, pp. 126–7; also B. Cerretani, *Storia Fiorentina*, in Schnitzer, *Quellen und Forschungen*, III, pp. 6–9.

[113] Landucci, *A Florentine Diary*, p. 54. Masi explained that the portentous lightning was caused by Lorenzo releasing a spirit that had been imprisoned in his ring; *Ricordanze*, p. 17.

[114] B. Cerretani, *Dialogo della mutatione di Firenze*, in Schnitzer, *Quellen und Forschungen*, III, pp. 97–8. See also P. Villari, *Life and Times of Girolamo Savonarola*, trans. L. Villari (London, 1896), p. 131 and note.

[115] Weinstein, *Savonarola and Florence*, pp. 135–7, 271–3; Trexler, 'Lorenzo de' Medici and Savonarola, Martyrs for Florence', *Renaissance Quarterly*, XXXI (1978), p. 294.

in 1478 to alienate the citizens and which had begun to take hold in the city during the Pazzi War were dug up and invested with new meaning. Out of the pro-Savonarola, anti-Medici sentiment grew as well the freshly remembered accounts, oft-repeated in Savonarolian literature, of how Lorenzo had summoned the prior of S. Marco to hear his deathbed confession but that Savonarola had departed abruptly when the Magnificent refused to restore liberty to the city, leaving the dying man unabsolved.[116] The negative image of Lorenzo as tyrant began to fade following Savonarola's execution,[117] and it was only a matter of time under changed political circumstances before those who hated Savonarola and his legacy would recast Lorenzo's image in a golden light.

The human mind has infinite capacity to telescope historical events in the course of its larger search for meaning, even to 'remember' and reinterpret them differently as their relation to the present changes. This is how myth becomes history and how history becomes myth. The dramatic changes which occurred in the early development of Lorenzo's posthumous image make a fascinating chapter in Renaissance historiography by themselves, but these changes also comprise an important stage in the larger process of the formation of Lorenzo's historical myth. The historians of the early sixteenth century began to interpret the significance of Lorenzo's life in the light of history. They elaborated the richly ornamented images they had inherited from the fifteenth century and added new material to his biography. The larger-than-life portrait of Lorenzo that they codified provided ready substance for successive reinterpretations and enlargements which eventually made Lorenzo into a bona fide symbol of the Renaissance.

The real ferment of the myth-making process, however, had already begun in the fifteenth century at the hands of Lorenzo's humanist eulogizers and through his own image-making efforts with the help of approving Florentines and foreigners. The contemporary images cast of him were by far the clearest and most compelling. They had been spawned in the midst of the drama of everyday life and mainly directed

---

[116] Fra Placido Cinozzi's version is given in Ross, *The Lives*, p. 340. In his biography of Savonarola, Villari still defended the story as factual, *Life and Times*, pp. 168–72. Condivi recounts another story, this time how Lorenzo's ghost, clad only in a ragged black robe, appeared twice to a friend of Michelangelo's with a warning to Piero de' Medici of his coming exile; Asconio Condivi, *The Life of Michelangelo*, tr. A. Wohl (Baton Rouge, 1976), pp. 17–18. For Condivi, Lorenzo was the 'father of all *virtù*' (p. 12).

[117] The image never entirely faded from political historiography. Sismondi picked it up in the nineteenth century in his *History of the Italian Republics*, where he compared Lorenzo's usurpations of power to those of a Napoleon III. It has also surfaced in more recent scholarly preoccupation with the collapse of the Florentine Republic and the origins of the Medici principate.

towards limited political and personal ends. But once the particular concerns and circumstances of the various myth-makers dropped away from memory or were obscured with the passage of time, the transcendent power of those images of Lorenzo emerged ever brighter and captured the imagination of subsequent generations of Renaissance devotees and Medici fanciers down to the present day. Looking back over the various constituent elements in the formation of Lorenzo's historical myth – the language of humanist praise, Lorenzo's deliberate crafting of his own magnificence, the validation of contemporaries, the codification of the myth in the early sixteenth century, and subsequent symbolic enlargements – it becomes evident that each stage of its history contained within it synchronic elements of human belief, the stuff of myth. The myth did not emerge at a certain point in time, during the dramatic events of the Pazzi Conspiracy, or immediately following Lorenzo's death, or during the crisis of Italy in the sixteenth-century. Elements of myth were present from the very beginning. Far from being opposed to one another, myth and history might best be considered two sides of the same coin. The remarkable survival of Lorenzo de' Medici into the late twentieth century with much of his mythic aura still intact certainly testifies to the power of the will to believe.

Political rhetoric and poetic meaning in Renaissance culture: Clément Marot and the Field of Cloth of Gold

PHYLLIS MACK

...men might say,
Till this time pomp was single, but now married
To one above itself. Each following day
Became the next day's master, till the last
Made former wonders its. To-day the French
All clinquant, all in gold, like heathen gods,
Shone down the English; and to-morrow they
Made Britain India: every man that stood
Show'd like a mine.

Shakespeare, Henry VIII

'The Field of Cloth of Gold' was the name given to a meeting between Francis I of France and Henry VIII of England in June, 1520. The meeting lasted for twenty days, during which the kings visited, dined, jousted and excelled in theatrical acts of courtesy and friendship. Henry held court in a specially built summer palace with an embattled gate ornamented with statues of men in various attitudes of war, ceilings covered with white silk, roofs studded with roses on a ground of gold, banners painted by Holbein, the whole supported by a great pillar wreathed in gold, surrounded by four gilt lions and surmounted by a blind Cupid. Francis rested in a tent 'as high as the tallest tower,' with thirty-two sides, covered in cloth of gold with stripes of blue velvet 'powdered' with golden fleurs-de-lis, and attached to the tent by violet taffeta imported from Italy. At the summit stood a life-size statue of St. Michael, patron saint of France and of the royal order of chivalry. Nearly four hundred other tents and pavilions surrounded that of Francis, 'an entire town of silver and gold, of silk and velvet, of floating tapestries,' all of them decorated with golden apples, their banners painted by Jean

I would like to thank Edward Morris, François Rigolot and John Elliott for helpful conversation and criticism. Thanks also to the Institute for Advanced Study, Princeton, and to the Rockefeller Foundation, for providing a supportive atmosphere in which to complete this essay.

Clouet. 'Their cloth of gold, devices and golden apples were very beautiful in the sunlight.'[1]

Although it was accompanied by the most opulent artistic and culinary display in recent memory, the Field of Cloth of Gold proved to be of little practical significance. The two kings' gestures of friendship had already been partially nullified at a meeting of Henry and the Emperor Charles V the week before, and were to be totally obliterated by another meeting of Henry and Charles less than a month after; on June 24th the kings parted and on July 5th, Henry met Charles near Calais, while Francis hovered on the frontier, waiting to be invited. There, 'the very sea-sands might have blushed' when Henry and Charles discussed a possible marriage alliance.[2] So Charles undermined whatever personal links had been established during the kings' dinner parties and embraces. 'In this meane while..., warre was earnestlie pursued between England and France... in so much that each part did what in them lay to hurt [the] other.'[3] Francis' tents – the ones that had not been overly damaged by the dust and rain at the Field of Cloth of Gold – were used to house his troops.

The Field of Cloth of Gold was not a momentous event in European history, but it was an intriguing one, because it illustrates both the importance and the difficulty of appreciating the character of Renaissance political culture. How should the historian deal with the crisis of credibility induced by the spectacle of so much conspicuous and seemingly frivolous display – both of words and of money? Reading through the State Papers of Henry VIII, we find passages like the following:

...the affection [the two kings] bear to each other in their hearts is the chief means to knit the assured knot of perseverant amity betwixt them...it is not to be marvelled that this agreeable consonance of semblable properties and affections do vehemently excite and stir them both, not only to love and tenderly favor each other, but also personally to visit, see and speak together...and finally make such impression of entire love in their heart that the same shall be always permanent and never dissolved, to the pleasure of God, their both comforts, and the weal of all Christendom. (Instructions to Wingfield, representative at the French court)

[1] Joycelyne G. Russell, *The Field of Cloth of Gold. Men and Manners in 1520* (London, 1969), esp. pp. 23–30. Also cf. Desmond Seward, *Prince of the Renaissance. The Golden Life of François I*, (New York, 1973), pp. 802–6.

[2] Karl Brandi, *The Emperor Charles V. The Growth and Destiny of a Man and of a World-Empire*, tr. C. V. Wedgwood (London, rep. 1967), p. 118.

[3] *Holinshed's Chronicles of England, Scotland, and Ireland*, ed. Raphael Holinshed, 6 vols. (London, 1807–8), III, p. 686.

Further on, we read in a letter from the Emperor's envoy in England, de la Sauch, to Charles' Councillor, Chièvres,

When we deal with men we give good words, and promise wonders; but having attained our object, there is an end of it. If you think that the English here will labour for us, out of pure love for our smiles and our good looks, and turn a deaf ear to others, *certes, monsieur*, you will find yourself very much mistaken. The French do not act in this way; for they talk and give at the same time, and make large promises besides.[4]

One's first impulse, in taking notes, is to delete the rhetoric and underscore the cynical analysis. Since we know that Renaissance diplomats devised elaborate spy systems to circumvent formal negotiations and displays of Christian brotherhood, it seems only common sense to view arguments over precedence and declarations of Christian love as a tissue of public relations, behind which the diplomats exercised rational, cold-blooded reason of state. 'How much is left of its glory', writes one historian, 'when we pierce the golden veil to discover the harsh reality of achievement? If the...[Field of Cloth of Gold] was immensely celebrated...neither then nor now can it have deceived anyone. A golden mountain had brought forth a mouse.'[5]

One's second impulse is to label all those gestures of chivalry and piety as 'medieval' and the spy systems and secret instructions to diplomats as 'modern.' When Charles plotted with Henry to invade France in 1523 (violating the 1520 agreements) he was being modern; when he challenged Francis to personal combat in 1534, causing a panic among the diplomats of both sides, he was being medieval. 'The Field of Cloth of Gold was a glorious excuse for the two courts to show off'; writes another observer, 'and the attempt at rekindling a departed chivalry was irrelevant to the problems of a nationalistic Europe.'[6]

A third approach, one currently favored by many historians, is to focus on the mode of communication – the political discourse – itself, and to ask what meaning verbal and artistic ornament had in a society where power was sought and expressed within a system of patron/client relationships: How did artifacts express social and political values? What did Renaissance culture mean for the people who lived it? One historian describes the 'big-man' system which existed in Renaissance Europe as

---

[4] *Letters and Papers, Foreign and Domestic, of the Reign of Henry VIII, 1509–1547*, ed. J. S. Brewer, 21 vols. (London, 1867), III, Part I (1519–1523), pp. 212, 255.

[5] Russell, *Field*, p. 45.

[6] Neville Williams, 'The Tudors, Three Contrasts in Personality,' in A. G. Dickens, ed., *The Courts of Europe: Politics, Patronage and Royalty, 1400–1800* (London, 1977), p. 156. On Charles V, see Brandi, *Charles V*, pp. 378–9.

well as in many non-western societies. 'The same elements are there: the growing accrual of power in the hands of Big Men; the evolution of patterns of deference and patronage; the competition between rivals and their client groups, both in politics and the arts.'[7] In this context the Field of Cloth of Gold could be seen not as a tissue of phony public relations but as a kind of royal potlatch, where social etiquette facilitated the dispensing of benefits and displays of deference, and where artistic spectacle served both to display and justify power in a language which contemporaries could easily understand.[8]

This approach seems both straightforward and value-free; in fact, it is laden with difficulties, because the culture which most directly reflects Renaissance political values – court festivals, and the art and literature of the courtier – is precisely the culture which is most inaccessible to modern sensibilities. Some scholars object, on ideological grounds, to history written 'from the top down'; history which focuses on the ideas and values of the ruling classes as a means of defining the ideas and values of the general culture. For these scholars, the ruling classes certainly had ideas and projects, but only the laboring classes had *mentalités*.[9] As children of both the Puritan revolution of the seventeenth century and the bourgeois revolutions of the eighteenth, some are also simply uncomfortable with the aesthetics of an aristocracy which adored splendor and found comfort and utility contemptible. They understand, even if they do not necessarily prefer, culture which reflects the bourgeois values of order, durability and cleanliness, as well as Puritan simplicity and depth of feeling – not to mention bourgeois and Puritan frugality; why waste all that money and talent on banners and golden apples, toys to be played with for a single fête?[10]

Even the great cultural historian, Lucien Febvre, trying to appreciate the beautiful women of Francis' court, had to throw up his hands:

[7] Werner L. Gundersheimer, 'Patronage in the Renaissance: An Exploratory Approach' in Guy Fitch Lytle and Stephen Orgel (eds.)
Patronage in the Renaissance (Princeton, 1981), pp. 12–13.
[8] On the potlatch as a type of 'prestige consumption' in Early Modern Europe, see Norbert Elias, *The Court Society*, tr. Edmund Jephcott, 1st American ed. (Oxford, 1983), pp. 66–8.
[9] Robert Darnton actually defines the historian of *mentalités* by distinguishing him or her from the historian of high culture: 'Instead of following the high road of intellectual history, [this] inquiry leads into the unmapped territory known...as *l'histoire des mentalités*...Where the historian of ideas traces...formal thought...the ethnographic historian traces the way ordinary people made sense of the world.' (*The Great Cat Massacre, and other Episodes in French Cultural History* (New York, 1985), p. 3.)
[10] On Puritan objections to all art as ephemeral, see Stephen Orgel, *The Illusion of Power: Political Theater in the English Renaissance* (Berkeley and Los Angeles, 1975), pp. 41–42.

...no effort of the will can make our own aesthetic sense coincide with that of our ancestors'. For us [their] face[s] hold neither charm nor grace nor beauty...But in all fairness, how could they have refined their features...while exposing themselves constantly, on horseback, to the out-of-doors, to the cutting wind,...traveling for weeks and weeks without real rest, without anything more than improvised lodgings?[11]

At least one contemporary of Francis agreed with Febvre, the Anglican bishop John Fisher, who used the Field of Cloth of Gold as the subject of a sermon in 1521. Fisher described the splendor – and the filth – which he experienced at the meeting:

For that lytell whyle that we were there, somtyme there was suche dust, and therewithall so great wyndes, that all the ayre was full of dust. The gownes of veluet, and of clothe of golde were full of dust, the ryche trappers of horses were full of dust, hattes, cappes, gownes were full of dust, the here and faces of men were full of dust, and briefly to speke, horse and man were so encombred with dust, that scantly one myghte se another.

Fisher used his fastidious disgust and 'lothesomenes' to criticize the values of the aristocracy. Many had filled their coffers, some had become sick and died; some learnt pride of apparel and could not shake it off; some learned envy.

Take away the glysteryng garment, take away the cloth of golde, take away the precyouse stones, and the other rychesse of apparell, and what dyfference is betwyxt an Emperour and another pore man...They be in them selfe but erth and asshes, and to erthe they retourne, and all theyr glorye well consydered, and beholden with ryght iyen [eyes], is but very myserable.[12]

Febvre and Fisher would probably have been equally distressed – and for the same reasons – by the food which was served at the Field of Cloth of Gold: the 'subtleties' or edible table decorations made all of sugar and shaped like heraldic beasts, allegorical figures, church interiors or hunting scenes; or the 'peacock in hackles royally' – a roasted peacock which had been flayed, reinserted in its own skin and plumage and served sitting, as if it were alive – the rich sauce masking the questionable condition of the meat.[13]

Other observers, seeking the central meaning or message of a work of art, have been bemused by a different kind of Renaissance opulence: the condensed images, the clusters of dissonant metaphors, the contradictory

---

[11] Lucien Febvre, *Life in Renaissance France*, tr. Marian Rothstein (Cambridge, Mass., and London, 1977), p. 17.
[12] Sermon of John Fisher, bishop of Rochester, pub. 1532 and quoted in Russell, *Field*, pp. 217, 218.
[13] *Ibid.*, pp. 149, 153.

and unresolved meanings often embodied in a single work. In allegory, mythological figures, as personifications of human qualities, are pitted against each other, while the human action is suspended. A poet might take a thoroughly immoral figure of mythology which he or she would cull from one of many source books, and show how it symbolized the soul in tribulation, searching for God. Venus, for instance, might be depicted as 'the intelligible beauty which is in the ideas,' a kind of celestial love, or as a personification of lust; if the poet were subtle, he or she would probably paint her both ways.[14]

It is one thing for a modern observer to laboriously decode the unfamiliar language of this allegorical symbolism; it is a much greater challenge to imagine how the poems, costumes and banners ornamenting the Field of Cloth of Gold were actually conceived and 'read'. Take, for example, one of the costumes worn by Francis:

The French King...[wore] purple velvet embroidered full of little bookes of white satin, and in the bookes were written *Ame*. About the borders...of the garments a chaine of blew like iron, resembling the chaine of a well or a prison chaine, which was interpreted to be *Liber*, a booke. Within this booke was written...*Ame*. Put the two together and it maketh *Liberame*.[15]

For Frances Yates, this sort of cryptic symbolism signified a coherent philosophical outlook inspired by Christian Neoplatonism. 'Life flowed into [these symbols]; from above through the contact with the dynamics of a living religion; from all sides, through the enriching commerce between poets, artists, architects, musicians, moving about their appointed tasks within a homogenous culture.'[16] But even within this 'homogeneous culture' of Latin-speaking humanists, there was confusion about how to puzzle out even the literal meaning of Renaissance artifacts; looking at Francis' garment, one contemporary observer thought the symbols, taken together, should read, 'Deliver me of bonds,' while another thought it should be 'Deliver me *not* of bonds,' although he could not be sure. Many others were surely indifferent to everything about the garment except its cost; Castiglione considered the French courtiers notable for their total indifference to humanist learning, and hoped that they would take a greater interest in their own education.[17]

---

[14] J. Seznec, *The Survival of the Pagan Gods. The Mythological Tradition and its Place in Renaissance Humanism and Art*, tr. B.F.Sessions, (New York, rep. 1940), p. 223.

[15] Holinshed, *Chronicles*, III, p. 653.

[16] Frances Yates, *The French Academies of the Sixteenth Century* (Nendeln, Liechtenstein, rep. 1968), p. 132, 151.

[17] Edward Hall, 'The Triumphant reigne of Kyng Henry the VIII' i, 207, quoted in Russell, *Field*, p. 134. On other costumes, and other misunderstandings, see Russell, pp. 138–9. Courtiers in France were noted for their unwillingness to educate themselves; Castiglione said he hoped the French court would participate in the Renaissance

For modern observers, the deeper meaning of Francis' garment to contemporaries must seem even more obscure. Is it (as Marc Bensimon says) that 'In [the] sixteenth century man relates not to the principle of immanence, but...seeks transcendence in the visible,' or is it (as Stephen Orgel says) that 'The pressure is not toward spiritualizing the physical, but toward embodying and sensualizing the moral and abstract'?[18] Did the reader or viewer, ruminating over these symbolic representations, hovering between levels of abstraction, ever feel a sense of vertigo?[19]

In the remainder of this essay I want to address one problematic aspect of Renaissance culture, the multiple images and meanings that characterize so many artistic works, by focusing on a single Renaissance experience, the Field of Cloth of Gold, through the prism of a single text, a ballad written by Clément Marot to commemorate the event. Marot was, in his time, the most important poet in France. In *our* time he is seen as a transitional figure between the late-medieval *rhétoriqueurs* (his father was the *rhétoriqueur* Jean Marot) and the Pléiade. He is admired for his later satires and for his translations of the psalms, written after he had become an evangelical Christian. But because he was a *valet de chambre* in the royal household (poet/secretary, different from the aristocrats who were called *gentilshommes de la chambre*), he is also dismissed as a fundamentally decorative poet, a man without an artistic soul:

One naturally compares Scève with Marot, the contemporary master: Scève writes for himself, careless of reputation and audience, whereas one can hardly

of letters. (Pauline M. Smith, *The Anti-Courtier Trend in 16th Century French Literature* (Geneva, 1966), p. 93.) In 1521 Budé complained that he was having trouble getting Francis to establish a school for Greek studies: 'I do what I can to rekindle the fire [in Francis]...but I lack the ability to influence the courtiers, who sometimes deride my plans and try unfairly to discredit me.' (R. J. Knecht, *Francis I* (Cambridge and New York, 1982), pp. 138–9).

18 Marc Bensimon, 'Modes of Perception of Reality in the Renaissance,' in R. S. Kinsman, (ed.) *The Darker Vision of the Renaissance. Beyond the Fields of Reason* (Berkeley, 1974), p. 249. Stephen Orgel, 'The Royal Theatre and the Role of the King,' in Lytle and Orgel, (eds.) *Patronage*, p. 264.

19 Marc Bensimon, for one, is sure that they did. He describes the fifteenth-century *chansons* with two voices, one singing in Italian, the other in French, or two texts with entirely different meanings. Bensimon interprets these texts as deeply problematic; 'In a sense, symmetrical representation reflects a heroic mode of coping with anxieties and time.' What Renaissance poets *do* capture by this glut of images is surface, not depth, 'mask[ing] an essential alienation from inner reality.' To support his contention that Renaissance literature is neurotic, Bensimon quotes the words of modern schizophrenics, who, like Ficino, use imagery of sun-worship, mountains, elevation, flying, gold, and angels. For Bensimon, the courtier Marot was a poet alienated from himself, while Rabelais' psychological attitude 'would have to be described, medically-speaking, as perversion and revolt' (pp. 238–9, 250, 251, 254, 270).

imagine Marot without his public...And though it would be unfair to deny
Marot's claims to write serious poetry when the mood took him, I doubt if one
can grant him the richness of inner experience that is so distinctive in Scève's
poetry.[20]

Whatever their opinion of Marot's later elegies and satires, most critics
agree that the early poems of Marot are those of a 'charming, feckless
courtier'; derivative, conventional, and mediocre works which rely on
complicated syntax and allegorical allusion to stimulate ingenuity, not
serious thought. C. A. Mayer writes in Marot's defence, 'the act of
seeing in our poet only the author...of rondeaux and ballades allows one
to relegate Marot to the Middle Ages and view his poetry as the art of
being agreeable.' Mayer is trying to rescue Marot from the Middle Ages,
but he leaves the early Marot who wrote rondeaux and ballades still in
his grave. Marot didn't break with the rhétoriqueurs or go to prison for
his beliefs until 1526; therefore he didn't become profound until 1526.
After all, a ceremonial poem, like a court pageant, couldn't have much
meat in it.[21]

I want to start by taking these critics at their word, and assuming that
Marot was merely a cipher, a purveyor of the dominant political and
aesthetic discourse; what can the ballad tell us about the meaning of
Renaissance culture for the people who lived it? I also want to speculate
about Marot's mentality and intent as a poet who was also a servant of
the state. Like Marot's literary critics, many historians of French society
display a strong antipathy to courtier culture, largely stemming, I
suspect, from reading the attacks on courtiers from the period immediately after Marot's, the regency of Catherine de Medici.[22] 'Competition

[20] I. D. McFarlane, A Literary History of France. Renaissance France, 1470–1589
(London and Tonbridge, 1974), p. 106–7.
[21] C. A. Mayer, ed., Clément Marot. Oeuvres Diverses (London, 1966), p. 5. Mayer refers
to Marot's ballade on the Field of Cloth of Gold as 'assez mediocre' (C. A. Mayer,
Clément Marot, (Paris, 1972), pp. 39, 138.) Elsewhere, Mayer defends Marot as a
courtier/poet and compares his oeuvre to Mozart's, who also worked for a patron
('Clément Marot et ses protecteurs,' Culture et Pouvoir au temps de l'Humanisme et de
la Renaissance (Geneva and Paris, 1978), pp. 259–69.) Also see Seward, Francis: '...in
some ways [Marot] remains the last French poet of the Middle Ages' (p. 169). Pauline
Smith wrote that Marot's early ballades showed the influence of the rhétoriqueurs, and
that his evolution after 1527 represents a break with the medieval poetic tradition.
(Pauline M. Smith, Clément Marot, Poet of the French Renaissance (London, 1970), pp.
66, 79.) McFarlane said the same thing (Literary History, p. 106–7). Robert Griffin
defends Marot's total oeuvre as a synthesis of court life, individual freedom and
spiritual insight; he doesn't mention Marot's ballade on the Field of Cloth of Gold
(Clément Marot). The most recent critical work on Marot is George Joseph, Clément
Marot (Boston, 1985). Joseph particularly values Marot's psalm translations, epigrams,
verse epistles and rondeaux (Preface, n.p.).
[22] For example, Norbert Elias wrote perceptively of the courtier/artist as extrovert,
distinguishing between the self-observation of the religious contemplative, seeking a

for patronage was the normal condition of most artists' lives,' Professor Koenigsberger writes, 'But in court society, as it developed in sixteenth- and seventeenth-century Europe, it became part of men's life-style in the sense that everything else was subordinated to it and to its rules and patterns.'[23] As nobles became more dependent on the monarchy and more financially strapped because of inflation, criticism of these quasi-professional courtiers became more and more barbed. During the French wars of religion courtiers, Henri II's *mignons* in particular, were accused of being 'murderous perverts' who corrupted princes and oppressed the people. Italians and *nouveau riche* hangers-on became the scapegoats for the economic and religious chaos that afflicted the older nobility and the peasantry – and also some poets, who resented the fact that courtiers received so much money for displaying so little talent. By 1576 Ronsard was attributing the ruin of France to Italians and courtiers, as well as Protestants, while Jean de La Jessée advised an aspiring courtier/poet not to study or work too much:

> No one wants to hear, in these superb courts,
> A long Aenead, or some high-flown discourse:
> A facile rime, a little song
> Is more to our taste, and in your interests...
> Don't break your neck working so hard.[24]

All of this hostility peaked in the works on 'hermaphrodites,' (actually the homosexuals surrounding the king) who were described as materialistic, decadent, cynical, and atheistic.

knowledge of hidden impulses, and the courtier, who thinks about himself in order to achieve self-discipline in his social life. His books are 'nothing else than direct organs of social life, a part of conversations and social games...' But after all this promising analysis, Elias simply dismisses court literature as superficial; the courts, he says, were not fertile grounds for literature or scholarship (Norbert Elias, *The Court Society* pp. 104–6). Likewise Sydney Anglo, in a study of anti-courtier literature, sums up his findings: 'And it is a sad fact that...systematic self-seeking...remains too clearly recognizable as the sempiternal reality of what may crawl away when the stones of political life and polite society are stirred' (Sidney Anglo, 'The Renaissance and Changing Ideals,' in Dickens, *Courts*, p. 53).

On anti-courtier sentiment during the sixteenth century, see Pauline Smith, *The Anti-Courtier Trend*. Also see Barbara C. Bowen, *Words and the Man in French Renaissance Literature* (Lexington, Ky., 1983): 'Renaissance humanists...were much concerned with the power of the spoken word, and in particular with the evils and dangers of *garrulitas*...very few emblem books did not include at least one emblem on the evils of misused speech' (pp. 96–6). In 1536 Guillaume de la Perrière published an emblem, or image-picture, of a courtier with his tongue held on a plate before him, his heart in his other hand, hidden behind his back (Anglo, 'The Renaissance and Changing Ideals', pp. 33, 44–49).

[23] H. G. Koenigsberger, 'Republics and Courts in Italian and European Culture in the Sixteenth and Seventeenth Centuries,' *Past and Present*, No. 83 (1979), p. 38.

[24] Quoted in Smith, *The Anti-Courtier Trend*, pp. 182, 185, 196–202.

Marot's own position as a courtier/poet was, on the face of it, much less problematic than that of the political sycophants who surrounded Catherine. King Francis' sister, Marguerite of Angoulême, in whose household Marot was living in 1520, was close to him in age and interests. More sympathetic, intellectual and introspective than Francis, and more dedicated to humanist scholarship, she was also free of the pressures of foreign policy and could devote herself entirely to cultural and spiritual concerns.[25] Francis himself was an accomplished poet, the author of some 209 *rondeaux*, *ballades*, *chansons* and other works. He also prided himself on the intellectual and aesthetic refinement of his court; it was at Francis' request that Castiglione wrote his flattering portrait of the courtier, depicting him as a well-rounded, wise and honest counselor of princes.[26] In short, Marguerite and Francis were ideal patrons for an aspiring artist; courteous, appreciative, and easy to praise. Throughout his career, Marot acknowledged his debt to the French court for educating him as a poet.[27]

But however congenial the atmosphere of court or household, however satisfying the courtier/artist's moments of identification with the values of his patrons, there was surely an inbuilt ambiguity in the position of the courtier, taking his themes from a relatively fixed menu, and that of the artist or thinker, reflecting and commenting on those themes. Because Marot and many other artists seemed to work comfortably within the patronage system, we should not assume that they were necessarily insensitive to the tensions inherent in that system, or that they were devoid of critical consciousness or moral integrity; we should look instead for ways in which they succeeded in resolving those tensions creatively.[28] In the final section of this essay, I would like to read Marot

[25] *Ibid.*, pp. 49–50.
[26] *François Ier, Oeuvres Poetiques*, critical ed., J. E. Kane (Geneva, 1984). R. J. Knecht, 'Francis I, Prince and Patron of the Northern Renaissance,' in Dickens, *Courts*, pp. 100–1, 106ff.
[27] Marot did criticize courtiers a few times during his career; he disdains their powdered faces, their mania for building houses which they couldn't keep up, and their demands for money. (Smith, *The Anti-Courtier Trend*, pp. 87, 90–1, 100, and Robert Griffin, *Clément Marot and the Inflections of Poetic Voice* (Berkeley, 1974), p. 171). Smith points out that while Marot was anti-clerical in his writing, he had very little to say against courtiers (p. 57). George Joseph remarks that Marot was not a 'courtier of the opposition; a member of the court who was secretly opposed to it...[he wanted to] control political events from the court's privileged position above all parties' (Preface, n.p.).
[28] See, for example, Lauro Martines, 'The Gentleman in Renaissance Italy,' p. 77: 'There are moments in history when the thrust of political power is such that it affords men few choices. They are either with the dominant wave or against it. To be different is almost akin to dropping out of the historical process. The Renaissance...made exhausting demands on the human spirit, particularly so in the 16th century. Personal integrity must have been doubly rare then.'

as a creative thinker and artist, linked to his audience by friendship as well as need, working within the constraints of his time to comment on the relation of beauty and power within his own culture. The critic George Joseph writes that 'The political nature of Marot's poetry cannot be dismissed as a mere excuse or superficial fiction permitting the poet to address more serious matters.[29] I want to suggest that the profusion of images and meanings in Marot's early poems, which appear to most modern observers as an impenetrable web of arcane symbolism, may reflect the courtier/artist's attempt to express the ambiguity of his own position.

II.

Du triumphe D'Ardres et Guignes, faict par les roys de France et d'Angleterre[30]

> Au camp des roys les plus beaulx de ce monde
> Sont arrivez trois riches estendars.
> Amour tient l'ung, de couleur blanche et munde,
> Triumphe l'autre avecques ses souldars,
> Vivement painct de couleur célestine:
> Beaulté après en sa main noble et digne
> Porte le tiers, tainct de vermeille sorte.
> Ainsi chascun richement se comporte,
> Et en tel ordre et pompe primeraine
> Sont venuz veoir la royalle cohorte
> Amour, Triumphe, et Beaulté souveraine.
>
> En ces beaulx lieux plus tost que vol d'aronde
> Vient celle Amour des célestines pars,
> Et en apporte une vive et claire unde,
> Dont elle estainct les fureurs du dieu Mars.
> Avecques France, Angleterre enlumine,
> Disant: 'Il faut qu'en ce camp je domine'.
> Puis à son vueil faict bon guet à la porte,
> Pour empescher que Discorde n'apporte
> La pomme d'or, dont vint guerre inhumaine:
> Aussi affin que seulement en sorte
> Amour, Triumphe, et Beaulté souveraine.
>
> Pas ne convient que ma plume se fonde
> A rediger du Triumphe les ars,
> Car de si grands en haultesse profonde
> N'en feirant onc les belliqueurs Césars.
> Que diray plus? richesse tant insigne

[29] George Joseph, *Clément Marot*, Preface, n.p.
[30] The ballad was published as part of Marot's book, *L'Adolescence Clémentine*, in 1532. A modern edition, edited by V. L. Saulnier, was published in Paris in 1958.

A tous humains bien démonstre et désigne
Des deux partiz la puissance très-forte.
Brief, il n'est cueur qui ne se réconforte
En ce pays, plus qu'en mer la Séraine,
De veoir régner (apres rancune morte)
Amour, Triumphe, et Beaulté souveraine.

ENVOY

De la beaulté des hommes me déporte:
Et quant à celle aux dames, je rapporte
Qu'en ce monceau laide seroit Hélaine.
Parquoy concludz que ceste terre porte
Amour, Triumphe, et Beaulté souveraine.

In 1520, Marot had just been 'given' by Francis to the household of Francis' sister, Marguerite de Valois, as a *valet de chambre*. Clément was moderately educated, and knew some Latin. As a boy, he had served as page to a nobleman and then as a clerk in the Paris law courts before he attracted Francis' attention by dedicating some poems to him. Marot probably attended the Field of Cloth of Gold as a member of Marguerite's entourage. It was his first big event; he was twenty-four.[31]

The ballad was a conventional, one might say proper poem, written probably to order. The ballad form had flourished for two centuries, sometimes through monthly competitions at the royal court. It was often used to express grave subjects, suitable for addressing princes. Distinguished by repeated refrains and grace of rhythm, the ballad was basically old-fashioned; du Bellay condemned it as an *espicerie*.[32] This ballad is an allegory of Love, Triumph and Beauty: Love dominates stanza 2; Triumph, stanza 3, and Beauty, the *Envoy*.

Marot may have read an official pamphlet, published in 1521 by Jean Lescaille, in which the author described the event in terms remarkably similar to those of the ballad.[33] Lescaille first recounts the opulence and pageantry of the jousting, and notes the importance of preventing *le dieu Mars* from entering, due to idleness and sedition in the camp. He then contrasts the interview of Henry and Francis, having friendship as its object, with the marriage of Peleus and Thetis, which ended in discord. Marot's poem begins with a processional, distinguished by its opulence and pomp; then comes an allegory, in which the fury of Mars is quenched by the clear wave of Love, who then stands guard at the door to prevent Discord from bringing in the golden apple. (The apple was,

31 Smith, *The Anti-Courtier Trend*, pp. 4–13.
32 Mayer, *Oeuvres Diverses*, p. 28. On the *ballade* form, see Griffin, *Marot*, p. 32.
33 Quoted in Brewer, *Henry VIII*, p. 308.

of course, thrown by Discord into the wedding of Peleus and Thetis and claimed by the three goddesses, Venus, Hera and Athena). Both pamphlet and ballad thus describe the Field of Cloth of Gold as a triumph of order and pomp, and both use the same allegorical framework.

Marot was Francis' favorite poet. What might the ballad have conveyed to him, or to any member of his court who was given to self-congratulation, on a first or second reading? 'the most beautiful kings in this world...' sounds like the inflated rhetoric of the diplomats, writing of the 'said serene princes...like in force corporall, beautie, and gift of nature,...and in the flower and vigor of youth...'[34] But this *was* an astonishing fact: two kings who actually looked like kings – young, vigorous and handsome, (Francis was twenty-five, Henry twenty-nine). Professor Koenigsberger has calculated that there was one chance in eight for a dynasty to produce three generations of healthy male rulers. In 1559 there was only one in Western Europe, Philip II. So the word *beaulx* must have evoked in Francis' mind a vivid, sensuous image of two handsome men, splendidly dressed.

Second, since the kings were *beaulx* and not *forts*, the reader might sense that the poem was written to celebrate the prevention of war, not a military triumph; *estandars* would make one think of a pageant, not a battle. *Triumphe* was part of the conventional decorative vocabulary of court pageants. It did not mean military victory, but a procession or pageant which glorified the ruler. *Souldars* might well be heralds, and 'heralds' might remind Francis of the aristocratic officials who arranged the jousting and acted as umpires; 'conservative practice had been that only kings, princes, and the great nobles...were permitted heralds... whose order, like that of priests, was held to be indelible.'[35] By using the colors blue, white and crimson, Marot might have also been referring to the first meeting of the French and English queens which took place at the joust; the ladies' clothes and accoutrements were of crimson, silver and azure (Mary, duchess of Suffolk and formerly queen of France, was known as 'the white queen'). *Triumphe* might, of course, be used ironically by a poet, since there really was no moral or even diplomatic triumph at the Field of Cloth of Gold. Most people, however – the king certainly – thought of a triumphal arch, or a procession. The Field of Cloth of Gold, especially the jousting or fake battles which climaxed the event, was really political theater with the kings and queens as both stars and spectators. In this sense it was a forerunner of the masques and displays of martial prowess produced at the English, French and Spanish courts, in which the royal audience, sitting on stage, was also

[34] *Ibid.*, p. 212.
[35] Russell, *Field*, p. 122.

on display to the rest of the aristocratic assembly, who watched the king and queen watching the performance and occasionally even acting in it.[36]

The words Love, Triumph and Beauty were also familiar to Francis as abstract concepts. Love, although represented as Cupid or Venus, might also mean harmony or peace. *Beaulté*, in abstract form, is not the earthly beauty of kings, but the quintessence of beauty which is the soul's vision of Truth. The colors are also symbolic: white is purity, and *célestine* is celestial blue, the perfection of those who follow virtue.[37] In this context *Souldars* might also suggest angelic heralds, especially since it is followed by *célestine*. Since the real-life pageant was decorated with allegorical figures, the poet has not ceased to describe it in concrete terms. He is saying to contemporaries, 'At the Field of Cloth of Gold, they carried around banners in symbolic colors' and also, 'The Field was taken over by higher elements, which are the subject of the poem.' The first stanza depicts the event both as it occurred in real life and as a starting point for allegory.

> Into these beautiful places comes,
>> more swiftly than the flight of the swallow
> Love from heavenly parts,
> Who brings with her a brisk and clear wave,
> With which she extinguishes the fury of the
>> god Mars.

Love quenches the fire of war. Mars was the god of the tempest and of the confusion and strife of battle. He was usually matched, in allegory, with Pallas Athene, the goddess of Wisdom and well-matched chivalrous fights. But since Venus was traditionally born of seafoam and was blown to shore on a wave, since she was worshipped both as Love and as

[36] Catherine of Aragon had a litter of crimson satin decorated with pomegranates. Claude of France wore silver. Many ladies in the English retinue came in wagons covered in cloth of gold on azure. Mary of Suffolk, 'the white queen,' was described as 'a nymph from heaven,' and 'one of the most beautiful young women in the world... it was she who led the dances and festivities...' (Russell, *Field*, pp. 5–6, 124). Du Bellay, talking about the Field of Cloth of Gold, said, 'I will not pause to tell you of the great triumphs and festivities which were made there' (du Bellay, *Mémoires de Martin et Guillaume du Bellay*, Vol. I (Paris, 1898), p. 100). The *Mémoires* of a bourgeois of Paris referred to 'la plus grande triumphe que jamais en France ne ailleurs fust veue' (Brewer, *Henry VIII*. p. 306, 310). On Renaissance monarchs' use of theatrical apparatus, see Orgel, 'The Royal Theatre,' p. 261. On court masques in sixteenth century England, see Orgel, *Illusion of Power*, pp. 8–10. On France under Catherine de Medici, see Yates, *French Academies*. On Spain in the sixteenth and seventeenth centuries, see Professor Elliott's essay in this volume, pp. 5–24.

[37] Frances Yates, *The Valois Tapestries*, (London, 1959), p. 246. George Joseph remarks on the ballad that, 'Marot...emphasizes moral categories as if to call the reader to see beyond flashy appearances and judge the meeting in terms of its success in bringing about peace and harmony' (p. 4).

goddess of the peaceful sea, these four lines would certainly suggest Venus and Mars. Francis might remember pictures of the sleeping Mars and Venus which depict peace after war and which, of course, are sensual. (The royal ordinance for the jousting, printed in Lescaille's pamphlet, said: 'chivalrous Mars has left behind delightful means of avoiding idleness in time of peace: by joyous tournaments jousts and combats...for the love of their ladies.')[38] This reference to Mars and Venus, although veiled, must have resonated in the mind of a man whose daily routine was dominated by hunting and romantic liaisons, who – more deliberately than his predecessors – used beautiful women as ornaments at court and as pawns in the dynastic marriage market, and of whom it was said that 'ladies more than years caused his death.'[39] Perhaps Francis also began to muse on the character of this profane love which might also mean the end of peace; the beauty of Venus, in this sense, would also be a warning of danger, an incitement to evil.

But *Amour* comes from *célestine pars*; this is also a passage about sacred or Platonic love. Francis, or any reader acquainted with the doctrines of Neoplatonism, might placate any self-doubts by remembering that sensual love, when united to virtue, was potentially a power for good, a stage in the soul's progress toward enlightenment. Through the contemplation of a beautiful person and the stimulation of desire, one might be led to the contemplation of Beauty itself. Through the exercise of reason and the taming of these same passions (the irrational part of the soul), romantic love might ultimately be transformed from desire for a person to a vision of God. As the facilitator of this aesthetic and spiritual ascent, the poet, in Neoplatonic philosophy, is depicted as the ideal personality. So Francis, reading this stanza, might be moved to appreciate Marot's excellence as well as his own.

> It is not fitting that my pen should
>   take part
> In writing out the artifices of this Triumph,
> For such great and exalted acts
> Not even the warlike Caesars ever accomplished.

Classical figures (*Césars*) were used in the same context as mythological heroes. The Caesars were grand and powerful, but Henry and Francis are more so. This is shown by the magnificence of the spectacle; since

---

[38] Quoted in Russell, *Field*, p. 109. Another interpretation of the Mars/Venus theme seems more far-fetched; Sydney Freedberg remarks that Rosso's drawing of Mars and Venus, intended for Francis, may be an 'allegory of Francis' giving up war to devote himself to the arts'; Francis hired him a few months after seeing it. (Sydney J. Freedberg, 'Rosso's Style in France and its Italian Context,' in *Actes du Colloque International sur L'Art de Fontainebleau*, André Chastel, ed. (Paris, 1975), p. 19.)

[39] Seward, *Francis*, p. 244.

magnificence is the nearest virtue to magnanimity, and magnanimity is keeping discord out, the present triumph is greater than Caesar's because it reflects the power of love, not of arms.

Why would Francis have wanted to see himself as Caesar or Mars? Why did the kings dress up as gods to play games at the Field of Cloth of Gold? During his youth, Francis and his courtiers enjoyed themselves by riding through Paris, disguised, at night, throwing eggs and stones at his subjects; at the Field of Cloth of Gold, the monarchs said they would leave the negotiating to their councilors and spend their time in frivolity and demonstrations of affection.[40] That arrogant frivolity should have been such a large component of Francis' persona, in contrast, say, to the solemnity and asceticism of Philip II, was partly due to personal temperament. It also reflected the fact that, unlike Philip, Francis presented himself, and probably perceived himself, as a quasi-divine being. The king took communion in both kinds; only priests did this. He also claimed the power to heal by touch; in 1530 Francis touched at least 1,731 people. When he died, Francis' meals were served to an effigy of himself, lying in state, for eleven days, while his real corpse lay in an adjoining room.[41] By treating the Field of Cloth of Gold as a setting for personal recreation rather than serious diplomacy, and by his resemblance to capricious, life-like mythological heroes, the king expressed his disdain for 'proving himself' in the arena of power politics. Perhaps Francis also believed, along with Lorenzo de' Medici, that praise could improve its subject, and that he might actually raise himself toward union with the divine by contemplating his own myth about himself.[42]

On the other hand, Francis' persona also reflected the fact that monarchy, as an institution, was less fully developed in Renaissance France than it was in sixteenth-century Spain. Philip II and Louis XIV celebrated their highly formalized political rituals like priests – the Escurial and Versailles being their temples. Francis had no temple in 1520, and the rituals of kingship at *his* itinerant court were far less reified; one high point of the Field of Cloth of Gold was a 'surprise' visit of Francis to Henry in his bedroom one morning, flaunting all the rules of precedent. For Francis, the royal mystique emanated solely from the king's person, not from a building or a set of rituals or institutions, implying both greater freedom to be capricious in his personal and public behavior and less actual authority as head of state.

[40] Du Bellay, *Mémoires*, p. 172.   [41] R. J. Knecht, 'Francis', pp. 102–3.
[42] See the essay by Professor Bullard in this volume, pp. 40–1. The degree of Francis' interest in humanist studies and philosophy is unclear. Knecht credits him with giving humanists large-scale patronage, and having several in his personal entourage in 1520; he also says that Francis' enthusiasm was sporadic (*Francis I*, p. 138).

Clémont Marot and the Field of Cloth of Gold

For the fact was that Francis had no large standing army, no centralized system of taxation, and – until much later in his reign – no central royal palace. 'France' was really a literary term, referring to a tradition of kingship, religion and culture which was certainly more vague than the awareness which the average person had of his or her strictly local affiliations and obligations. So Francis' self-image as king must have been complex, to say the least. Far from being an outmoded ritual from the Middle Ages, the sheer fact of association with a saint or divinity was powerful propaganda – and powerful self-affirmation – in an era when rulers were trying to narrow the gap between their inflated, almost sacred authority as holders of the royal office and their very limited concrete power over lands and peoples. By establishing a mythological genealogy, the king validated his own dynasty; mythological ornament also validated the use of military power as a heroic exploit. In an era when Mirrors for Princes still stressed the mellower Christian virtues of charity and humility, the trappings of pagan gods were helpful in portraying Francis and Henry as pious princes who, because they were also god-like, might legitimately excel at war.[43]

> What more shall I say? Such signal richness
> demonstrates and shows, to all people,
> The great power of the two parties.

More than beauty, wealth means power, and power, as we know, meant patronage. So the magnificence of Wolsey's wardrobe and his twelve chaplains, fifty gentlemen, 238 other servants and 150 horses reflected something besides the size of Wolsey's ego; it indicated to Francis' entourage that Wolsey was in favor with Henry and therefore a man to be reckoned with. Money also reflected the social hierarchy: the orders given in 1519 laid down 'that no man should wear prince's apparel, in order that the King's estate might be above all as to his pre-eminence... all nobles were to come apparelled as belonging to their degree...'[44] The gentlemen were to wear silk; the yeomen, cloth. What impressed Italian observers most about the Field of Cloth of Gold was the English noblemen's golden chains or collars; Sir Thomas More, on going to the Tower, refused to part with his.

> In brief, there is no heart that is not consoled in this land,
> more than the siren in the sea,
> To see reign (after the death of rancor)
> Love, Triumph and sovereign Beauty.

[43] Orgel remarks that it is no accident that the Jesuits, leaders of the church militant, were the mythographers of the seventeenth century ('The Royal Theatre,' p. 264).
[44] Russell, *Field*, p. 96.

The siren was a common literary and artistic device. In Conti's contemporary manual on mythology, the sirens are interpreted in a bad sense. 'Their half-animal form suggested the predominance of the irrational part of the soul. Their song is the allurement of sensual pleasure and also flattery, a great danger to princes.'[45] But sirens were also symbols of goodness; they could sing the praise of good and great men and incite those who heard them to follow and imitate such goodness. Sirens might also be daughters of a muse. In Neoplatonic terms, they might be seen guiding the celestial spheres which emitted music (harmony); this might, in turn, symbolize moral and political harmony under the king.

In Marot's poem, the king would no doubt have recognized the song of praise and peace offered by the deities of nature. If Francis thought about the common meaning of 'siren,' the creature living on cliffs who bewitches mariners, he would have remembered that the Argonauts got away by concentrating on the divine music of Orpheus, and perhaps be drawn back to contemplation of true poems (not flattery) like the ballad he is reading about himself. The death of rancor would remind him, perhaps, of the Hundred Years' War, and the attempts of England to maintain her lands on the continent, or just of general tension and the expectation of peace.

The *Envoy* refers to Helen, classical symbol of beauty and, as everyone knew, a classic cause of war. If she seemed, for a moment, inappropriate as a symbol in a poem about peace, Francis had only to remind himself that in Neoplatonic thought, immoral creatures might be shadows of divine truths. Moreover, Helen fits in with the preceding images because she is connected with the sea (a thousand ships, etc.). Sea creatures and water shows were a common feature of court festivals (one of Henry's costumes – and his horse's – at the Field of Cloth of Gold was decorated with 'waves' worked in gold; this was held to signify mastery of the seas),[46] and the theme of the sea runs through the second half of the ballad: Venus coming in on a wave and quenching the fire of Mars, the siren's song of loyalty and peace, and Helen. Also, Helen is part of the same myth: the golden apple was awarded to Venus, who then promised Paris the most beautiful wife in the world. Paris then sailed to Sparta and won Helen. (In 1518, Francis had won Françoise de Foix, the first of his great mistresses.)

This was Marot's praise of Francis. Both the Field of Cloth of Gold and the ballad reflected an historical moment of high pretensions and

[45] Yate, *French Academies*, p. 241.   [46] Russell, *Field*, p. 128.

considerable optimism – but it was only a moment. In both poem and pageant, Francis was presented, to himself and to others, as a virile athlete and a connoisseur of women: in 1520 the sexuality of French court society was pervasive and flamboyant enough to be noticed by contemporaries, while fifty years later it was not only noticed, but slandered as outrageous and perverted. In 1520 contemporaries also noticed and approved the fact that women were more influential in Francis' court than they had been in earlier reigns – the king's mother and sister in particular; a few decades later Catherine de Medici's influence over *her* court was attacked as unnatural, even monstrous.[47] In 1520 Francis was successfully portrayed as a philosopher-king, using art for self-enlightenment as well as self-advertisement, his body literally decorated with books; just one year later, in 1521, the father of letters banned all books not approved by the Sorbonne faculty of theology. Pageant and ballad also portrayed Francis as both a lover of peace and a military conqueror; the king *had* beaten the Swiss at Marignano in 1515, and he and Henry VIII really *did* admire each other in 1520, but Francis suffered defeat at Pavia just five years later, in 1525, and his hatred of Charles V would embroil him in destructive military campaigns for the rest of his reign. At the Field of Cloth of Gold Francis appeared as both pious and majestic, dwelling at the summit of an admiring and unified populace; the *affaire des placards* would shatter that illusion in 1534. Marot himself was summoned by the magistrates, his house ransacked, his books confiscated; with Marguerite's help, the poet fled the country in 1535.[48]

During the French civil wars, court fêtes replicated actual conflicts by casting nobles from different factions in allegorical battles, which were then resolved by a goddess (Catherine de Medici). The figure of the siren also acquired heavier political connotations: at one festival, the sirens overthrew the monster of war, represented by a whale, and in 1589, the Catholic League issued a satirical print called, 'Portrait of a Politique,' in which a double-tailed siren was featured; she symbolized flattery and two-faced behaviour.[49] In 1520, however, the conflicts in French court

---

[47] Knecht writes that Francis, observing that women were considered an essential adornment of court life in Renaissance Italy, along with literature and the arts, gave both women and art greater prominence at his own court (*Francis I*, p. 91).

[48] George Joseph, *Clément Marot*, p. 13.

[49] Yates, *Valois Tapestries*, p. 57, and *French Academies*, p. 261. Rachel Weil writes that the idea of reconciling opposites became a moral and aesthetic principle under Catherine; it was seen in the androgynous dress of courtiers, in the obsession with harmony and geometry, and in a treatise on monsters and hermaphrodites by the king's surgeon. 'What could not be realized in religious and political reality flourished in the arts and in the imagination of courtiers' (unpublished paper, Princeton University, 1984, pp. 11–12).

politics were still only implicit, as they were in Marot's ballad. In typical
Renaissance fashion, the poem raised up images which were confused,
even contradictory, but the overall effect was sure to leave a pleasant
taste.

III.

We now have, I hope, some notion of how Francis might have read
Marot's ballad; but what was Marot thinking when he wrote it? One
critic insists that Marot 'writes with his eye on his audience, he is more
concerned with what its members think than his own inmost feelings.'[50]
Was it really possible, given the constraints of both the literary genre and
the patronage system which supported him, for Marot to make a critical
statement of any sort? What modes of personal reflection were feasible
for an artist so closely identified with the court culture of his time?

Reading the *ballade* once again, we see that it is not really a conventional
allegorical poem at all.[51] Marot's concern is not to depict the conflict
between *Amour* and Discord and *Amour's* triumph at the Field of Cloth
of Gold; in fact, he abandons the allegorical drama after the second
stanza. Looking at the poem as a whole, the movement, through levels
of abstraction, is as follows: from men (*les roys*) to the level of greatest
abstraction (*Amour*, not Venus) which is sustained throughout the first
stanza. The second stanza begins again with *Amour*, but her arrival in
a clear wave and, especially, the reference to Mars, betokens Venus. So
we have, now, a mythological tale with Venus, Mars and the golden
apple – one step 'down' from abstract *Amour*. In stanza three, we are
nearer earth, with Caesars and half-human sirens. The Envoy is about
Helen, whose beauty is corporeal, like that of the two kings. Talking
about beauty in the first and last lines, we are thus led in a circle,
beginning and ending with physical beauty, with people. The overall
impression is not upwards – from human to divine ideas – but ultimately
downwards – from *Beaulté* to Helen.

Reading closely, I am not sure that Marot is talking about abstract
Amour and *Beaulté* even in the first stanza: *beaulx, riches, noble, digne,
richement, ordre, cohorte, pompe primeraine, de ce monde,* – one's impression, after all this, is not of abstract, purified love and beauty. Rather,
it is a totally visual impression, like looking at a tapestry. Triumph's
standard is 'painted' blue, Beauty's is 'tinted' red; but abstract Triumph
isn't painted blue, it *is* blue. I can't discard the impression that the first
stanza reads almost like a set of instructions, or an accompaniment for a

[50] McFarlane, *Literary History*, p. 113.
[51] C. S. Lewis, *The Allegory of Love. A Study in Medieval Tradition* (London, 1951), p.
251. Lewis speaks of a 'weakening' of allegory in Chauceriana, where the poet is
concerned with allegory as trapping, which is secondary to satire or rhetoric.

pageant, where the main event is a parade of three allegorical figures carrying painted banners, and where everything is very richly done. Moreover, the sense of *chascun* is ambiguous; do the kings richly comport themselves, or do the abstractions? In short, the author *seems* to pass from one universe of discourse to another, from a universe of earthly ornamental beauty to one of pure beauty which needs no ornament. Actually, the reader is suspended between them. The poet himself is two steps away from the event: the first step is from the kings to the abstractions or emblems; the second is from them to the poet, who sees them as painted set pieces, as people dressed up as allegorical figures. The poet seems to view the pageant as an undeniably aesthetic experience, but as an artificial experience; he suggests this in so delicate a fashion (using *painct*, *tainct*) that one almost misses it. Marot may have even intended an ironic reference to Petrarch's *Six Triumphes*, which both he and his father read in Robertet's French translation. Petrarch depicted love, as Cupid, in absolute triumph over kings and gods:[52]

> Cupid prostrates with his dart
> Jove, Neptune and Pluto crowned,
> Kings pursuing wild love and pleasure,
> Triumphing over them, notwithstanding their own power.
> Princes, rein in your pleasures,
> For immoderate sceptres
> Soon fall and are not at all stable.

Perhaps Marot had a similar notion in mind when he placed Triumph's banner between those of Love and Beauty.

The rhythm of this first stanza reinforces the sense of a pageant or processional, rather than a meditation about abstract concepts. The first seven lines are measured, smooth and almost unbroken. The *trois riches estendars* (the subjects of the stanza) must be emphasized in speaking the lines. The hard sound of *sorte* ends the processional of the three figures. The *ainsi chascun* – beginning a line with an adverb and a pronoun whose reference is obscure – is a letdown, because every other line until now has begun with an emphatic, bell-like sound – *Amour, Triumphe, Beaulté*. The high points of the next two lines are *richement* and *pompe primeraine*, (the *primeraine* is reminiscent of Rabelais' 'Tresillustres et treschevaleureux' – both are too much of a good thing).

In the second stanza the allegory is sustained, but the confusion gets worse. *Amour* (Venus) quenches the fire of Mars; harmony triumphs over discord. Love's quality, however, is very delicately sensual, (delicate,

[52] 'Les Six Triumphes de Petrarque,' Jean Robertet, *Oeuvres*, ed. Margaret Zsuppán (Geneva and Paris, 1970), p. 179. I owe this and several other points to Professor Rigolot.

because Venus isn't mentioned, and because *Amour* in the courtly tradition is usually a god, not a goddess. Marot has chosen to make Love, *celle Amour*).[53] Next, *Amour* (Venus) takes over the camp and watches the door to keep Discord out. At this point the allegory breaks down, and we see why Marot said *Amour* and not 'Venus'. According to the myth, the golden apple saying 'To the most beautiful,' was claimed and won by Venus. But it seems both ridiculous and futile for Venus to stand guard against herself. Since vanity is the cause of war, the sense of the poem has now altered, and we see that the pomp, opulence and artistic display which were supposed to reflect ultimate values may also be the greatest threat to peace. In fact, the *beaulx roys* are potentially like the three goddesses (if not, why does *Amour* need to set up a guard?); eventually, they will compete for highest honors because they are beautiful and proud, and therefore vain. It is difficult to see how Discord could fail to get in the door.[54]

In the third stanza, the irony between *Beaulté* and Venus (as vanity) comes very close to being explicit. As Francis might have read it, this stanza says, 'I am not worthy to relate the triumph which has taken place, so much more exalted than those of the warlike Caesars. After all I'm only human. You, however, are better than Caesar. Your richness shows how great you are. Nature herself, in the siren's song, echoes the praise of the poet.' But the lines might also read, 'It is not possible for me to continue this allegory because I have just implied that your beauty is likely to attract, not repel, discord. To compare you to Caesar is to insult you; you are supposed to exude pure Christian love, yet you are comforted by the siren's song, which is especially dangerous for kings, who are vulnerable to flattery. "Love" and "beauty" mean, simply, power. Your magnificent gesture is a show of force and all human beings know it.'

When Marot refuses to continue the poem (*Pas ne convient...*) he seems to be pulling back from the subject, telling the reader that he has nothing more to say. Actually, by putting himself into the poem (*ma plume...*) he is changing the mode of communication from that of allegory to that of introspection.[55] He not only breaks the mood of the

[53] I owe this and other points to Professor Morris.

[54] Marot may have been thinking of the popular poet Eustaches Deschamps, who wrote two ballads which argued against holding tournaments: Christian authority says that they lead to the sins of pride and envy while classical sources say that tournaments are used only as training for war. (Laura Kendrick, 'Rhetoric and the Rise of Public Poetry: The Career of Eustaches Deschamps,' *Studies in Philology*, LXXX (Winter, 1985), No. 1, p. 12.)

[55] Griffin remarks on Marot's interjection of himself into his later poems, 'The intricate relationship of the so-called real author with his various official versions of himself, and the picture the reader gets of his presence, are among the most important effects of his poetry' (*Marot*, p. 246).

processional, but introduces a new statement about the event which is more direct, and hence more forceful. At the command, *Pas...*, the figures and banners evaporate, as if they were made of paper. The poet then *tells* the reader (he doesn't suggest it) what *richesse* (not *Beaulté*) means *à tous humains* – to *all* people, not to the connoisseur who understands the symbolism of the tapestry, but to everyone: such conspicuous wealth (*richesse insigne*) denotes power. The emblematic quality of the poem is sustained by other words *démonstre, désigne*; these words have been implicit all along, they describe how the poem is built. *Célestine* denotes (demonstrates) virtue; *Amour* denotes harmony; the clear wave denotes Venus. But the language is now not implied, but stated. It is also more prose-like, more everyday: (*Que diray plus? Brief..., Pas ne convient*). It is reminiscent of Marot's first *rondeau*, where the poet talks in abstract terms about poetry at the beginning and then 'gets down to business' and tells us how a poem is put together.

In the *Envoy*, beauty no longer has a capital letter. It is about the physical beauty of men and women, and about Helen, who caused the Trojan war – by which Marot concludes that love, triumph and beauty exist on this earth. The *Envoy*, it seems to me, is very strongly and openly ironic. The word *laide* after so much *beaulté* (seven times) comes as a jolt. It is absurd to think that Marot intended Helen as a symbol of peace, or as an earthly symbol of pure beauty. On the contrary, Helen was the greatest siren of them all – she sank the most ships. Her name, therefore, recalls the *Séraine* of the preceding stanza, and effaces the 'good' sense in which the figure was sometimes meant. Perhaps Marot was also thinking of his own translation of the poetry of François Villon, published the year after the ballad. Villon depicted sirens, and Helen, as temptresses, their gorgeous bodies destined for decay:[56]

> Be it Paris or Helen who dies
> Whoever dies dies in such pain
> The wind is knocked out of him
> His gall breaks or his heart
> And he sweats God knows what sweat
> And no one can lighten his pain.
>
> Body of woman so tender
> So polished, so smooth, so dearly loved
> Must you too come to these agonies?
>
> That queen white as a lily
> Who sang in a siren's voice
>
> Where are the snows of last winter?

[56] François Villon, 'Le Testament,' in *The Poems of François Villon*, trans. Galway Kinnell (Boston, 1977), lines 313–52.

Considered in this way, Marot's allegory (meaning both the poem and the pageant itself) emerges as a purely aesthetic, not a moral experience. On Earth at least, beauty does not mean goodness.

If the Field of Cloth of Gold was 'about' anything, it was about beauty. I think that Marot wanted, first, to write a poem which would convey an aesthetic experience similar to the one conveyed by the event itself. To this end he used only visual images – colors, richness, pomp – which induce in the reader a vision of the pageant. He does not introduce any of the popular virtues which would have been appropriate, such as wisdom or prudence, but uses only those gods who personify beauty. For Marot, the pageant was an undeniably splendid experience, to which the poem pays the tribute of imitation.

With this aesthetic experience as a background, I think that Marot was less interested in commenting on the significance of the event (Was it an empty show? Is Francis susceptible to flattery? Does Helen's presence mean that Marot thinks there will be war?) than in writing about the different meanings which 'beauty' may have. As a metaphysical poet, he is exploring the notion that an aesthetic experience may be both spiritually elevating and psychologically destructive. On the one hand, beauty *is* somehow related to goodness; it inspires love and a sense of serenity, which are good things. But beautiful clothes also intimidate people and make them subservient; beautiful people incite desire, which makes them heartless; in the political arena, beauty is a sign of power. Marot does not make a statement about the meaning of beauty; his poem is suggestive, not didactic. *Beaulté* and Helen are both real.

We should remember that Marot had good reason to be concerned with this ambiguity, this problem of beauty. As a courtier, a consciously independent artist, and an evangelical Christian, Marot's own life was full of ambiguities. He always displayed both deference and arrogance toward the court, and affirmed his artistic and spiritual independence while tailoring his style to suit his patrons' tastes.[57] Not surprisingly, Marot was also fascinated by the idea of paradox; he actually began a popular fashion for a new type of blazon, an emblematic poem both praising and abusing its subject (e.g., Marot's 'The Beautiful Breast' and 'The Ugly Breast'). 'The blazon preserved the duality of its tone in its appreciation; in other words, it could render praise ironical and flatter that which was usually not to be flattered.'[58] So Marot knew and

[57] George Joseph, *Clément Marot*, Preface, n.p and p. 139.
[58] Mikhail Bakhtin, *Rabelais and his World*, tr. Helene Iswolsky (Cambridge, Mass. & London, 1968), p. 427. Bakhtin saw these blazons as indicative of Marot's and Rabelais' alienation from court culture. 'Rabelais' images have a certain undestroyable

probably relished the difference between art as a siren's song (whether of flattery or loyalty is irrelevant) and art as the music of Orpheus. His ballad is both things; in this stately, adulatory poem, the opposing qualities of pure love and self-love are virtually conflated in the cryptic symbolism of the siren, and of Helen.

Of course Marot may have simply believed that Helen and this ugly earth are shadows of *Beaulté*. This may be a poem about Neoplatonic beauty; Marot was surely conversant with Neoplatonic ideas through his association with Marguerite. But Marot would have been more a man of his time if, as I believe, he was more fascinated by the ambiguity of the aesthetic experience than by the possibility of resolving it; why else did he end his poem so enigmatically – 'Here is Helen, therefore there is on earth...' (If he were being a Neoplatonist, why didn't he say, '...therefore there is in heaven...')? Think of the different guises in which we see beauty. There is *Beaulté* (harmony), *beaulx roys* (physical beauty), Venus (love overruling discord; vanity), *richesse* (power), *séraine* (flattery, loyalty), Helen (destructive beauty). Marot would have written a better allegory if he had pitted these different aspects of the personality against each other. Had he done so, he would not have been doing his job – writing a ballad to celebrate his patron's glory. More important, his poem would have been about conflict, whereas this poem does two things: it implies that a conflict of values exists, but it sustains the sense of visual beauty which the Field of Cloth of Gold conveyed in real life. Marot's choice was to suggest the conflict in a manner so delicate that we may enjoy the beauty of the poem without resolving the problem.[59] In this way, the subtlety and creative tension of a youthful ballad, written in the service of the state, foreshadowed the more pronounced irony and introspection of Marot's later work, written in the service of an evangelical Christianity.

nonofficial nature...[they] marked the suspension of all hierarchical rank, privileges, norms, and prohibitions...' (p. 3). Bakhtin doesn't mention that Rabelais himself was part of the patronage system; Francis I had *The Inestimable Life of the Great Gargantua* read aloud to him, and presumably he enjoyed it, because he gave Rabelais a sinecure, making him a Master of Requests.

[59] Griffin's interpretation is slightly different from mine: 'Marot maintains the individual characteristics of classical and biblical sources while refusing to see the value systems they represent as mutual contraventions' (p. 177).

The unlikely Machiavellian: William of Orange and the princely virtues

GUY WELLS

> And yet these schollers of Machiavell, would here bleare our eyes, with these
> goodlie shewes of loyaltie, fidelitie, naturall clemencie, and such golden
> and glorious words, and yet notwithstanding they make no difficultie, to
> play with the othes which they take, & and with the wordes that they
> give...[1]

Having already compared the King of Spain and his advisers to an
impressive array of villains both biblical and classical, the author of
Orange's *Apology* probably did not expect this denunciation to hold
much shock value for his readers. Once invoked, the Italian is not
mentioned again, and the reference to him is easy to miss. But its mere
presence has tantalized later readers for the possibilities it suggests. How
much did the prince of Orange know of Machiavelli's creation? What did
it mean to him? How might it have influenced his own political
assumptions and techniques? Alas, four centuries later we cannot even
be sure that Orange knew any more about *The Prince* than the reference
above. Although released in William's name and with his approval, the
Apology was the work of other hands. For the rest, William the Silent
is true to his sobriquet regarding his views, if he had any, on the ideas
of the Florentine republican.

Still, the relationship between the prince and *The Prince* has long
fascinated and bedeviled historians of the Netherlands revolt. Even for
writers to whom William had all the makings of an heroic type, the
nagging undercurrent of Machiavellianism could not be ignored. The

Parts of this essay were read in a discussion of Orange at the Sixteenth Century Studies
Conference in St Louis in November, 1984. I am grateful to the participants in the session
for their comments and discussion. Thanks also to Professor Koenrad Swart for his initial
encouragement to me to pursue this idea; and to Telluride Association, R. C. Martens,
J. M. Snodgrass, Scott Swanson, and John Najemy for their assistance and advice in the
course of its preparation.

[1] *The Apologie of Prince William of Orange Against the Proclamation of the King of Spain,*
   H. Wansink, ed. (Leiden, 1969), p. 68.

Apology itself affirms by indirection that Orange's good faith was far from univerally accepted even in his own time. Whenever his agents promised undisturbed practice of religion or exercise of public office to the Catholics in a newly conquered area, it seemed like a promise made to be broken; Orange's treatment of the many accusations of double-dealing that arose from such situations is weak.[2] More important, Orange claimed that during the negotiations for Cateau-Cambrésis, he became aware of a secret agreement between Henry II and Philip II to set aside their differences in order to concentrate on wiping out the Protestants and introducing the Inquisition in their respective realms. At that time, he says, he inwardly resolved to thwart their designs, while temporarily dissimulating his agreement until the opportunity for open opposition arose.[3] Were it true, this claim would impart a chilling constancy of purpose and thoroughness of deception to all of the prince's activities in the years before the revolt broke out. Schiller accepted Orange's story at its face value, and the resulting sketch of his character borders on the sinister:

The calm tranquillity of a never varying countenance concealed a busy, ardent soul, which never ruffled even the veil behind which it worked, and was alike inaccessible to artifice and to love; a versatile, formidable, indefatigable mind, soft and ductile enough to be instantaneously molded into all forms; guarded enough to lose itself in none; and strong enough to endure every vicissitude of fortune... Not by making Machiavelli's *Prince* his study, but by having enjoyed the living instruction of a monarch, who reduced the book to practice, had he become versed in the perilous arts by which thrones rise and fall.[4]

Less stereotyped is the treatment the prince received at the hands of Prescott and Motley. For both historians, Orange was one of the great men of his age, albeit one with some Machiavellian blemishes. Prescott does not shrink from repeating the folklore that Orange read Machiavelli more often than any other author, but forgives his deviousness because of his precocious espousal of religious toleration.[5] Motley's conception is more nuanced, and his synthesis of the conflicting aspects of Orange's character has been heavily influential on later biographers. For Motley, the young Orange is indeed a morally shallow dabbler in the evils of Machiavellianism. But Orange's purposes came to sanctify his tactics as

[2] *Ibid.*, pp. 109–10, 118–19. On this, see Koenigsberger, 'The Organisation of Revolutionary Parties in France and the Netherlands', in *Estates and Revolutions: Essays in Early Modern European History* (Ithaca, 1971), p. 237.

[3] *Apologie*, pp. 61–2.

[4] F. Schiller, *History of the Revolt of the Netherlands*, tr. A. J. W. Morrison (New York, 1847), pp. 68, 70.

[5] William Prescott, *History of the Reign of Philip the Second, King of Spain* (Boston, 1855), I, pp. 486–91.

he used 'the subtleties of Italian statesmanship' and 'the Machiavellian school' to frustrate Philip's 'knavish purposes'. The purity of Orange's patriotism and his lack of selfish ambition shed a halo of righteousness over the shadiest of his tactics. It was only in the crucible of the revolt that his character developed the complex of political subtlety and moral grandeur which befitted the nineteenth-century ideal of a proper *Pater Patriae*.[6]

Most subsequent writers on Orange have used some form of Motley's synthesis in dealing with a figure who was continually subtle in his politics and whose 'true' feelings on basic issues are often elusive. For Felix Rachfahl, Orange's gradual adoption of his world-historical role as the bearer of the *ständische Tendenz* either blots out or explains the anomalies and vagaries of his activities. A generation ago, C. V. Wedgwood's portrait of Orange presented us with the fully developed figure of *Vader Willem*, the canny but benevolent father figure whose charisma inspired his rebellious countrymen to unexpected heroism, and whose personal greatness of soul and selfless devotion to the Netherlands' cause made the earlier allegations of Machiavellianism seem overly cynical, if not downright sacrilegious. Robert van Roosbroeck's more recent biographies continue in the same vein.[7]

Nevertheless, unfashionable though it may seem, I think it is time to raise the issue of Orange's Machiavellianism once again. I do not mean by this to investigate the extent of any alleged influence the Italian may have had on Orange, for the hard evidence we have is too thin and too circumstantial to go much further than Schiller's allusion. Looking at how Orange's career and practices fit into the models and theories which Machiavelli advanced, however, can give us some helpful insights into how the prince thought, what unspoken habits of mind lay behind his actions, and how his career both fit into and emerged from the fabric of early modern politics.

The Machiavelli to whom we return, however, is not the stereotype invoked in the *Apology* or by the biographers of previous centuries. A generation of intense scholarship has produced a range of interpretations of the Florentine's ideas, which have injected entirely new content into

---

[6] John L. Motley, *The Rise of the Dutch Republic* (New York, 1883), II, pp. 241–4; III, pp. 622–4.

[7] Felix Rachfahl, *Wilhelm von Oranien und der Niederländischen Aufstand*, 2 vols. (Halle and the Hague, 1906–24); C. V. Wedgwood, *William the Silent: William of Nassau, Prince of Orange, 1533–1584* (New York, 1968); Robert van Roosbroeck, *Willem de Zwijger, Graaf van Nassau, Prins van Oranje: Een Kroniek en Een Epiloog* (Antwerp, 1974), and *Willem van Oranje* (The Hague, 1976). For other comments on Orange's biographers, see K. W. Swart, *William the Silent and the Revolt of the Netherlands* (London, 1978), p. 40.

the old word 'Machiavellian'. While it is impossible within the scope of this essay even to summarize all the recent developments in Machiavelli studies, our discussion of Orange requires a look at what have emerged as two key concepts in the modern discussion of *The Prince*; *Virtù*, and Fortune.[8]

The intellectual and political worlds which Machiavelli inhabited, and his own experience in them, gave him a keen sense of the fragility of human institutions before the flow of events, and the limitations on man's power to control that flow. Fortune – constantly and unpredictably changing – either governs or is involved with all human actions: she is '...the ruler of half our actions, but...she allows the other half...to be governed by us.'[9] But it is not easy to lay claim even to that half which Fortune allows to be subject to human endeavour. Fortune must be constantly overcome, guarded against; time and again, the fall of princes and republics is ascribed to the failure to observe and adapt to her alterations.

The way to master and control Fortune, for Machiavelli, is through the exercise of *Virtù*. But that word, in *The Prince*, has a whole new configuration of meanings. Gone are virtue and the virtues in their normal significations. *Virtù* is simply what makes a prince able to withstand and manipulate Fortune. Like the latter, its specific content is ever-changing. Its general character is flexibility of mind and the ability to adapt to continually differing necessities. Above all else, the prince's mind must be 'disposed to adapt itself according to the wind, and as the variations of fortune dictate...'[10] The interplay of Fortune and this newly conceived *Virtù* (or its absence) underlies virtually all the discussions in *The Prince*.

Turning to the realm of historical princes, we can find few political careers which have been as subject to dramatic turns of fortune as that of William the Silent. Some of the most decisive events of his life can

[8] The following discussion is based principally on Felix Gilbert, *Machiavelli and Guicciardini: Politics and History in Sixteenth-Century Florence* (Princeton, 1965); J. H. Hexter, 'The Loom of Language and the Fabric of Imperatives: The Case of *Il Principe* and *Utopia*', in *The Vision of Politics on the Eve of the Reformation* (London, 1973), pp. 179–203; Neal Wood, 'Machiavelli's Concept of *Virtù* Reconsidered', *Political Studies*, xv (1967), pp. 159–72; I. Hannaford, 'Machiavelli's Concept of *Virtù* in *The Prince* and *The Discourses* Reconsidered', *Political Studies*, xx, pp. 185–9; Thomas Flanagan, 'The Concept of *Fortuna* in Machiavelli', in Anthony Parel, ed., *The Political Calculus: Essays on Machiavelli's Philosophy* (Toronto, 1972), pp. 127–256; and Quentin Skinner, *Machiavelli* (New York, 1981). Another highly suggestive interpretation of these themes is that of Hannah Pitkin, *Fortune is a Woman: Gender and Politics in the Thought of Niccolo Machiavelli*, (Berkeley, 1984).

[9] Machiavelli, *The Prince*, tr. Luigi Ricci, in Max Lerner, ed., *The Prince and the Discourses* (New York 1950), p. 91.

[10] Ibid., p. 65.

easily be relegated to that half of events which Machiavelli's Fortune does not allow men to govern: he had no control over the accident of his birth into a relatively obscure German noble family, or his falling heir as a child to one of the great aristocratic fortunes of Europe, including the principality from which he subsequently took his name. (That his Lutheran parents were willing to see him raised as a Catholic in the court of Charles V in order to receive this bounty might itself be deemed a triumph of *Virtù* over religious principle, but it is an instance for which the young prince cannot himself be given credit.) Similarly, at the end of his life, Orange was the victim of two assassination attempts. The first, by chance, barely failed. The second, in a final unkind stroke of ill fortune, brought his life to its end. Between his inheritance and his death, however, Orange's career derived much of its unique quality from his constant efforts to position himself favourably in relation to possible chance events, and to reshape his most basic aims in response to adverse circumstance. In the space which remains, I will discuss how this characteristic can be seen at work in Orange's behaviour during the Year of Wonders, 1566–7, and how it shaped his later career.

The political upheavals of 1566 were the culmination of nearly a decade of growing tension in the Netherlands.[11] During that time, the problem the central government saw facing it was the spread of heresy, especially Calvinism. By 1562, France had already slid into what would be a long period of civil war and turmoil, and all parties in the Netherlands were acutely aware that they were subject to the same dangers. On the ruler's side, the religious unrest occasioned several controversial actions, above all the twin attempts thoroughly to reorganise the Netherlands church, and to introduce more effective mechanisms for enforcing orthodoxy. But the ecclesiastical reforms touched on a large number of deeply entrenched aristocratic interests, while the other measures looked suspiciously like an attempt to introduce the much-dreaded Spanish Inquisition, with all the violations of local autonomies and legal privileges which that might entail.

It was in the storm of protest which these measures entailed that Orange, now in his late twenties, began to spread his political wings. It was clear from the beginning that he did not envision himself in any but a primary role in whatever drama might unfold. His marriage projects, first with Christina of Lorraine and later with Anna of Saxony,

---

[11] The most recent general survey of Netherlands politics in the 1560s in English is Geoffrey Parker, *The Dutch Revolt* (Ithaca, 1977), which summarises a huge mass of secondary literature. For positions taken here which are at variance with Parker's, I have detailed documentation in a still-unpublished doctoral dissertation, *Antwerp and the Government of Philip II, 1555–1567* (Cornell University, 1982), *passim*.

signalled not only his claim to standing among the greatest aristocratic families of Europe, but also his independent, if not frankly adversarial, stance in relation to Philip II. As the Guise and Montmorency had done earlier in France, Orange worked steadily and assiduously through the 1560s to build up a body of followers in the Netherlands who would look to him for patronage and protection, and whose collaboration would be a prerequisite for the effective exercise of political power by any ruler.[12] Whatever the specific content of his causes and intrigues might be, the prince, a sovereign in the service of Philip II, had set out to play politics on a grand scale, to build up a store of *réputation* which would make him a central figure in the government of the Netherlands.

The immediate crisis in 1566 was precipitated by Philip II's decision to denounce the modifications which the aristocratic party thought they had induced him to make in his policies. The famous Segovia letters of October, 1565, embodied a hard line on virtually every issue with which the Netherlanders were involved and – completely aside from the wisdom of Philip's approach to the problem of heterodoxy – embodied a direct challenge to the political credibility of Orange and the other *Grands Seigneurs*.[13] They reacted by putting the squeeze on Philip's regent in Brussels, Margaret of Parma. On one side, they encouraged a league of lesser nobles and gentry, which, in collaboration with much more openly Protestant elements, was preparing to demand a change in religious policy. The threat of armed resistance was implicit if the group, later named the Beggars, failed to achieve satisfaction. On the other side, just as the unrest they countenanced put Margaret in desperate need of their collaboration, they threatened to withdraw from participation in the government unless the hard line was abandoned. This was not just Orange's doing; he was the essential and most illustrious member of a united aristocratic front. The regent had little choice. Through the summer of 1566, Philip's orders remained a dead letter while she attempted to find a solution which would satisfy both king and nobles.

The force of Orange's position in the political confrontation was his apparent ability to mediate between what were actually irreconcilable groups. Through his openly Protestant brother, Louis, who kept his own rooms in Orange's palace in Brussels, he stayed in close touch with the Beggars and managed to maintain the image of their great hope among

[12] On this, see H. G. Koenigsberger, 'Orange, Granvelle, and Philip II' in *Bijdragen en Mededeelingnen tot het Geschiedenis der Nederlanden*, n. 99 (1984), esp. pp. 578–9.
[13] The Segovia letters, dated 17 October 1565, are printed in J. S. Thiessen, ed., *Correspondance française de Marguerite d'Autriche* (Utrecht, 1925), I, pp. 98–105; on their formulation, see P. D. Lagomarsino, 'Court Factions and the Formulation of Spanish Policy towards the Netherlands' (unpublished diss., Cambridge University, 1973), pp. 164–206.

the upper aristocracy. At the same time, he was trusted by most Catholics to protect their interests and remained an indispensable member of the central government councils, however much Philip and Margaret might distrust him. It was an extremely unstable position, though, and it began to crumble as it became apparent, by the early summer of 1566, that the more popular elements of the dissident movement were out of control.

The threat of social chaos drove most of the magnates back into the regent's firm allegiance by the end of the summer. The outbreak of the Iconoclasm in August only hastened a movement which had begun a month or so earlier. Orange, however, moved to take an independent stance from which he could continue to pose as the essential mediator with the dissident elements. In early July, he maneuvered Margaret and the city council of Antwerp into accepting him as her special representative in that city, probably averting attempted *coups* by both Beggars and alarmed Catholics in so doing.[14] This situation had the advantage of distancing him from affairs in Brussels, putting him in control of the county's largest and richest city, and keeping him in close touch with the Calvinists there. In short, he was positioned so that he would be the most likely agent of reconciliation if the conflict could still be brought to reconciliation, if it could not, and open civil war erupted, he would still occupy a key strategic position, from which he could maneuver in whatever situation might develop.

Orange failed in his attempt to be the central figure in the resolution of the crisis of 1566. His prestige on all sides had rested on potentialities – the twin possibilities that he could rein in the dissidents for the regent, or that he could secure government concessions for the dissidents. With the iconoclasm, both sides began to insist on actualities, which the prince was unable to deliver. This meant a final loss of confidence in him at court, both in Spain and Brussels, and enormous pressure to adopt some kind of rebellious stance or face complete political isolation.

In mid-1567 and after, this is in fact what Orange did do, and many of his biographers have held that he followed a consistent course in this direction after late 1566. Rachfahl dates the decision to leave the Low Countries and make war on the Spanish system from a meeting with Egmont and Horn in October. By then, Philip's decision to send an army to the Netherlands was becoming known, and it was clear that Orange was one of many marked men as a result of his apparent collaboration with the rebels.[15] Nevertheless, it is hard to argue that Orange's actions

---

[14] On the origins of Orange's mission to Antwerp, see my *Antwerp and the Government of Philip II*, pp. 414–38.
[15] Rachfahl, *Wilhelm von Oranien*, II, pp. 794–7.

after the iconoclasm point in any clear direction. Certainly he did not embrace Brederode's rebellion on its own terms, at least until after he was in exile. As late as mid-March, some things he did gave the impression that he 'sided openly with the government,'[16] especially when he kept the Antwerp Calvinists from rushing to the aid of their co-religionists at Oosterweel. At the same time, many of his actions were far from those of an obedient servant. Immediately after the battle of Oosterweel, he negotiated a new, more liberal agreement with the Protestant groups in Antwerp, one which outraged the Regent. During his tour of Holland between October 1566 and the following February, he enforced his own interpretation of Margaret's accord with the Beggars, including the toleration of preaching in cities where none had taken place earlier. The fact that he sold much of his plate and otherwise raised great sums of money before he left for Germany can also support the idea that he was planning rebellion during the winter.[17]

Nevertheless, I suspect that Orange did not commit himself to exile and rebellion until at least the end of March. To be sure, he hedged his bets heavily toward the direction he finally took. But his main policy through the winter was a holding action, to preserve as much of his position as he could and be able to maneuver to best advantage if events took any sort of encouraging turn. Enforcing his liberal version of Margaret's accord in Holland and Zeeland made him few new enemies and earned him the extravagant gratitude and praise of the Estates of Holland.[18] Any number of highly plausible events could have altered completely the course in which Netherlands politics were running. Coligny and Condé might have decided to come to the aid of the beleaguered Calvinists at Tournai and Valenciennes, and transformed their rebellion into an international religious war. The incessant maneuvering of factions at Philip's court might have turned against Alva's hard line and undermined his mission to the Netherlands. More drastic still, Philip II might always have died (as three other strongly Catholic monarchs, Mary of England, Henry II and Francis II of France, had done at crucial moments within the previous decade), and his entire policy could have been thrown into question in the infighting that would have surrounded his unstable son Carlos. In any of these eventualities – as in numerous, less drastic scenarios – Orange's political position could have turned round overnight. Waiting for such a revolution of Fortune's

[16] Parker, *The Dutch Revolt*, p. 97. But Parker also notes the vacillating, inconsistent nature of Orange's behaviour in 1566–8 on p. 290, n. 17.
[17] Wedgwood, *William the Silent*, pp. 93, 95.
[18] *Ibid.*, pp. 91–2; Rachfahl, *Wilhelm von Oranien*, II, p. 816.

wheel, the prince held on as long as he could, only abandoning the Netherlands at the last possible moment.

It might not be immediately clear how such a story of failure would fit into the Machiavellian ideal of princely practice. After all, the ultimate test of *Virtù* is success: if *Virtù* is by definition what is necessary to master Fortune, failure to do so should automatically indicate its absence. But sometimes success against Fortune is a matter of simple survival, of preserving one's essential forces in order to fight another day. In that, Orange succeeded where the other great aristocratic dissidents failed. Egmont and Hoorn died on the scaffold in 1568, while Orange kept both his independence and his head. Indeed, the very failure of Fortune to turn in his favour in the months leading up to his exile reveals the care with which he chose his positions to take advantage of its potential vagaries. His constant equivocation on issues ranging from the king's new loyalty oaths to his true confessional allegiance can appear in retrospect as inconsistency and vacillation. But seen from *in media res*, I think they represent calculated decisions *not* to burn bridges, *not* to close off options, *not* to relinquish potentialities. Right up until he began his exile – indeed still for a time after that – Orange was in a position to retake the initiative if the circumstance changed. And even if his worst-case option were to become a reality – which it did – he had set things up so that he could still keep his ability to maneuver and play in the great game.

The manner in which Orange handled his failure is where he had a chance to show the extent of his *virtù*. In the late 1560s, it looked as though he had hit bottom. Five years later, he had re-emerged as a central figure in the Netherlands, whose actions would transform the country's history even into our own age. Even his later success was salvaged out of the ruins of his original strategy. In 1572, he planned an invasion of the southern Netherlands from both Germany and France, with only minor diversions in the north. Another revolution of Fortune – in this case, the St Bartholomew's Day massacre in France, which wiped out Coligny and his Huguenot allies – turned the prince's grand designs into ashes. The success at Brill, the success which finally took hold and from which the rest of the Netherlands revolt grew and flourished, was equally fortuitous. Orange's ability first to survive the failure and then to recognise and capitalise on the success, I would argue, are both later developments of the same strain of *Virtù* we see operating in 1566–7. Throughout Orange's career, a latter-day Machiavelli could find a steady succession of instances in which the prince managed to make the most of unexpected good fortune (for example, the death of Requesens, the Spanish bankruptcy, Don Juan's inability to master his own fortunes) or to salvage what he could from unfavourable turns of events (defeats like Gembloux, Alençon's treachery, Jaguéray's attempt on his life). Throughout the prince's life, in short, the Florentine would find a welter of instances he could use to illustrate the central interplay of Fortune and *virtù* in *The Prince*. William of Orange had not only mastered all the individual tricks of the princely trade, but also firmly grasped its underlying sense and logic.

Finally, looking at Orange in this new, Machiavellian light, we can get a glimpse of how, in actual practice, the author of *The Prince* might have integrated that treatise with the theoretical world of the *Discourses*. Certainly the Dutch republic which emerged from Orange's lifetime of endeavour was no paragon of an ideally mixed state such as Machiavelli discusses. Moreover, much of the prince's appeal to the burghers of Holland lay precisely in the fact that he did *not* set out to be a lawgiver, but rather a preserver of the old privileges. William did not just set up a perfect state and then retire into obscurity like some Hellenic patriarch. When he met his death, it was by no means clear if, or how, or in what form the new state would survive. But he was a founding father nonetheless, and in many ways an ideal one. Machiavelli's *Discourses* on ideal states are fraught with dilemmas of reality: how to produce a lawgiver powerful enough to found a good state, yet virtuous enough to retreat from power and prominence once his work is done; how to arrange a state in which people have liberty, and yet preserve enough discipline to defend themselves; how to achieve a balance in which strong leadership can emerge when it is necessary, but which does not degenerate into tyranny and despotism. A daunting, if not impossible task, even for a man of the greatest virtue and *Virtù*. And yet, through the revolutions of his fortunes and the flow of necessity, William turns out to have done all of that. Our latter-day Machiavelli looking back would see Orange as a near-ideal study in *virtù* mastering *fortuna* to bring forth the *felix respublica* of which his own land and age had despaired.

The Estates of Brabant to the end of the fifteenth century: the make-up of the assembly

EMILE LOUSSE

Since their inception, under the reign of the Duchess Jeanne (1356–1406, the last of the House of Louvain) and the 'Joyous Entrance' of Philip the Fair (1494–1506, the elder son of the Emperor Maximilian and father of Charles V), the Assemblies of the Estates of the Country and Duchy of Brabant (*die Staeten van Brabant*), which were modeled after the French, exercized their mandate through the princes, first of a junior branch, then later the elder branch of the House of Burgundy–Valois, e.g., Antoine of Burgundy (1406–15), Jean IV (1415–27), Philippe de Saint-Pol (1427–30), Philip the Good (1430–67), Charles the Bold (1427–77), Marie of Burgundy (1477–82) and Maximilian of Austria (first as husband of Marie, then as tutor and Regent until the majority of Philip the Fair). The protocols, derived from the practices of the preceding century and a half, were observed without major alteration up until the demise of the *Ancien Régime*.

From beginning to end, the Assemblies of Brabant were made up of representative from three groups: the Prelates (*die prelaeten*), the Barons and the Knights (*die baenrodsen ende ridderen*), and the cities and the townships (*die steden ende vriheden*). They were frequently convened by summons of the Prince – such was the practice – or else gave advice under their own initiative in exceptional circumstances. However, few who were summoned responded to the call; there were many more members called than representatives deputized to appear. The Assemblies were constitutionally required to be held in the territory of Brabant, along an accessible route in one or another city, freely chosen for convenience and interest.

The Prince would convene the Estates; such was the general rule in Brabant. However, as always, there were exceptions. Under extraordinary circumstances, even the tax commissioners were given sufficient powers to convene the representatives to the Assemblies, so as to be heard. In other cases – not imaginary – if the Duke could not or would

95

not convene an Assembly without undue delay – perhaps, to delay sur-
render of the receipts for the tax collectors – the cities would take it upon
themselves to call the Assembly, be it of representatives of the first two
orders or only of the Barons and Knights.

In the case of a dynastic crisis, the Estates would assemble, be it at
the initiative of a Prince or under their own authority. If the heir
presumptive was under age, they could either institute a Regency or give
him full authority right away. If he was not found to have the right of
direct lineage, they would take into consideration other titles, finding
perhaps that he was the head of some defunct collateral line. If the ruling
prince displeased them, or became an uncontrollable tyrant, they quickly
forced him to moderate his ways – or replaced him. In 1420, they thus
declared the removal of Jean IV in favor of Count Philippe de Saint-Pol,
a younger brother, whom they proclaimed *ruwaert* of the Duchy. In
1427, and 1430, they instituted one coup after another – and there were
two new Dukes: Philippe de Saint-Pol to succeed Jean IV, and then
Philip the Good (the elder of the superior branch of Burgundy), to
replace Philippe de Saint-Pol, who died young. Their regular inter-
ventions at particularly decisive moments – from the earliest occasion by
Antoine at the end of the fourteenth century, until the accession of
Charles V in 1515 – had considerable influence on the tradition of
succession and the good reputation of the House of Burgundy–Habsburg
in Brabant. Perhaps the Joyous Entrance did not become a recognizable
charter, for it would have had to have been renewed many times
afterward with the assent of the Assemblies or under pressure from them
in order to extricate the Estates of Brabant from the five or six dynastic
crises which occurred subsequently.

The meetings of the Assemblies were neither long-winded nor
solemn, for the object of contemplated deliberation was often formulated
in rather vague terms, and occasionally only fleetingly addressed. We are
lucky, however, for the dates and places were described scrupulously,
as this was indispensable. In 1427, it was decreed that the cities would
be notified at least fifteen days in advance, so as not to give anyone an
advantage; otherwise, the meetings had only to be convened in a safe
and convenient place, within the borders of Brabant, so that the
representatives could make their way there and attend to business
without being molested or made uneasy. Brussels, Antwerp, Bois-
le-Duc, Vilvorde and Lierre were often chosen; Louvain was chosen for
the whole of the Joyous Entrance – and also at other times, it goes,
without saying. Nowhere was exclusively reserved; Des Marez, however,
thought that 'the Chamber and Hall of the City of Brussels', 'oft-cited

in the texts, could some day have become the Palace of that Chancellor of Brabant. But only a little later? How long would it be?

The Assemblies of the Estates remained obligatorily within the frontiers, but certain summonses were addressed to outside: to Saint-Trond, to the Comte de Nassau, Master of Breda; to the abbeys and monasteries of Bonne-Espérance, Floreffe, Lobbes, Cambron. And indeed, why? It would have been ridiculous and detrimental to omit the great fortunes – among the most considerable in all Brabant – simply because the Master of that fortune had his principal residence abroad. It was imperative to wait, to insist that he attend the meetings, so that he would not decline to contribute to the regularly endorsed supports, assizes and collections, pro-rated for each intended province. Was it not essential to be satisfied with less, rather than to lose all?

The towns and personages, ecclesiastical and secular, which were placed within the six 'corporations' of the country of Brabant, followed the custom of convoking assemblies from the Three Estates of the same country. The following is a list from which it is possible to derive and discuss figures and other valuable information about the composition of the Assemblies of the Estates of Brabant in the fifteenth century. Indeed, in this list we find Saint-Trond, Nassau-Breda, Bonne-Espérance and others given below.

Reflected in the following chart, 174 summonses to the Assembly were addressed as follows:

	To					
	Prelates of communities of		Barons and		Town-	
From	Men	Women	Knights	Cities	ships	Total
Town Hall of Louvain	6	2	9	5	1	23
Ammanie of Brussels	3	4	20	2	6	35
Marquisate of Antwerp	2	2	14	6	2	26
Town Hall of Bois-le-Duc	4	3	11	3	7	28
Town Hall of Tirlemont	4	1	13	3	1	22
Bailiff of the 'Roman Pays'	12	4	14	4	6	40
Total		47	81		46	174

Barring mistakes, this is complete. A total of 174 summonses were sent: 47 to Prelates, 81 to Barons and Knights, 46 to cities and small townships. There were 81 noblemen versus 93 from all the other orders.

One can note, besides, that the cities and townships divide up about 50–50, with the Marquisate of Antwerp having 6 cities and the Town Hall of Bois-le-Duc with 7 townships. There were 16 Prelates in the 'Roman Pays' – otherwise known as Brabant Walloon – 20 Barons and Knights within the Ammanie of Brussels. *Quid hoc sibi vult?* A map would be useful; it would retain the language and surely give a clearer picture.

For those who prefer sorting by corporations rather than by orders, in descending quantity it was necessary to send:

40 summonses to Brabant Walloon
28 to the Great Town Hall of Bois-le-Duc
26 to the Marquisate of Antwerp
23, only, to the Town Hall of Louvain
22 to the Town Hall of Tirlemont.

The relatively small Town Hall of Tirlemont received 22 summonses: that is, less than the Marquisate of Antwerp (26) and the Great Town Hall of Louvain (23), and the Ammanie of Brussels (35), and Antwerp (26) with Bois-le-Duc (28); the equilibrium logically maintains at 58 to 54. But it is shattered entirely when one compares the four southern 'corporations' (Brabant Walloon, Brussels, Louvain, Tirlemont) with their 120 summonses to the 54 summonses to the North (Antwerp, Bois-le-Duc) – much more vast, to be sure, but less fertile – a population less dense and poorer.

The list does not reflect the summonses sent to the Duchy of Limbourg nor the other countries of Outre-Meuse, which found themselves in a unique alliance with Brabant, holding special Assemblies.

The frontier cities of Maastricht and Saint-Trond had mixed loyalties: half to Liège and half to Brabant. The former, for example, had two special magistrates seated face to face, in the same Town Hall (Andorre-sur-Meuse?). Saint-Trond is given in the list of recipients of summonses, Maastricht is not, even though it is known (by other means) that the deputies of Maastricht were an effective presence at various Assemblies at the beginning of the fifteenth century.

In the list of summonses (and this was typical of other documents dating from the fifteenth century) there was no question – as in other countries – as to the usage of the *Ordo ecclesiasticus*, but solely the Prelates (*die Prelaeten*) designated and deputized the representatives of the Church (*die geestelicken, die geestelicke persoenen*). Fifteenth-century Brabant had no bishops other than those of Liège and Cambrai, who were also princes; consequently they were formidable neighbors politically. The secular clergy, even the canons of the diocesan chapters, fell under the same aegis, seemingly for the same reasons. On the other hand, the rural pastors were so poor, reduced to such a meager allowance, and therefore dependent on their masters and lords, that they were kept well in line no matter which village they hailed from; it was no longer a question of Dominicans, Franciscans or Carthusians – for all were renowned beggars. In the first of the three Estates of Brabant, one includes in the generic term 'Prelate' nothing other than the Superiors – male and female – of the religious communities: the convents (*cloosters*) of the Benedictines, Cistercians (female), Norbertins (male) and the ordinary Canons of Saint Augustine. All told, the ratio of men to women in these communities was 2:3. From the ecclesiastical point of view, Brabant was, *par excellence*, a land of Prelates; this remains today little more than a memory: footprints, outlines, echoes.

If it was the city and not the head of the convent (*clooster*) of Nivelles that was summoned, it was because the religious community ('mother of the city') was a *reichsinmittelbares Stift*, of venerable Carolingian origins (seventh century). On the other hand, we see that at Gembloux, the summonses were not addressed to the city, but to the Abbot of the Benedictine monastery, from which the bourgeois community had grown: it was the elders of the Prelates of Brabant who later adorned themselves with the title Count-Abbot. Crowned and mitered, they walked with the first rank, in the Order of the Barons and Knights, rather than in those of the Prelates. In this group without symmetry, all found their place, as if naturally, by successive shudders, and so the Assemblies of the Estates of Brabant also kept in step with the spirit of the times.

Many were called, few were chosen: in any event, more were called than showed up. In fact, from the heads of the Houses of God (*Godshuisen*), we know that there were in fact only 10 members in 1415, 15 in 420, 7 in 1484 and 10 in 1490. The Barons and Knights who claimed to be unable to support themselves alone, asked and were granted the power to charge at least part of traveling expenses to their subjects. Each of the three groups was represented by a member of the magistracy, and was guarded by a retainer. At first, it was the seven Town Heads (*die zeven hoofsteden* of Louvain, Brussels, Antwerp, Bois-le-Duc, Tirlemont, Léau and Nivelles); later, these were only the deputies of the four principal Town Heads (*die vier principale hoodsteden* of Louvain, Brussels, Antwerp and Bois-le-Duc, respectively the capitals of the four 'quarters' (*kwartieren*) of the Duchy. At the Brussels Town Hall, fashioned in the eighteenth century manner after the model of the Assembly of the Estates of Brabant, it is a tight fit for the forty-odd communal advisors of today. This is a metaphor, a paradigm, an occasion for reflection. Compared to our trim forerunners in the fifteenth century, today's parliamentarians are but bloated shadows. *Virtur in medio? aut in nihilo?* The value of the assemblies came from the quality, not the quantity, of their membership.

SOURCES

PRIMARY SOURCES

Archives de l'Abbaye du Parc, Héverlé-Louvain, *Etats de Brabant,* Liasse 1324–1494.

Archives communales d'Anvers, *Staeten van Brabant,* 1404–1577.

Archives générales du Royaume, Brussels, Mercy-Argenteau, Reg. No. 32.

Bibliothèque royale de Belgique, Brussels, *Section des Manuscrits,* No. 5562, Th. Schotte, *Swert Boek van de Staeten van Brabant.*

Brabantsche geesten, Les Gestes des Ducs de Brabant. Chronique en Vers thyois du quinzième Siècle, Vol. III, Bk. 7, 1406–30, ed. J.-H. Bormans, (Brussels, 1869).

Ch. Butkens, *Les Trophées tant sacrés que profanes du Duché de Brabant,* 3rd ed., (The Hague, 1724–46).

Placcaeten ende Ordonnatiën van de Hertoghen van Brabandt, I, (Antwerp-Brussels, 1648).

L.-P. Gachard, *Mémoire sur la Composition et les Attributions des anciens Etats de Brabant, Mémoires de l'Académie royale de Belgique,* Sér. in-8, Vol. XVI, (Brussels, 1843).

E. Poullet, *Mémoire sur l'ancienne Constitution brabançonne, Mémoires de l'Académie royale de Belgique,* Ser. in-4, Vol. XXXI, (Brussels, 1863).

SECONDARY SOURCES

Emile Lousse and L. Wils, *Les Etats du Pays et Duché de Brabant,* in *Anciens Pays et Assemblées d'Etats,* XXXIII, (500 *Ans de Vie parlementaire en Belgique, 1464–1964. Assemblées d'Etats*), pp. 5–14, and two plates, (*Louvain-Paris,* 1965).

De Staten van Brabant tot het Einde van de XVde Eeuw. De Prelaten, in *Vriendenboek, Dr G. Renson,* s.l.n.d. (Brussels, 1979), pp. 97–103.

Brabantse Prelaten en Kloosters onder de Tachtigjarige Oorlog, De Brabantse Folklore (Brussels, Sept.–Dec. 1980), Nos. 227–8, pp. 342–9.

De Staten van Brabant tot het Einde van de XVde Eeuw. Contributie en Convocatie van de Prelaten, in *Recht en Instellingen in de Oude Nederlanden tijdens de Middeleeuwen en de Nieuwe Tijd. Liber Amicorum Jan Buntinx* (*Symbolae Facultatis Litterarum et Philosophiae Lovanensis,* Ser. A, Vol. X (Louvain, 1981), pp. 211–23.

De Staten van Brabant tot het Einde van de XVde Eeuw. De Prelaten, Stichting van en Bevoorrechting van de Kloosters onder hun Gezag, Notre Comté. Bulletin timestriel du Cercle d'Histoire, d'Archéologie et de Folklore du Comté de Jette et de la Région, XII Nos. 1–2, Jan.–June, 1982, pp. 23–31.

Presents and pensions: a methodological search and the case study of Count Nils Bielke's prosecution for treason in connection with gratifications from France

RAGNHILD HATTON

The fellow-scholar whom we honour in this volume and the present writer have an interest in common, in what might loosely be labelled 'bribery and corruption in international relations', though our periods do not quite overlap and we have concentrated on different areas of Europe in our investigations. My own initial curiosity was aroused by the sweeping assertions of some historians of the seventeenth and eighteenth centuries that bribery and corruption was prevalent among all those connected with foreign affairs, from the lowest to the highest,[1] whereas in my own researches, at that time limited to a single decade in the early eighteenth century and to Dutch, French and English archives only, had pointed to a clear division between customary, legitimate gratifications to men of stature, and secret presents and pensions meant to corrupt. The only examples I had come across of the latter were limited to minor officials: copyists and clerks who could sometimes be prevailed upon to give the clauses of a treaty before it was published, preferably with one or more of its secret articles – or the contents of an important letter – and to postmasters or their assistants who permitted the opening of mail and the perusal or the copying of specific despatches.[2]

The legitimate presents soon sorted themselves out. They were not concealed, though at times the recipient had to obtain the permission of his own sovereign before acceptance. First: the present given to a

---

[1] See e.g. J. W. Thompson and S. K. Padover, *Secret Diplomacy* 1500–1815 (London 1937), and – on the popular level – Nancy Mitford, *Frederick the Great* (1970) pp. 16–17; with more experienced historians the assumption is usually due to too facile an acceptance of diplomatic excuses for the lack of success of their own efforts compared with those of the 'opposite' side, with more money to spend.

[2] These conclusions were reached during the research for my *Diplomatic Relations between Great Britain and the Dutch Republic*, 1714–1721 (London 1950) where, like Ph.D. candidates before and after me, I found it essential to go both back and forward in respect of the years covered in the thesis.

diplomat on taking his congé of the ruler or state to whom he had been accredited – this was rarely given in coin or bills of exchange in the second half of the seventeenth century, apologies being offered when there was not sufficient time to turn the leaving present into medals of silver or gold.[3] Rough tables for the value of the present in accordance with the rank of the individual diplomat concerned persisted, however: a portrait of the monarch to whom he had been accredited might range from a routine copy turned out by pupils of the original painter in his studio to the most magnificent original in a diamond-studded frame, again the value of the stones being finely graded according to rank, the personal acceptability of the diplomat and the state of relations between his host country and the home government.

Second: the reward, generally given in coin or bills of exchange, presented to negotiators or mediators who had successfully helped to conclude a treaty or covenant between two or more rulers or states. The 'cash' element was permissible because this present was looked upon as financial compensation for extra work and expense incurred in arguing and fashioning the clauses of the treaty – on the analogy that fees were regarded as legitimate perquisites for services rendered in branches of domestic administration. This second customary present often amounted to the parties concerned rewarding each other's negotiators; but increasingly some monarchs (and Louis XIV was one of the innovators here) preferred to reward their own negotiators, fearing undue gratefulness on the part of their subjects to a foreign ruler. If a monarch was known to be reluctant to give permission for a money present, the customary reward became nearly indistinguishable from the present of politeness discussed below. To give but one example, George I offered the Premier Commis Pecquet of the French foreign ministry a ring valued at £1000 upon the conclusion of the Quadruple Alliance of 1718, while he rewarded his own main negotiator, James Stanhope, with plate worth £2000[4]. Negotiations as to the size of possible future presents and pensions frequently took place in wartime between diplomats and statesmen or officials in the host country whom they hoped to secure as mediators, without the individual involved taking umbrage: after all, he was discussing a customary present to be rendered in the future, with payment only on completion of his legitimate and formal services.[5]

[3] The custom in Sweden of giving the leaving-present in sheets of copper was dying out towards the end of the century; and regulations of 1692 specified the value for different ranks of diplomats: for a summary of these see Algemeene Rijks Archief (ARA), Archief Heinsius 622, Rumpf to Heinsius, Stockholm 2 May 1699.
[4] R. Hatton, *George I. Elector and King* (London and Harvard UP 1978) p. 272 and *footnote.
[5] See e.g. the discussions between Avaux and Bengt Oxenstierna during 1693 and 1694:

In general presents of politeness were often regarded as permissible, especially where they were known to the individual's head of state. They often developed from soundings in the realm of presents of politeness to be exchanged between sovereigns since it was deemed sensible to ascertain what would be a welcome gift: as an old Scandinavian proverb has it, 'When it rains on the clergyman, it drips on the verger'. The go-between was also thought worthy of a gift. The valuable presents to crowned heads or members of their families was a matter for discreet research: expensive horses and carriages, rare falcons, specific breeds of hunting-dogs, valuable tapestries, carpets, clocks and watches, rare maps, books or manuscripts, were the most popular, and – on request – sought-after medicines, such as the Duchess of Kent's powder from England.[6] Fine wine, fashionable wigs, good materials not easily obtained in the host country, were acceptable presents for courtiers and ministers who had proved helpful, or – for their ladies – pieces of jewellery, mirrors and fashionplates. At times presents of politeness were offered to governesses and secretaries, but at this level the distinction between a proper present of politeness and one that was meant to pave the way for a quid-pro-quo, more or less innocent, when demanded, becomes clear. If the present was kept secret we reach the subtle but significant distinction of one which was meant to induce services not fit to see the light of day, in contrast to well-deserved rewards for public services rendered to a common cause. We need only instance the way in which successful generals proudly displayed finely engraved swords and sheaths adorned with diamonds presented to them by grateful foreign monarchs,[7] and the furtive way in which many presents of politeness to lesser subjects were negotiated and concealed.

It is noteworthy that scrupulous men in high office declined all presents of politeness even when, as in the case of the Swedish statesman

PRO, FO 95 vol 577, Louis XIV to Avaux, Versailles, 10 May 1694; Avaux to Louis XIV, Stockholm, 30 June 1694; for presents of politeness being accepted by Countess Oxenstierna at this time (a pendant, a lace 'coiffeure', and three fine diamonds) see J. A. Wijnne (ed.), *Négociations de M. le Comte d'Avaux, ambassadeur extraordinaire à la Cour de Suède pendant les années* 1693, 1697, 1698 (3 vols, the last in two parts, Utrecht 1882–3) I, pp. 125, 319; Avaux to Louis XIV, Stockholm 8 April, 10 May, and 22 July 1693.

[6] This powder was much in demand by ladies of the Swedish court; and it was used to revive Bengt Oxenstierna when the Chancellor (who was already 74) fainted during the seven hour long coronation ceremony of Charles XII: PRO, SPF 95 vol 15, Robinson's letter from Stockholm of 22 December 1697.

[7] It was well known that the Duke of Marlborough stipulated in his will that the sword given to him by Emperor Leopold I should be kept in the family 'for always'; and Prince Eugene of Savoy was much gratified by the sword (valued at £4,000) presented to him by Queen Anne (during his, unsuccessful, diplomatic mission to London in 1712) as a reward for his services in the War of the Spanish Succession – which has also been labelled that of the Protestant Succession in Great Britain.

Friherre Lars Wallenstedt, his sympathy lay with France during the Nine Years' War.[8] Yet diplomats increasingly chose to regard a present of politeness to the wife of an official or minister, who had firmly refused to accept a money present or pension, as a substitute for a 'bribe' to the husband. A good example of this comes from the camp of Charles XII at Altranstädt during the Duke of Marlborough's visit there in 1707. The Duke and the British diplomat accredited to the Swedish king on campaign failed to persuade Count Karl Piper, head of the Field Chancery, to accept a pension from Queen Anne. A plan was therefore hatched to present a pair of diamond earrings to his Countess; and when this succeeded those involved on the British side assumed that a significant contact had been established with Count Piper and that 'other stratagems' could be devised for the next installment of the 'pension'.[9] Whitehall was not aware that Count Piper had explained his dilemma to Charles XII and had received the King's permission for his wife to accept the gift, lest the good relationship with Sweden's ally – then under some stress – should deteriorate further.[10]

By diplomatic convention the dirty work of paying for spies was usually left to non-accredited agents, working in close contact with and guided by the minister in charge of foreign affairs in the home-country. At times one comes across in the accounts of the 'extraordinaries' of a diplomat that he has paid minor sums to a spy or a postmaster,[11] but the expenditure of big money was reserved for rulers and their closest collaborators.[12] In centuries of soaring costs of warfare, close watch was kept on outgoings, whether for official subsidy treaties to make sure of auxiliary troops, or ships, or for secret presents and pensions to statesmen and ministers and officials who – it was hoped – might influence the policy of their own ruler. Again, we find a clear distinction between the two, equally important, items of expenditure. The subsidy

---

8 For evidence see Hatton (full details, text and note 14 below) 'Gratifications and Foreign Policy', pp. 72 and 80. n32; Karl Piper was also one of those who gloried in their independence both of factions at home and of foreign rulers.

9 R. Hatton, *Charles XII of Sweden* (London and New York 1968) p. 224 based on evidence in PRO, SPF 88 vol 17; cp R. Hatton, ed. *Captain James Jefferyes's Letters from the Swedish Army 1707–1709* (in Historiska Handlingar 35:1, Stockholm 1954), introduction, pp. 15–16.

10 S. E. Bring, 'Till frågan om Pipers politiska hederlighet', *Historisk Tidskrift* (Sweden) 1909.

11 These can be traced in the printed *Calendar of Treasury Books*, and searched for in the unprinted Treasury Papers, PRO.

12 An illuminating example of how a network of spies was attempted (with varying success) in France and Switzerland during Nottingham's secretaryship in William III's reign is found in the, as yet, unpublished papers of the Finch MSS, Historical Manuscript Commission collection (London).

treaties were concluded in formal terms whether a treaty or a convention was signed, delineating every detail as to numbers and composition of troops, time of due arrival, and – if relevant – the substitutes permitted, whether in ships or money.[13] Even if secret or semi-secret at the time, these surfaced as archives, have been made accessible to scholars and collections of treaties published. Conversely, the attempts, whether successful or unsuccessful, to gain by secret money-presents and pensions men assumed to have the ear of their own sovereign, and with use of strategems and subterfuges intended to mislead political opponents and curious gossipmongers, have been shrouded in mystery. Many of these transactions were so well concealed that it has been difficult for historians, in ascending degree, to show (a) that money-presents and/or pensions were offered, (b) that such offers were accepted, and (c) that sums offered and accepted were actually handed over to the would-be recipient.

In my own case I was brought up against these problems when it dawned on me – working in the 1950s on Anglo-French rivalry in Sweden for commitment at best, and neutrality at worst, in the Nine Years War – that here if ever was a case of money expended in large quantities, secretly, on men in high office. I vowed to get to the bottom of it, but not to regard any case as proved unless the three criteria listed above were met. My search became entertaining, time-consuming and at times exasperating; and only a combination of persistence and luck brought me to the point where I could eventually reveal the facts and assess the role of 'Gratifications and Foreign Policy: Anglo-French Rivalry in Sweden during the Nine Years War', in *William III and Louis XIV. Essays 1680–1720 by and for Mark A. Thomson*, who had helped my postgraduate research at University College, London, and who had become a dear friend and critical mentor.[14]

The French side had proved relatively straightforward, since French diplomats were at this time in the habit of sending whole letters enciphered if they dealt with sensitive material and persisted in using the 'ordinary cipher' even when they had been warned by the French foreign minister that this cipher had been broken. Louis XIV himself ordered the Comte d'Avaux – one of the ablest diplomats accredited to

[13] An unusual, but interesting case, is the one where William III asked and was granted permission to substitute English cloth for Swedish uniforms instead of money due to Charles XII under the Anglo-Swedish treaty of Jan 1700: a sample of cloth of amazing quality and its blue quite unfaded after so many years, intrigued me when I came across it in the Swedish War Office archives (Krigsarkivet) in Stockholm: see Hatton, *Charles XII*, pp. 112–13, 142.

[14] Published, in 1968 (Liverpool UP and Toronto UP). ed. Ragnhild Hatton and J. S. Bromley.

the court of Charles XI – that he must use the grand cipher, held to be unbreakable, and not let the key to the box in which it was kept out of his own hands. Avaux protested that the grand cipher was too complicated and would delay urgent news because of the time consumed in enciphering and persisted with the ordinary cipher. Neither diplomat nor ruler knew at this time how the leak occurred, though the French mended their ways in the years after the Nine Years War.[15] The historian's task was thus rendered easy since the *en clair* version was neatly written in between the lines of the enciphered material; and this was done when, as a temporary safeguard, Avaux had been given a new number code for certain Swedish individuals. Moreover, the presence of the papers of Jean Antoine de Mesme, Comte d'Avaux in the Foreign Office section of the Public Record Office (acquired at a date and in a manner which is not known in any detail), elucidated the French case further.[16] Three volumes of the Avaux correspondence, for the years 1693, 1697 and 1698, had been published by J. A. Wijnne in 1882 and 1883; and historians interested in the Nine Years War had hitherto assumed that this was all that was available, just as Swedish scholars had assumed that the extracts copied from the French Quay d'Orsay archives deposited in the Swedish Riksarkiv by historians of the nineteenth and early twentieth centuries (the Wahrenberg, Stråle, and Palme collections) exhausted the material significant for Swedish history. London being closer to Paris than Stockholm it was easier for me to make a thorough search of the papers of the *Archives des Affaires Etrangères*, where both the *Correspondence Politique, Suède* volumes, as well as the volumes of Supplements yielded up many secrets; while the Foreign Office Avaux collection with its original letters received, its drafts for, or copies of, memoranda, and letters from the diplomat added to what was known from the printed Wijnne volumes as well as giving vital information for the years 1694, 1695, 1699 not covered in the Wijnne edition (again for reasons not known).

The rub for me remained the ciphered instructions in the Public Record Office State Papers, Sweden, where the enciphered sections of

---

[15] That Louis XIV learnt his lesson is evident from the careful use of cyphers between Versailles and important generals and diplomats from papers I later examined e.g. those to and from General Boufflers in the Spanish Netherlands in 1700, 1701 and 1702. The French correspondence via Germany remained vulnerable, however, because of the Hanoverian opening of letters which continued throughout the eighteenth century; see e.g. K. L. Ellis, *The Post Office in the Eighteenth Century* (1958) and the same author's article on the same century, in *Bulletin of the Institute of Historical Research (BIHR)* (1958) 'British Communications and Diplomacy'; Bengt Peterson's article in Swedish, but with English summary, *Scandia* 1961, 387–99.

[16] Call number FO 95, vols 576 and following.

copied instructions in the Foreign Entry Books defeated my no doubt amateur attempts to decipher them once my search in the PRO for a cipher-key of the period that fitted had proved fruitless. The diplomatic despatches from Stockholm gave me some valuable clues in that here enciphered words, or parts of words, were often deciphered on receipt, and more especially the names of individual Swedes; the number 1194 for Bengt Oxenstierna, the Chancellor whose responsibility for foreign affairs, became engraved on my brain if not on my heart. Other Swedish high officials and members of King Charles XI's Council cropped up again and again: though only two of those of particular interest to me, Count Fabian Wrede, head of the College of Commerce, and Samuel Åkerhielm, 'la plume de la Chancellerie' and an expert on trade, had numbers of their own.[17] Others, like Count John Hastfer, a field marshal at this time governor-general of Livonia; Baron (from November 1690 Count) Nils Gyldenstolpe, second-in-command of the Chancery; Thomas Polus, a Chancery official well versed in German affairs; Baron Karl Piper, particularly influential in domestic affairs; Count Lars Wallenstedt, the legal expert in charge of the resumption of crown lands; the Court Marshal Count Johan Stenbock; the clever Johan Olivekrans who, out of favour with Charles XI, held no office but was valued by ministers for his wide correspondence abroad; and his son-in-law, the diplomat Nils Lillieroot, had their names made up from enciphered numbers interspersed with *en clair* letters. So did Count Nils Bielke, a soldier of Swedish and European fame, a personal friend of Charles XI, a count and a field marshal since 1690, and a governor-general of Pomerania, who will be the subject of the case study of the second part of my contribution.

My attempts from the deciphered numbers to construct a cipher-key of my own was a dismal failure and regretfully I laid my file marked 'POSSIBLE MONEY-GRATIFICATIONS' aside. Some years later I had a stroke of luck while looking for something else in the Blathwayt Papers in the British Museum's manuscript collection for the campaign of 1693 when William Blathwayt (whose office was that of Secretary at War) was acting Secretary of State to King William III in the Low Countries. I became aware of something folded and heavy towards the end of the volume.

---

[17] We have already noted that Wrede accepted no money, but he dealt with sensitive matters, such as the problems of Swedish trade and navigation. Åkerhielm was hard pressed to accept money from England but declined: eventually he accepted what was considered a flattering and valuable present of politeness; his son studied at Oxford for three years at the expense of the English government; see Hatton, 'Gratifications', p. 85; and Hatton, *Charles XII*, p. 235; for quote on Åkerhielm see Wijnne, III (2) p. 152 Avaux to Louis XIV Stockholm 5 June 1697.

Unfolded and laid flat, there was my cipher-key: the tell-tale 1194 for 'Oxenstiern' was sufficient proof.[18] During my wait for the xerox copy which would enable me to penetrate the PRO secrets, I had time to ponder the ingeniousness not only of the cipher, but of the use made of it. Below its initialed signature W, the number 93276 was written in ink as well as the following memorandum: All numbers ending in o are blanks, [as are] All numbers under 13 and above 1341.[19] The cipher was divided into 13 columns, with the 26 letters of the alphabet from A–Z beginning with 14 printed vertically in the first column with the numbers allocated to individual letters (varying from two to six) written in ink running along all 13 columns. The next 12 columns had printed words or parts of words with their respective numbers inked in. Blank spaces were given in the 12 other squares deriving from the crossed vertical and horizontal lines, though the inked numbers continued without interruption from 14 to 1341. In some of these blank spaces names of individuals were inked in, in general following the alphabet; but permitting the insertion of new names as need arose, particularly in the last three columns, broader than the rest. I noted that rulers were catered for in printed form in rubric K with country added: K. France Spain, K. Poland Swead, K. Portugal Denmark.

I knew that William III, when he was *Stadhouder* of the United Provinces, had been let into the secret of the Brunswick–Lüneburg interception of enciphered diplomatic correspondence (and in particular that between France and the Scandinavian courts) at Nienburg and Gifhorn where skilled decipherers had broken the French cipher just because there was so much of it. Copies of the deciphered material had frequently been put at William's disposal by Duke George Wilhelm of Celle and Duke Ernst August of Calenberg since they had interests in common: opposition to Catholic France and concern both for the Ninth Electorate (Ernst August obtained the Electoral title in 1692 from Emperor Leopold I and received his coveted cap, but general recognition was slow to come) and for the English Protestant Succession.[20] It seems

---

[18] He is entered as Oxenstiern Benou: foreign diplomats frequently left out the final 'a' in his family name.

[19] BM (now BL) Add. MS 35105 fol 11.

[20] S. P. Oakley in the Mark Thomson volume mentioned above (text and note 14) has in his 'The Interception posts in Celle 1694–1700'; pp. 95–116 given proof of this intercepted correspondence reaching both William III and the Grand Pensionary, Antonie Heinsius, of the Dutch Republic; Professor G. Schnath in his *Geschichte Hannovers 1647–1714* (4 vols 1938–82) gives many instances of the interceptions. Georg Wilhelm and William of Orange met first in 1617: in 1672 Georg Wilhelm joined the anti-French coalition, as did Ernst August (then princebishop of Osnabrück) in 1674 and both, as well as the future George I of England (from 1675) took part in the campaigns of the Dutch War: for this and for the joint interests referred to in text, see Hatton *George I*, pp. 32 ff, 39 ff, 69 ff, 85 ff. Note that William visited Celle in 1680,

to me highly probable, though I have no direct evidence, that this influenced the English instructions to diplomats in William III's reign to be very sparing indeed in the use of their ciphers; only once was a particular number for a given letter permitted in any one despatch, which explains the need for ingenious strategems to convey the necessary secret information without infringing this rule. It also explains its success: the cipher was never broken during William's reign. Nor were the French able to discover where the Nine Years War correspondence with Stockholm was opened and deciphered. England had splendid cipher-makers and in time became independent of their Hanoverian decipherers, though Hanover never lost its preeminence in forging so perfectly the seals to reclose the despatches.[21]

Armed with the cipher-key from the Blathwayt papers I was able to get at the facts in respect of English money-gratifications and pensions during the Nine Years War, the hardest remaining tasks being to figure out the complex routing and rerouting of bills of exchange (to avoid detection of eventual recipient of money) and the search for clinching evidence that the money had actually been received.[22] My objective had not been that of seeking for guilty men; indeed, I had gone out of my way to analyse why at that particular time Swedish ministers and officials were tempted to mislead foreign rulers and diplomats about their willingness to serve them in return for money-presents, and had deduced the rules of the game for those who accepted such presents or pensions. As one cynic among them put it: 'If you served your country and your king and acted in their best interest, there is no harm in profiting as a private subject, as long as you do not receive money from both sides.'[23]

1681 and 1698 and that Georg Wilhelm visited William III in the Netherlands in 1696 and 1701.

[21] The initial W in the cypher-key mentioned above indicates the mathematician and skilled cyphermaker John Wallis who was William III's keeper of archives from 1690. I am indebted to Miss Uta Richter (University of Göttingen) for the information that skilled Hanoverian decypherers were called to England in George II's reign and settled there; proof of increasing self-sufficiency lies in the very title of Helle Stiegung's study (in Swedish) of which he examines the political spying of the *Londonkabinett* in respect of Sweden, in particular for the years 1770–2 (*Historisk Arkiv (HA)*, 1961).

[22] That phrases could be so innocent and unimportant to editors of correspondences as to be left out altogether, was made clear to me when I used the original Finch papers of the Historical Manuscript Commission while vol II was in the press. I found a one-line letter 'Your friend has been satisfied' which, because of its date, its addressee and signature, gave proof of the safe delivery of Count Oxenstierna's annual pension, while in the published volume this letter was omitted without any indication that there was any break in the sequence of letters.

[23] This was said by Gyldenstolpe, who had himself taken English and French money, but

I had analysed why sympathies with one side or the other of the belligerents in the War had developed in individual recipients and had assessed the way in which changes in the European power balance and Sweden's own needs had affected the advice they rendered Charles XI. Yet I could not help being impressed by the contrast between the fates of Count Oxenstierna, the main recipient of William III's money, who had received the bulk of it, some £20,000, in the war years and whose annual pension continued even after Charles XI's decree of December 1699[24] that it was henceforth an act of high treason if a minister or official, high or low, accepted money-presents or pensions from a foreign ruler and whose secret, with the active connivance of Whitehall, was kept inviolate till eventually disclosed in 1968 – and Count Bielke, against whom a legal prosecution for treason on nine different counts was started in 1698. The most serious in the eyes of contemporaries was the accusation of having received a pension from France, when the sources which I will cite below render it reasonably certain that he did not accept one after December 1696, and that he had received far less than contemporaries assumed in the course of the war.

Bielke came of an old Swedish family, noble from at least the thirteenth century, and whose branch of the family received the new titles of barons and counts when it decided to support the Protestant Duke Charles (later King Charles XI) against the Catholic Sigismund Vasa of Poland. Its members had a long tradition of service to the crown in administration and in the armed forces, and most of his direct ancestors had been made members of the Council. His own parents, however, died young, and his education was entrusted to his uncle Count Sten Bielke (1624–84). In 1661 it was arranged that Nils (born in 1644) should accompany his cousin Klas Tott on his embassy to Paris, as a page; and Nils spent three years in France, learning the chivalrous arts and absorbing French culture and manners, and was entrusted with delivering the King of Sweden's congratulations to Louis XIV on the

who once he had received a second money present from France, accepted that it would be dishonorable to receive more from William III: see Hatton's 'Gratifications', pp. 81–3 (for £1,000 in 1690 from William III, with a particularly lavish present of politeness to his wife, a portrait of Queen Mary valued at £500); 3,000 livres from Louis XIV 1691, 12,000 ecus in several instalments during 1695 and 1696, and 4,000 ecus in 1697). Note that the livre was the money of account, there being one ecu to three livres. The relationship between French and English money varied with the exchange; a pound sterling being worth between 12 and 15 livres.

24 Officially the decree was motivated by the acceptance of bribes by a Swedish secretary at the Emperor's court at Vienna. Some Swedish historians have therefore argued that it was not aimed at men in high places; but the papers I have examined convinced me that the decree, urged on Charles XI by Wallenstedt, was intended to put a stop to the rumours, and practice, of councillors and high officials accepting money presents and pensions.

birth of the Dauphin. His French education and other travels proved very costly in terms of money and eventually his uncle called him home. Nils had been born with the hereditary title of baron and had already in 1649 been given a barony of his own; and his parents had left him several large estates, but 14,455 riksdaler stretched his income to its limits. Some years of service at court (the child King's and that of the Queen Mother) and in good regiments followed; then several years of travels – to Germany, Italy, the Netherlands, England and France, where he made influential friends, before his marriage in 1669 to Eva Horn (1643–1740), daughter of the high court official Gustav Horn. She brought him riches, gave him two sons and three daughters and remained loyal and supportive when misfortune hit him in 1698.

Bielke's personal friendship with Charles XI dated from the Scanian War, when – since the regents of the King's minority, having accepted subsidies for Sweden from France, became, without meaning to and by degrees, involved in the continental warfare that followed Louis XIV's attack on the Dutch Republic in 1672 – Sweden's enemies, in particular Brandenburg and Denmark, took the opportunity of trying reconquests of Swedish provinces gained in the Thirty Years War and by Charles X Gustavus. Sweden's former Danish and Norwegian provinces were at stake, and Bielke's bravery and recruiting and organizing ability won him the favour and gratitude of the young King. He accepted, as the saying went, 'that Sweden's fate had hung on the tip of Bielke's sword', embraced him in public before his troops and promised him in private that he would never forget his bravery and that he could count on his royal help if he met with difficulties. At the end of the war for Scania, Bielke was sent to France as ambassador where he renewed old friendships and made new connections, especially with military men. He felt, however, out of sympathy with the political development in Sweden where the power of the high nobility was curbed, and sought and obtained leave from Charles XI to serve in the war against the Turks, first with the Bavarian army and then with the Imperial cavalry. He won renown for his outstanding bravery, and achieved an all-embracing European reputation. In 1686 he was rewarded by Leopold I with the title of Count of the Holy Roman Empire, and was then called home by Charles XI, who created him a Swedish count and a field marshal before the end of the year and in 1687 made him governor-general of Swedish Pomerania, with the task of carrying through the resumption of crown land in that province. This was not congenial work for Bielke, who soon requested leave to take military service abroad once more. This was firmly denied; a European war threatened, and Charles XI argued that he needed his friend close enough to call him to Sweden for consultation and advice. One of the King's well-known *banne-brev* (curse-you-letter) convinced Bielke that he just had to get on with *reduktionen;* but he was gratified by the several diplomatic missions to North German states, like Hanover, Saxony and Brandenburg, to Holstein-Gottorp and to Denmark which were entrusted to him during the Nine Years War – this was work for which he had a special aptitude and which he enjoyed. He remained governor-general but, at Charles XI's orders, spent long periods in Stockholm most years of the war (once at least the whole winter season), hunting with the King, holding confidential talks with him before and after important Council meetings which was resented by his political rivals. Bielke was not as 'out-and-out French' as these argued; and he certainly did not merit their accusation that he put the interests of Louis XIV above that of his own country and gave Charles XI 'bad advice'. Bielke, who had after all seen the Austrian and Imperial cause at close quarters, held Louis XIV to blame for the outbreak of the Palatinate War (as the Nine Years War was known at its outset). He expressed his fears that France might, after all, aim at 'universal monarchy', laying down the law to all Europe. But he changed his mind once the attempt by William III to place his wife Mary (and himself) on the throne of England in 1688–9 proved successful. To him, as to other Swedes, such as Wrede, the combination of the Two Maritime Powers under the same ruler destroyed the balance of power in Europe, particularly for Sweden which could no longer play England and the Dutch Republic off against each other. They now found their trade endangered by combined Anglo-Dutch opposition to Scandinavian attempts at enlarging their trade and navigation and felt obliged to form 'armed neutralities' with the old enemy Denmark to protect their shipping against England's interpretation of its maritime right.[25]

Bielke's political opponents were not principally motivated by envy of the man considered 'the richest man in Sweden'[26] and who had also had the King's friendship; they firmly believed that Sweden had more to expect from the Allies than from Louis XIV. They wanted from the Maritime Powers solid support for the Duke of Holstein-Gottorp against Denmark[27] as well as compensation for ships taken as prizes and promises of free trade for the future; while from Emperor Leopold they

[25] For Bielke's career there are good articles by Georg Wittrock in *SBL* (*Svensk Biografisk Leksikon* 1918, in progress) and also in the later publication *Svenska Män och Kvinnor* (1942–55); for the so-called first armed neutrality see Hatton, 'Gratifications' p. 71 and note 7.

[26] HMC, *Downshire Manuscripts*, I, p. 558 Robinson to Trumbull, Stockholm, 2 October 1695.

[27] For this issue see Hatton, 'Gratifications', p. 90 (briefly) and in more depth Hatton, *Charles XII*, pp. 21 ff, 60 ff, 86 ff, 108 ff.

desired the inclusion of the town of Bremen and the principality of Hadeln in the Swedish German dominions as well as the succession to the duchy of Welden. With Louis XIV they had already in the early stages of the war arranged payment of subsidies outstanding from the war of 1675–9, had obtained favourable treatment of Swedish trade and shipping, and assurances of French willingness to make Charles XI a mediator of the peace. All they could further expect was the restitution of the King of Sweden's personal possession of Zweibrücken (Deux-Ponts), the victim of French reunion policy.[28] They were mistaken in their belief that Bielke did not share these objectives; and became convinced that they had made some impression on Charles XI with their complaints that Bielke was in French pay and not faithful to Sweden when it transpired, on the King's will being opened, that he had not included Bielke's name on the list of regents during Charles XII's minority. It was then generally rumoured that the late King on his deathbed, in April 1697, had warned the future Charles XII against trusting those who had 'French stomachs'.[29]

By this time the division between pro-French and pro-Allied Swedes had to a large extent lost its meaning. Exasperated by the unwillingness of Charles XI to come down firmly on one side or the other, William III and Louis XIV had arranged their own peace terms though Swedish diplomats were the official mediators at the Congress of Ryswick.[30] If one wished to count heads among the six regents named by the late King there were three or four of pro-French sympathies (Wallenstedt, Wrede and Gyldenstolpe) who could balance the other three votes, the one of Bengt Oxenstierna with the two votes given to the Queen-Grandmother, Hedvig Eleonora, born of the Holstein-Gottorp House.

It is my contention, however, that these regents feared Bielke on another count, and even the pro-French among them presented a united front here: the very reform of the Swedish constitution by the introduction of the absolutist regime, the breaking of the high nobility's political and economic power, seemed to them threatened by men like

---

[28] Hatton, 'Gratifications', p. 88 ff; by this time Charles XI and his advisers had given up their most sanguine hopes, namely guarantees – from whatever side, but preferably from the Emperor – of the Swedish Baltic possessions outside the Holy Roman Empire: Ingria, Estonia and Livonia – they had found no takers.

[29] For a more probable admonishment, not to listen to the advice of those who were out for their own gain, see Hatton, *Charles XII*, p. 65: still one that might have been aimed at Bielke who, when interrogated during his prosecution, admitted that this had been one of his faults.

[30] These were Lillieroot, named at an early stage, and held to have been rewarded by William III (see Hatton, 'Gratifications', pp. 89 and 77, 91) and Count Carl Bonde (whose secretary received a French gratification of 1500 livres, 1697): ibid p. 91 and 43, p. 82.

Bielke who was thought capable of leading an attack on the work of Charles XI, aiming – it was held – at a reversion or at least the non-completion of the *reduktion*.[31] Bielke, suspended from his governorship of Pomerania to permit investigation of his financial administration of the province, had been replaced by the sixth regent, Nils Gyllenstierna. It was felt that he had to be stopped decisively in his tracks. The recent example of William III attempting to save the Elector of Brandenburg's minister, Danckelmann, from disgrace awoke fear that Louis XIV might interfere in Swedish domestic affairs by support of Bielke.[32]

Even so, the criminal case against Bielke might not have materialized, but for the fact that he drew suspicion on himself which could be used to discredit him with the young Charles XII. While Bielke was still governor, an order was given for the promotion of a Swedish officer in a Pomeranian regiment. The governor, whether biased against the man (who had once been in his service) or inadvertently, passed on the order to the Pomeranian Estates. This was construed with some right as disobedience to a royal order and secured Charles XII's consent to a general investigation into Bielke's conduct as an official of the Swedish crown.[33]

The legal process that followed, from January 1698 until judgement was pronounced in April 1705, has been the subject of several Swedish investigations, the most searching being that by Georg Wittrock who was the first historian to examine the separate protocols and documents covering the most sensitive of all the accusations, that of treason by receipt of foreign money and secret correspondence with foreign rulers; these papers were, by order of Charles XII, sealed and deposited in the archives 'until further orders', which were never given.[34]

Of the nine points levied against Count Bielke, some were easily disposed of by the committee of legal experts.[35] For instance, number 1, which accused him of having given himself undue importance by the description of his office on a medal as *Pomerania produx* instead of *generalis gubernator*; and number 4, whether his unfavourable comment

[31] Hatton, *Charles XII*, pp. 70 ff.
[32] Georg Wittrock, 'Förräderipunkten i Nils Bielkes Process 1704–5', *Karolinska Förbundets Arsbok (KFA)* 1917, p. 44 referring to Ranke's research into the English diplomat Stepney's mission to Brandenburg in 1698.
[33] Georg Wittrock's articles in the two biographical lexica cited in note 25 above.
[34] Wittrock, *KFÅ* 1917, p. 41, note 1.
[35] *Ibid.* pp. 41 ff for the names (shifting with time as death and change of office took its toll). The main prosecutor, most biased against Bielke, was Henrik Heerdhielm (later vice-president in the Supreme Court); and the most independent and penetrating young Peter Scheffer, who later reached high office. Charles XII was anxious to emphasize from his campaign headquarters that the accused must be given fair treatment with access to all relevant documents and other rights guaranteed by law.

on the behaviour of the Maritime Powers in a private letter to the then Swedish envoy in Vienna was worthy of punishment, took little time to decide in Bielke's favour. The investigation into his diplomatic activities gave more work, since they dealt with disobedience in respect of a second, initially unauthorized mission to Hanover, in 1690; and his negotiations with Saxony and Brandenburg where he was suspected of attitudes inconsistent with royal policy. On all these counts Bielke could prove by witnesses or by original letters that he had acted either with Charles XI's permission or been given later approbation. The one case where he had been guilty of independent action – a grandiose scheme for Swedish reconciliation with Denmark at the expense of the Duke of Holstein-Gottorp (to be compensated with lands elsewhere in Germany) thus robbing Sweden of her back-door entry into Denmark, the committee did not question him, probably on orders from higher authority.[36]

As far as his financial misdemeanour was concerned, Bielke admitted that he had allowed a German adventurer to stay longer than the year granted by Charles XI in Pomerania from where he had flooded the North German states with inferior coin;[37] and the conclusion was easily reached that Bielke had paid insufficient attention to Charles XI's personal wishes on the Güstrow-Schwerin succession dispute.[38] This was hardly sufficient to find him guilty under the medieval definition of treason which listed rebellion against the king, attempts at murder of the royal person, or the bringing of foreign troops to act against Sweden. It all depended therefore on the issue of the point that accused him of treasonable contact with foreign powers. It was hoped that evidence would be found among Bielke's papers that he had received money-presents or pensions from Louis XIV after December 1696. By early 1705 the committee, with expert help, had managed to decipher the greater part of letters from Bidal d'Asfeld, the French diplomat, which dealt with presents in the early 1690s. In 1699 they had already received a statement from Christian Braun that he, as Bielke's secretary in 1690–1, had received from Bidal's brother, the abbé d'Asfeld, in Paris, 50,000 ecus, worth 47,000 riksdaler. When examined by the commission,

[36] Denmark was a sensitive subject for Charles XI who had adored his Danish Queen and for Charles XII who hoped to marry the Danish princess – to whom he and his family felt he was unofficially engaged – after the Great Northern War was over; just as Charles XI, who had been officially engaged to Ulrika Eleonora before the Scanian War, married her after the Scanian War.

[37] Wittrock, *SBL* for details.

[38] The details of this dispute do not concern us (they are treated with lucidity in Wittrock, *KFÅ* 1917); there was a family element in that one of the parties to be protected was Charles XI's maternal aunt.

Braun gave a different explanation: that the money was the remnant of a sum paid, by Bielke, for the estate of Harzfeld in Swedish territory, belonging to Bidal d'Asfeld, soon to be resumed by the crown. No proof of Bielke having bought the estate was forthcoming, and the conclusion once the cipher evidence was *en clair* was that this was Bielke's pension from France. It was assumed that this vast sum was Bielke's annual pension from 1690 onwards; but though no evidence could be found for later years, individual opinions on whether there was now sufficient proof that Bielke had acted to the detriment of his country makes fascinating reading in the protocol. The judges could not agree, but by a majority it was decided that Bielke did deserve punishment. Loss of life and estate was the verdict on 15 April 1705, on the grounds that he had carried on a secret correspondence with foreign diplomats; he had moreover exceeded his instructions in several cases, and been too concerned to amass a fortune for himself. The punishment was not put into effect as far as the loss of life was concerned; Charles XII decreed that Bielke should not in future reside in Stockholm or wherever the Court of Sweden stayed, and that his estate should be forfeit. Bielke had, however, had time to dispose sensibly of his land and his money, with the help mainly of relatives, and especially one of his sons-in-law.[39] His main estate, 'Salsta', was in his wife's name, and to this he retired and lived peacefully till his death. His shame was lessened by the undeniable fact of a judgement at least semi-political: he was regarded as a possible leader for anti-absolutist conspiracies and therefore capable of treason in the future. His children did not suffer, they were received at court during the legal investigation and afterwards; his daughters married well and both sons distinguished themselves in Charles XII's campaigns. One of them, Ture Bielke, was the officer used to keep secret the King's route on his famous ride from Turkey to Stralsund: dressed in the uniform of Charles XII and carrying some of his well-known appurtenances, like his *etui* of mathematical instruments, he rode in some state and was treated like a king by those who accompanied him, and the deceit worked.[40]

It remains to note what Nils Bielke did receive from Louis XIV. Of the 150,000 livres (the 50,000 ecus of the accusation) paid in Paris, 60,000 went to Bielke, equal to three years' pension at 20,000.[41] His pension

[39] Wittrock, *SBL* for details.
[40] Hatton, *Charles XII*, pp. 385, 388.
[41] Hatton, 'Gratifications', p. 81 and note 35 correcting older authorities from AAE Corr. Pol. Suède vol 71, Bethune to Louis XIV, Stockholm 16 July 1692; and PRO FO 95 vol. 576, mémoire Avaux of 16 April 1693.

for the years 1693, 1694 and 1695 was paid at one go in 1696, being put directly into a fund at the Hôtel de Ville, together with a sum which Bielke added, intended to be the equivalent (but he could not quite manage to raise all the cash) to the pensions already received; from this fund Bielke was to receive annual interest.[42] No pension seems to have been paid for 1696. Louis XIV agreed that his ambassador should pay Bielke's pension for this year, but there is no evidence that it was paid.[43] The knowledge of Charles XI's decree of 1696 may well have inhibited both sides. The decree certainly made a stir in Europe and was much discussed.[44]

[42] Hatton, 'Gratifications', p. 90 and note 82.
[43] *Ibid.* for Louis XIV's authorization to pay of 3 Jan. 1697: PRO, FO 95. vol 578.
[44] For reasons of space I have not dealt in this contribution with the dédommagement of 24,000 livres annually by Louis XIV for Bielke for the two regiments he withdrew from allied service. This compensation was not regarded by contemporaries as a money-present and is covered in 'Gratifications', p. 76 with note 16 and p. 90 with note 82.

Between Bruni and Machiavelli: History, Law and Historicism in Poggio Bracciolini

FREDERICK KRANTZ

In 1453, nine years after Leonardo Bruni's death, Poggio Bracciolini, his friend and fellow-student of Salutati, succeeded him as chancellor of the Florentine Republic. Poggio, by then seventy-three years old, had, like Bruni, received his early intellectual formation in the circle of humanists around Salutati, and, again like Bruni, had as a young man left Florence for a career in the Papal Curia.[1] Poggio was to remain with the Curia for the greater part of his life, never, however, cutting himself off from his Florentine friends, or, for that matter, from Florentine life generally.[2]

[1] The most important modern work is that of Ernst Walser, *Poggius Florentinus, Leben und Werke* (Leipzig and Berlin, 1914). Biographical information in what follows is drawn largely from Walser and: L. Martines, *The Social World of the Florentine Humanists, 1390–1460* (Princeton, 1968); R. Roedel, 'P. B. nel quinto centenario della morte', *Rinascimento*, XI (1960), pp. 51–68; Curt Gutkind, 'P.B.s geistige Entwicklung', *Deutsche Vierteljahrsschrift*, X (1932), pp. 548–96; V. Rossi, *Il Quattrocento*, rev. ed. (Milan, 1956), pp. 25–58, 80–172; Nicolai Rubinstein, 'P. B. cancelliere e storico di Firenze', *Atti e memorie dell'accademia Petrarca di lettere, arti e scienza di Arezzo*, n.s., Vol. XXXVII (1965), pp. 215–33; two essays by P. Bacci (*P. B. nella luce dei suoi tempi* [Florence, 1959] and *Cenni biografici e religiosi di P. B.* [Florence, 1963]) are sketchy. See also Francesco Tateo's *Tradizione e realtà nell'umanesimo italiano* (Bari, 1967), pp. 251–77; the chapter on 'Rhetoric, Ethics, and History: Poggio Bracciolini' in Nancy S. Struever, *The Language of History in the Renaissance. Rhetoric and Historical Consciousness in Florentine Humanism* (Princeton, 1970), pp. 144–99; Riccardo Fubini, referring to much recent literature, 'Il "Teatro del Mondo" nelle prospettive morali e storico-politiche di Poggio Bracciolini', in *Poggio Bracciolini 1380–1980. Nel VI centenario della nascita* (Florence, 1962, no ed.: Instituto Nazionale di Studi sul Rinascimento, Studi e Testi, VIII), pp. 1–92, with an edition of Poggio's *Oratio ad Reverendissimos Patres* of 1417 (during the Council of Constance) at pp. 103–32, and of the *Proemium in Historiarum Florentini Populi Libris Octo* at pp. 134–5.

[2] Poggio left Florence for Rome in 1403, where through the good offices of Salutati and the help of Bruni he obtained a post as Curial *scriptor* and *abbreviator* under Boniface IX (see F. Novati, ed., *L'Epistolario di Coluccio Salutati*, 4 vols. [Rome, 1891–1911], Vol. I, XII, p. 15). Poggio remained at Rome until 1414, when he went with John XXII to the Council of Constance; during this period, he remained very close to the Florentine circle, corresponding with Salutati (until his death in 1406), Niccoli, Bruni, and others, and travelling with Bruni in 1407 to inspect the monastic library at Montecassino. His great manuscript finds of 1415–17 were forwarded to Florence, to Niccoli, and an intimate correspondence with his Florentine friends continues through his English stay

In 1453, at a critical moment in the war then raging between Florence and Milan on the one hand, and Venice and Naples on the other, Poggio accepted the Signoria's offer of the chancellorship and, in a context not unlike that pertaining during the tenures of Salutati and Bruni in the period of the earlier Visconti wars, returned amidst popular acclaim to the city of his youth.[3]

There is, then, a kind of symmetry in the lives of Salutati, Bruni and Poggio. Poggio, although born at Lanciola, near Terranuova, was brought up in Arezzo, the town of Bruni's birth, and, like Bruni, was sent to the Florentine *Studio* to study notarial law. Like Bruni he seems to have become part of the circle around Salutati while studying law; and while he passed his notarial examination in 1402, enrolling subsequently (like Bruni) in the guild of the *Giudici e notai*, he soon sought to escape from a professional career into the more congenial realm of the emerging

of 1418–22 and his return to Rome. He was highly thought of in Florence, and in 1429 was offered the chancellorship, but turned it down; in 1436 he married into the Buondelmonti, a leading Florentine family. From 1434 to 1436 he resided in Florence, with Eugene IV, and again from 1439 to 1442, during and after the Council of Florence. And throughout his Curial period, Poggio assiduously acquired properties and invested money in Florence; by his death in 1459, 'the Bracciolini family figured among the richest families in the city' (Martines, *Social World*, p. 126); see Walser, *Poggius Florentinus*, 'Dokumente', pp. 325–559 *passim*. for records of Poggio's acquisitions of land and houses, his investments of sums of money (above all with the Medici bank), and his loaning of money, supplemented now by the new information contained in Ms. Horne 2805 (Museo Horne, Florence) discovered by P. O. Kristeller and edited by Renzo Ristori ('Il Ms. Horne appartenuto a Poggio Bracciolini' in *Poggio Bracciolini 1380–1980*, pp. 271–80). All of this makes Hans Baron's efforts to show that Poggio 'shar[ed] Florentine views' (*The Crisis of the Early Italian Renaissance* [Princeton, 1965], 2 vol. ed., I, pp. 238–40, 353–5, II, 465–8; 1 vol. rev. ed. [Princeton, 1966], pp. 407–9, and 454–5, 479–90) seem unnecessarily forced: Poggio was indeed a Florentine, and while his long stay at the Curia no doubt contributed much to his development, his return to the city in 1453, despite some initial adjustments, was generally a natural transition. As George Holmes puts it in *The Florentine Enlightenment 1400–50* (New York, 1969), 'He enjoyed the society of the Curia, but he remained essentially a Florentine' (p. 83). It should be noted too that Poggio maintained a long and intimate friendship with Cosimo de' Medici, supporting him as early as his temporary banishment from the city by the Albizzi faction in 1433 (see T. Tonelli, ed., *Poggii Epistolae*, 3 vols. [Florence, 1832], V, xii, xxi; x, ii, for a series of adulatory letters covering the period 1433–49. The Tonelli edition of the *Epistolae* is reprinted in Vol. III of R. Fubini, ed., *Poggius Bracciolini Opera Omnia*, 4 vols. (Turin, 1964): all citations to Poggio's works will henceforth be to the Turin edition unless otherwise noted.

[3] Garin, in his 'I Cancellieri umanisti della repubblica fiorentina', *Rivista storica italiana*, LXXI, ii (1959), 185–208, maintains that Poggio's recall was largely ceremonial, that he was an 'ornamental' figure (p. 204); Nicolai Rubinstein, in his important 'P. B. cancelliere e storico di Firenze', holds that Poggio's appointment had political import, coming as it did during the war against Venice and Naples, and that this was recognized in Florence at the time (see pp. 215–18). Poggio himself seems to have been aware of the parallels, for it is after his appointment that he begins work in earnest on his *Historia Florentina*: again, the Bruni parallel.

studia humanitatis. In 1403 an opportunity presented itself in the form of a post at Rome with Cardinal Maramaldo; subsequently, with the help of Salutati, he was named apostolic *scriptor* in the Curia, under Boniface IX. With interruptions, Poggio would maintain the Curial connection for fifty years.[4]

I

Like Salutati and Bruni, Poggio had had formal legal training, and was well-versed in Italian legal realities, Florentine, papal, and peninsular. All his writings indicate this, as we shall see, and, like Salutati, but unlike Bruni, Poggio also devoted a number of pieces to specific discussions of law (above all, the centrally important *Secunda Convivialis Disceptatio, Uttra Artium, Medicinae an Iuris Civilis Praestat* – 'Which Science, Medicine or Civil Law, is more Excellent' – of 1440). Generally, how-ever, Poggio's distinct – and distinctively radical – legal thought is embedded in his humanist writings, and is, indeed, to a very large extent a function of the philological, rhetorical, and historical elements charac-teristic of his humanism. In order, therefore, to place his legal thought in context, some discussion of the major characteristics of Poggio's humanism is in order.

All students of Poggio's works are struck by a number of characteristics which seem, despite certain fundamental similarities, to set him off from his predecessors. Walser refers repeatedly to his 'inductive', realistic approach, Gutkind speaks of his 'historical relativism', Roedel of his orientation towards historical reality; Charles Trinkaus, in a more recent work, emphasizes Poggio's 'historical and social realism', and Riccardo Fubini notes 'the indubitably "Epicurean" (or sceptical, relativistic) propensities'.[5] There is indeed in Poggio's work a kind of consistent

---

[4] Poggio came to Florence in the late 1390s, and while studying seems to have earned his way as a copyist, and this in turn commended him to Salutati (he had already developed the late Carolingian cursive for which he would later be famous: see Walser, pp. 11–12, and Gutkind, 'P. B.s geistige Entwicklung', pp. 554–5). Unlike Bruni, he did not study Greek with Chrysoloras, but picked it up later (somewhat imperfectly, as his translation of Xenophon's *Cyropaideia* later indicated [see Walser, p. 230, and Poggio's discussion of the problems of translating from the Greek, *Epist.*, IX, xxv, xxvi]), as he did the rudiments of Hebrew.

[5] Walser, p. 250, for Poggio's 'rein Induktiv' method, a..d *passim*. Gutkind talks at length about 'die historische relativierte Erkenntnisgesinnung Poggios' (p. 561), and Roedel stresses Poggio's rootedness 'nella realtà storica', his 'realismo sensuale' (pp. 56–57). Trinkaus in *'In Our Image': Humanity and Divinity in Italian Humanist Thought*, 2 vols. (London, 1970), I, p. 270, calls Poggio's 'historical and social realism' a 'true product of his humanist scholarship'; with Manetti, if differently, Poggio's works reveal 'a distinctly Renaissance quality in their stress upon the actuality of human behaviour or achievement.' Trinkaus here presents an interpretation of Poggio's thought similar to the one found in his early *Adversity's Noblemen: The Italian Humanists on Happiness* (New York, 1940, re-issued 1965); both works turn largely on

nominalism, a tendency, even a drive, to view reality, past and present, in terms of concrete particulars. This thrust, also evident in Bruni, in Poggio is pushed to an extreme, and one major result is a kind of integration of all human experience, an implicit assumption of the secular relatedness and comparability, indeed, the interchangeability, of that experience.

This tendency is manifest very early in Poggio's work, and can be seen in his dispute (1405–6) with Salutati regarding the relative merits of Petrarch and the 'learned ancients'. While Poggio's letter has not survived, Salutati in his first reply paraphrased his pupil's position, that no comparison could in fact be made between the great classical writers and famous contemporaries.[6] Salutati was moved to reply at length, using first Luigi Marsili and then Petrarch as models of the conjunction of Christian wisdom and literary eloquence. For Salutati, Petrarch was superior to the ancients, because, in addition to being able to write eloquently in both prose and poetry, he was a Christian, and hence possessed a truth unavailable to the pagans. Poggio's position on this point was to deny that possession of the 'truth' necessarily meant literary superiority.[7]

> Poggio's late *De Miseria Humanae Conditionis* (1455), producing a rather dark picture of Poggio and his concerns. See also Fubini ('Il "teatro del mondo"...in P. B.', cited in n.1 above), p. 28. Nancy Struever, stressing the comparative nature of rhetorical method in Poggio, observes (the context is a discussion of the *Facetiae*, but the point is generally applicable) 'The development of the free sceptical spirit with its surgical skill in separating out the established hypocrisies of society...' (*The Language of History in the Renaissance*, pp. 186, 192.) Eugenio Garin, in his discussion of Poggio's defense of acquisitiveness in the *De Avaritia*, his earliest systematic treatise (1428–9), cites approvingly Filelfo's portrayal of Poggio's praise of the 'concretezza della *res*, che sono quasi le tangibile espressione dell' attività umana' (*Commentationes Florentinae de Exilio*, ms. Bibl. Naz. di Fir., II, ii, 70, ed. Garin, *Testi inediti e rari* [Florence, 1949]: *L'Umanesimo italiano*, 2nd ed., pp. 55–6, 55. n.1) (Filelfo, of course, was Poggio's enemy, and his presentation of Poggio in the *Commentationes* is generally less than flattering.) What is important here is that these attempts to characterize Poggio's thought generally (many others could be adduced) share a common emphasis upon its striking realism, concreteness, and historicity.
>
> [6] F. Novati, ed., *L'Epistolario di C.S.*, 4 vols. (Rome, 1891–1911, IV, XIV.19.126–45; 22, 158–70 [1405–6]. See also Jerrold Seigel's *Rhetoric and Philosophy in Renaissance Humanism* (Princeton, 1968), pp. 88–98. Baron's approach to the exchange should also be noted (*Crisis*, 1-vol. ed., pp. 264–7; 2-vol. ed., I, pp. 238–40, II, 238–9). Baron's point of view is close to that expressed by Bruni's 'Niccolò Niccoli' in his *Dialogus* [II], [1402–4]: see 'Ad Petrum Paulum Histrum Dialogus', in Garin, ed., *Prosatori latini del Quattrocento* [Milan and Naples, 1952], pp. 44–99, at 94). See too Walser, pp. 32–6, and Ronald G. Witt, *Hercules at the Crossroads. The Life, Works, and Thought of Coluccio Salutati* (Durham, N.C., 1983), pp. 266–71, 401–05, 422–3, where the exchange is placed in the context of the increasingly religious emphases of the last decade of Salutati's life.
>
> [7] Novati, IV, 145. Seigel, *op. cit.*, p. 97, alludes to the possibly sceptical implications of Poggio's attitude towards truth as a function of faith; what seems at stake here is, rather, Salutati's assertion of Petrarch's literary supremacy *because* of his Christianity;

In addition to the by now common humanist assumption of the intimate connection between thought and expression, form and content, Poggio's position in the controversy also implies a rejection of the traditionalist sense of a gulf between antiquity and Christianity, of a kind of ideological dividing-line or buffer between two world-views, the former of which being devoid of ultimate truth is necessarily inferior to the latter. Here Poggio, although close to Bruni, characteristically tends to push the principle further, to etch it more sharply.

Poggio's tendency to view experience and thought, past and present, as essentially 'equatable' realities is also clear in two other early pieces, his letters, dating from his stay at the Council of Constance, describing the baths of Aargau, near Zurich, and the burning of the Hussite heretic Jerome of Prague.[8] In the spring of 1416, during his manuscript-hunting travels through Germany and Burgundy, Poggio and his small party stopped at the baths near Zurich. The public bathing made a strong impression on Poggio, and lead him to write an essay which is surely one of the finest pieces of early Quattrocento cultural analysis.[9]

The letter, to Niccoli in Florence, opens with Poggio stating his desire to 'describe the mores of these people, and their custom of bathing.'[10] Men and women bathe nude in the Swiss baths, joyfully and without any shame.[11] Poggio remarks that this reminds him of that place 'in which the first man, which the Hebrews called Gamedon, was created, that is, the Garden of Delights. For if pleasure can constitute a blessed life, I do not see what is lacking in this place for perfect and complete pleasure.'[12] Here the monks and priests honestly give themselves over to pleasure, and all are of one mind, to flee sadness and seek joy; and

this the young Poggio would not accept (one is reminded here of Bruni's insistence on the beauty and human truth of Plato and Aristotle in his *Prologus in Phaedonem Platonis* [1404–5], in Hans Baron, ed., *Leonardo Bruni Aretino Humanistisch-Philosophische Schriften* [Leipzig and Berlin, 1928], pp. 3–4).

[8] Fubini, ed., *Opera*, I, pp. 297–301, 'Pogii Florentini de balneis prope Thuregum sitis descriptio ad Nicolaum suum' (Spring, 1416), and pp. 301–5, 'Pogii Florentini de Hieronymi haeretici obitu et supplicio descriptio ad Leonardum Aretinum' (29 May, 1416). See now Helene Harth, 'Eine kritische Ausgabe der Privatbriefe Poggio Bracciolinis', *Wolfenbütteler Renaissance-Mitteilungen*, II-III (1978), pp. 72–5, and her new edition of Poggio Bracciolini, *Lettere*, I, *Lettere a Niccolò Niccoli* (Florence, 1984).

[9] I know of no other short treatise or discussion in the early Quattrocento which adopts such a consistently 'comparative' cultural perspective. Just as in the exchange over Petrarch Poggio sought to compare contemporary and ancient writers on the same basis, so in the letter on the baths Roman, Northern and Florentine 'mores' are viewed comparatively (and so, in the discussion the heretic Jerome of Prague, heretic, Christian, and pagan will be viewed on a kind of 'neutral' comparative basis).

[10] *Opera*, I, p. 297.

[11] *Ibid.*, I, pp. 298–9.

[12] *Ibid.*, I, p. 300.

despite the size of the group (almost a thousand people) there is no discord, no dissidence, no abusiveness.[13]

Men and women take up with one another, even those married, yet there is no jealousy; indeed, the very term ('zelotypus') is lacking since, the thing being absent, the word does not exist.[14] This then leads Poggio to compare his subjects' mores with those of his fellow-countrymen.[15] The Swiss live contentedly from day to day, enjoying their possessions, not worrying about the future, bearing whatever comes with a good spirit, and having as their motto the simple 'Vixit dum vixit bene.'[16]

The second letter of this period, describing the trial and execution at Constance of a Hussite heretic, Jerome of Prague, while dealing with a quite different subject, displays the same kind of observational, comparative approach. Poggio tells Bruni, to whom he is writing, that he is moved to describe the event both 'because of its seriousness and because of the man's eloquence and learning...I have never seen anyone who approached more closely to the eloquence of the ancients, whom we so greatly admire.'[17] Jerome in Poggio's version of the event rejects the right of his judges to judge him, arguing that 'you are men, not gods, not immortal, but mortal, subject to indecision, error, deception, deceit, to being lead astray',[18] and refutes the charges laid against him. He places himself within the context of the history of persecution, both classical and Biblical (Socrates, Plato and Zeno were persecuted, as was Moses, 'liberator of his people and legislator'), and shows too how the Apostles were persecuted, 'not as good men, but as seditious agitators of the people, scorners of the gods, and doers of evil deeds.'[19]

The heretic then goes on to say that he came to the Council willingly, that it was the custom of the doctors of the Church to debate questions of faith not in order to harm it, but better to arrive at truth: 'So Augustine and Jerome differed, not only believing diversely, but even appositely, and yet there was no suspicion of heresy between them.'[20] Yet now, while his audience expected him to recant, Jerome went on to maintain his innocence, and even to praise Hus, calling him a 'good, just and holy man.'[21] Jerome is then condemned to death and goes courageously and almost gladly, to meet the flames: 'O man worthy of human memory forever!...none of the Stoics ever sought out their death

[13] *Ibid.*   [14] *Ibid*, I, p. 301.
[15] *Ibid.* These lines should be read against Antonio's defense of avarice in the *De Avaritia* of 1428; see below pp. 126-7.   [16] Ibid.
[17] *Ibid.*, I, p. 301. Poggio was evidently not in Constance when John Hus was burned; there is no mention of the event in his correspondence.
[18] *Ibid.*, I, p. 302.
[19] *Ibid.*, I, pp. 303-4. Again, the lumping together of pagan, Hebrew, and Christian martyrs is typical.
[20] *Ibid.*, I, p. 304.   [21] *Ibid.*

Poggio Bracciolini

with so constant and strong a soul...nor did even Socrates drink the hemlock as willingly as he sought the fire.'[22]

What has struck most critics about this letter is Poggio's evident sympathy for a professed heretic (Bruni too noted this and was quick to get off a warning to his younger friend).[23] What is important for our purposes here is the underlying manner, or 'method', of treating the event.[24] Poggio's Jerome likens himself to earlier martyrs, classical, Biblical, and Christian, while Poggio compares him with classical orators and with Socrates. The approach to the whole problem is dispassionate and historical, and has in common with the letter on the Aargau baths a certain analytically detached, observational quality.

Both the 1416 letters and the exchange in 1405–6 with Salutati turn on a clear sense of the historicity of things, a kind of natural 'placing' of individuals and concepts (Petrarch and the ancients are indeed worlds apart, the Swiss bathers are interesting precisely because of their sheer 'otherness', Jerome of Prague, a Bohemian heretic, reminds one of Moses and Socrates).[25] Yet at the same time, it is precisely this historical specificity which provides Poggio with a common ground for comparative and judgemental analysis (literary evaluations of the pagans should not be colored by religious considerations, the mores of Swiss bathers throw light on contemporary Italy, and the heretic Jerome is *like* Socrates, Moses and the Apostles even while different from them). A sense of human and historical particularity becomes the basis for a kind of 'historicist' awareness, which becomes even more marked as Poggio's thought matures, assuming the form of a general, if not always clearly articulated, method.[26]

[22] *Ibid.*, II, pp. 304–5.
[23] Cited in Fubini, 'Il "Teatro del Mondo"...di Poggio', p. 21, n.46. Nancy Struever notes that, concerning Jerome of Prague, 'Poggio can accept the Church's charge of heresy without letting it affect his judgment that Jerome expresses genuine religious feeling, and that such an expression has great meaning for his contemporaries' (*The Language of History*, p. 189). See, generally, Renée N. Watkins, 'The Death of Jerome of Prague: Divergent Views', *Speculum*, LXII (1967), pp. 104–29.
[24] Gutkind, 'P. B.s geistige Entwicklung', p. 574, refers to Poggio's 'religiös indifferenter Relativismus.' It should be noted, however, that Poggio in the text is careful to maintain a certain distance from Jerome, despite his admiration for his courage and eloquence: *Opera*, I, pp. 301, 305. The *veritas–doctrina* distinction has already been encountered in the 1405–6 Petrarch controversy.
[25] A minor element in Poggio's rather awed stance toward Jerome is perhaps precisely the fact that he is a Bohemian; not being an Italian, his eloquence is even more impressive than would otherwise be the case. Also, he was a cleric, which, given Poggio's general attitude towards the religious (see his *Contra Hypocritas Dialogus* [1448], *Opera*, II, pp. 43–80, for a fair, if late, example) must have made him all the more remarkable. See G. Vallese, 'Umanisti e frati nella prima metà del'400: P. B. e il contra hypocritas', *Italica*, XXIII (1946), pp. 147–51, and Cesare Vasoli's recent article, cited in n.27 below.
[26] The observations of Donald R. Kelley's *Foundations of Modern Historical Scholarship*:

FREDERICK KRANTZ

An examination of three important works, one comparatively early, the second written at the height of his Curial career, and the third from the later period of his Florentine chancellorship, is necessary before we can examine Poggio's explicitly juridical thought. The *De Avaritia* (1428–9), Poggio's earliest important work, has one of its interlocutors espousing what some critics have taken to be a strikingly radical defense and justification of avariciousness and of the desire for wealth generally; the *De Nobilitate* (1439–40) is perhaps the most systematic Quattrocento examination of a much-vexed problem; and the *Historia Florentina* (unfinished at Poggio's death in 1459) is an explicitly historical text, clearly undertaken as the crowning effort of his life's work.

Poggio wrote the dialogue *De Avaritia* in 1428, dedicating it to the Venetian humanist Francesco Barbaro, to whom it was sent a year later. Its immediate cause was Poggio's reaction to the preaching in Rome of San Bernardino of Siena, following his acquittal there on charges of heresy related to his *Nome di Gesù* cult.[27] Taking up a theme already touched upon by Bruni, Poggio, arguing *in utramque partem* in good Academic fashion, examines the nature and consequences of the desire for gain.[28] One of the interlocutors, Bartolomeo da Montepulciano,

Language, Law, and History in the French Renaissance (London and New York, 1970), p. 46. concerning Lorenzo Valla's 'historicism' – his '...recognition of individuality, of...temporal change, and of a kind of cultural relativism...' – fit Poggio as well. As has been demonstrated for Bruni (see F. Krantz, *Florentine Humanist Legal Thought*, 1375–1450 [unpub. doctoral diss., Dept. of History, Cornell Univ., 1971], Ch. II, 'Leonardo Bruni: Philology, History, and Law', pp. 99–205, philological method and an historical approach to law were emerging in Florence before and independently of Valla, and are highly developed by Poggio as well. On the problem of historicism, see Friedrich Meinecke, *Die Entstehung des Historismus* (Munich, 1965, orig. ed. 1936); see also Carlo Antoni, *Dallo storicismo alla sociologia* (Florence, 1940; Eng. trans., Detroit, 1959). Kelley sums up its elements in terms directly applicable to Poggio as 'humanism, individuality, pluralism, relativism, and mutability' *op. cit.*, p. 4) and Franco Gaeta, referring to Valla, defines the consequences of early 'historicism' nicely: for Valla – and again, as for Poggio – both Aristotle and *Digest* 'sono nella storia, sono produzioni storiche...'. (*Lorenzo Valla. Filologia e storia nell'umanesimo italiano* [Naples, 1955], p. 126) See too Salvatore I. Comporeale, *Lorenzo Valla: Umanesimo e teologia* (Florence, 1972), *passim*. Nancy Struever shrewdly observes that, while for Bruni 'the key antinomy...was private vs. public, it is the contrast of *labilis–stabilis* in Poggio' (*The Language of History*, p. 164).
[27] San Bernardino's sermons evidently made a serious impression on some of Poggio's Curial colleagues, prompting his reply: see Walser, pp. 128–34, and J. W. Oppel, 'Poggio, San Bernardino of Siena and the Dialogue "On Avarice"', *Renaissance Quarterly*, xxx (1977), pp. 564–87; for the dialogue's relation to Poggio's life-long anti-monastic preoccupations, see Cesare Vasoli, 'Poggio e la polemica antimonastica', in *Poggio Bracciolini 1380–1980*, pp. 163–205. On San Bernardino, see *Bernardino predicatore nella società del suo tempo* (Todi, 1976, no ed.); R. Roedel, 'P. B. nel quinto centenario della morte', pp. 55–7, gives examples of contemporary views on wealth.
[28] On the utility of wealth, see Bruni's 'Praefatio in Libros Oeconomicorum [Pseudo-] Aristotelis' (Baron, *Schriften*, pp. 120–1) and *Epist.*, V.iii. See too n.34 below.

126

mirroring San Bernardino's traditionalist teachings, denounces avariciousness as an evil thing, full of fraud and malevolence, rendering man
wicked and cruel and an enemy of common utility.[29] Antonio Loschi
replies, maintaining that not only is avariciousness natural, but that
without it those things essential to the preservation of human society
would be destroyed. 'For what all desire, should be considered to issue
from nature, and to be owed to her suasion.' Everyone desires more than
sufficiency – 'Therefore avarice is natural.' Cities are built by those
adept at conserving the human race, not by the inert and larval; and if
they did not produce more than their needs, we would have to labor in
the fields. After all, how engage in pious and charitable acts, how give
to another, when one has only enough for oneself?[30]

And beyond the naturalness and necessity of the desire for wealth in
terms of the individual, what else are cities, republics, provinces and
kingdoms – 'if you perceive rightly' – than a kind of 'public workshop
for gain'?[31] Indeed, wherever one looks, there are proofs of both private
and public greed, such that refuting the avaricious means holding the
whole world to be reprehensible, and that everyone's morals and way of
life must be changed. For the desire for wealth is so extensive that
avarice should be considered a virtue, not a vice, and whoever, as a
result, becomes wealthier, should be the more honored.[32]

Of course, the *De Avaritia* as 'Academic' dialogue turns on the
expression of conflicting views, and Antonio's striking position (clearly
the dramatic focus of the piece) is countered by the other interlocutors.[33]
One need not commit the 'intentional fallacy' and uncritically identify

[29] *Opera*, I, pp. 4–7; also see Eugenio Garin, *Prosatori latini del quattrocento* (Milan and
Naples, 1952), pp. 248–301 for an edition of the main body of the work; an English
translation is available in Benjamin G. Kohl and Ronald G. Witt, eds., *The Earthly
Republic. Italian Humanists on Government and Society* (Philadelphia, 1978), pp. 241–89.

[30] *Opera*, I, p. 13. Poggio's identification of the 'natural' with 'what everyone desires'
is extended in the *De Miseria Humanae Conditionis* (1455) to law: 'naturae legem, hoc
est sensus nostros'. The juxtaposition of what might be termed urban 'surplus
production' with rural 'sufficiency production' is striking. It is tempting to see here
an early, and in Italian terms quite remarkable, sense of the economic distinction
between a still-'feudal' agrarian world and the proto-'capitalist' realm of urban
production and exchange. For a discussion of the complex general issues involved in
conceptualising the Italian late-medieval and Renaissance economy, see Frederick
Krantz and Paul Hohenberg, eds., *Failed Transitions to Modern Industrial Society:
Renaissance Italy and Seventeenth Century Holland* (Montreal, 1974), Introduction,
and especially pp. 1–34.

[31] *Opera*, I, pp. 13–14, with the Poggian 'si recte animadvertas'.   [32] *Ibid.* and p. 15.

[33] On the *De Avaritia* as dialogue, and Poggio's use of the form in terms of a vision of
the freedom of discourse and 'the independence of truth from individual ethical
limitations', see David Marsh, *The Quattrocento Dialogue. Classical Tradition and
Humanist Innovation* (Cambridge, Mass. and London, 1980), pp. 11, 38–54. Insofar
as the conclusions of humanist dialogues are concerned, Marsh notes (p.11) that they
do not 'establish an unchallengeable finality'.

Antonio with Poggio in order to sense the importance of the issues drawn here. For our purposes the *De Avaritia* is crucial because it turns on a sharpening of the interpretive techniques already evident in the earlier letters. Received opinion, classical and Christian, on the subject is compared with contemporary 'reality' and what is 'natural', in a context reflecting Poggio's 'civic' values.[34] Antonio's discourse assumes the individual and his observed mores as the focus of attention, and a kind of structural parallelism is also assumed between individual and institutional–public patterns of behavior. What is 'natural' is strictly utilitarian: it is that which is done by most people most of the time, and in his attack on San Bernardino's preaching and the avariciousness of clerics pagan materials are as much grist for Poggio's mill as are those of his Christian contemporaries.

Twelve years later Poggio turned from the problem of wealth to the related question of nobility. In the *De Nobilitate*, a dialogue set in Florence, Poggio himself, his close friend Niccolò Niccoli, and Lorenzo de'Medici, the brother of Cosimo, discuss the nature of nobility. Niccoli quickly strikes the typically Poggian theme: if one examines the opinions and usages of men, nobility will be found to have no possible basis, for 'While the name is found among all peoples, the thing itself always differs.'[35] Since nobility would surely be considered a virtue, rather than a vice, it should satisfy the minimal conditions governing true virtue, that is, it should be one and the same thing everywhere, and should not vary with usage: but this is not so, for examples of 'nobility' are diverse and mutually contrary: Even the Italians, from whom '*humanitas, virtus* and all reason and discipline of right living flow to the other peoples', differ markedly among themselves in this regard.[36] And the nobilities of

---

[34] Antonio's defense of avarice is situated within a clearly 'civic' context, the praise of those contributing to the 'conservationem generis humanis', to the 'conservatio civitatis'. Bruni had already defended *liberalitas* and the *vita activa* (see his Pseudo-Aristotelian *Oeconomicus* 'Preface'; wealth is also discussed in the *Isagogicon Moralis Disciplinae* [1421–4]). Characteristically, where Bruni asked 'Quid avaritiae?' and answered that a brake must be imposed upon it, that *liberalitas* is the goal (see Baron, *Schriften*, pp. 31–2), Poggio has Antonio make a virtue of the vice, seeing in it a kind of model of the social virtue of acquisitiveness generally. Cesare Vasoli ('Poggio e la polemica antimonastica', pp. 181–3) places the dialogue, and Poggio, squarely within the Florentine civic tradition.

[35] *De Nobilitate Liber (Opera*, I, pp. 64–83 [1440], p. 66. This formulation recalls the earlier discussion of the absence of the term 'jealous [husband]', *zelotypus*, among the Swiss, because they lack the reality it describes. Poggio generally gauges language against the given thing or concept to which it refers; meaning changes as its concrete referents change, which implies a kind of historical approach to language as well (see also below, nn. 106 and 128).

[36] *De Nob.*, I, p. 67. See I, pp. 67–9 for a striking 'sociological' comparison of the Neapolitan, Roman, Florentine, Genoese, and Venetian 'nobilities'.

other nations – Germans, French, English, Spanish, Byzantines – differ little from the variety evident in Italy. Rulers everywhere, from Pope to Emperor, kings and princes, confer nobility with scraps of parchment, as if a few words and a bit of wax really meant anything.[37] Such contrariety demonstrates that the concept is without any firm and stable basis.[38]

Lorenzo responds to this attack on nobility by likening nobility to law, which although it varies is universal and necessary, and to custom generally, 'magistra morum', which while exhibiting local variants can also be seen to have certain uniform elements.[39] Thus nobility, while varying, is judged by all to exist either in ample patrimony or honorable life, in freedom from work or in praise of martial valor, in a magnificent mode of living or in a dignity higher than that of others.[40] Niccoli rejects this 'social' line of argument, noting that wealth often corrupts, office is abused, and that the children of old and honest families are often lazy and reprobate. Indeed, nobility is not something extrinsic, but is rather a function of one's own efforts, one's own virtue; 'nobility' as Lorenzo uses the term is in fact nothing, and is unrelated to the true goods of life.[41]

Lorenzo then advances Aristotle's dictum from the *Politica*, that nobility consists in the possession of virtue and inherited wealth, adding that one opposing such wisdom would be deemed foolish. Niccoli rejects this too, refusing to bend to an 'authority' with whom he disagrees; besides, Aristotle in the *Politica* is not speaking his own mind, but rather is reporting common opinion, 'for in the *Ethica*, where he expresses that which he feels to be true, he calls that man generous who by nature discerns truth and seeks the good...this he calls true and perfect nobility.'[42] True virtue consists in action, efficacious action, 'and it therefore follows that nobility resides in that which employs the functions of virtue...I call him noble who is resplendent on the basis of his own

[37] *Ibid.*, I, 68–9.
[38] *Ibid.*, I., p. 69.
[39] *Ibid.*, I, 69. On Poggio's use of dialogue generally, see F. Tateo, 'Il dialogo "realistico" di Poggio Bracciolini', in *Tradizione e realtà nell'umanesimo italiano* (Bari, 1967), pp. 251–77, and David Marsh, *The Quattrocento Dialogue*, pp. 38–54. Also see Tateo, *op. cit.*, 'La disputa della nobiltà', pp. 355–89, and P. O. Kristeller, 'Introduzione' in V. Branca, ed., *Lauro Quirini umanista* (Florence, 1977 – Fondazione Giorgio Cini, 'Civiltà Veneziana', Saggi, 23), pp. 21–42.
[40] *Opera*, I, p. 70.
[41] *Ibid.*
[42] *Ibid.*, I, pp. 74–5: 'Fateor Nicholaus inquit istum principem appellari Philosophorum, sed tamen nulla me cuisvis impediet autoritas, quin quod mihi simile vero videatur et loquar, et sentiam...' The interpretation of Aristotle is a good example of Poggio's independent stance towards his classical sources generally.

virtues, not he who enumerates his excellent parents.'[43] Citing the Stoics and Plato, 'the prince and author of [philosophical] wisdom', Niccoli concludes that

nobility is a kind of splendor issuing from virtue, which adorns its possessors whatever their social condition... For we deserve praise and nobility on the basis of our own, and not another's, merits, and through those actions which issue from our own will... Socrates was not a patrician, and Philosophy did not receive Plato noble, but made him so. Spirit makes him noble to whom, of whatever condition, it is permitted to rise above Fortune.[44]

Poggio's method in the *De Nobilitate* is, due allowance being made for the rhetorical dialectics of the dialogue as form, once again primarily historical. The examination of the contradictory concrete forms 'nobility' takes leads to the conclusion that the reality of the concept is so diverse that it is quite useless as a normative description of a general social class. True nobility is a function of virtue itself, and virtue is the autonomous product of an 'active' life in which learning and goodness are combined, and in relation to which birth, place, and wealth are largely irrelevant.[45] Thus, historical method in the *De nobilitate* is not simply 'relativistic', but is linked to the affirmation of an ideal of human dignity and worth; historical investigation here becomes the basis for a 'destructive-constructive' critique of received opinion, classical and contemporary, in the interest of this ideal.[46]

---

[43] *Ibid.*, I, p. 75.

[44] *Ibid.*, I, pp. 79–80: Of Diogenes Laertius' quadrapartite definition of nobility (*Vita Platonis*), Niccoli prefers the fourth, 'qui non aliena, sed sua virtus et animi magnitudo nobilitatem donarit...'.

[45] On one level, the *De Nobilitate* reflects the 'career open to talents' ideology of Bruni's *Laudatio* and his *Oratio Funebris* for Nanni degli Strozzi (1428). On another level, Poggio is concerned as well to defend the contemplative life, without, however, denying the excellence of civic involvement (*Opera*, I, p. 82, an argument not dissimilar from Bruni's view twenty-five years earlier, in the *Cicero Novus*, that study and commitment are mutually beneficial [see Baron, ed., *Schriften*, pp. 113–20, at p. 115]). Indeed, Poggio's general emphasis throughout the treatise on the necessity of implementing virtue 'in actionibus', calls to mind the teacher of both men, Coluccio Salutati (see his *De Nobilitate Legum et Medicinae*, 8.19–20).

[46] It is important to note that the basic attack on Lorenzo's defense of nobility is the historical-'comparative' demonstration of the concept's evident contradictions; the critique of Aristotle, and the appeal to Plato, come late in the work and are secondary. The defense of human freedom, and the emphasis on will as the source of victory over external circumstances, are central elements in all of Poggio's writings (cf. especially the defense of individual freedom against the buffeting of Fortuna in the *Historiae de Varietate Fortunae* [1442/3–1448], *passim;* and the formulation in Poggio's *Oratio in Funere Laurentii de Medicis* [1440], *Opera*, I, pp. 278–86, at p. 286: 'Nam dum in mundo sumus probamur quotidie in acie'). See the observations of Riccardo Fubini on the *De Varietate* in his 'Il "Teatro del Mondo"...di Poggio', p. 63.

After his return to Florence in 1453 as chancellor of the Republic, Poggio, with Bruni's example clearly in mind, began to work on his last important piece, the *Historia Florentina*.[47] He had earlier thought of writing a history of Venice, a resolve which would issue later, in a period of disenchantment with Florentine affairs, in his 'Oration in Praise of the Republic of Venice' (a kind of turning inside-out of Bruni's *Laudatio Urbis Florentinae*),[48] and he had throughout his life been interested in history, both as a literary form and as a central element in the understanding of human events. We have already seen the gradual emergence of a kind of historical method in Poggio's earlier works; in the *Historia* this method, and its consequences, assumes a particularly clear form.[49]

While largely a continuation of Bruni's *History*, which had closed in 1402 with Florence's triumph over Giangaleazzo Visconti, Poggio initially recapitulates Bruni's story, opening with a short discussion of Florence's ancient beginnings, and then moving quickly to 1350, where a detailed narrative begins (a narrative which, for the fifty-two years down to 1402, is also a kind of [rhetorical] competition with Bruni).[50]

[47] I have used the first printed edition of the work, Jp. Baptista Recanati, ed., Jacobi Pogii Florentini, *Historia Florentina* (Venice, 1715, reprinted in Fubini, ed., *P. B. Opera Omnia*, II, pp. 85–480); the Recanati edition is reproduced in Muratori, *RRIS*, xx (1731). In referring to the text, I shall give both the 'book' and the pagination of the 1715 and the page of the *Opera Omnia* editions, for easier reference. While never achieving the eminence of Bruni's *History*, Poggio's work became a well-known part of the Florentine historiographic tradition (see generally Rubinstein's 'P. B. cancelliere' for contemporary interest in and use of the work, down to and including Machiavelli, and Eugenio Garin's 'Presentazione' in Leonardo Bruni and Poggio Bracciolini, *Storie fiorentine* [Arezzo, 1980], which reprints the Venice, 1476 translation by Poggio's son, Jacopo Bracciolini).

[48] *Oratio in Laudem Rei Publicae Venetorum* (Opera, II, pp. 925–37, based on Firenze, *Bibl. Naz.*, cod. Magl. XXVII. 65, cc. 1r-14v). I accept Walser's dating (p. 291) of the text as 1459; Rubinstein's attempt ('P. B. cancelliere'), on palaeographic grounds, to date it 1449 (1450 Florentine style) seems inconclusive.

[49] Like Bruni and other humanists, Poggio's historical practice differs from his explicit conceptualization of 'history': see the 'Proem' to his translation of Xenophon's *Cyropaedeia* (Walser, p. 230, n.1, citing *Cod. Laur.* 45, 18), *Epist.*, X.xix, 39–40 ('...non enim historiam Cyri conscribere [Xenophon] voluit, sed optimum principem, qualis nunquam fuit, effingere') and the later *Epist.* XI.xxxii, 103–5 [post-1453], where he notes that the portraits of Cyrus painted by Xenophon and Justinus are diverse, '...alterum non ad veritatem historiae, sed ad normam justi imperii, ut refert Cicero, locutum; alterum historiae veritatem secutum esse.' For Bruni on 'history', see Mehus, ed., *Epist.*, 2.VIII.ix.112: 'Aliud est enim historia, aliud laudatio. Historia quidem veritatem sequi debet, laudatio vero multa supra veritatem extollit...'

[50] For the element of competition with Bruni in Poggio's work, see Rubinstein, *art cit.*, p.224 ('l'occasione eccellente per gareggiare col suo predecessore la cui opera era ormai riconosciuta come "storia ufficiale" di Firenze'). Donald J. Wilcox finds Poggio's *History* more 'psychological' and less 'institutional' than Bruni's (*The Development of Florentine Humanist Historiography in the Fifteenth Century* [Cambridge, Mass.,

FREDERICK KRANTZ

Poggio, unlike Bruni (and perhaps in part for political reasons)[51] limits his history to a narrative of external political events, with the long series of wars against the Visconti, from 1350 to 1427, providing the primary narrative structure, supplemented by the war against Venice and Naples from 1452 to 1454, and ending with the peace proclaimed in 1454. Very importantly, Poggio continues the Brunian theme of Florence as *defensor Tusciae*, emphasizing the Republic as not only defender of Tuscany, but protector of the *libertas Italiae* generally.[52]

The *Historia* opens with a demonstration of Florence's foundation under the Roman Republic, and Bruni's work as well as architectural evidence is cited in support of this view. There follows a narration of the evolution of Florence's republican institutions, from their inception in the constitution of the consuls to the foundation of the 'priores artium' in 1282, which order 'has persevered down to the present day.'[53] Then, in a rapid sketch the period from the 1290s to 1350 is outlined, and the stage is set for the subsequent playing out of the history by the advent, in 1350, of Giovanni Visconti, 'whose soul burned with desire for the imperium of the Etruscans...whence the war began.'[54]

After 1350, Poggio's *History* is the story of Florence's leadership of the struggle against Milanese tyranny down to and beyond the final defeat of the Visconti in 1427. It is a completely 'secular' approach to historical change, the motor of events being construed as the desire for power and domination on the part of the Visconti, which creates a kind of countervailing force in the desire of Florence and other states not to be subjected to conquest. Very interestingly, in the period between the

1969], pp. 130–53); C. Baudi di Vesme, *Brevi considerazione sulla storiografia fiorentina e sul pensiero nel XV secolo* [Turin, 1953], on the other hand, gives Poggio higher marks than Bruni *qua* 'historian'. For an analysis of Bruni's *Historiarum Florentini Populi* and its influence, see Riccardo Fubini, 'Osservazioni sugli "Historiarum Florentini Populi Libri XII" di Leonardo Bruni', in Marina Serena Mazzi and Sergio Raveggi, eds., *Studia di storia medievale e moderna per Ernesto Sestan*, I, Medioevo (Florence, 1980), pp. 403–48.

[51] Rubinstein, *art. cit.*, p. 232. Poggio's relationship with Cosimo de' Medici was good: Cosimo was responsible for Poggio's tax-exemption in 1434, and Poggio was always regarded as an adherent of the Medici faction. The period from late 1454 to early 1458, which saw considerable political turbulence in the city, seems related to the high tax-assessment Poggio received in 1458, despite his earlier exemption (see Walser, pp. 289–90, and n.66 below).

[52] This theme runs throughout the work, finding its final consummation in the very last pages, with the peace guaranteed by Florence and Venice (*H.F.*, VIII, pp. 381–2 [1715 Recanati ed.], pp. 477–8 [Fubini ed.].)

[53] Recanati I, 4/*Opera* II, 100.

[54] *Ibid.*, I, 7/II, 103. Poggio refers here to the Imperial mantle which Giovanni sought to wear, thus tying the conflict in to the earlier Guelph–Ghibelline issue; like Bruni however, he tends to read the Imperial–Papal struggle in terms of power-politics, rather than of 'ideology'.)

defeat of the Visconti in 1427 and the outbreak of war again in 1452, Poggio turns this approach around on the Florentines in his description of the Florentine war against Lucca in 1427; then, in 1452, the same framework is applied to the Venetians and Neapolitans once again.

A few examples will have to suffice here to demonstrate Poggio's historical technique in the *Historia*. In 1375, during a momentary break in the war against Milan, another crisis breaks out, a confrontation with the Papacy. The depredations of Papal agents in areas under Florentine control lead to discussions in the city as to what actions to take.[55] The Priors then call a meeting to debate the issue, and the Gonfalonier, an Aldobrandini, 'putting before all things the safety of the country', speaks in favor of war. '...all things desire liberty...and how much more does man', the Gonfalonier begins, 'whom God, by giving him reason, prudence and intellect, wishes to excel all other beings, and for whom nothing is more excellent than liberty.'[56] He then goes on to draw an analogy between the struggle against the Emperor, and the present struggle against the Church: Florence, which gained her hereditary liberty in driving out Imperial servitude, must now maintain it against sacerdotal wilfulness.[57] Aldobrandino goes on to conclude that everyone recognizes the 'jus gentium', the right to repel force by force, and to go to war all else failing; 'and how much more just it is, to fight for liberty, and to avoid coming under the domination of others.' After his speech, the Eight of War is created, and the 'Otto Santi' War begins.[58]

Poggio's handling of the despatch of the jurist Donato Barbadoro and the scribe Domenico Silvestri as Florentine ambassadors to the Papal court to plead the city's case before the Pope provides further material for this presentation of his historical awareness.[59] Barbadoro's speech to the assembled Curia stresses the hardships imposed upon his city by the

[55] *Ibid.*, II, 47/143 (1375).

[56] *Ibid.*, II, 48/144. Note the reference to the 'superstitious souls' in the passage referred to in n.55, preceding, and here to those who speak in the guise of religion: Poggio in the *Historia*, as elsewhere, tends to have an instrumental, 'Machiavellian' approach to institutionalized religion.

[57] *Ibid.*, II, 50/144. The power and beauty of Poggio's style is most evident in his inserted *conciones*, with their rhetorical arguments *pro* and *con;* little in Bruni compares with his re-created debates. The republican theme struck here is found across his works; see his 1428 letter to the Milanese Duke Filippo Maria (*Epist.*, VIII.i.179–88, at 184) and his denunciation of Caesar as a tyrant in the *Defensiuncula contra Guarinum Veronensem* [1437–8] (*Opera*, II, pp. 367–90, at 370–2). The *Defensiuncula*, following in the footsteps of Bruni's *Laudatio*, is a remarkable attempt to relate socio-political context to literary–intellectual activity, and constitutes an early expression of a kind of cultural history.

[58] Recanati, II, 50/*Opera*, 146. See also p. 25 and n.101 below.

[59] *Ibid.*, II, 56/152 (1376). Poggio here departs from Bruni, who couples another jurist, Alessandro d'Antella, with Barbaro (see Bruni, *Hist.*, VIII, 211, pp. 24–32). See too Rubinstein, *art. cit.*, pp. 223–4.

actions of the Papal vicars, but quickly proceeds to an impassioned defense of Florence's defiance. He maintains that 'nothing is more just, more commendable, than that which is done to defend the liberty of one's country, which encompasses one's home, children, wives, fortune, church and everything human and divine.' The Florentines are compelled to defend themselves not willingly so much as by necessity, and for this reason they should be praised, rather than condemned, by the Pope.[60] Shortly after the audience the Florentines are, nevertheless, condemned by the Pope, and Poggio gives a very clear description of the practical consequences, especially the economic hardships, stemming from the Papal ban.[61] Despite the Papal interdict and its dire economic consequences the Florentines continue the war, seeing to it too that church services continued uninterrupted throughout. In 1378 peace follows Gregory XI's death and Poggio notes that while in Florence this was viewed as miraculous, his own experience and knowledge of history indicate that this kind of conjunction occurs frequently.[62]

The treatment of the Florentine–Papal war can stand as a model for Poggio's technique throughout the *Historia*. Conflict is seen in starkly political and military terms, and its political and economic consequences are carefully delineated. The role of individuals is given full weight, especially rulers' lust for conquest, while no explanatory appeal is made to external causation, divine or occult. 'Ideological' factors are taken into account, obviously where Florence is concerned, especially the communal energies flowing from her desire to retain the freedom bequeathed her from the Etruscans and the Roman Republic. Poggio has a good eye for significant detail, and a sense of the dramatic which makes his history good reading.[63]

[60] Recanati II, 57–8/*Opera*, 153–4. Poggio's handling of the oration is 'tougher', more 'ideological', than Bruni's; and, generally, he shows less respect for both Pope and canon law. He uses the 'natural law' right of repelling unjust force with force throughout the *Historia*, speaking too of the *jus gentium* concerning the necessity for states to keep faith: the use he makes of such concepts is discussed below, p. 142 and n.101.

[61] *Ibid.*, II, 63/159. See also his *De Avaritia* (*Opera*, I, p. 15).

[62] Recanati, II, 76/*Opera*, 172 (1378). See *ibid.*, IV, 152–4/248–50, for similar handling of Giangaleazzo Visconti's death in 1402.

[63] His sensitivity to physical setting and detail is striking and can be seen in a number of other works as well (above all in Book IV of his *Historiae de Varietate Fortunae*, where he gives a remarkable composite account of the travels of the merchant Niccolò Conti [see W. Sensburg, 'P. B. und Niccolò de Conti in ihrer Bedeutung fur die Geographie des Renaissancezeitalters', *Mitteilungen der k. k. geographischen Gesellschaft* (Vienna), XLIX (1906), pp. 257–372, for a study of Poggio's account and its influence, especially through Paolo Toscanelli, on Columbus (pp. 360–1)]); see also for Poggio's ability to use landscape to create psychological mood, the description of the ruins of ancient Rome at the beginning of Book I of the *Historiae de Varietate Fortunae*, and *Epist.* XIII.xxx, pp. 229–39, a letter clearly dating from the post-1456 period, where a storm

At the same time, and unlike Bruni, he has the ability to transcend, at times, his ideological thematics, or at least ironically to turn them around on the Florentines themselves. The clearest example of this is his handling of the discussions prior to the declaration of war against Lucca in 1427 (he is probably helped here by the fact that the major proponent of this war was Rinaldo degli Albizzi, his patron Cosimo's early enemy, and by the fact that the failure of the war itself was the immediate cause of Cosimo's rise to power in 1434). Rinaldo, addressing the assembled communal councils, employs all the rhetorical and 'civic' elements characterizing Barbadoro's speech to Gregory XI prior to the Eight Saints' War. Florence has always done what was necessary to defend her liberty; the war against Lucca will ensure the maintenance of Florentine freedom and, Rinaldo soothingly concludes, it will be neither long nor arduous.[64] Niccolò da Uzzano, a leading political figure in the city at this time, answers Rinaldo. He argues against war, stressing that such things are inherently uncertain: 'men's minds are changeable...much that is unforeseen can occur to lengthen the war and make it more difficult than now seems to be the case.'[65] Human affairs are uncertain, and no one should be too sure of Fortune's favor; and what of other considerations? what if the Sienese should fear for their liberty, and come to the aid of the Lucchese, perhaps bringing others with them? Besides, the war is patently unjust, and victory rarely follows unjust arms.[66] In the debate following the orations, however, 'as often happens, the better part was overcome by the greater', and war as declared, to be followed by all of the dire consequences of which Da Uzzano had warned.[67]

The interesting thing here is the way in which Poggio turns the treatment usually reserved for Florence's enemies around upon the city itself. This lends a kind of dramatic realism to the narrative, while simultaneously reinforcing the general theme of the essential 'openness' of Florence and of her republican traditions (such debate and airing of differences obviously being unthinkable, for instance, at the court of the Milanese tyrant).[68]

which has ravaged the Arno valley stands as a kind of symbol of Poggio's disenchantment with the city's political turbulence.

[64] Recanati VI, 256–9/*Opera*, 352–5 (1429).

[65] *Ibid.*, VI, 259–65/355–61, esp. 262–3/358–9.

[66] *Ibid.*, VI, 263–5/359–60, 277/363. For an analysis of the factional strife leading to the Medici ascendancy in 1434, see Dale Kent, *The Rise of the Medici. Faction in Florence, 1426–1434* (Oxford, 1978), especially pp. 211–52, 234–5.

[67] *Ibid.*, VI, 265/361. Again, one is tempted to see an ironic reference here to Bruni's allusion to the *maior/sanior pars* distinction (in the *Laudatio*, ed. Baron, p. 250), to show that the Florentine constitution ensured similar, rather than antithetical, interests.

[68] Here, as elsewhere, Poggio's expressive abilities must be given adequate weight when comparing his *History* to Bruni's: Poggio's is a more literary, more artful narrative,

When Poggio reaches 1432 in his narrative, he places the coronation of Emperor Sigismund at Rome by Eugene IV in a double perspective: first, in terms of the perversion of a Republican honor by Caesar and his Imperial successors, and second, as a 'new invention' imported into Italy by a German Pope. His handling of Imperial coronation reflects, in turn, his approach to the 'Emperor' and 'Empire' in the *Historia* generally: there, the Emperor is simply a German political factor entering into the Italian political equation, and the Empire is in no sense seen as a legitimate supra-Italian juridical entity.[69]

Poggio's historical method, then, exemplified in the *Historia Florentina*, enables him to 'place' persons and problems in well-defined contexts. Assuming here, as elsewhere, the fundamental secular comparability of all human actions and experience, Poggio tends to draw general conclusions from his materials even as he is sensitive to individual specificity. Employing rhetorical technique, and imbuing his descriptions with a strong visual–metaphorical dimension, Poggio's *Historia* conveys a coherent sense of movement and dynamics, of individuals caught up in historical unfolding. If his *Historia* is, chronologically and 'ideologically', a continuation of Bruni's *Historiarum Florentini Populi*, there is nevertheless a nuanced, distinctly 'Poggian' element constantly at work in it. This is reflected in a certain distancing from the republicanist theme, and is perhaps best expressed by saying that the work verges on being not only a history of *Florence*, but a *history*, as such. In this sense, as in much else, Poggio seems to anticipate Machiavelli.

II

Poggio's *opera* also exhibit an important, and revealing, juridical dimension. Given his own legal training and wide juridical and political experience, this is to be expected.[70] Poggio's legal thought, however,

and his 'inventationes' are generally more dramatic that Bruni's, as is befitting the author of the expressive *Facetiae*, the collection of droll and often pornographic tales, drawing on vernacular traditions, which was one of Poggio's most-read works in the fifteenth and sixteenth centuries. See Francesco Tateo, 'La raccolta delle "Facezie" e lo stile "comico" di Poggio', in *Poggio Bracciolini 1380–1980*, pp. 207–33, and Lionello Sozzi, 'Le "Facezie" e la loro fortuna europea', *ibid.*, pp. 235–59.

[69] Recanati, VII, 298–9/*Opera*, 394–5. See too the earlier (1433) *Epist*, V.vi.15–22.
[70] Poggio's legal experience should be emphasized here. He studied notarial law in the Florentine *Studio*, passing his notarial examination and becoming a member of the *Giudici e notai* guild in 1402 (Martines, *Social World*, pp. 123–4, also has him devoting 'a brief period of legal study at Bologna', seemingly on the basis of Walser's references [pp. 7, n.4, 310, n.1]). Poggio maintained his connection with the judges and notaries, being named in 1439, and again in 1455, first consul of that guild; in January 1456 he and his four sons were enrolled as well in the *Lana* guild. Poggio received the highest

while related to and reflecting his Florentine civic connections, goes well beyond this context, developing into an historicizing critique of contemporary juridical practice and theory. The comparative-historical thrust which characterizes his work generally is especially marked in his observations on law, imparting to this dimension of his thought perhaps the most radical vision of the 'real' nature and dynamics of law before Machiavelli.

Most generally, Poggio shares with Bruni a rejection of (or, perhaps, a simple lack of concern with) the traditionalist, hierarchical philosophy of law characteristic of their teacher, Salutati. Like Bruni, he retains to a certain extent a general emphasis on *aequitas* as a basic criterion of 'good' law, seeing in it primarily the Roman law principle of 'ius suum cuique tribuens.'[71] And, particularly in his orations and more formal works, Poggio maintains the centrality of *iustitia* in human affairs: 'For justice is that virtue which embraces all others. No city, no group of men, no society can long endure without justice. It is indeed a benefit to republics, and conservator of human and divine right.'[72] And again, in his *Oratio in Laudem Legum* (before 1440; 1436?), Poggio makes a similar point: the laws, born together with men themselves, were necessary for the right-reason of living, which without them is impossible.[73]

In a late work of 1456/7 where, outraged by what he considered an

honour, election to the Priorate, in July-August 1455, and he was, of course, active as Chancellor until 1456. Walser's documents, appended to his life of Poggio, indicate a varied legal activity in or in relation to the city throughout Poggio's Curial career, and, of course, his curial activities, where in the course of his career he moved from being a *scriptor penitentiarius* to the office of *scriptor apostolicus* and, finally, before leaving for Florence, where he was *apostolicus secretarius*, involved him in much legal and diplomatic work as well.

71 See the *Oratio in Funere Domine Francisci Cardinalis Florentini Habita* (*Opera*, I, 252–61 [1444?], at 257, and *Historia Florentina*, II, 57/153. Generally, however, Poggio uses the *aequitas* concept far less frequently, and with far less specificity, than does Bruni. This is particularly true of his *Historia Florentina*, which, quite unlike Bruni's, does not, as we shall see, insist upon equity as the cardinal feature of Florentine institutions and legal process. On Bruni's use of *aequitas*, see Ronald G. Witt, *Coluccio Salutati and His Public Letters* (Geneva, 1976), pp. 86–7, and 'The Concept of Republican Liberty in Italy', cited in n.94 below; for the fundamental role of *aequitas* in Salutati's legal thought, see F. Krantz, diss. cit. above, Ch. 2, pp. 26–98.

72 *Oratio in Funere Laurentii de Medicis* (*Opera*, I, pp. 278–86 [1440]), at p. 284. Also see *Hist. Flor.*, II, 57/153; *Defens. contra Guar.*, I, 370; *Epist.*, VII.ii, p. 182.

73 For the *Oratio in Laudem Legum*, I have used the critical edition prepared by Eugenio Garin in his *La disputa delle arti nel quattrocento* (Florence, 1947), pp. 12–15 (and reprinted in Fubini, ed., *Opera*, II, pp. 825–9). The beginning of the quoted passage sounds quite Machiavellian: 'Parum foris proficiunt arma, nisi vigeant domi leges.' My own examination of this text leads me to date it earlier than does Garin, ca. 1436 rather than 'before 1440'; this may be the inaugural dissertation for a candidate in civil law which Walser (pp. 253–4) mentions Poggio as having written.

unfair tax assessment, Poggio condemns the Florentine magistrates for their lack of *fides*, he returned to the same theme. Never, he says, was there a people so barbarous and wild 'that they did not maintain the laws of good faith in the holiest fashion'; *fides* is 'the basis of justice, and without it, no virtue can exercise its function.'[74] And, finally, *iustitia* as the 'foundation of the polity' is made the basis of Poggio's *In Laudem Rei Publicae Venetorum* (1459), a work in which Venice becomes a kind of mirror-image of Florence for the disillusioned chancellor and which concludes, '...considering the causes behind this ancient and enduring republic, one above all occurs to me; justice, which Aristotle calls the most certain foundation of republics [*Ethica*, V.1.13], is honored in that city above all others, there the laws, and not men, rule.'[75]

Justice, then, is seen in these works as a fundamental, indispensable social framework, and equity is viewed as its essential normative basis. It should be noted, however, that the orations and the anti-Florentine invective of 1456/7 adopt an essentially static perspective, justice here being seen as a given; when, as we shall see shortly, justice and law are viewed dynamically, as part of a larger historical process, Poggio's historical realism quickly comes into play, with results diametrically opposed to the rhetorical *laudationes* we have so far been dealing with.

Poggio also develops another critical distinction (already made generally by Petrarch, and consistently developed by Bruni), between the *studia humanitatis* as a professional discipline with its own method and claims to wisdom, and law as a *scientia*. On one level, this takes the form of comparing the 'end' or purpose of the *studia humanitatis* with that of the legal profession (Poggio, in a by-now typical humanist *topos*, characteristically divorces jurisprudence as a profession from justice as a fundamental social necessity). In the *De Infelicitate Principum* of 1441, as in the *De Nobilitate* of the same period, the 'disciplines' of the liberal arts and the *studia humanitatis* alone are held to perfect man and to teach true virtue.[76] And in a letter of 1436 Poggio affirms that such studies 'are sacred, worthy of worship and veneration.'[77] Law, on the other hand, is a lucrative and mercenary skill; no one seeks it out on its own account, but rather merely from hope of gain.[78] At best, one can perfect legal *scientia* through the study of eloquence;[79] at worst, one can make a living at it.[80] Petrarch and Bruni (and, by implication, Poggio himself) deserted

---

[74] *Contra Fidei Violatores* (*Opera*, II, pp. 891–902), at 895.   [75] *Opera*, II, p. 937.
[76] *De Infelic.*, I, p. 418, and *De Nob.*, I, p. 83.   [77] *Epist*, VI.iii.83.
[78] *Ibid.*, II.xiii.118, and again at *ibid.*, VI.viii.98 (to the jurist Benedetto di Arezzo, 1436).
[79] *Ibid.*, Vi.xi.104 (to the Bolognese jurist Bornio, 1437).
[80] See Poggio's rather sarcastic advice to his friend, Francesco di Arezzo, a lawyer: 'Si sapies, ibi jus tuum vende, ubi non pollicitationibus, sed nummis tibi satisfiat' *Epist.*, X.xx.41). Poggio's attitude towards law as a vile, money-grubbing profession is found

the study of law for the cultivation of letters at the first opportunity, natural enough given the obvious superiority of the latter over the former.[81] And, as if all of this was not bad enough, legal method, departing from the eloquent ancient jurisconsults, is confused, marked by differing opinions and superfluous terms, so full of contrarieties and cavilling that any perception of truth is precluded.[82]

Indeed, as Poggio points out in his 'Oration in Praise of Venice', what is wrong with law (elsewhere) is its internal inconsistency, a problem heightened by conflicting interpretations; at Venice, the laws are simple, and the magistrates interpret them using equity, reason and balance, rather than with 'manuals and the callid interpretations of the jurisconsults.'[83] And in the facetious tale 'Of a Certain Judge Who Objected to an Advocate Mentioning the "Clementinae" and "Novellae"', Poggio pokes fun at a jurist whose knowledge of law and Latin was so spare that he thought a lawyer's references to Roman Law were casting aspersions on the concubines he kept at home.[84]

A central element in Poggio's legal thought is his awareness of the historicity of law, both as a science and as a human institution. He repeatedly, throughout his works, makes invidious comparisons between contemporary jurists and the 'prisci legum latores', the early Roman jurisconsults. All later Roman law flowed from the Twelve Tables, the earliest compilation;[85] among the Romans, the republican jurisconsults are the best, for they lived before the perversion of the laws and magistracies under Caesar and his successors.[86] The 'prisci legum conditores', the founders of the Roman law, are to be praised: unlike contemporaries, they knew how to legislate so that social bonds endured.[87] Later, the barbarous medieval commentators, with their mangled Latinity, misinterpreted the early, pristine texts.[88]

in extreme form in his story about the notary turned pimp (*Opera*, I, p. 470, 'De lenone facto ex notario'), who had embroidered on his sleeve, in silver, the motto 'De bene in melius' (all references to the *Facetiae* are to vol. I of the Fubini, ed., *Opera*).

[81] *Epist.*, XIII.iii.185. 82 (after 1453). The letter defends the great Florentines as self-taught men, and pertains to younger men trying to fill the Florentine Studio's now-empty chair of rhetoric.

[82] *Ibid.*, VI.viii.98 (1436), to the jurist Benedetto d'Arezzo: 'Immensum quiddam est civilis juris perceptio, tum propter rerum varietatem, ac sententiarum, cum plures inter se dissideant legum scriptores, tum vero maxime propter commentantium infinita pene volumina, quae mentes legentium diversis implicant opinionibus...absunt enim ab omni cultu orationis, ut priscos illos juris-consultos eloquentissimos viros numquam legisse appareat...'   [83] *In Laud. R.P. Ven.*, *Opera*, II, p. 937.

[84] *Opera*, I, p. 472.   [85] *Oratio in Laudem Legum*, ed. Garin, p. 12.

[86] *Defens. contra Guar.* (*Opera*, I, p. 372).   [87] *Contra Fidei Violatores*, I, p. 174.

[88] In the *Secunda Disceptatio*, Poggio mocks the 'doctores legum' (ed. Garin, p. 18/*Opera*, ed. Fubini, p. 39) and ridicules Dinus, Bartolus, and Cinus, '...qui aliquando nesciunt latine loqui, ubi sit legum diversorum ignorant' (Garin, p. 24/*Opera*, p. 44). See also *Epist.*, X.xiv.32 (1450).

As an institution, a necessary human framework, law is for Poggio
pre-eminently something suited to human needs, and hence, by definition, changing. A constant theme in his work generally is the variability
of time and the changeability of all things human, and it is an *idée fixe*
which he does not fail to apply to law. 'Things human change', 'human
affairs vary, never remaining long in the same state', 'opinions vary with
the changing times', 'earlier friendship lost because of the times' – all
various ways of expressing the ineluctable mutability of things and the
force of external circumstances.[89] In the *De Nobilitate* the concept is
applied to law, 'Not all laws are relevant to all cities, but rather they vary
in terms of public usefulness and utility',[90] while in the Venetian oration
it is precisely the unique nature of Venetian laws, unlike all other states'
in that they are 'solid, stable and ancient [and] not varying from day to
day', which attracts Poggio's attention.[91]

Poggio's awareness of the variability and mutability of law is also
manifest in the *Historia Florentina*, which we have initially approached
in terms of its general 'historical' dynamics. Viewed juridically, this
work reveals a view of law as above all a function of human will and
political circumstances.

The legal world of the *Historia* exists on two rather uncomfortably
co-existing levels. The first level is, loosely speaking, 'ideological'; it is
embedded in the glorious deeds of the free Florentine Republic, inheritor
of Etruscan liberty and the freedom of Republican Rome, and defender
of her own and of Tuscany's independence. Here, the juridical independence of Florence as a *civitas sibi princeps* and free republic is a given,
something so obvious that it needs no conscious justification. Florence
is politically and legally independent of the Empire, whose 'servitude'
she had long before thrown off, and of the Papacy and its claim to
jurisdiction,[92] and she seeks to maintain this independence in the face
of expansionist foreign powers.[93] And as a free republic, the Florentine

[89] While Poggio's *Opera* is generally rife with such references, see especially *De nob.*, I,
p. 76, 'res hominum...variantur, nec in eodem stat diutius perseverent'; *Epist.*,
VII.i.145, 'Commutantur enim tempora, variantur hominum mentes', and *Hist.
Flor.*, VIII.383/479, 'amicitiam culpa temporum intermissam'.
[90] *De nob.*, I, pp. 69–70. In this work (1440), Poggio still sees 'aequitas et iusticia' as the
common basis of law (p. 70); when he wrote the *Secunda Disceptatio* ten years later,
even this last remnant of Salutati's teachings was to drop away.
[91] *In Laud. R.P. Ven.*, II, p. 932.
[92] *Hist. Flor.*, II, 50/146. On the problem of church–state relationships generally in the
period covered by Poggio's account, see the article of Marvin B. Becker, 'Church and
State in Florence on the Eve of the Renaissance (1343–1382)', *Speculum*, XXXVII [1962],
pp. 509–27.
[93] Indeed, the narrative spine of the *History* is the story of Florence's successful efforts

state elaborates political institutions and juridical usages relevant to her own needs: she is a city-state 'sui juris'.[94]

This concept of the city-state ruled by its own laws will be encountered again in the *Secunda Disceptatio*; it already played a major role in Bruni's earlier *History of the Florentine People*. In Poggio's hands, however, it becomes a basic criterion for gauging the legal independence of other states. Tyrannies, above all that of the Visconti at Milan, are not really juridically independent; indeed, the making of one's own laws is seen to constitute the essence of *libertas* and the juridical definition of a republic.[95] And in her diplomatic dealings with other states, legal independence becomes for Florence a *sine qua non* governing the possibility of alliances and political relationships generally.[96]

This leads to an aspect of Poggio's work which constitutes a major departure from Bruni's earlier *History*, the persistent concern with the nature of inter-state relationships. Partially because of his emphasis on *res gestae fori*, but perhaps also reflecting his European-wide experience, Poggio repeatedly pauses to remark upon the making of treaties and alliances, and the difficulties with which such understandings are fraught. Giangaleazzo in 1389, 'contra jus gentium, et datam fidem', violates a peace effected by Pietro Gambacorta of Pisa;[97] earlier the Florentine ambassadors remind the Pope that their defense against the aggression of his own agents is justified by the 'jus divinum' and the 'jus gentium',[98] while in 1429 Niccolò da Uzzano, turning the argument

to maintain her independence, against the Visconti of Milan, Ladislaus of Naples, and then, finally, against a coalition led by Venice.

[94] Poggio, while not devoting much attention to internal events and dynamics, does follow Bruni in emphasizing the theme of Florence as a 'civitas sui juris'. This is very clear in the first book of the *History*, where he describes the elaboration of the machinery of republican government. For the role of Bruni in connecting the general juridical notion of *libertas* with republican 'equality before the law', see Ronald G. Witt, 'The Concept of Republican Liberty in Italy', in *Renaissance Studies in Honour of Hans Baron*, pp. 175–99.   [95] See too Recanati VI, 258–9/*Opera*, 352–3.

[96] *Ibid.*, VI, p. 267/363, where a 1429 Genoese aid request is rejected because she is a 'civitatem natura servam, neque tunc sui juris...'. The fiction of ultimate Imperial sovereignty was maintained into the fifteenth century (see Gino Capponi, *Storia della repubblica di Firenze*, 2 vols. [Florence, 1875], I, pp. 405, 570–5.) Practically, Florence exercised juridical autonomy: see L. Martines, *Lawyers and Statecraft in Renaissance Florence* (Princeton, 1968), especially Chs. 4–5.

[97] Recanati (III, 88/*Opera*, 184). The Florentine ambassador Giovanni Ricci notes, in 1389, that Giangaleazzo in killing his relative Bernabo went against 'ipsa natura lex' (*ibid.*, III, 92/188); earlier (*ibid.*, I, 13/109), the right of repelling force by force is justified.

[98] *Ibid.*, II, 57–9/153–5. This passage illustrates nicely Poggio's tendency to run terms together. This, and his usually vague use of the term 'lex natura', remind one of his 'naturae legem, hoc est sensus nostros' in the contemporary *De Miseria Humanae Conditionis* of 1455 (see above, n.30), a work related in tone to the *In Fidei Violatores* and *In Laud. R.P. Venetorum* and which, like them, must be seen in the context of Poggio's increasing disappointment with Florentine affairs (see pp. 137–8 above, and n.100 below).

around, argues that Florence's planned attack upon Lucca would violate the 'divine law'.[99]

Poggio uses the terms 'jus gentium' and 'lex natura' throughout the *History* to refer simply to the 'sacred' obligation of maintaining faith on the one hand, and the right of resisting unjust aggression by force on the other. Florence's enemies, being either tyrannies or tyrannous, tend not to abide by the 'jus gentium', while Florence, resisting unjust aggression, is generally conformable to the 'lex natura'.[100] This rather simplistic and 'ideological' handling of matters aside, the *History* is interesting in terms of its view of international relationships as a kind of juridical problematic and its relatively consistent application of the term 'ius gentium' to usages governing inter-state relationships.[101]

But there is another level upon which Poggio's legal conceptions in the *History* function, a level free from republicanist ideology and in implicit, if not open, conflict with it. The *History* is, more consciously than Bruni's, the story of Florentine expansion as well as of her 'defense' of republican values.[102] Here, where conquest is at stake and force decides, a pragmatic, 'Thucydidean' (and 'Machiavellian') analytic, reminiscent of the *De Avaritia*, the *De Nobilitate*, and, as shall be seen, of the *Secunda Disceptatio*, comes into play.[103] Those opposing Florence are urged to

[99] Recanati VI, 264/*Opera* 360.

[100] One senses, again, in this aspect of Poggio's analysis, the bitter assertion of the equivocal centrality of *fides* in human and political relationships, and of Florence's abrogation of it, expressed in the contemporary *Contra Fidei Violatores* (1456–7) and in the *In Laud. R.P. Ven.* (1459), which is, as we have seen, a kind of reversed invective insofar as Florence is concerned; themes from the earlier *De Infelicitate Principum* (1440) also reappear in the *Historia*, particularly the emphasis upon the faithlessness and inconstancy of princes and of friends, as in his 1437 letter to the Marquis of Mantua [*Epist.*, VII.i.145]). The relationship of the *De Infelicitate* to Machiavelli, and particularly to his *De Principatibus*, needs study.

[101] Poggio's general use of the 'ius gentium' as a kind of international law is, of course, not new. The term itself is used in the *Corpus Iuris Civilis*, generally for those usages established among men by *naturalis ratio* (*Dig.*, 1.1.9), and in the late medieval period was much commented upon by both civilians and canonists; see generally Gaines Post, *Studies in Medieval Legal Thought* (Princeton, 1964), pp. 241–309, 494–561, and B. Tierney, 'Natura Id Est Deus: A Case of Juristic Pantheism?', in *Journal of the History of Ideas*, XXIV (1963), pp. 307–22; Salutati's contemporary, the Neapolitan jurist Luca da Penna, also uses the terms in a fashion similar to Poggio, although Poggio characteristically never, either in his *History* or elsewhere, refers to the Roman law *per se* as a 'ius commune' (on Luca da Penna, see Walter Ullmann, *The Medieval Idea of Law as Represented by Lucas de Penna* [London, 1946]; on *ius gentium* and *ius naturale* in relation to Salutati, see F. Krantz, diss. cit. above, pp. 27–57).

[102] Bruni too, it should be remembered, was not unaware of Florence's 'imperial' mission in Tuscany: see *Hist. Flor. Pop.*, ed. Santini, II, p. 34 and VI, p. 140.

[103] See Recanati I, 15/*Opera*, 111, and Florence's 'rational' plea for submission made to the Pisans in 1405, *ibid.*, IV, 164/260. The whole debate on the Lucchese war (see above, p. 135) is a clear application to the Florence ruled by the Albizzi faction of the 'ideological' treatment usually reserved for the city's tyrannous enemies, as the bitter

view the situation 'rationally', and to submit to greater force; the 'civitas sui juris' principle somehow does not apply to cities like Pisa and the sister-republic of Lucca, which the Florentines seek to acquire either through conquest or purchase.[104] Nor does Florence's selfless devotion to republican fraternity prevent her, through the agency of Cosimo de' Medici, from supporting the rise to power in Milan of Francesco Sforza, even at the cost of destroying the short-lived 'Ambrosian Republic' there.[105]

In short, on this more pragmatic (and more 'Poggian') level, law, like 'nobility', is seen to be a convention, in this case a function of force and power. Here, Florence's legacy from Rome is as much the expansion of the Republic as its liberty. The 'safety of the Florentine Republic', latitudinarily understood to include her expansion, is, far more importantly than the 'libertas Tusciae', the central interpretive key to an understanding of Poggio's *Historia*. The term is used frequently, and it is an important link to the *Secunda Disceptatio*'s mocking, and decidedly *un*-'civic', juxtaposition of law and power. In this respect, the *Historia Florentina* is fully consonant with the historical approach to law which characterizes Poggio's work generally.

III

Poggio in 1450, using his villa in Terranuova as the setting, put together three dialogues, the *Historia Tripartita*, wherein he himself, his friend the jurist Benedetto Accolti (the then-chancellor of Florence), Carlo Marsuppini, and Niccolò Tignosi da Foligno, doctor and Aristotelian, discuss a number of problems.[106] The second dialogue, the *Secunda*

remarks of a Lucchese orator, seeking aid from Siena after the Florentines have declared war, make clear: *ibid.*, VI 267/363.

[104] The use of Livy and Sallust by Poggio in the *Historia* is noted by many critics; but the influence of Thucydides (available in Greek mss. early on, and translated into Latin by Valla in 1450–2), seems possible as well, especially in terms of passages like the 'Melian dialogue' between Athenian 'Realpolitiker' ambassadors and the Melians jealous of their independence. On Thucydides in the early Quattrocento, see R. R. Bolgar, *The Classical Heritage and Its Beneficiaries: from the Carolingian Age to the End of the Renaissance* (New York, 1964), pp. 278 and 435; for the 'Machiavellian' dimensions of Poggio's thought, see nn. 56 and 73 and p. 142 above, and below, pp. 149 and n. 124, 150 and n. 151. For a discussion of the relation of Thucydides (and Plato) to Machiavelli, see Gennaro Sasso, *Studi sul Machiavelli* (Naples, 1867), pp. 50–80.

[105] Poggio makes clear the 'popular' resistance in Florence to the alliance with the condottiere Francesco Sforza, and – in a relatively unusual reference to 'internal' politics – emphasises the role of Cosimo de' Medici in overcoming this resistance (Recanati and *Opera*, VIII, 369/465, 371/467).

[106] Garin, ed., *La Disputa*, pp. 15–33, and *Opera Omnia*, I, pp. 35–7; for ease of reference, all citations to this work will give pagination for both Garin and Fubini editions. On the dialogue (and third *Disceptatio*), see Walser (*op. cit.*, pp. 248–62). Also, see Lynn Thorndike, *Science and Thought in the Fifteenth Century* (New York, 1929), pp. 24–58,

Disceptatio, is devoted to the question, 'Utra Artium, Medicine an Iuris Civilis, Praestet' ('Which Science, Medicine & Civil Law, is more Excellent?'), and clearly refers to the earlier handling of this question – and defense of the superiority of law, broadly understood as the *vinculum societatis*, over medicine – by Salutati in his *De Nobilitate Legum et Medicinae* (1398).[107] In the dialogue, Poggio's role is that of moderator, but here his sympathies clearly lie with the views of Niccolò Tignosi.

In the opening pages of the discussion, the jurist Accolti (to whom Poggio in 1436 had written a letter attacking legal *scientia*) develops a defense of the nobility and dignity of law, terming justice the foundation of republics and the laws its handmaidens, which is a paraphrase of Salutati's work fifty years earlier.[108] Niccolò begins his attack on Benedetto's position by invoking the greater utility, age and philosophical certainty of medicine,[109] but he soon proceeds to a clearly historical argument, in which we can see, precisely and powerfully articulated, many of the earlier *loci communes* of Poggio's thought. The laws, even those of the ancients, far from embodying the good, often permitted the worst crimes, and were far from rational; besides, laws are made by the will of the greater. Most men abstain from them; kingdoms and peoples live according to their own traditions, obeying either the will of their rulers or their customs, or usages handed down by their ancestors.[110]

But, more important even than this is the fundamental fact that law varies, so that even the much-vaunted Roman law is limited in its application:

and Gutkind (*art. cit.*, pp. 592–4). Garin's introductory references in the *Disputa* edition, pp. xlvii–xlix, are brief (Garin mentions the work in his *Filosofi italiani del Quattrocento* of 1942, but in the later *Umanesimo italiano* deals largely with Poggio's *De Avaritia*, with only a passing reference [p. 43] to the *Secunda Disceptatio*; the subsequent literature on Poggio generally accords the work only sporadic references.

107 The *De Nob. Leg. et Med.* was one of Salutati's more popular works, and there is much evidence to show that it was known and read throughout the fifteenth century. Printed at Venice in 1452, it was explicitly referred to in 1490–1 by Antonio de' Ferrariis, called 'Il Galateo', in his work *De Dignitate Disciplinarum* (see Garin, ed., *De Nobilitate*, pp. lii–liv); Poggio was well aware of the work and, indeed, seems to 'quote' it at points throughout the *Secunda Disceptatio* (see following note).

108 *Secunda Disceptatio.*, 19–21/40–1. This part of the treatise should be read in conjunction with Salutati's *De Nobilitate*, *passim;* aside from general similarity of conception and expression, there are numerous 'quotations' (see, e.g., Salutati, *De Nob. Leg. et Med.*, 18, and *Secunda Disceptatio, ibid.*

109 *Secunda Disceptatio.*, 16.40. Poggio himself, in his introductory remarks (15–16/40), gives the palm to medicine, remarking that in an earlier work (the *Oratio in Laudem Legum*) he had jejunely praised law.

110 *Ibid.*, 17/38. Poggio refers to Spartan and Egyptian laws justifying stealing, and to a Roman law enabling creditors to divide up the body of a defaulter. The 'law is founded by the will of the greater' idea is developed at length in the discussion.

For laws have an uncertain foundation, and indeed are so diverse, that they are often seen to be in conflict. Each city makes its own law, to such a degree that they reject our civil law, so that it is only understood by a few, and that in some circumscribed narrow corner and small place. For how many people hold to your civil laws? Look at all of Asia, Africa and the greater part of Europe. Do you think, aside from a few provinces, any mention or reference is made to your laws? Only the Italians, and not all even of them, obey your civil law. For the Spaniards, French, English, Teutons, Germans and all the other northern nations make their own laws, suitable to their own needs.[111]

This clear demonstration of the variability of law, and of the quite restricted applicability of the Roman law itself ('our civil law'), calls to mind a similar demonstration by Bruni, in his 1437 letter to Niccola Strozza.[112] But it should be remembered that Bruni's general purpose was to reject the assertion that law as a *scientia* partook of the same *philosophia* as did the *studia humanitatis*, not to discredit the general importance and necessity of law itself. Poggio, characteristically, pushes the argument much further, fastening upon its historical element in order to arrive at conclusions quite different from those of Bruni.

The Roman laws, Niccolò continues, were legislated 'pro tempore', made not by 'nature' but by men: 'Your commentators' seek to interpret away differences in the civil law, due to the fact that they were made in diverse periods by diverse men, as if the legists were infallible Phoebuses.[113] Put together later by 'some Greek' in several books, and given Imperial sanction,

it is new, inasmuch as invented by the Romans and approved by the Emperors, and holds no utility save for those to whom that law was given. It embraces only those who are subject to the Roman *imperium*, if indeed they wish to conform to it. But how widely now the Roman *imperium* extends! Almost the whole world has withdrawn from it, each nation makes laws for itself. Moreover, any city under Imperial jurisdiction makes its own laws for itself, which are preferred to your civil laws, because none can be forced unwillingly to obey.[114]

[111] *Ibid.* As with Bruni, Poggio's approach to the Roman law is conditioned by his low estimation of the Empire itself, both in terms of 'civic humanist' rejection of the Empire as the corrupter of Republican virtue and culture, and of the solid awareness of the historical and juridical weakness and ineffectiveness of the 'translated' German 'Empire'. Here, historical awareness, civic ideology, and 'juridical radicalism' are mutually reinforcing.

[112] Bruni, *Epistolae*, ed. Mehus, VI.vi.50.

[113] *Secunda Disceptatio*, 21/42.

[114] *Ibid.*, 21–2/40–1, passage beginning 'Haec ab nescio quibus Graeculis postmodum in plures libros scissa...'. The reference is to the compilation of the *Corpus Iuris Civilis* under Justinian by Tribonian (see too *Epist.*, XIII.iii.85). Poggio was familiar with Valla's work (both exchanged a series of invectives), and with Valla's assertion that the inept Tribonian had mangled the pristine Roman jurisprudence in his compilation (see Valla's *Elegantiae*, VI, p. 35 [*Opera Omnia*, ed. E. Garin, 3 vols. (Turin, 1962), vol. I,

With the decline of the Empire as a legal and political force, independent nations and cities make their own laws. The point is made more sharply later in the dialogue,

Each city makes its own civil laws, each town its own private law. The Florentines employ private more than public (that is, Roman) law. Many laws made in her foundation-period have now, over time and with changes in the city, been altered. Thus necessity compels different cities to make laws suitable to their needs, which are preferred to Roman law.[115]

The argument becomes even more interesting when Niccolò, accepting Benedetto's rather weak defense, that without law man would be like the brute animals, a beast,[116] turns the statement around to demonstrate that force and power indeed reign supreme in human affairs, and that law is either ineffectual in face of this, or is indeed merely a function of it. Niccolò at the beginning of the discussion had remarked in passing that 'laws are made by the will of the stronger',[117] and now this concept is taken up again, with a vengeance.

Echoing a theme struck twenty years before in the *De Avaritia*, Poggio notes that the really fundamental things of life, food, clothing, shelter,

p. 216]; and, on 'anti-Tribonianism' generally, the references in D. Maffei, *Gli inizi del umanesimo giuridico* [Milan, 1964], and L. Palazzini-Finetti, *Storia della ricerca delle interpolazione nel corpus iuris giustineano* [Milan, 1953]). For Poggio's attitude towards some of Valla's legal ideas, especially his claim to write a better gloss after three years' study than Accursius, see 'Invectiva in L. Vallam Primam' (1452), *Opera*, I, pp. 188–205, where Valla's presumptuousness, rather than his criticism, is ridiculed. The criticism of Tribonian fits in nicely with Poggio's earlier juxtaposition of the pristine republican jurisprudents and the later, barbaric commentators, with his criticisms of Constantine and his successors for removing the seat of the Empire to the East (see Walser, p. 307), and with his dislike of the 'Graeculi' generally (his rejection of post-Imperial Greek historians' pro-Caesar judgements in the *Defens. contra Guarinum* should be recalled here).

[115] *Secunda Disceptatio*, 30/49. This passage picks up a point made earlier (18/39), in relation to pre-contemporary usage, which deserves noting: 'Non enim iidem sunt mores semper, et quae utilia aliquando [leges] putantur, tempore fiunt persaepe contraria. Ita et leges videntur. Variae enim sunt, vel potius diversae, cum civitates fere singulae suum ius, quod appellant civile, sibi constituant. [The Spartans, Athenians, and Thebans, like the Romans after the Twelve Tables, had different laws and lawgivers, just as the Etruscans, Picts, Umbrians, Samnites, and Campanians had their own usages and laws.] Iureconsulti in urbe solum docti habebantur; extra urbem indocti.' This last point may reflect Bruni's earlier '...jus autem locis et temporibus variatur, ut saepe quod Florentinae legitimum est, Ferrariae sit contra legem' (*Epist.*, ed. Mehus, 2, VI.vi.50 [1430/4 (1437?)]). One is reminded, given Poggio's placing of the common law of cities and states above the surviving Roman law, of J. N. Figgis's contrasting description of Bartolus, for whom 'Common law of course means...here and always, Roman law...' ('Bartolus and the Development of European Political Ideas', *Transactions of the Royal Historical Society*, New Series, XIX [1905], pp. 147–68); see too C. N. S. Woolf, *Bartolus of Sassoferrato* (Cambridge, 1913), pp. 43–5, 64.

[116] *Secunda Disceptatio*, 27/47.   [117] *Ibid.*, 17/38.

are sought naturally by all, without compulsion: here, law is unnecessary. Indeed laws are generally repugnant to men, since they feel obedience to them to be a kind of servitude. Therefore (and here again an earlier motif is repeated), 'the first legislators always attached a numinous element to their laws, in order to overcome the objections of the people by fear of the gods.'[118] He then gives examples of this procedure, from Menes King of the Egyptians through Moses and Lycurgus and Numa Pompilius, concluding that 'only the plebes and lowly' uphold the civil laws, while 'the powerful and the rulers of the city' transgress them.[119]

Indeed, it is a law of history that states grow and become powerful by force and arms, not through laws. The empires of the Assyrians, Persians and Medes, of the Athenians and the Romans (like those of contemporary states, as Poggio will note later) were put together not by respect for law, but by power and military expansion entailing the destruction of people and cities:

What might I say about the Roman Republic? Did she not become great through the despoiling and devastation of the whole world and through slaughter, all prohibited by the laws? What of the rape of the Sabine women, with which we begin the city's origins? Would you say this was done legally?...Yet nothing is more contrary to the civil laws than force and violence....Did equity, justice, right – your laws – impel these deeds? The same is true of the Athenians, whose rule extended far and wide [and underlay their cultural greatness]. For great power always produces literature and learning ....all admirable works, creativity, architecture, would cease if, submitting to your laws, man were content with what he had and spent his life in tranquillity. For everything excellent and worthy of memory springs from force and injustice, in contempt of the civil laws.[120]

'For everything excellent and worthy of memory springs from force and injustice': at this point Salutati's concern with *aequitas* as the foundation of law is stood upon its head, and Bruni's tentative 'the laws vary from place to place' argument pales into insignificance.[121] Further, Poggio

---

[118] *Ibid.*, 28/48. See also the *Contra Hypocritas* (1448), another work which exemplifies the consistency of Poggio's thought, and helps to explain the context in which the second *Disceptatio* was written.

[119] *Secunda Disceptatio.*, loc. cit.: 'Sola plebecula et inferioris urbe tenentur legibus vestris...potentiores et civitatum principes illarum vires transgrediuntur.'

[120] *Ibid.*, 29/48. Here again, a related theme is developed in an earlier work, in this case the *De Infelicitate Principum* of 1440, in which Poggio repeatedly emphasizes the unquenchable desire for power of rulers, and its *dire* consequences for human life and culture generally (*Opera*, I, p. 404); he also makes the comparison between individuals, who obey the law, and rulers, Christian and non-Christian, who are a law unto themselves. The social critique of *otium* here also recalls Antonio in *De Avaritia*.

[121] The argument is striking, and while elements of it are already present in the earlier works (above all the *De Infelicitate Principum*, a work of marked political and historical realism), it receives in the *Secunda Disceptatio* an extraordinarily lapidary and powerful

immediately, and characteristically, moves to illustrate his point with contemporary examples: the Milanese, Venetians and Florentines increase their territories through conquest, to which no civil laws impel them:

> Do I believe that when the Florentine people, or the Venetians, make war that they first call the jurisconsults together and, on their advice, declare war, or, rather, that they are guided by their own utility and the expansion of their republics? Away with these laws and your 'right', which are imperial propaganda, an impediment to acquiring kingdoms and extending republics; they pertain only to private matters, and to ordinary and weak men, who need their protection against the more powerful and waste their time in disputes and litigation. Serious, prudent, and sober men have no need for laws. They confer a law of right living upon themselves, established for virtue through nature and study. The powerful reject and despise them, as suited to weak, mercenary, manual-laboring, money-grubbing and cowardly men of meager means, who are indeed ruled more by force and fear of punishment than by laws.[122]

The treatise ends with Marsuppini cutting off the jurist Benedetto's halting attempt to reply to Niccolò's peroration, to ask Niccolò what he thinks of canon law. And here Poggio, drawing on his own Curial experience, sharpens the preceding attack on Roman law: the canon laws issue from the will of the Popes; what one issues, another abrogates, there is little worthy of the term *scientia* in them; they are a recent invention, being introduced scarcely more than 300 years ago.[123]

Law now assumes a double, and doubly ironic, aspect: it is the will

---

form. I know of no other humanist work in the Florentine tradition prior to Poggio where force as the basis of law is so dramatically propounded. Marsilius of Padua emphasises law's coercive power, but he consistently maintains that temporal authority issues from the popular will, and has responsibilities toward the people, something quite different from Poggio's view here: see A. Gewirth, *Marsilius of Padua, the Defender of the Peace*, 2 vols. (New York, 1956), I, pp. 132–66, and Nicolai Rubinstein's excellent 'Marsilius of Padua and Italian Political Thought of His Time', in J. R. Hale, et al., ed., *Europe in the Late Middle Ages* (Evanston, Ill., 1965), pp. 44–75. As for 'models', it is entirely possible that Poggio was familiar with Thrasymachus's arguments from Book One of the *Republic* and with Thucydidean political realism (for instance, the Melian dialogue) in the *History* (Bruni had a Greek manuscript of the latter by 1407, and manuscripts in Greek of the former were in Florence by 1424); and Aristotle's discussion of the problem of submission to law, and of some men who are a law unto themselves, in Book III of the *Politics*, was also at hand; see n.104 above.

[122] *Secunda Disceptatio.*, 29–30/49.

[123] *Ibid.*, 31–2/50–1. Poggio here develops another topos already touched on by him elsewhere: the 'historical-realist' critique of canon law. In the letters dealing with law, Poggio generally subsumes canon law under the more general heading, and applies to it criticisms similar to those directed at Roman law and lawyers generally (lack of eloquence and linguistic correctness, gain rather than wisdom as an end, power and force as the basis of promulgation rather than 'right', and so on: see, for example, *Epist.*, X.vi.50 [1420] and X.xiv.33 [1450]; and *De Avaritia*, I, 14); but in the *Secunda Disceptatio.*, the criticism is much more radical, and much more historical.

of the strong, a manipulative instrumentality for holding the state (*any* state, including republics) together, and at the same time it plays this role by providing the weak with the illusion that they can place their hopes for protection from the strong in it. As the former, law in Poggio's view is a kind of twisted fulfilment of the legists' old *summa ius, summa iniuria* tag; as the latter, it is a pitifully (and pitilessly) utilitarian rendering of the noble Salutatian view of law as Divine *aequitas*, the fundamental guarantor of human society. Here, to the extent that one can isolate Machiavelli's instrumentalist approach to law from his republican vision of its potential efficacy, Walser's observation is to the point: Poggio is "Machiavellian" before Machiavelli.[124]

IV

The *Secunda Disceptatio* may thus be seen to tie together the earlier themes and critical techniques of Poggio's work. Law here, to borrow a term from Biblical criticism, is effectively 'de-mythologized': it is no longer a God-given rule, but is rather a manipulative instrument given a divine aura by shrewd rulers; no longer a given of Nature, but rather simply a utilitarian set of 'natural' and changing norms, relevant to particular peoples and places. The Roman law is no longer an august and universal 'ius civile' bequeathed to contemporaries by Rome, but is rather the ever-more irrelevant usage of a decayed, shrinking, and impotent 'Empire'. Powerful rulers, nations, and cities make their own laws, and where, as in Italy, some vestiges of the Roman law linger on, they are inferior to the evolving urban common law, and are violated whenever necessary.[125]

In a sense, Poggio in this work, while never explicitly mentioning it, accepts the Roman law 'quod principi placuit' principle which had exercized Salutati, extends it to ruling groups in republics, and makes

---

[124] Walser, *Leben und Werke*, p. 258: 'Poggio Bracciolini legt in seiner Schrift Machiavellismus vor Machiavelli dar.' For brief references to Machiavelli's familiarity with the *Historia Florentina* see Felix Gilbert, *Machiavelli and Guicciardini. Politics and History in Sixteenth-Century Florence* (Princeton, 1965), pp. 237–8; Gennaro Sasso, *Niccolò Machiavelli. Storia del suo pensiero politico* (Naples, 1958), pp. 316–17; Donald J. Wilcox, *op. cit.*, pp. 20–3; and John M. Najemy, '*Arti* and *Ordini* in Machiavelli's *Istorie Fiorentine*', in Sergio Bertelli and Gloria Ramakus, eds., *Essays Presented to Myron P. Gilmore*, 2 vols. (Florence, 1978), I, pp. 161–91, at 161–2. A closer analysis of the general relation of Poggio's thought to Machiavelli's is long overdue.

[125] Bruni, too, as we have seen, was quite aware of the autonomy of Italian urban 'common law': see his letter of 1430/4 (1437?) cited above, n.115, and Santini, ed., *Hist. Flor.*, II, pp. 27–49, and IV and V, *passim*. But, characteristically, such awareness did not lead him to break completely with the Roman law seen as a body of continuing juridical relevance, nor to develop a philosophy of law as, essentially, a function of 'natural' circumstance, or force, or both.

a virtue of it.[126] The will of rulers expressed in force and conquest becomes here a kind of higher 'law'; the powerful are a law unto themselves, and were this not so, nothing humanly great and worthy of memory would ever be achieved.

The *Disceptatio*, then, which in formal terms begins as a kind of continuation of Salutati's older, somewhat naive 'de dignitate' debate-discussion,[127] turns into a fundamental 're-vision' and re-statement of the problem of law, one which would probably have been repugnant, if not incomprehensible, to Poggio's former teacher. In terms of time, fifty years separate the discussions of law of Salutati and Poggio; conceptually, they are worlds apart. In terms of Poggio's own development, however, there is an evident connection between this late work and his earliest efforts. One can discern a common thematic and critical thread running from the Petrarch dispute with Salutati of 1405–6 through the letters of 1416 on the Swiss baths and the heretic Jerome of Prague, to Antonio's naturalistic defense of greed in the *De Avaritia* of 1428–9, and through the *De Nobilitate* 1440 (1436?) and *De Infelicitate Principum* of 1448 to the *Historia Tripartita of* 1450. These works share an emphasis on the common historicity of all human events and values, an acceptance of observed reality as the starting point of analysis, and the implicit assumption of the comparability of all human experience and discourse.[128]

---

[126] *Inst.*, 1.2.6, *Dig.*, 1.4.1; for Salutati, see Novati, ed., *Epistolario*, II, pp. 33–4, and Garin, ed., *De Nob. Leg. et Med.*, 242, pp. 13–25.

[127] The 'de dignitate' debates continued in Florence and elsewhere, carried on after Salutati's death usually in terms reminiscent of Salutati's own framework, that is, medicine standing for Aristotelian natural science, law for the humanistic, Ciceronian emphasis on the connection between eloquence and social life. Garin reprints a number of these debates in his *Disputa*, including the Salutatian *An Medicina Sit Legibus Politicis Praeferenda* of the Florentine Giovanni Baldi de Faenza (1415) (pp. 3–4, excerpted), and the *De Medicinae et Legum Praestantia* of the physician Giovanni d'Arezzo, ca. 1468 (pp. 36–101, especially at 78 and 82). The latter work, while far more Aristotelian and 'philosophical' than Poggio's *Secunda Disceptatio*, has obviously been influenced by it, as careful textual comparison reveals.

[128] One of the striking elements of this critical stance is the way Poggio uses his humanistic classicism. Here again he reminds one of Machiavelli, for 'experience' is on an equal plane with 'literature' as a source of both *exempla* and wisdom, and the two share a comparative-historical method. Much the same is true of Poggio's Latinity, which, while classical in tone, is also 'open' and stylistically alive and contemporary, like Machiavelli's *volgare*. Poggio is quite sensitive, as we have seen, to philological considerations, and this from quite early on, e.g., his *michi-mihi* dispute with Salutati of 1405, where Poggio used philological evidence to argue against Salutati's retention of medieval usage (see Gutkind, *art. cit.*, pp. 550–61), and his well-supported argument later, in the third dialogue of the *Historia Tripartita*, demolishing Bruni's earlier assertion of two distinct languages in classical Rome, one popular, one literary (see Walser, *P.F.*, *Leben und Werke*, p. 262, who concludes 'So steht Poggio...als ein moderner romanischer Philologe da'). Two other attitudes of Poggio to language are also instructive, and typical: his almost Erasmian interest in adapting Latin to

These 'historicist' elements in the humanism of Poggio Bracciolini come together clearly, coherently, and powerfully in the 1450 discussion of law, and constitute, as we have seen, a kind of 'sub-text' running beneath the 'civic' republican surface of his last great work, the *Historia Florentina*. Yet, if the historicist thrust of Poggio's humanism does indeed have a 'relativist' dimension, Poggio himself, despite the views of some critics, is not in any consistent sense a relativist. Without illusions, finally, about the role of power, force, and hypocrisy in the public realm, sceptical about the direct utility of classical learning ('human life is not weighed on the scales of philosophy'[129]), and consistently refusing to invoke transcendental compensations, Poggio yet remains committed to a still-humanist vision of an individual, personal 'nobility' and of a possible this-worldly felicity.[130]

In his historical and analytical realism, his reliance on the utility of contemporary experience ('for we learn more from experiencing than from reading'[131]), and his independent, critical stance towards antiquity, Poggio calls to mind, again, Machiavelli. He remains, finally, very much part of the movement that Charles Trinkaus, commenting on the Renaissance role in the emergence of modern 'structures of conscience', calls an outlook

which increasingly was rejecting the negativity and passivity of the older 'structures' of conscience for a structureless ideal of personal autonomy, where the individual was daily challenged to establish his dignity in a world of chance, nature, history, and the inscrutable operation of divine providence.[132]

ordinary, 'popular' discourse (in the preface to the *Facetiae*, probably post-1453: *Opera*, I, p. 420), and his observation, after the birth of his second son, Scipione, in 1440, that 'balbutire incipit, et ipsa verborum corruptio est mihi eloquentia jocundior' (*Epist.*, VIII.xvi, 219).

[129] *De Avaritia, Opera*, I, p. 16: '...vita mortalium non est exigenda nobis ad stateram philosophiae.'

[130] See Fubini, 'Il "Teatro del Mondo"...in Poggio', p. 29: 'La "virtù" infatti rappresenta per lui un margine residuo di certezza, senza la consistenza oggettiva di una dottrina o il conforto di modelli, quali il proverbiale paradigma stoico del sapiente, e coltavibile pertanto solo in una sfera soggetiva ed empirica.'

[131] *Epist.*, VIII, 12 (1439): '...nam magis experiendo quam legendo cognoscuntur' (the context is a critique, based on his own experience, of Francesco Barbaro's anti-marriage *De Re Uxoria*, but the observation is emblematic of much of Poggio's thought).

[132] *The Scope of Renaissance Humanism* (Ann Arbor, Mich., 1983), p. 458.

Constitutional discourse in France, 1527–1549

SARAH HANLEY

For centuries the *Lit de Justice* of the kings of France, one of the most celebrated events in the ancien régime, has been interpreted in terms of eighteenth-century historiography: as a ceremonial appearance of the king in the Parlement of Paris used chiefly to exercise arbitrary power and quell parlementary remonstrances.[1] In the mid-eighteenth century the parlementaire Louis-Adrien Le Paige reflected this view.

You ask me what a *Lit de Justice* is? I will tell you! In its origins and according to its true nature, a *Lit de Justice* [assembly] is a solemn session of the king in the Parlement [of Paris] which is convoked to deliberate on important affairs of state. It is a tradition which originated in ancient general assemblies held in earlier times...[But today] the convocation of a *Lit de Justice* [assembly] is an occasion of mourning for the nation...[2]

Abbreviations: A.N. – Archives Nationales, Paris; B.N. – Bibliothèque Nationale, Paris.
   I express appreciation to The Institute for Advanced Study, Princeton, where work on this chapter was completed.

[1] See Adolphe Chéruel, *Dictionnaire historique des institutions, mœurs et coutumes de la France* (Paris, 1855), II, 670–3; Marcel Marion, *Dictionnaire des institutions de la France aux XVII*e *et XVIII*e *siècles* (Paris, 1923), pp. 336–8; Gaston Zeller, *Les Institutions de la France au XVI*e *siècle* (Paris, 1948), pp. 156–60; and Roger Doucet, *Les Institutions de la France au XVI*e *siècle* (Paris, 1948), I, 186. The same view appears in older works: Charles Desmaze, *Le Parlement de Paris, son organisation, ses premiers présidents et procureurs généraux...*(Paris, 1859); J. J. M. Blondel, *Mémoires du Parlement de Paris...*(Paris, 1803 [?]), quoting passages verbatim from Louis-Adrien Le Paige (n. 2 below); Ernest D. Glasson, *Le Parlement de Paris, son rôle politique depuis le règne de Charles VII jusqu'à la révolution* (Paris, 1901), I, II; Édouard Maugis, *Histoire du Parlement de Paris de l'avènement des rois Valois à la mort d'Henri IV* (Paris, 1913–16), I, II, III; Joseph H. Shennan, *The Parlement of Paris* (Ithaca, 1968); and Roland Mousnier, *The Institutions of France under the Absolute Monarchy, 1598–1789* (Chicago, 1979), I, 757, in the glossary.

[2] Louis-Adrien Le Paige, *Réflexions d'un citoyen sur les Lits de Justice par L–A Le Paige* (n.p., n.d. [c. 1787]), pp. 5–12, first published as *Lettre sur les Lits de Justice*, 18 *Août* 1756 (n.p., n.d.). Following the ubiquitous legend of the *Lit de Justice*, Le Paige considered all great assemblies as *Lits de Justice* from time immemorial, whether they were called *Champ de Mars, Champ de Mai, Placités Généraux, Cours Plénières, plein Parlement, Grand Conseil*, or finally, *Lit de Justice*.

In his opinion the contemporary format given the ancient *Lit de Justice*
betrayed the pristine French constitution, and that image of the assembly
as unconstitutional became fixed in French history following similar
denouncements in the decades just preceding the French revolution.[3]
The research of modern scholars in the nineteenth and twentieth
centuries was cast in this shadow and thus continued to perpetuate an
inaccurate interpretation of the *Lit de Justice*,[4] which is now in need of
revision. Accordingly, this study investigates first, the actual convocation
of *Lit de Justice* assemblies in the early sixteenth century and the
invention of a legend legitimizing them; and second, the competing
modes of discourse, royal and parlementary, through which constitutional precepts were articulated between 1527 and 1549.

HISTORICAL EVENT AND LEGEND

In early modern France the historical interaction of two processes, the
repeated convocation of *Lit de Justice* assemblies and the invention of a
national legend about them, stimulated constitutional discourse and
provided a public forum wherein constitutional ideologies – juristic,
dynastic, and absolutist – were disseminated.[5] Contrary to received
notions about its medieval origins, however, the *Lit de Justice* assembly
appeared first in the early sixteenth century, not in the fourteenth
century; and it was distinguished from the Royal *Séance* (the usual type

[3] For example, see the published speech of the parlementaire Antoine-Louis Séguier, *Discours de M. Antoine-Louis Séguier...prononcé au Lit de Justice...au château de Versailles le treize avril* 1771 (n.p., n.d.), and compare that with the parody issued on the speech with its deadly criticism: *Discours de M. Séguier...prononcé au Lit de Justice...* 13 *avril* 1771. *Nouvelle édition...*(n.p., n.d.).
[4] In addition to works cited in n. 1 above, review Ennemond Fayard, *Aperçu historique sur le Parlement de Paris* (Paris, 1876–8), and Félix Aubert, *Le Parlement de Paris, de Philippe le Bel à Charles VII* (1314–1422) (Paris, 1886), especially I, 196–7, which cites the Royal *Séance* of Charles V in 1369 as 'the first *Lit de Justice*.' Particularly influential is Maugis, *Histoire du Parlement*, I, 22, 120, 524, and 628, adjudging the *Lit de Justice* a 'customary ceremony' by 1581. Other works which adhere to the legend of the *Lit de Justice*, particularly its medieval origins, are Roger Doucet, *Étude sur le gouvernement de François Ier dans ses rapports avec le Parlement de Paris* (Paris, 1921–6); Robert J. Knecht, *Francis I and Absolute Monarchy* (London Historical Association, 1969), and *Francis I* (Cambridge, 1982); Simon H. Cuttler, *The Law of Treason and Treason Trials in Later Medieval France* (Cambridge, 1981); and Ralph E. Giesey, 'Models of Rulership in French Royal Ceremonial,' in *Rites of Power*, pp. 54–58 (see n. 5 below).
[5] For the complete study, consult Sarah Hanley, *The 'Lit de Justice' of the Kings of France: Constitutional Ideology in Legend, Ritual, and Discourse* (Princeton, 1983); and 'Constitutional Ideology in France: Legend, Ritual, and Discourse in the *Lit de Justice* Assembly, 1527–1641', in *Rites of Power: Symbolism, Ritual and Politics since the Middle Ages*, ed. Sean Wilentz (Philadelphia, 1985). For a comparative view of 'constitutions,' see Helmut G. Koenigsberger, 'Monarchies and Parliaments in Early Modern Europe – Dominium Regale or Dominium Politicum et Regale,' *Theory and Society*, v, No. 2 (1978).

of parlementary session attended by the king) on constitutional grounds. The first three *Lits de Justice* were convoked in July 1527, December 1527, and January 1537 to treat issues touching French Public Law (that is, constitutional law), raised in the bitter contest between Francis I and the Emperor Charles V.[6] In those extraordinary assemblies important precepts of French Public Law were articulated through the medium of ceremonial ritual and discourse,[7] and not long after their appearance these *Lits de Justice* were defended ably as tried and true French custom.

In renaissance France historians and legists, convinced of the indigenous nature of French laws and institutions, resurrected and studied archival documents in order to reconstruct the ancient French constitution. Already an avid sleuth in the 1520s, the clerk of the Parlement of Paris and scholar, Jean du Tillet (d. 1570), executed the most formidable work of reconstruction in his major historical treatise, *Recueil des roys de France*, which was circulated in manuscript from the 1540s through the 1570s and published posthumously between 1577 and 1618.[8] Insisting that the key to the French national past lay in documents which were officially signed, sealed, and preserved in archival repositories, he derided colleagues who trusted chronicle lore or fancy rhetoric as a guide to the past. Du Tillet called attention to the unique historical method which informed his research and scoffed at those who cited 'fabricated fables committed to chronicles' and wrote refinéd rhetoric which emphasized 'text rather than context, appearance rather than reality.' No 'ornaments' (elegant prose) decorated his treatise, he stated, because historical arguments rest on their own 'compelling force.'[9]

Du Tillet's compendium of sources proffered a typology of royal visits to the Parlement of Paris from the mid-fourteenth century which divided sessions into Royal *Séances* (honorary visits) and *Lit de Justice*

[6] For the first assembly, see Hanley, *The 'Lit de Justice' of the Kings of France*, Chap. II; for the second and third, below.   [7] The ceremonial ritual is analyzed in *ibid.*
[8] Jean du Tillet, *Recueil des roys de France, leurs couronne et maison* (Paris, 1607), the most complete edition. The work was first published posthumously under the title *Les Memoires et les recherches* (1577 and 1578), then in a version expanded and titled as above (1580, 1586, 1587, 1588, 1602, 1607, 1618). For the importance of this treatise in French historiography, see Donald R. Kelley, *Foundations of Modern Historical Scholarship: Language, Law, and History in the French Renaissance* (New York, 1970), pp. 215–38, and André Lemaire, *Les Lois fondamentales de la monarchie française d'après les théoriciens de l'ancien régime* (Paris, 1907), 82–91, who point to Du Tillet's merits as a founder of the historical school of French law. Du Tillet exemplifies the admirable scholarly bent of early modern times. As the conceptual organization of his work shows, he was interested in both current practices and historical precedents, and scholars in the next century admitted their debt to him; see Hanley *The 'Lit de Justice' of the Kings of France*, Chaps. IV and XI.
[9] Du Tillet, *Recueil des roys de France* (preface), fols. Aii^v–aiii^r–v and p. 365; and *ibid.*, *Pour l'entière majorité du roy très chrestien contre le légitime conseil malicieusement inventé par les rebelles* (Paris, 1560), fol. d^v.

assemblies (constitutional sessions) and created in the process, despite his careful scholarship, a historical fiction about the existence of a medieval *Lit de Justice* assembly. That fiction gave rise to certain assumptions about periodization in French constitutional history: glorious decades when Royal *Séances* and *Lit de Justice* assemblies flourished (the 1360s to 1413) followed by a dark lull when the tradition was suppressed (from 1414–1526), interim decades when the Royal *Séance* was revived (1484–1526) followed by a French constitutional renaissance when the *Lit de Justice* assembly reappeared (in 1527).[10] In this handbook of French constitutional history, Jean du Tillet legitimized the first three *Lits de Justice* as a revival of French tradition and set a powerful legend in motion, and the *Recueil des roys de France* was consulted by virtually every commentator from the sixteenth century to the present.[11]

As might be suspected, however, when one turns to the sources in the registers of Parlement which supplied the evidence for Du Tillet's thesis, the historical case for the medieval *Lit de Justice* assembly vanishes. The fact is that there was no medieval *Lit de Justice* assembly in the fourteenth and fifteenth centuries, even though commentators from the sixteenth century on have insisted on its feudal origins. This point must be emphasized because it challenges conventional wisdom which has escaped critical evaluation right through the twentieth century. As it turns out, the ephemeral medieval phrase *lit de justice* signified nothing more than the drapery paraphernalia (canopy, drapes, and pillows) which was constructed by parlementary ushers in the Grand-chambre of the Parlement of Paris to cordon off royal space for the king. The idiom appeared around the 1360s in the popular jargon of ushers who prepared the Grand-chambre for Royal *Séances*, and it was incorporated briefly into parlementary vocabulary between 1387 and 1413 by clerks who wrote minutes of those sessions.[12] One perceives here the

---

[10] See Table 1 below. Du Tillet's *Recueil des roys de France* contains three sections paginated separately. The two used here are (1) *Recueil des roys* (same title as the whole treatise), pp. 1–456; and (2) *Recueil des rangs des grands de France* (entitled here, *Recueil des grands*), pp. 1–130. The treatise compiles sources in the antiquarian fashion of the day with very little analysis.

[11] For a complete view of the legend told by commentators from the sixteenth to the eighteenth centuries, see Table One in Hanley, *The 'Lit de Justice' of the Kings of France*; for modern commentators, see nn. 1, 2, and 4 above.

[12] The idiom is written in the ushers' accounts, A.N. KK 336 (Comptes de l'Hussier), of Jehan Baure, Raoul Le Noir, and Pierre Belle, fols. 1ʳ (1388), 6ᵛ, 7ʳ (1390), 10ʳ (1394), 22ʳ (1396), 53ᵛ (1400), 55ʳ (1401), 165ʳ⁻ᵛ, 168ᵛ, 173ᵛ, 174ʳ, (1413). For a description of the drapery paraphernalia, see A.N. Xla 1469, fol. 146ᵛ (24 July 1366). The clerks of Parlement, Jean Willequin and Nicholas de Baye, recorded six events which used the idiom *lit de justice* and led Du Tillet astray: see A.N. Xla 1473, fol. 293ᵛ (2 March 1387); A.N. Xla 1477, fol. 14ʳ (3 December 1392); A.N. Xla 4784, fol. 87ʳ (10 April

development of a conceptual vocabulary of short duration, not a constitutional assembly of ancient origin; and the trivial nature of the idiom then, as compared to the constitutional import impressed upon it later, strikes an ironical chord. Indeed, the appearance of that odd phrase would not even elicit historical interest except for the fact that early modern commentators interpreted it as evidence for the medieval origins of the *Lit de Justice* assembly, bemoaned the loss of that pristine tradition, and invoked the fictive medieval *Lit de Justice* as the prototype for its supposed renaissance counterpart.

The first three *Lit de Justice* assemblies, born of political crises and legitimized by historical suppositions about the ancient constitution, were not welcomed by all parties. It is evident from the case studies here (the *Lits de Justice* of December 1527 and January 1537, and the Royal *Séance* of 1549) that the stance taken for the validity of the *Lit de Justice* and the rising crescendo of concern against it coincided. The modes of discourse apprehended in writings and speeches in those assemblies warrant close attention, because they shed light on the *mentalité* of the participants, the institutions they molded, and the relationship between constitutional practice and theory.[13] In the ensuing debate one can delineate two strands of consensus and conflict: consensus between the royal party and Parlement on tenets of French Public Law and the juristic nature of kingship and conflict between them over the provenance and purpose of the *Lit de Justice* assembly.

CONSTITUTIONAL DISCOURSE IN THE *LIT DE JUSTICE*
ASSEMBLIES OF DECEMBER 1527 AND JANUARY 1537

Francis I (1515–47) convoked a second *Lit de Justice* in the Grand-chambre of the Parlement of Paris on 16 and 20 December 1527 to discuss the annullment of the Treaty of Madrid for a new peace treaty consonant with the Law of Inalienability, a tenet of French Public Law.[14] The *Lit de Justice* publicized the constitutional case against the

1396); A.N. U 513 (26 December 1407); A.N. Xla 1479, fol. 243^v–244^r (26, 27 May 1413), and Xla 4789, fol. 458^v (26, 27 May 1413); and A.N. Xla 4789, fol. 514^v (5 September 1413), and Xla 8602, fol. 285^r, 286^v (5 September 1413). All dates have been converted from old to new style.

[13] On the critical formulation of conceptual vocabularies, consult the works of John G. A. Pocock, 'Languages and their Implications: The Transformation of the Study of Political Thought,' in *Politics, Language and Time: Essays on Political Thought and History* (New York, 1973), pp. 3–41; and Quentin Skinner, *The Foundations of Modern Political Thought* (Cambridge 1978), I and II; 'Conventions and the Understanding of Speech Acts,' *The Philosophical Quarterly*, XX, 79 (April 1970), 118–38; 'Some Problems in the Analysis of Political Thought and Action,' *Political Theory*, II, 3 (August 1974), 277–303.

[14] A.N. Xla 1531, fols. 26^v–33^v [recess, fols. 33^v–46^r] and fols. 46^r–53^v (16 and 20

SARAH HANLEY

treaty negotiated with the Emperor Charles V, secured a wide network of national support for the treaty, and raised ransom monies for the royal hostages held in the king's stead (the dauphin and his brother). Francis I considered the proper maintenance of French Public Law as a royal prerogative, had already repudiated the Treaty of Madrid for a new treaty which would not flout Public Law, and convoked the *Lit de Justice* so that interested parties could give counsel on its merits and raise the ransom. The king formulated the case carefully, characterizing the assembly as a consultative forum seeking advice, not consent, from orders of the realm (clergy, nobility, city officials, and Parlements) and invoking for that purpose language reminiscent of the well-known medieval principle of limited representation, *quod omnes tangit* (what touches all [should be approved of by all]). He emphasized the public nature of the French polity by differentiating the *king's two bodies*, one public and corporate, the other private and familial, and by announcing that he had convoked this particular forum, the *Lit de Justice* assembly, in place of a meeting of Estates to resolve a case of pressing 'necessity.'[15]

Francis I emphasized several points: the obligation of the monarch to maintain Public Law, the constitutional nature of the issue (involving inalienability of Crown lands) which 'touches not only the said lord and his children but also the entire universal monarchy of the kingdom of France...the *chose publique*...,' and the voluntary convocation of a consultative assembly with community representation to give counsel.[16] This idea of the public nature of a polity which rested on specific constitutional foundations stood in sharp contrast to the older notions of individual relations in a feudal nexus. In laying the groundwork for repudiation of the Treaty of Madrid and the collection of public monies for a royal ransom, Francis I did not base his case solely on feudal prerogative but emphasized instead the monarch's obligation to observe

December 1527); portions in Théodore [and Denys] Godefroy, *Le Cérémonial françois* (Paris, 1649) [Reg. Parl.], II, 478–501 [recess, 488–490]. The account of François-André Isambert, et al, eds. *Recueil général des anciennes lois françaises depuis l'an 420 jusqu'à la révolution de 1789* (Paris, 1821–1823), XII, pp. 285–301, is totally garbled with inaccurate transcriptions and improper dates.

[15] For the king's speech, A.N. Xla 1531, fols. 29^r–32^v (16 December 1527); reprinted in Godefroy, *Cérémonial françois* [Reg. Parl.], II, 481–7. Ernst H. Kantorowicz, *The King's Two Bodies: A Study in Medieval Political Theology* (Princeton, 1957), treats English and continental political theory in the later middle ages but has few examples of this separation of king and polity for France. Ralph E. Giesey, *The Royal Funeral Ceremony in Renaissance France* (Geneva, 1960), shows how funerary practices delineated the *king's two bodies* in the 16th century. On the notion of limited representation, *quod omnes tangit ab omnibus comprobetur*, see Gaines Post, *Studies in Medieval Legal Thought: Public Law and the State, 1100–1322* (Princeton, 1964), Chaps. III and IV; and on *necessitas*; *ibid.*, pp. 241–309, and Kantorowicz, *King's Two Bodies*, pp. 235–8.

[16] A.N. Xla 1531, fols. 29^r–32^v (16 December 1527).

158

Public Law, that is, the constitution. When he stressed his adherence to Public Law, his recognition of the consultative principle, his voluntary request for counsel in the discharge of his *dignité*, and his decision to convoke a *Lit de Justice* assembly (rather than a meeting of Estates) as a consultative forum, the king adopted a constitutional platform. Clearly the *Lit de Justice* had been convoked to exhibit the monarch as legislator and guardian of French Public Law, the Parlement as a judiciary body and advisory group among the other Estates. But the Parlement of Paris ignored the consultative tenor of the king's request and proceeded to rule on Public Law as if the Court was co-guardian with the king of the French constitution. In the meantime, the dissonance sounded over the procedural issue (locating legislative authority in the king at the *Lit de Justice*) contrasted oddly with the resonance heard regarding shared precepts of the French constitution.

The first president of the Parlement of Paris, Jean (II) de Selve, presented at the *Lit de Justice* a detailed brief which outlined the constitutional grounds for annullment of the Treaty of Madrid. The president's presentation, like that of the king, touted French Public Law, not feudal prerogative, as the basis for action that day. Amidst a litany of axioms reminiscent of the *king's two bodies*, he described the structure of the polity as a *mystical body* composed of king and subjects as head and members. 'The kingdom is in the king and the king is in the kingdom,' he stated, invoking the organological notion of the body politic and mystic used to characterize the relationship between people, or Estates, and the king throughout the fifteenth and sixteenth centuries. Then President De Selve introduced a new constitutional axiom to the French scene in the guise of a marriage metaphor to describe the King's relationship to the realm:

Apropos of that, a *marriage is made between the said lord and his said subjects* and the law of that marriage which the said lord must keep is to uphold and to maintain the [Public] Laws of his Crown, not the least of which is the Salic Law which has been maintained over time as a holy and just law and according to which the [Public] Laws of the Crown are themselves inalienable...the said lord must seek peace and must raise the ransom...because the...dauphin and the Duke of Orléans are natural children of the said lord and are also children of the French people and of the *chose publique*...[17]

[17] For De Selve's speech, A.N. Xla 1531, fols. 46^r–53^v (20 December 1527); recounted in Godefroy, *Cérémonial françois* [Reg. Parl.], II, 493–9 [italics added]. Jean (II) de Selve became president of Parlement in 1520. These axioms provide evidence for the French scene, which is missing in Kantorowicz, *King's Two Bodies*, pp. 207–31, 363–4 (*corpus mysticum*); pp. 214–22, 347–58 (marriage metaphor and inalienability); pp. 13, 215–23 (prince in the state, state in the prince).

President De Selve's evocation of the marriage metaphor describing the relationship of the king, as well as the princes, to the kingdom marks a very early instance of that juristic rubric in France. Perhaps he drew inspiration from the work of the medieval jurist Lucas de Penna, whose metaphor illustrated the inalienability of fiscal property.[18] But the crucial twist which De Selve gave to the expression made it particularly apropos for the circumstance of 1527. The president not only wed the king and the realm (identifying the dauphin and his brother as issue of that union), but also predicated the duration of that fictive espousal upon the monarch's successful maintenance of French Public Law. At this *Lit de Justice* of December 1527 President De Selve evoked a most unusual image of the French constitution for the time. He proffered the concept of a corporate body politic and described the king's relation to the realm in terms of the marriage metaphor; then he gave a juristic definition of French kingship as a royal *dignité* whose incumbent was charged with upholding the French constitution. It is noteworthy at the same time, however, that the president did not acknowledge the assembly underway as a *Lit de Justice*, distinct from an ordinary Royal *Séance*, or admit to the monarch's sole authority in constitutional affairs. This difference of opinion over the locus of constitutional prerogative was not resolved in 1527 and would crop up again in the *Lit de Justice of* 1537.

Francis I convoked a third *Lit de Justice* assembly in the Grand-chambre of the Parlement of Paris on 15 January 1537.[19] Once again the problem discussed there touched French Public Law, because it involved disposition of the royal domain. After a decade of strained political relations, Francis I (suzerain of Flanders and Artois) moved to deprive Charles V (vassal of the French king) of those Crown lands.[20] To that end the Treaty of Madrid was rescinded and the emperor was tried and convicted (*in absentia*) of the charge of 'notorious felony,' a lesser charge

18 Lucas de Penna (c. 1320–90) applied the marriage metaphor in conjunction with the notion of the state as a *corpus mysticum* in *Commentaria in Tres Libros Codicis*, published six times in France during the sixteenth century (first edition, Paris, 1509); see Kantorowicz, *King's Two Bodies*, pp. 212–32, who discussed the canonistic transfer of this metaphor to secular legal and political thought probably around 1300.
19 The original record made by Du Tillet in the civil registers of Parlement disappeared in the mid-sixteenth century. An abbreviated version survives in Du Tillet, *Recueil des grands*, pp. 93–5 (15 January 1537), and a fuller version in papers of Barnabé Brisson, reprinted in Godefroy, *Cérémonial françois* [Brisson], II, 501–3. Finally, there is another account written by a pleadings clerk, Pierre Le Maistre, now in the records of the Chambre des Comptes, A.N. P 2306, fols. 353^r–382^v (15 January 1537), extracts in Godefroy, *Cérémonial françois* [Le Maistre], II, 503–17. Barnabé Brisson was *avocat* of the king in 1575, president of Parlement in 1580.
20 Hearings had been held earlier against the emperor: A.N. Xla 1524, fols. 95^r–97^r (15 February 1522), and A.N. Xla 1525, fols. 275^v–277^r (30 June 1523); extracts in Godefroy, *Cérémonial françois* [Reg. Parl.], II, 455–63.

of treason within the rubric of *lèse-majesté*.[21] Once again the extraordinary nature of this assembly was in contention from the outset, considered as a *Lit de Justice* by the royal party, alternatively as a Royal
Séance by the Parlement of Paris. Yet as before there was definite agreement on the constitutional issue at stake.

The *avocat* Jacques Cappel pronounced the Treaties of Madrid and
Cambrai null and void for two reasons: they were obtained by Charles
V through extortion (holding Francis I prisoner, then his sons as
hostages); and second, they required the illegal alienation of Crown
lands. Cappel's main thesis, the monarch's constitutional obligation,
provided the guide for legal action. Harking back to the marriage
metaphor introduced by President De Selve in the *Lit de Justice* of
December 1527, the *avocat* Cappel developed that constitutional concept
further. First, he appended the *dowry-domain* analogy to that metaphor;
then he identified the coronation oath as the ceremonial ritual which
confirmed transfer of the French domain into royal safe-keeping. Cappel's
extended version of the marriage metaphor held that

By its nature the Crown is inalienable... because according to the Law of France,
which is called the Salic [Law], and customary, divine, and positive laws, the
sacred patrimony of the Crown, the ancient domain of the prince, cannot be
divided among men. [Rather] it is transmitted to the king alone who is the
husband and political spouse of the *chose publique* which brings to him at his *sacre*
and Coronation the said *domain as the dowry* of his Crown. Kings swear solemnly
at their *sacre* and Coronation never to alienate that dowry for any cause
whatsoever, because it is itself inalienable... Consequently, since [Public] Law
not only forbids kings the right to alienate the domain but also prohibits the
alienation of patrimonial or domainal property itself, and since such prohibition
concerns the public welfare, it is obvious that contracts [the treaties of Madrid
and Cambrai] which contain clauses of alienation as heretofore mentioned are
invalid from start to finish and cannot be validated by consent or oath.[22]

As President De Selve before him, Cappel too molded the marriage
metaphor into a French constitutional adage by linking it to the 'Law
of France,' the precept of inalienability in the Salic Law.[23]

21 Du Tillet, *Recueil des grands*, pp. 93–5 (15 January 1537); Godefroy, *Cérémonial
français* [Brisson], II, 501–3; A.N. P 2306, fols. 353ʳ–382ᵛ (15 January 1537), extracts
in Godefroy, *Cérémonial français* [Le Maistre], II, 503–17.
22 A.N. P 2306, fols. 356ᵛ–379ᵛ (15 January 1537) [italics added]; and in Godefroy,
Cérémonial français [Le Maistre], II, 505–11. Jacques Cappel became *avocat* in
Parlement in 1535.
23 *Ibid.* It has been suggested that recourse to precepts of private law (in this case,
inheritance and dowry notions) signalled a 'proprietary' notion of kingship and the
state; Herbert H. Rowen, *The King's State: Proprietary Dynasticism in Early Modern
France* (New Brunswick, 1980). But that suggestion fails to consider first, that the
participants had no appropriate vocabulary available for discourse on Public Law in

The pleading issued a two-pronged constitutional prohibition against alienation of the French domain, one tenet based on the definition of the inalienable domain itself, the other on the regulation of the king's relation to the domain expressed through the marriage metaphor. This case against Charles V rested firmly on French Public Law. Finally, Cappel suggested that the Coronation oath legalized this juristic notion of French kingship (that is, the fictive marriage between king and kingdom; the domain of the Crown as the dowry of a marriage). That suggestion was formalized later when that ritual was implicitly expressed in the Coronation order of Henry II in 1547 and then explicitly enacted through the rubrics of the Coronation order of Henry IV in 1594.[24] Once again, however, though there was amiable agreement between king and Parlement on the juristic nature of French kingship in 1537, the *avocat* Cappel, as President De Selve before him, made no reference to the extraordinary *Lit de Justice* assembly underway.

Until now historians have assumed that in France the simplest formulation of the marriage metaphor (designating the king as the *spouse of the kingdom*) first appeared in a legal treatise of Charles de Grassaille published in 1538; that the metaphor then found its way into the Coronation ceremonies of 1547 and 1594 (connected with the bestowal of the ring); and that its elaborate formulation (likening the *domain* of the kingdom to the *dowry* of a marriage), appeared in the last three decades of the sixteenth century in the writings of legists such as René Choppin, François Hotman, Pierre Grégoire, and Jean Bodin.[25] Yet here the first version of the metaphor (the king as *spouse of the kingdom*) actually emerged decades earlier, not in a legal treatise but in a speech actually tendered by President Jean (II) de Selve during the *Lit de Justice* assembly of December 1527. Likewise, the complex version of that metaphor (adding the equation of *domain* and *dowry*) also appeared several decades earlier than supposed, not in the writings of legists of the late sixteenth century but in a speech set forth during the *Lit de Justice* assembly of January 1537. This public discourse, a language framed by royal and parlementary speakers, outlined early in the sixteenth century a French version of the *king's two bodies* which

the early sixteenth century; and that they succeeded admirably in fashioning (from private-law precepts) a new language of Public Law suitable for constitutional discourse. The important emergence of a language of French Public Law became increasingly evident as the century wore on.

[24] Now the juristic usage of the marriage metaphor can be dated earlier than the Coronation rubrics. For a discussion of the metaphor and the precept of inalienability in the context of the Coronation, see Kantorowicz, *King's Two Bodies*, pp. 221–3, n. 83; and Richard A. Jackson, *Vive le Roi! A History of the French Coronation from Charles V to Charles X* (Chapel Hill, 1984), Chap. VI.

[25] Kantorowicz, *King's Two Bodies*, pp. 221–2.

articulated the ideology of Juristic kingship stressing the obligation of the monarch as holder of the royal *dignité* to maintain French Public Law. Given the appearance of these juristic rubrics at such an early date in France, the genesis of this genre of constitutional thought must be moved back from the late sixteenth century to the 1520s; and given the linkage of such rubrics with the extraordinary *Lit de Justice* which appeared at the same time, the constitutional nature of that assembly must be stressed.

The *Lit de Justice* was born of international political crises and nurtured by growing historical suppositions about the ancient constitution, but the attempt to delineate two types of parlementary sessions, the *Lit de Justice* (constitutional) and the Royal *Séance* (honorary), was resisted by some and became the focus of debate at mid-century. Despite the admittedly constitutional nexus of the assemblies, none of the parlementaires acknowledged them as *Lits de Justice*. This cast of mind, the tacit refusal to recognize the *Lit de Justice* as constitutionally different from the Royal *Séance*, was couched in the abstruse form of silence. It was not until a decade later that the incipient debate about the origin and function of the *Lit de Justice*, which was muffled in the *Lits de Justice* of 1527 and 1537, burst forth publicly on the scene.

THE DEBATE FROM HISTORY AND RHETORIC IN THE ROYAL
SÉANCE OF 1549

During a Royal *Séance* of 1549 held by Henry II (1547–59) in the Grand-chambre of the Parlement of Paris, the place of the *Lit de Justice* in the ancient constitution was debated.[26] The chancellor, François Olivier, and the first president of Parlement, Pierre Lizet, elucidated two different versions of Parlement's history and function, both directly related to unsettled contentions about the novelty or historicity of a *Lit de Justice* assembly.

Chancellor Olivier related an institutional history of the Parlement of Paris which employed archival evidence probably obtained from Jean du Tillet's historical treatise.[27] Olivier divided the history of Parlement into four distinct stages. First, he noted that the origin of 'parlements' was somewhat obscure, because

---

[26] A.N. Xla 1565, fols. 203ᵛ–212ʳ (2 July 1549). Extracts of the *Séance* are contained in Du Tillet, *Recueil des grands*, pp. 98–9; and in Godefroy, *Cérémonial françois* [Reg. Parl], II, 518–30, who incorrectly entitles the *Séance* as a *Lit de Justice*.

[27] Henry II issued a research commission to Du Tillet on 22 December 1548 that ordered the clerk to deliver his findings to the chancellor; Godefroy, *Cérémonial françois*, I, fol. E ivʳ. Francis II renewed the commission (mistakenly dated 12 May 1562 but issued in 1559 or 1560); B.N. ms. fr., n. a. 20256, fol. 55ᵛ.

...it is not ascertainable either from histories or from ancient records exactly when this Parlement [of Paris] originated and was organized or how the sovereign justice of France was administered in early times; but it is generally conceded that it [the Parlement of Paris] formerly consisted of an assembly of varied persons chosen by the king, convoked intermittently, and called 'parlement.'[28]

Second, he recapitulated the uneven growth of the 'parlements,' when sporadic convocations of ambulatory feudal courts took place during the reigns of Louis IX (1226–70) and Philip III (1270–85), and the first attempt to regulate convocations in the reign of Philip IV (1285–1314). Third, Chancellor Olivier fastened upon the reign of Philip VI (1328–50) as the era in which a recognizable institution, the Parlement of Paris, issued from these diffuse 'parlements.' That change occurred when a division of chambers (Grand-chambre, Enquêtes, Requêtes) took place and a specified number of secular parlementaires were appointed to staff them. Since the king, princes, and peers often joined the Court to discuss important affairs, the jurisdiction of the Parlement of Paris then comprehended a wide variety of cases, domestic and foreign, private and public, civil and constitutional. After establishing the institutional roots of the Parisian Parlement around the 1340s and showing the comprehensive nature of the Court's jurisdiction over private and Public Law at that time, Olivier identified a fourth and final stage in Parlement's history.[29]

The final stage of Parlement's institutional evolution focused on a historical moment in the 1350s when the Parlement of Paris became a specialized judicial body and a concomitant separation of powers, judicial and constitutional, took place.

King Jean II [1350–64] realized that affairs of state were no longer accorded the secrecy due them and that the Parlement [of Paris] was increasingly burdened with judicial affairs, so he decided to limit the cognizance and jurisdiction of Parlement. He ordained that it [Parlement] would rule thenceforth only on cases of the peers of France...and [on cases] of persons who by privilege or precedent were heard in the Court of the domain of the king...From that time on there were no affairs of state treated *in the Court* [the Parlement of Paris] except by *special commission*. And the Court concerned itself with justice only according to the terms of the ordinance of King Jean.[30]

This interpretation of parlementary history was very radical in conception. Chancellor Olivier allowed that originally feudal parlements of

---

[28] A.N. Xla 1565, fols. 205^r–207^v (2 July 1549). François Olivier, formerly a president of Parlement, was chancellor from 1545 to 1551.

[29] *Ibid.*

[30] *Ibid.* [italics added].

French kings had treated both private and Public Law, as did the new institution, the Parlement of Paris, at the immediate outset; but then he correlated the first decades of the Court's institutional status with a concomitant shift in its sphere of jurisdiction. Some time in the 1350s King Jean II issued an ordinance which in effect removed affairs of state, or constitutional matters, from the Parlement's normal jurisdiction, and thereafter the Parlement of Paris functioned to contemporary times solely as a judicial institution and retained only one aspect of its former constitutional role, that is, its judicial function as a Court of peers. By invoking the example of Charles V (who promulgated the Law of Majority in 1375), Olivier juxtaposed the king in the role of legislator to the Parlement of Paris as adjudicator, noting that Parlement's source of authority was not inanimate ordinances but the animate king (the *lex animata*), the 'living and speaking law' of the realm.[31] His insistence that after the 1350s affairs of state would be treated *in the Court* by a *special commission*, that is to say, by an extraordinary assembly convoked in the Grand-chambre for that purpose, certainly suggested that an assembly like the *Lit de Justice* had existed in feudal times and could be convoked again when constitutional business arose.

The parlementaires had shrouded the *Lit de Justice* in conspicuous silence in 1527 and 1537; now they shifted that stand in 1549 by confronting directly the term *lit de justice* in French historical discourse. The first president of Parlement, Pierre Lizet, spoke after the chancellor and presented the opposing view of French constitutional history. Yet even though President Lizet broke the earlier silence by speaking openly about a *lit de justice*, he maintained a skeptical stance by refusing to acknowledge it as an ancient constitutional assembly. As opposed to Chancellor Olivier's historical formulation (based on Du Tillet's theory), President Lizet's interpretation of Parlement's history emphasized linguistic structure. He argued that the medieval idiom *lit de justice* simply served as a metaphor for the Parlement of Paris. In his ken kings had sometimes used the phrase *lit de justice* not as a title for a special constitutional assembly but as an allusion to the Court of Parlement itself ensconced in the Grand-chambre along with the monarch and peers.

When great assemblies or convocations of the peers of France were held [in the Court of Parlement], your [Henry II's] predecessors called it [the Court of Parlement] the *lit de justice*, indicating by that reference the presence there of

---

[31] Olivier's formulation points to the antithesis between animate king and inanimate law rendered in the late thirteenth century by Aegidius Romanus, *De regimine principum* and repeated by others, including Lucas de Penna; see Kantorowicz, *King's Two Bodies*, pp. 134–6, for the medieval antecedents.

both your royal Majesty and your subjects. Sire, in it [the Court of Parlement, or the *lit de justice*], you effect repose, because when you...exercise sovereign justice [there]...you maintain concord, union, and the bond of human society among your subjects; consequently, it is also for them the *lit* where they repose.[32]

President Lizet took direct issue with Chancellor Olivier's presentation of parlementary history. He gave no quarter either to the notion of a historical separation of judicial and constitutional powers or to the possible existence of any *special commission, Lit de Justice* assembly or other, which differed constitutionally from a Royal *Séance* in Parlement. He did not correctly trace the term *lit de justice* to the medieval drapery paraphernalia, but he located its usage in figurative rather than in procedural language. Lizet thus stated explicitly in 1549 the principle that Parlement had harbored implicitly in 1527 and 1537: that historically the phrase *lit de justice* was a metaphor which brought to the mind's eye a vision of the Parlement of Paris conjoined with monarch, princes, peers, and others in the Grand-chambre, that is, a traditional Royal *Séance* in which all matters, judicial and constitutional, were comprehended. In the Royal *Séance* of 1549, therefore, there were finally expressed outright two diametrically opposed views about the locus of constitutional power and by inference the legitimacy of a *Lit de Justice* assembly held in the Court to treat constitutional business.

In the Royal *Séance* of 1549 Chancellor Olivier and President Lizet elucidated two different versions of Parlement's history and the origins of the *Lit de Justice* assembly. Lizet's argument from rhetoric stressed universal likenesses and continuity in historical events over time. He maintained that king, peers, and Parlement assembled in the Royal *Séance* constituted a body which comprehended both constitutional and judicial matters; and he insisted that the phrase *lit de justice* was not a procedural term for an assembly but a simple figure of speech which signified the Grand-chambre of the Parlement of Paris filled with those notables gathered to treat affairs of state in France. According to Lizet, therefore, the French constitution knew no *Lit de Justice* assembly and witnessed no separation of powers. The rhetorical argument of the parlementaires had its convincing aspects, but it paled in contrast to the powerful historical case advanced by the royal party. Speaking for the king, Chancellor Olivier fixed upon the phenomenon of historical change (as told by Jean du Tillet's research) and noted discontinuity in historical events over time. By this reckoning Parlement first achieved institutional status not in the late thirteenth century but around the 1340s and then became a specialized judicial institution in the 1350s when the *Lit de*

[32] A.N. Xla 1565, fols. 207^v–210^r (2 July 1549). Pierre Lizet, a councillor in Parlement in 1514, an *avocat du roi* in 1517, replaced Jean (II) de Selve as first president in 1529.

Justice assembly was instituted in the Court to deal with constitutional matters. According to Olivier, the French constitution in the mid-fourteenth century witnessed a separation of powers, the judicial vested in Parlement, the constitutional vested in the *Lit de Justice*.

In the early sixteenth century the powerful force of historicism, nominalist and philological in conception, bred in its adherents a new mode of perception and a surety of purpose which shaped the *mentalité* of the times. In building the foundations for modern historical scholarship, the new historical method required forays into the archives and interpretation of original sources to uncover the roots of the ancient constitution. As will be recalled, one of the greatest proponents of that method, Jean du Tillet, disdained the study of 'text rather than context, appearance rather than reality,' and insisted on the 'compelling force' of historical facts in reconstructing the past. On this platform in the Grand-chambre of the Parlement of Paris, bounded on the one side by royal policy and historical research and on the other by parlementaire reservations and rhetorical tradition, two opposing theories about a separation of powers under the French constitution emerged from the debate about the *Lit de Justice* assembly and competed for place throughout the ancien régime.

Table 1. Jean du Tillet's sources: *Recueil des roys de France, leurs couronne et maison* (Paris, 1607)

	Date		Location	[*Recueil des roys*], p. and *Recueil des grands*, p.
1	1310	(Winter)	Unknown	35
2	1332	—	Louvre	42–45
3	1366	(21 February)	Saint-Pol	48
4	1366	(27 July)	Saint-Pol	48–49
5	1367	(13 February)	Saint-Pol	50
6	1367	(15 November)	Louvre	50–51
7	1369	(24 April)	Saint-Pol	52
8	**1369	(9, 11 May)	Parlement	51–52, [256]
9	*1369	(10 December)	Parlement	52
10	1374	(19 March)	Saint-Pol	53
11	**1375	(21 May)	Parlement	52–53, [277]
12	**1378	(9 December)	Parlement	11, 14, 18, 53–55, 65-66, [368–9, 371]
13	**1387	(2 March)	Parlement	12, 55, 66, [368–9, 371]
14	**1392	(3 December	Parlement	58
15	**1396	(10 April)	Parlement	16, 20, 59
16	1404	(23 August)	Saint-Pol	59

Table 1 (*cont.*)

	Date		Location	[*Recueil des roys*], p. and *Recueil des grands*, p.
17	**1407	(26 December)	Parlement	60, [279]
18	1412	(18 February)	Saint-Pol	60
19	**1413	(26 May)	Parlement	60–61, 62
20	**1413	(5 September)	Parlement	61–62
21	1458	([10] October)	Vendôme	13, 14, 15, 16, 19, 67–8, [314, 370–1]
22	*1493	(22, 25 February)	Parlement	75–76
23	*1493	(8, 11 July)	Parlement	76–77
24	*1498	(7 July)	Parlement	78
25	*1499	(13 June)	Parlement	78
26	*1502	(24 February)	Parlement	78
27	*1504	(3 December)	Parlement	78
28	*1504	(5 December)	Parlement	78
29	*1504	(16 December)	Parlement	78
30	*1505	(2 January)	Parlement	78
31	*1508	(13 November)	Parlement	79
32	*1508	(16 November)	Parlement	79
33	*1510	(18 March)	Parlement	79
34	*1515	(14 March)	Parlement	79
35	*1515	(29 March)	Parlement	79
36	*1517	(5 February)	Parlement	79
37	*1522	(15 February)	Parlement	80
38	*1523	(30 June)	Parlement	80
39	*1524	(8, 9 March)	Parlement	81
40	**1527	(24, 26, 27 July)	Parlement	14, 19, 81–86
41	**1527	(16, 20 December)	Parlement	14, 86–92
42	**1537	(15 January)	Parlement	12, 14, 15, 19, 93–95
43	*1549	(2 July)	Parlement	98–99
44	*1551	(12 November)	Parlement	99–100
45	*1552	(12 February)	Parlement	100–1
46	1558	(5 January)	Saint-Louis	68
47	*1558	(15 January)	Parlement	105–6
48	1559	(10 June)	Augustins	106–7
49	*1563	(17 May)	Parlement	107–8
50	1563	(17 August)	Rouen	[280]

** Double-starred events were designated as *Lit de Justice* assemblies by Du Tillet.

* Starred events were designated as Royal *Séances*.

Lieuwe van Aitzema : a soured but knowing eye

HERBERT H. ROWEN

One encounters some of the most interesting figures of history while
venturing down the bypaths of one's researches. I found one such while
cutting through the thickets of seventeenth-century Dutch history.
Lieuwe van Aitzema is hardly unknown to specialists, to be sure, but he
has been for them little more than a richly informed chronicler, if one
whose pen was dipped in the acid of total cynicism. How that attitude
squared with his apparent conversion to Catholicism late in life has been
a puzzle ever since the sources indicating his change of religion were
discovered a few decades ago.[1] Historians of the Cromwellian regime
have long known some of his work but not the man himself, for his secret
dispatches from The Hague that are printed in John Thurloe's *Collection*

---

[1] There has been no full-length study of Aitzema. E. H. Waterbolk, ed., *Proeven van
Lieuwe van Aitzema, 1600–1669* (Leeuwarden, 1970) is a collection of essays written
by students of Professor Waterbolk in his seminar at the University of Groningen.
Devoted to a variety of themes concerning Aitzema and of varying quality, it gives the
fullest picture of Aitzema yet published; none of the essays, however, addresses itself
to the theme that is my subject in these pages. J. D. M. Cornelissen published three
informative and thoughtful articles on Aitzema: 'Brieven van Aitzema in het archief
der Brusselsche nuntiatuur (1665–1666), '*Bijdragen en Mededelingen van the Historisch
Genootschap*, XLIX (1928), 126–86; 'Het pessimisme en de waarheids-liefde van
Lieuwe van Aitzema (1600–1669), gezien in het licht van de international aan te wijzen
gedachten,' *Historisch Tijdschrift*, XX (1941), 5–19;' 'Lieuwe van Aitzema en Hugo de
Groot,' *Bijdragen voor de Geschiedenis der Nederlanden*, I (1946), 47–71. Robert Fruin,
'Geheime briefwisseling van Lieuwe van Aitzema, 1654–1660,' in his *Verspreide
Geschriften* (11 vols.; The Hague, 1900–5), vol. VIII, 54–67, is fundamental for the
evaluation of Aitzema. J. J. Poelhekke, 'Enkele aantekeningen over Lieuwe van
Aitzema,' *Mededelingen der Koninklijke Nederlandse Akademie van Wetenschappen,
Afdeling Letterkunde*, Nieuwe Reeks, XXIII no. 15 (Amsterdam, 1960), is probably the
most insightful short work on Aitzema; it is reprinted in Poelhekke, *Met Pen, Tongriem
en Rapier* (Amsterdam, 1976), 85–114, with a postscript. Pieter Geyl discusses
Poelhekke's article in his essay, 'Aitzema de kroniekschrijver en nieuwsleverancier,' in
his *Figuren en Problemen I* (Amsterdam, 1964), 38–45. W. Wilde, 'Lieuwe van
Aitzema', in *Studiën*, LXIII (1904), 99–118, is a vigorous examination of Aitzema from a
Catholic viewpoint. I have not read J. J. Kalma, 'Liuwe fan Aitzema (1600–1669),' in
Dit wienen ek Friezen, II (1964), which is in Frisian.

of State Papers are without his signature. As for historians of the Dutch Republic, they can do no work on the middle decades of the seventeenth century without drawing upon Aitzema's *Saken van Staet en Oorlogh* ('Affairs of State and War') as their fullest and best contemporary printed source. Yet, within the pages of that work, scattered in the midst of documents printed *in extenso* and arid, if highly useful detailed accounts of events, are to be found commentaries of great pungency and highly personal character on history, politics and religion. It is Aitzema's mind as revealed in these *obiter dicta* which is the object of my attention in these pages.

The *Saken van Staet en Oorlogh* was a controversial work, especially in its first appearance in twelve in-quarto volumes in the years 1657 to 1668. Aitzema's publication of state documents that were formally secret was a venial offense that would not of itself have brought down upon his work the ban and confiscation imposed upon it in 1668, on its completion; after all, the wall of privacy about affairs of state in the Dutch Republic was so porous that its penetration was commonplace and little commented upon. It was rather Aitzema's caustic asseverations and animadversions about the official Calvinist church and its doctrines that drew fire, and these offensive remarks were supposedly, but not always, removed in the new in-folio edition in seven volumes (plus an index volume) that appeared after Aitzema's death, between 1669 and 1672.[2] The immediate reprinting of the large and expensive work was proof of its wide readership among the political class of the Netherlands; it was, indeed, the only comprehensive account of events available to the public, and it was so valuable that a manuscript translation was prepared in the mid-eighteenth century at the French foreign ministry.[3]

The *Saken* was an indirect outcome of Aitzema's public career. Born at Dokkum in Friesland in 1600, he came from a distinguished family of the province. In 1621 he accompanied the Dutch army under Prince Maurice in the expedition into Germany to oppose the Spanish forces under Spinola. It was his first sight of war, and he did not like what he saw, repeating the Erasmian adage, *Dulce bellum inexpertis*.[4] In 1624 he was admitted to the bar in his native province and in the province of

[2] I have used in the in-folio edition: Lieuwe van Aitzema, *Saken van Staet en Oorlogh, in, ende omtrent de Vereenighde Nederlanden* (6 volumes in 7 parts, plus index volume; The Hague, 1669–72). The differences between the two editions and their relative worth are discussed in Geyl, 'Aitzema de kroniekschrijver,' and D. J. Mennink, 'Kwarto- of folio-uitgave,' in Waterbolk, 12–19. Mennink finds Geyl's preference for the quarto edition unfounded.

[3] Albert Waddington, *La République des Provinces-Unies, la France et les Pays-Bas espagnols de 1630 à 1650* (2 vols.; Paris, 1895–7), I, iii.

[4] Aitzema, *Saken*, I, 5. See also v, 775.

Holland as well. Three years later, with the support of his uncle, Foppe van Aitzema, one of the chief Dutch diplomats in Germany, he took up a new career as an agent for the minor German city of Magdeburg. In 1629 Foppe obtained for him the residency in The Hague for the Hanseatic towns, but this minor post was the highest rung he ever reached on the diplomatic ladder.[5] His diplomatic status was important less for his negotiations, which never concerned major matters, than for providing some cover for his work as a news-correspondent for foreign potentates. Much of the material he transmitted was obtained in at least technical violation of the law, by bribery of deputies and clerks. During the First Anglo-Dutch War (1652–4), however, he overstepped the boundary of legality. He continued to inform John Thurloe, the secretary of the English Council of State whom he had met during a visit to England on the eve of the war, of events in the Dutch Republic. His reports about naval and political developments were sent secretly, partly in cipher and without signature; he had become a spy for the enemy of his country. Yet he was a spy with a difference. His reports were not just accounts thick with facts and documents; they were replete with warnings that the continuation of the war threatened the existence of the republican regime in the Netherlands and might well lead to the restoration of the Orange stadholderate, and hence to Dutch support of the fallen Stuart dynasty in England. His reports therefore provided a sustained argument for making peace on terms acceptable to the government in power, which from July 1653 was under the leadership of John de Witt, the councilor pensionary of Holland.[6]

Aitzema departed this life on 23 February 1669, with an unsavory personal reputation. He was fond of the pleasures of eating and dressing well, but it was his enslavement to the needs of the flesh that came to the attention of the authorities after his death. He never married but took in mistresses – concubines would be the more exact word, since they were of much lower social class – to live with him, three in all. The second bore him two children, who were baptized in the nominally covert Catholic church in The Hague. According to the testimony of his servant, he even arranged 'cover' marriages for the ladies of his house.[7] Curiously, it was not these irregularities which made trouble for him in his own time or besmirched his reputation in later centuries but only his refusal to play it safe in religion and his flirtation with treason in his news-reporting business.

[5] Wilde, 100.
[6] Poelhekke, 'Aantekeningen'; G. N. van der Plaat, 'Het "Verraad",' in Waterbolk, 32–58, an excellent piece of research and analysis.
[7] Waterbolk, Bijlage II, 169–70.

He was proud of his history, of its truthfulness even more than of its wealth of information. He asked his readers to condone his failure to state softly the hard facts of a 'harsh time.' He had the advantage for a historian of not being a member of government (what the Dutch called a 'regent'), so that he could present what he had heard and seen 'nakedly and without flattery.' His book was like a stage play, in which the characters act and speak according to their roles, but the playwright himself is not heard. He spared the reader, too, the rhetorical devices of Italian and French writers, who described battles that were fought 'not just with ships upon the water but on land with every kind of poetry, figures and emblems.'[8] Although his boasted impartiality did not deter him from commentaries that reveal a distinct intellectual personality with strong judgments about the events of his time, his sincere commitment to truth seems beyond serious question.[9]

It is, however, as a thinker, not a historian, that we are interested in Aitzema, and his significant ideas range over the fields of politics and religion – as does his chronicle. His political conceptions were complex, but contemporaries saw in them primarily his unabashed acceptance of the doctrine of reason of state. They saw a man who said that in matters of high policy it was vain to appeal to law: 'necessity has no law.'[10] Promises are not kept unless the anticipated advantages continue to be present. Each side in a conflict claims to have right on its side, but the only 'just decision' will be that which God will give on Judgment Day.[11] Secular rulers are no more bound by their promises than the council of Constance was by the safe-conduct it had given to John Hus. 'Kings and potentates do as they please.' Religion, one's word, oaths – none mattered. 'When piety yields profit, then men will be pious.[12] Arguments from right and law are either hypocrisy or a waste of time. 'The big fish eat the little fish. He who has power uses it. Everyone speaks of honesty, sincerity and affection, and it is all deceit and hypocrisy.[13] Those who possess both opportunity and power do not 'break their heads' with findings pretexts for action.[14] 'Therefore we must conclude that everyone acts and speaks according to his passions, and that the passions follow

[8] Aitzema, *Saken*, III, 780–1.
[9] Wilde, 102.
[10] Aitzema, *Saken*, III, 531, 885. See also Aitzema to Thurloe, July 21, 1654, *A Collection of the State Papers of John Thurloe, Esq; Secretary First, to the Council of State, And afterwards to the Two Protectors, Oliver and Richard Cromwell* (7 vols.; London, 1742, II, 480.
[11] Aitzema, *Saken*, VI, 296. See also III, 731.
[12] Aitzema, *Saken*, I, 905.
[13] Aitzema, *Saken*, I, 655. The Latin tag ('Pisces minutos magnus comest') is repeated in IV, 471.
[14] Aitzema, *Saken*, III, 1272.

each one's interests and advantage. Everyone loves that which he finds profitable.'[15] 'Men in general strive to keep what they have...Whatever Princes can keep or protect is just, and what I say is based on what happens in practice. Having is having, indeed having is honorable.'[16] As for the common welfare, the darling of moralists and political theorists, it was an 'orphan' whose fate was in the hands of those who had power.[17]

Aitzema rang the changes on the theme that in politics it was not justice but power that prevailed. He spoke words that in their terseness are worthy of Machiavelli. 'He who is strongest always has the best rights'[18] is echoed even more simply in the epigram, 'Where might is, there is right.'[19] This was not the result of accidental circumstances but of the very nature of man, who is driven by *Libido dominandi*.[20]

This Dutchman was able to display extraordinary neutrality about the most important event in his country's history. To ask who had been right in the contest between Philip II of Spain and the founders of the Dutch Republic was 'foolishness.' The test lay in the outcome: 'One gains the crown, the other the gallows, both in the same cause.' The success of the Dutch Revolt 'proved' that William the Silent had been right.[21] Had Philip crushed the rebellion, he would have been praised even in Holland. But he failed.[22] 'The King of Spain was a man, Count William was a man, angels and perfect beings dwell in heaven, and *the winner is pleasing to God*.'[23] Elsewhere, Aitzema painted William of Orange as an opportunist who took advantage of religious turmoil to put himself at the head of those who created the Dutch state. 'It was a *coup d'état*, such as provides French and other political writers with material for whole books,' he wrote. 'Changes in states are the result only of chance and opportunities. Whoever wants to explain them by divine or human laws has his work cut out for him.'[24]

It was not sentiment but armed force that counted.[25] Where was the country, Aitzema asked, 'that does not bend, interpret and explain' laws, oaths and instructions 'according to passions and interests'? Where was the country where the people did not say, openly or implicitly, that they would keep their oaths and follow the laws 'to the extent that they are observed and practiced'?[26]

None of this was really new, of course. But seldom since Machiavelli

[15] Aitzema, *Saken*, IV, 649. See also III, 741, VI, 450.
[16] Aitzema, *Saken*, III, 525.   [17] Aitzema, *Saken*, IV, 1059.
[18] Aitzema, *Saken*, III, 1192.   [19] Aitzema, *Saken*, III, 428.
[20] Aitzema, *Saken*, III, 1171.   [21] Aitzema, *Saken*, VI, 157–58.
[22] Aitzema, *Saken*, I, 1035.   [23] Aitzema, *Saken*, IV, 653.
[24] Aitzema, *Saken*, VI, 157–58.
[25] Aitzema, *Saken*, III, 667. See also Aitzema to Thurloe, 10 Sept. 1655, Thurloe, III, 747.
[26] Aitzema, *Saken*, II, 779. See also III, 1250, IV, 1125.

himself had such notions been stated with such plain force, and outside the exculpatory principle that those who violated the moral law in the service of God or some other higher good were guilty of nothing more than 'holy pretence.'[27]

Aitzema was more original when he turned to questions of the day. During the last two decades of his life, the central issue in Dutch politics was the place of the stadholderate in the Republic. More precisely, it was whether the absence of the stadholderate in the five principal provinces, including Holland, after 1650 was constitutional and proper. It has generally been held that Aitzema was a friend of the so-called 'republican' or *Staatsgezind* (pro-States) party, and a foe of the House of Orange.[28] Yet Aitzema vehemently denied that he was more pro-Holland than pro-Prince. He knew no one, he said, who was either really *Prinsgezind* or *Hollandsgezind;* there were plenty who were *Eygen of self-gezinde,* 'in favor of themselves.'[29] It might better be said, however, that Aitzema was sometimes *Prinsgezind* and sometimes *Hollandsgezind,* depending on circumstances, but neither upon the basis of emotional commitment.

For Aitzema the conflict between Orangists and *Staatsgezinde* was less a conflict of principles than of interests. 'If someone had been promoted by the Prince, then he thought well of the Prince.' But since such favors could not be bestowed upon all who yearned for them, those who were left out proved to be a majority when William II died in November, 1650. They believed that they would do better 'standing on their own feet,' and that this would be to the benefit of the country as a whole. This occurred not only in Holland but also in the other provinces, notably Zeeland. Those Zeelanders who accused Aitzema of not being in favor of the Prince were as little committed to the Orange cause as he was himself. They had been the Prince's creatures and turned against his son after his death; he, Aitzema, on the contrary, 'spoke the language of both Prince and Holland, and did harm to neither.'[30]

On both sides of this conflict, he wrote, ambition was the driving force, 'everyone wanted to be the boss,' and commitment to either Prince or liberty was 'a pretext and a cloak.'[31] When the stadholderate was abolished outright in Holland in 1667 – until then it had merely been left vacant – Aitzema poked fun at the 'plausible names of liberty and privileges.' What really moved those in power was 'nectar autocraticum.'[32] In such matters, subtle arguments of history and

[27] See George L. Mosse, *The Holy Pretence* (Oxford, 1957) for an insightful study of this doctrine in England in the seventeenth century.
[28] Cornelissen, 'Brieven van Aitzema,' 137–8.
[30] Aitzema, *Saken*, III, 744.　　　　　　　　　　[31] Aitzema, *Saken*, III, 829, 1171.
[32] Aitzema, *Saken*, VI, 169.

political theory matter less than brute force. 'The correct explanation always comes from him who is strongest, compelling him who is weakest to believe what he wishes.'[33]

Aitzema was led by the presence of the force which may be called 'Orange democracy' – the support for the restoration of the stadholderate and the authority of the Prince of Orange by the people, both the burghers and the plain folk beneath them – to broader considerations of the place of the people in the Dutch polity. The fact that the populace was Orangist was not for him an argument in the Prince's favor. In their 'blindness' the people preferred to be governed by a Prince of Orange rather than by their 'equals'[34] – equals, of course, only so far as simple subjects and patrician regents were all commoners, not nobles. Aitzema was no admirer of the common folk, least of all when they broke out in riotous violence. 'If the shout goes up among the people in the street, "The dog is mad," then it is lost.'[35] He was pleased that Admiral John Evertsen, maltreated by the mob in 1665 on coming ashore after the loss of a naval battle, was found innocent by the court. 'Little trust can be put on the *Arbitrium popularis aurae...*'[36] The populace was not only cruel in conduct but also fickle in judgment, and it did not act on its own but on behalf of one or another faction of regents.[37] Aitzema scorned equally the rule of the mob and the weakness of governments that had to give in to them.[38] He denied that the voice of the people was the voice of God. Had not the children of Israel given their unanimous voice against Moses?[39] The people had a native tendency toward sedition; envy and concealed hatred were in their nature, as mistrust was in that of governments.[40] Yet he could display compassion for the toiling populace, if not sympathy for their political role. 'How many artisans,' he asked, 'must work and sweat from early morning until evening to pay the excises, the imposts and the land tax, and how many poor widows must toil at the distaff until midnight?' At least they contributed to the needs of the state, not, as in monarchies, to the upkeep of 'impecunious courtiers and officers.'[41]

The controversy over the stadholdership was of narrowly Dutch significance, but because it was usually equated with monarchy in general, Aitzema was led into the much broader debate over the relative advantages and disadvantages of monarchy and republicanism. Totally absent from his discussion, it may be noted, is the kind of civic republicanism that consists in a commitment to selfless citizenship; for

[33] Aitzema, *Saken*, III, 1083.
[34] Aitzema, III, 828, 912.
[35] Aitzema, *Saken*, IV, 800.
[36] Aitzema, *Saken*, V, 449.
[37] Aitzema, *Saken*, III, 743–4.
[38] Aitzema, *Saken*, VI, 619.
[39] Aitzema, *Saken*, I, 591, V, 787.
[40] Aitzema, *Saken*, I, 680.
[41] Aitzema, *Saken*, I, 679.

Aitzema monarchy meant simply government by 'one head' and republicanism rule by States assemblies without a single head of state possessing sovereignty. Monarchy and republicanism were categories of political analysis that were familiar to both Aitzema and his readers, although they did not fit the constitutional situation of the Dutch Republic.[42] It was accepted doctrine that sovereignty belonged to the States, but with two complications. The first was the question whether the States General shared the sovereignty with the provincial States; the second, whether it could be exercised without the participation of a stadholder. Although the stadholderate was usually equated to incipient monarchy, or at least monarchy in potential and aspiration,[43] there was virtually never any proposal for abolition of the States, as was happening in so many places in Europe during the seventeenth century. Aitzema's judgments on monarchy and republican government, sharp and perceptive when addressed to the situation in other countries, therefore lacked some focus and definition when applied to his own country. Nonetheless they hold interest because they are more penetrating and biting than was common in most political discourse.

Where in the question of the stadholderate Aitzema had been of two minds, in the larger debate over forms of government he came down clearly on the side of the republican regime. Although he was strongly impressed by the changeability of politics,[44] he believed equally strongly in the importance of a regime of order and inequality. Experience taught him that they were both necessary. The longer a government endured, the more was it worthy of praise.[45] Citing the difficulties of the English after the execution of Charles I, he observed that it is easier to break than to build.[46] When Oliver Cromwell died, Aitzema felt compelled to praise the skill and courage of the Lord Protector in military and political affairs. 'But it soon became apparent in his son that his valor, wisdom and good fortune had not been hereditary,' he added. 'The love that he bore his son was blind, for he could not foresee that he would have shoulders too weak for carrying such a heavy burden.'[47] But this was a

---

[42] Ernst H. Kossmann, *Politieke Theorie in het Zeventiende-eeuwse Nederland* (Verhandelingen der Koninklijke Nederlandse Akademie van Wetenschappen, Afdeling Letterkunde, Nieuwe Reeks, LXVII, no. 2 [Amsterdam, 1960]) is a brilliant study of the discordance between the dominant political theory taught in Dutch universities and the political practice of the country.

[43] I discuss the distinction between stadholdership and monarchy in my article, 'Neither Fish nor Fowl: The Stadholderate in the Dutch Republic,' in: Herbert H. Rowen and Andrew Lossky, *Political Ideas & Institutions in the Dutch Republic* (William Andrews Clark Memorial Library, University of California at Los Angeles, 1985), 1–31.

[44] Aitzema, *Saken*, IV, 705.   [45] Aitzema, *Saken*, III, 863.

[46] Aitzema, *Saken*, I, 323.   [47] Aitzema, *Saken*, IV, 301–302.

fault to be found wherever there was hereditary rule, whatever the form of government.[48]

He was not given to flattery of kings. Praising the 'heroic virtues' of King Christian IV of Denmark, he noted that even he, for all his great knowledge and long experience, was dependent upon his servants. A monarch, 'seeing through the eyes of others and hearing through their ears, became what his servants wanted him to be,' Aitzema wrote. 'He *rules*, but his *ministers rule* him (hy *regeert* soo als hy wert *geministreert*).[49] The European monarchs did not even possess a decent sense of solidarity. They had no hesitation, Aitzema observed, about sending congratulations without delay to the new republican regime of England, although they were related by blood to the beheaded Charles I and his son, the exiled Charles II.[50] He contrasted the books written in defense of the royalist cause by such then famous authors as Salmasius and Boxhorn with the deeds of these monarchs, who did nothing but 'talk and sing and achieved nothing.' They preferred to wage their own wars among themselves and courted the victor in England, 'and all in fact brought themselves to call the harlot "Miss."' Only 'someone named Milton (eenen Milton)' had refuted Salmasius's *Defensio pro Carlo I*, and one Dutch scholar, Aitzema added, commented that Salmasius had defended a 'very good cause very badly, but Milton a very bad one very well.'[51] Aitzema did not doubt that there was greater wisdom in many heads than in one. Among the English Republicans there had been 'very stout-hearted, valiant and heroic men who did great, even Roman things.' But it had come to naught, for they quarreled among themselves, everyone wanted the biggest part of the booty for himself, everyone wanted to be boss. 'That is what happens when many rule.' Leadership and responsibility ordinarily fall to a single man, but with authority comes envy. 'Authority only multiplies enemies.'[52]

He castigated the hunt for office and preference and the attendant corruption in the Dutch Republic but thought it was an incurable evil. Offices ought to be given for services, 'without consideration of kith and kin' – but where does that happen?[53] The quest for offices was like the state of marriage. Of the latter it was said, 'Everyone who is in it wants to get out, but everyone outside wants to get in.' He reversed this saying for offices:' Everyone who is outside wants to get in, but those who are in want to stay in.'[54] Two who are friends when out of office split when

---

[48] Aitzema, *Saken*, IV, 653. [49] Aitzema, *Saken*, II, 443
[50] Aitzema, *Saken*, III, 328. [51] Aitzema, *Saken*, III, 497.
[52] Aitzema, *Saken*, III, 497.
[53] Aitzema, *Saken*, III, 497, 529, 1171. See also I, 585, 591.
[54] Aitzema, *Saken*, II, 182.

one gains office and the other does not.[55] Oaths against corrupt practices were like forbidding beer but not other drinks, or debauching women for money but not otherwise, and similar evasions. 'It is as if what is sought is to forbid corruption for all who are not in government but to leave those who are in office free to practice it.'[56] In fact, corruption was nothing more than the practice of gratitude for good deeds.[57] Was such a remark an expression of Aitzema's realism or his cynicism? Probably of both – and also of his fondness for the ironic epigram.

Offensive as Aitzema's views on politics were for the common – or the commonly asserted – morality, even more so were his thrusts at the Calvinist church and faith, the official religion of the Dutch state.[58] More than anything else, they aroused the preachers of the Reformed church against him. They knew only of his caustic analysis of their beliefs and status and his reiterated praise for the Roman faith and institution; that he also found fault with Mennonites, Quakers and other Protestant dissenting sects, which they abhorred, mattered little to them. Had they anticipated that he would secretly transform a candidly stated preference for Catholicism into an apparent deathbed conversion, they would have been even more horrified.[59]

Aitzema considered that the political troubles in both France and the Netherlands began over the question of religion; the difference was that the new religion succeeded in winning in the one and did not in the other. 'The outcome tests all things.'[60] This was a notion he repeated many times over: that the issue in the competition of religions was not which was true but which succeeded... and success was determined by which had more political force behind it.

In the struggle between the Gomarians and the Arminians – the great internal conflict of Dutch Calvinism in the first two decades of the seventeenth century – Aitzema saw religion at work as the pretext for those who were really driven by a craving for domination.[61] Holy Scripture had been misused in the struggle. 'One must be blind not to see that the clergy have their passions no less than the politicians.'[62] Predestination, however, he found beyond belief. 'All animals, even those with the least reason, love their children. How could God, who is the father and creator of us all, hate his own creations and children? It was even more horrible when Calvin argued that God created man for eternal death.' Such 'hard and cruel' talk was contrary to all Scripture.

[55] Aitzema, *Saken*, II, 304.
[56] Aitzema, *Saken*, III, 530.
[57] Aitzema, *Saken*, IV, 977.
[58] See Poelhekke, 'Aantekeningen,' and J. Drewes and D. J. Mul, 'Godsdienstige opvatting van Lieuwe van Aitzema,' in Waterbolk, 59–70.
[59] Cornelissen, 'Brieven van Aitzema,' 141.
[60] Aitzema, *Saken*, I, 428.
[61] Aitzema, *Saken*, I, 702. See also II, 873.
[62] Aitzema, *Saken*, I, 1022–3.

He cited to the contrary the Jewish prayer for the dead, according to the formula communicated to him by the synagogue in Amsterdam, which corresponded to the wish and words of the Apostle (II Tim. 1)[63] The Remonstrants (as the Arminians came to be called) had been foolish to lose so much for the sake of their opinions about matters which surpassed their understanding or at least that of the common people. 'Father' Cats – the poet-politician Jacob Cats – had taught a very useful lesson: 'Be members of the Church and friends of the State,' without saying what church or what state. The Christian religion was like schools: all produced learned men, but that school was best which had the 'best discipline and best order,' and hence one must conclude that this is the prevailing or public church. There were too many needless disputes in the matter of religion; the real causes of the existence of so many sects and splits was the 'ambition and vanity' of the theologians, who accused others of what they themselves were guilty of.[64] The 'subtle five points of predestination' were for the most part only 'logomachy, a dispute over words.' Each side pulled the words of the other by the hair. All that was really necessary was the catechism, although it was but child's learning. All rested upon implicit faith in the translators of the States Bible.[65]

Aitzema treated the doctrinal distinctions between Catholicism and Calvinism as minor. Except for the name the papist confessional and the Reformed 'visit' were virtually the same. The Calvinists had their equivalent of Catholic saints in their 'militant and peregrinating earthly saints.' But neither were necessary, 'for God already knows before we pray what we will seek in prayer and what we need, better than we do ourselves.' Yet it pleases Him that we should pray in or through the name of those beloved of Him, like Abraham, Isaac, and others.[66] Learned theologians Aitzema saw as like painters, who can easily find subjects in the Bible by which they can lend attractive colors to their own opinions.[67] He mocked the use and misuse of the Bible as a 'lid for pots of every kind.' Biblical texts could be read in a hundred thousand different ways.[68] He was deeply opposed to 'subtle distinctions' in theology which 'throw more darkness than light' upon the subject of God's justice and man's reconciliation with Him. How could the ordinary man understand what the theologians disputed? 'Or should he judge for himself who is right?' Most of the disputes were over words and concerned formulas. 'It is like *fashion* in clothes. Everyone finds something new. Everyone maintains that his owl is a falcon. But the purpose of clothes is to protect us against the cold, and the more simply

---

[63] Aitzema, *Saken*, II, 705.
[64] Aitzema, *Saken*, I, 1094.
[65] Aitzema, *Saken*, II, 572–3.
[66] Aitzema, *Saken*, I, 384.
[67] Aitzema, *Saken*, I, 1079.
[68] Aitzema, *Saken*, II, 874, IV, 921.

the better.' By bringing such high questions as predestination, election, God's providence and eternal decrees, and justification into the pulpit and among the people, who then assumed a right of judgment for themselves, even raising new questions from their own reading of the Bible, theologians did great harm. Aitzema cited the English situation of 1647 and that in Holland. The preachers by their disputes gave over discipline from themselves to the political authorities, 'and were it not for the town hall, the division in the church would be even greater.'[69] Discussing the difference between the Roman and the Lutheran conceptions of the eucharist, he faulted each side for imputing to the other things that were not true. 'It is all a dispute over expressions: in the matter itself, the *Symbolum* [the Apostle's Creed], they are agreed.'[70]

He reproved the Puritans in England for making their explication and presentation of the Bible a 'more infallible canon' than the Catholic interpretation. After all, the canonical books of Scripture were made such by the Church, for nowhere in the Bible itself is any canon to be found. Where do the Puritans find their own liturgy, formularies of prayer, eucharist, baptism, marriage, etc. in the canonical books? he asked. Liturgy, formularies and ceremonies had to come from outside the Bible, for neither Christ nor the Apostles gave any.[71] He also criticized formularies of prayer required in the Netherlands that recommended the East and West India companies, trade, industry and the like to God. 'It is as if we wish to prescribe an instruction and order to God.' But God is not bound by them.[72] But in the world political power determined who would make decisions in the matter of religion.[73] Aitzema therefore accepted the principle of *cujus regio*, transferring it from Germany to the Dutch Republic. 'Town hall and church must be in agreement.' If preachers called for one way and the burgomasters for another, division, 'which is the mother of downfall,' arose.[74]

There had to be order in the church, whether Reformed or Catholic. 'What difference is there between a President [of a synod] and a Pope or primate, between assessors and cardinals, but the name? The principal difference lies in the profits and revenues.' Among the Reformed, in fact, 'everyone claims to be a bishop, each preacher is one in his own congregation, but his revenues are much less.'[75] The Reformation had decapitated the church, stripping it of authority, power and prestige. But Aitzema added a proviso: 'I speak of these things politically, not theologically.'[76] He rejected therefore the argument of Brownists,

[69] Aitzema, *Saken*, III, 172.
[70] Aitzema, *Saken*, IV, 1183.
[71] Aitzema, *Saken*, IV, 1183.
[72] Aitzema, *Saken*, IV, 1182. See also IV, 1005.
[73] Aitzema, *Saken*, III, 497.
[74] Aitzema, *Saken*, II, 875.
[75] Aitzema, *Saken*, VI, 70.
[76] Aitzema, *Saken*, III, 505, 1083.

Puritans and Quakers that only what was found explicitly in the New Testament was acceptable, especially ranks, services, ceremonies and rites: these were necessary for the honor and unity of the church, which they had maintained from the beginning.[77] In England what had been called the 'Anti-Christian tyranny' of the episcopal church had been replaced by the 'anarchy of the Independents.' How different from the Roman church order, where succession and duration over many hundreds of years provided 'clear experience' of its stability.[78] The churchmen in England discovered that the Protestant Reformation had taken the right of judgment in religious controversies from their hands and put it in the hands of 'every churchgoer, weavers, furriers, old wives, and the like.' It was as if a court of justice had been taken from the judges and given to the common people. 'But it is clear and certain that the church is *the firmament and pillar of truth.*'[79] Calvin and Luther, 'politically speaking,' had done great harm by abasing the ecclesiastical order, giving all the property of the church to the secular princes and hence magnifying their power. What had it served to elevate the princes? Luther had acted like the worst of court flatterers, and the people who had failed to see that it would result in their own oppression had been blind. It was better before, under the rule of the Popes, who were never elected from the same house as their predecessors, which is 'a good sign and result of liberty.' 'Politically speaking,' he went on with his pet phrase, 'papal hierarchy or government is one of the finest and most durable republics that there has ever been or can be.' How different was that of England, which had fed fanaticism and Quakery.[80] The Roman church had avoided the hereditary element in monarchy while meeting the need for one at the head. Abuses like flattery, tyranny and the like were the fault not of order or rank but of the one to whom it was given.[81]

What Aitzema disliked in any form was religious inquisition, whether Roman or Genevan. He noted that the inquisition had been in decline in the Netherlands before the Revolt. It had been remarked that 'a good life is good religion,' and the rule, 'do good and avoid evil,' was the best proof of the Christian faith.' All that was required of belief from the time of the Apostles was their creed, which was taught by Reformed, Lutherans, Mennonites and all Christian sects alongside the 'Our Father' and the Ten Commandments. 'The rest is only ceremonies,' maintained by public authority in the churches. He praised the practice of the Dutch Republic, where the Reformed formulary excluded members of all other sects from Heaven, but not from the city where they

---

[77] Aitzema, *Saken*, III, 533.
[78] Aitzema, *Saken*, III, 328, 863.
[79] Aitzema, *Saken*, IV, 921.
[80] Aitzema, *Saken*, III, 896–7.
[81] Aitzema, *Saken*, II, 874. See also IV, 1008.

lived, worked and traded. Aitzema reaffirmed that his purpose had not been to slander the Reformed church, as the preachers seemed to imagine, but to put events within history and to show that the welfare of the country consisted in a multitude of residents of all sects. 'Public tolerance is my justification...My single, simple aim has been to praise this maxim of state, tolerance and unity.' To give the preachers a free hand would be to reenact the old tragedy.[82]

Aitzema's conversion – whether a total ritual acceptance of the Roman faith, although that is probable, or just a clear preference for it – may be explained by the interplay of personal character and the widest considerations of public life. Cynicism and skepticism are usually the traits of the disappointed idealist, and Aitzema's disappointment had to begin with himself. It is difficult to believe that a man who saw through all the cloaks of self-interest in others did not do so to some extent in himself. From the deepest self-doubt and even self-loathing, he may have sought solace and respite in faith. Although he did not explicitly engage in the debate over Pyrrhonism so important in seventeenth-century thought, his cast of mind was deeply skeptical, and he may well have made the leap from doubt to faith that R. H. Popkin has revealed to us in so may Pyrrhonists.[83] We may also speculate that his yearning for order and hierarchy in public life was fed by the disorderliness of his private life. Short of a full-scale biography, however, we cannot be sure how much truth there is in such guesses, however suggestive and plausible.

Does the picture of Aitzema the thinker sketched in these pages mean that I have discovered a hidden genius, a forgotten Locke or Hobbes, or, in view of his religious ideas, a Dutch Bossuet? Hardly. Aitzema's ideas lack the necessary deep originality for such a place in our annals, and they are presented almost incoherently. Pierre Bayle may also have hidden his thoughts under a mountain of barrels in his *Dictionnaire*, but they are still fresh and fruitful. Aitzema's ideas, whatever impact they may have had in the last years of his life when his great work was published, had none that has been detected in subsequent generations. Aitzema was a mirror of ideas, not their source – but a mirror that did more than just transmit, a mirror that intensified the images it displayed.

[82] Aitzema, *Saken*, IV, 203–4, 1008–9.
[83] Richard H. Popkin, *The History of Scepticism from Erasmus to Spinoza*. Rev. ed. (Berkeley, 1979).

John Calvin's contribution to representative government

ROBERT M. KINGDON

H. G. Koenigsberger, through his many publications and through his devoted service to the International Commission for the History of Representative and Parliamentary Institutions, has made many important contributions to our knowledge of the forms of representative government in early modern Europe. But most of the institutions to which he has drawn our attention have been subordinate parts of royal governments, helping to govern nations and provinces under the sovereign rule of a king, as the Sicilian and Netherlandish estates in the realms of the Spanish crown. There was, of course, another form of representative government in the period, of similar age and importance. That was the form of government dominated by representative councils that developed in cities, particularly in those parts of Europe in which cities claimed independence of any sovereign lord – such as Italy and Switzerland – or even in those areas in which cities conceded sovereignty to a distant emperor in order to deny it to any local lord – such as the Holy Roman Empire. It is upon this second type of representative government that this chapter concentrates.

This chapter concentrates, furthermore, upon the period of the early sixteenth century, because many of these representative city governments then became intimately involved in the initial stages of the Protestant Reformation with consequences of some importance for their forms of government. Bernd Moeller has forcefully drawn our attention to the special appeal Protestantism had for the free cities of the Empire and he has also tried to develop an explanation for this appeal, an explanation connected to the sacral nature of the communities protected by their

Some of the material in this essay was used earlier in a paper, 'John Calvin's Contribution to Constitutionalism,' prepared for the 1984 meeting of the Conference for the Study of Political Thought, and some of it was also used in a lecture in the 1984 T. V. Moore series at San Francisco Theological Seminary, titled 'Calvin and Constitutionalism: his work on the laws of Geneva,' and scheduled for publication in the *Pacific Theological Review*.

governments.[1] His argument can easily be extended, indeed was extended to a degree by Moeller himself, to the Swiss cities.

Within these cities which had been governed for centuries by representative institutions and to which the Reformation proved to be particularly appealing, a new form of Protestantism developed, a form that might fairly be labelled civic Protestantism. It was developed first in Zurich under the leadership of Ulrich Zwingli, introduced soon after in Strasbourg under the leadership of Martin Bucer, and spread before long to several other cities. But it came to be dominated in the second generation by the example of Geneva under the leadership of John Calvin. Indeed by the time civic Protestantism was reaching its zenith in Geneva, with Calvin's triumph in 1555 over the last of his local adversaries, it was beginning to fade in the imperial cities. So the specific form of this civic Protestantism that had the most enduring impact on other countries and later generations was the form developed by Calvin. And the type of representative government with which early Calvinism was most obviously associated was the type developed within the city of Geneva. It is upon this specifically Calvinist form of urban representative government that this chapter concentrates. It concentrates even more specifically upon Calvin's personal contribution to that type of government. For it should be recognized that Calvin himself assisted the development of early modern representative government in important ways, specifically in the form it took within cities, and that his assistance took a very concrete form – he drafted the constitution of the independent Genevan state. That, at least, is the argument I wish to develop here.

Calvin, of course, was best known in his own day and since as a theologian. But we should not forget that he was also a lawyer and had, in fact, received more formal training in the law than in theology. We should also not forget that contemporaries knew of his legal skills and valued them. It can be argued that the city of Geneva in calling him back in 1541 and employing him for the second time, now not merely as a public lecturer but also as the general director of its newly Reformed church, was hiring him for his legal skills as well as for his theological skills. If the rulers of Geneva had simply wanted an eloquent preacher, they could have recalled William Farel or hired Pierre Viret, both of whom had preached the Protestant message in Geneva and both of whom were arguably more effective than Calvin in reaching the general population with this message. But the Genevans called Calvin instead,

---

[1] B. Moeller, *Imperial Cities and the Reformation*, tr. from an expanded French version of the German original of 1962 by H. C. Erik Midelfort and Mark U. Edwards, Jr. (Philadelphia, 1972).

John Calvin

because he could do more than simply preach. And in the beginning they used his legal skills intensively. A significant portion of his time from 1541 to 1543, the two years after his definitive return to Geneva, was spent in drafting laws for the city-state. It is upon those laws that I want to concentrate in this essay, for I suspect that they reveal Calvin's really decisive contributions to the development of representative government.

There were three sets of laws Calvin drafted for the Genevan city-state in these years, and each was of such fundamental importance that it can fairly be called a part of the Genevan constitution. The first set of laws was the *Ecclesiastical Ordinances*, adopted on 20 November 1541. They provided a constitution for the Reformed Church, a new ecclesiastical structure to replace the Catholic structures that had collapsed when the prince-bishop of Geneva had been driven out of the city in the political revolution that proved to be the first step toward Protestantism. This new ecclesiastical structure included important new provisions for representation of the Genevan community. The second set of laws was the *Edict of the Lieutenant [of Justice]*, adopted on 12 November 1542. It provided a structure for the administration of justice in Geneva to replace the Savoyard structure that had collapsed when the agents of the duke of Savoy had been driven out of the city with their ally, the bishop. The third set of laws was the *Ordinances on Offices and Officers*, adopted on 28 January 1543. It provided a structure for the government of Geneva by elected magistrates and councils designed to be more nearly representative of the general city population than the ecclesiastical and monarchical government of the prince-bishop it replaced. It created a true constitution for the Genevan state, a constitution that was to continue in force with little change down to the time of the French Revolution.[2]

Some have doubted that Calvin was the true author of these three sets of fundamental laws. It is true that the passages in the registers of the city council that record the details of the commission to draft both the laws on justice and the ordinances on offices do record the names of others who were assigned to work with Calvin. We do, however, also have drafts in Calvin's own hand of at least parts of all these laws – a complete draft of the ecclesiastical ordinances, a draft of about three-quarters of the judicial edict, and a draft of a fragment of the ordinances on offices.[3] Each of these drafts corresponds almost exactly with the

[2] *Les sources du droit du canton de Genève*, E. Rivoire and V. van Berchem (eds.), (Arau, 1930), II, pp. 377–90 (*Ordonnances ecclésiastiques*); pp. 394–408 (*Edit de lieutenant*); pp. 409–34 (*Ordonnances sur les offices et officiers*).

[3] *John Calvin, Ioannis Calvini Opera quae supersunt omnia*, G. Baum, E. Cunitz and E. Reuss (eds.) (Brunsvigae, 1863–1900), x/1, cols. 15–30 ('Projet d'ordonnances ecclésiastiques'); cols. 132–9 and 144–6 (fragments of the *Edit de lieutenant*); cols.

185

recorded texts of the laws as finally adopted. There are changes but most of them are so minor as to seem cosmetic or accidental. In addition, one of the passages in the council register on the drafting of the civil law mentions that Calvin was relieved from most of his duties in the church to work on these laws for a period which may have lasted as long as two months in the fall of 1542. Another such passage notes that Calvin was rewarded with a cask of wine shortly after the judicial edict was adopted.[4] All these bits of evidence persuade me that Calvin was indeed the principal author of these laws, and that in them we may find pretty solid evidence of his legal thinking. I do not, in other words, buy the theories of some that he was merely a secretary for a committee of local old-timers, jotting down their recollections of how things used to be done.[5] He was rather a creator of law, who had a powerful effect on his community. Even if Calvin was not the primary author of these laws, however, the important consequence is the end result. For they clearly codified and formalized a type of representative government for the city of Geneva, a type that proved to be both influential and durable.

This is most obviously documented by the first and the third of the sets of laws Calvin drafted. For the *Ecclesiastical Ordinances* created a church with a limited role for representative institutions and the *Ordinances on Offices and Officers* created a state with a really central role for representative institutions. What was the specific content of these laws?

The *Ecclesiastical Ordinances*, to look at them first, built a Reformed church around four ministries: pastors, doctors, elders, and deacons. All were chosen by the elected councils that governed the city, and each type can be regarded as representing the general population in some way. The pastors and doctors, however, were chosen more for their special skills and could hold their positions for relatively long periods of time, while the elders and deacons were chosen from among the lay citizens of Geneva for only a year at a time. So clearly the bodies within which the elders and deacons worked have a more representative character.

The function of the pastors was to preach the Word of God and to administer the sacraments. Each was assigned to a pulpit in one of the three large parishes into which the city of Geneva was divided after the

---

126–8 (fragment of the *Ordonnances sur les offices et officiers*). The latter two sets of fragments are not identified by the editors as parts of laws actually adopted.
[4] Quoted in *Ibid.*, cols. 125–6.
[5] For a thoughtful statement of a view of this type, see A. Roget, *Histoire du peuple de Genève depuis la réforme jusqu'à l'Escalade* (Geneva, 1870–83), 2/1, 64–8, who concludes that Calvin served as an editor rather than a legislator in preparing these texts. Roget in general supplies the best narrative history and the most authoritative description of Genevan institutions of this period.

Reformation or in one of the small villages in the Genevan hinterland still remaining under the control of the city. Each was chosen by co-optation, after passing a rigorous examination administered by the established pastors, subject to approval first by the city council and then by the members of the parish congregation to which he was assigned. Each became a civil servant, provided with housing, a food allowance, and a small quarterly salary by the state, and subject to instant dismissal if he ever displeased the reigning magistrates. The pastors met once a week, in a group called the Company, to study theology together, to plan the schedule of religious services, to criticize each other, and, later, to oversee a program for the evangelization of France.

The function of the doctors was to teach the Word of God, to the pastors and to the laity. They were expected to be experts in Holy Scripture, accomplished in the original languages in which it had been written. In the beginning, Calvin was the principal doctor, and fulfilled his teaching obligation by delivering public lectures several times a week on selected passages of Scripture. He had originally been hired primarily to do this back in 1536, when Farel first persuaded him to stay in Geneva and help in the reformation of its local church, and he resumed these duties after his return in 1541. Toward the end of his career other doctors were hired, and together they constituted the faculty of the Academy of Geneva, the nucleus from which later grew a university. They were chosen in the same way as the pastors, by co-optation, subject to approval by the city Council. They were also civil servants, supported by the state.

The function of the elders was to see to it that the inhabitants of Geneva lived by the Word of God. They met once a week, together with the pastors, in a semi-judicial body called the Consistory. They were selected so as to represent the different neighborhoods into which the city was formally divided and each elder was supposed to keep close watch on his neighbors. If an elder spotted any deviations in belief or behavior, he was supposed to try to resolve the problem on the spot. If that did not prove possible, the sinner was summoned to a meeting of the Consistory. There the problem would usually be resolved by discussion, with the sinner admitting the error of his ways and promising to sin no more. But if the problem was serious or the sinner stubborn, he or she could be excommunicated or referred to a secular city court for trial and punishment. The Consistory operated, in brief, like a compulsory counselling service and petty court. The elders were lay-business and professional men, elected to the position once a year from a slate drawn up by the outgoing city Council in consultation with the pastors. They constituted one of the many standing committees of the

ROBERT M. KINGDON

city government. They were public servants and received no pay. Most of them were relatively well-to-do and either middle-aged or elderly, thus in a position to let sons and other younger relatives manage their private businesses while they tended to the public business. Their functions made them representatives of their neighbourhood: their election made them representatives of the entire city. From either point of view, their presence in the Consistory made it a representative body.

The function of the deacons was to administer charity for the poor and unfortunate in Geneva. There were two types: a hospitaller who was a permanent and paid civil servant, living in the General Hospital from which most charity was dispensed, and a group of procurators who met with the hospitaller once a week and supervised his activities. The procurators were elected by the outgoing city council in consultation with the pastors, in precisely the same manner as the elders. They constituted another standing committee of the city government. They were also relatively well-to-do and of mature age. Like the elders, they were representatives of the city, and their board might thus be regarded as another representative body.

After describing each of these offices, the *Ecclesiastical Ordinances* then go on to describe its functions in some detail. There are sections on the administration of sacraments, on marriage and burial, on visitation of the sick and the prisoners, and on the catechism of children.[6]

The representative bodies that exercised sovereign power over the entire state of Geneva including its ecclesiastical institutions, however, are the ones described in the later set of laws, the *Ordinances on Offices and Officers*, so let us now turn to them. Unlike the ecclesiastical structure described in the earlier laws, much of the secular structure described in these ordinances had existed at least in a skeletal form for some time. It had developed through the middle ages as a part of the episcopal government and had been described in the 1387 franchises promulgated by bishop Adhémar Fabri[7] and elsewhere. But this medieval structure had been limited to controlling purely local matters of secondary importance – guarding the city walls, cleaning the streets, regulating the periodic fairs, and chores of that sort. The more important functions of government had been reserved to the bishops and their Savoyard allies. The bishops had controlled foreign policy, the coinage of money, and certain kinds of justice. The appointees of Savoy had

6 See E. W. Monter, *Calvin's Geneva* (New York, 1967), Ch. 5, for more general information on how each of these ministries operated, and 'The Consistory of Geneva, 1559–1569,' *Bibliothèque d'Humanisme et Renaissance*, XXXVIII (1976), pp. 467–84, for a particularly good examination of that institution. For additional bibliography, see the items listed in R. M. Kingdon, 'Genf,' *Theologische Realenzyklopadie*, XII (1984), 3/4, de Gruyter.   7 *Les sources du droit du canton de Genève* (1927), I, 190–237.

188

controlled military defense and other kinds of justice. Now the city councils made up of elected representatives had to take over all of these functions and thus needed a more developed and more formal legal structure. That is what Calvin provided for them.

This structure was basically a hierarchy of elected councils. At the apex was an executive council which met several times a week, called the Narrow or Small Council, or often simply the Council. Its activities were directed by four elected magistrates called syndics, arranged in order of seniority, with the first gaining precedence over all the other offices of government. At the next level was the Council of Sixty, which met only occasionally, at the call of the Small Council, to handle certain types of problems, most commonly in the realm of foreign policy. At a similar level was the Council of Two Hundred, which also met only occasionally, at the call of the Small Council, to handle certain types of problems and to participate in the electoral process. At the bottom level was the General Council, made up of all the city's bourgeois – all the male inhabitants who possessed enough property and had a business of good enough reputation to justify their inscription in a book of the bourgeoisie. The General Council met once a year to elect all the officers in the city government. It also met to ratify laws of special importance. The *Ecclesiastical Ordinances*, the *Edict of the Lieutenant*, and the *Ordinances on Offices and Officers* were all adopted at meetings of the General Council.

New syndics were elected every year. The members of the Small Council, the Council of Sixty, and the Council of Two Hundred were also elected every year, but it was usual to elect many of the same people year after year to these bodies. Membership in Small Council and most of the executive offices attached to it, down to its secretaries and porter, were limited to citizens. So were the offices of the lieutenant and his assistants described in the *Edict of the Lieutenant*, and so were a number of other offices in the city. The status of citizen in sixteenth-century Geneva was quite restricted. Only a native-born bourgeois could be a citizen. Immigrants, no matter how wealthy or distinguished, were barred from this status. Thus Calvin, as an immigrant from France, could and did become a bourgeois, albeit rather late in his career,[8] but never could become a citizen. Membership in the larger councils and in certain less sensitive offices was open to all the bourgeoisie.

These councils are all described in Calvin's *Ordinances*. So are a great number of more specific offices ranging from syndics down to jailers and janitors. The *Ordinances* first describe the method of election to each

[8] *Le livre des bourgeois de l'ancienne république de Genève*, A. L. Covelle (ed.) (Geneva, 1897), p. 266.

office and supply the text of the oath tendered to each type of officer at his induction. They then describe the duties of each council and each office, sometimes in considerable detail.

Out of what material did Calvin construct these ordinances? He would have answered that he constructed the *Ecclesiastical Ordinances* out of the Word of God, specifically from the fragmentary descriptions of the apostolic church one can find in the New Testament, primarily in the book of Acts and in certain of the Pauline epistles. There is some evidence, however, that he also integrated customs and practices that he had observed in other Reformed communities in which he had lived, specifically Basel and Strasbourg, or that he found already in operation in Geneva. The Genevans had already deputed the administration of charity to a hospitaller and a board of procurators, for example, before Calvin arrived in the city. He called these officers deacons, and in so doing sanctified their calling, but he did not create their positions or devise the way in which they were chosen.[9]

The *Ordinances on Offices and Officers* incorporate in even more obvious ways existing practice. It is possible that Calvin may again have been influenced on points of detail by governmental arrangements he had observed in other free cities in which he had lived, but if he did there is little evidence of it in the text of the laws he drafted. He saw his job to be primarily the description, codification, and formalization of existing Genevan practices and institutions. In describing some of the offices, he displays a considerable control of received legal principles, a control even more evident in the text of the *Edict of the Lieutenant*. For example the *Ordinances on Offices and Officers* include a particularly careful description of the duties of the Procurator General, a legal representative of the city, who, among other duties, was expected to appear as a representative of the people in trials before the Lieutenant, to arrange for tutors or guardians or orphans, to enforce certain zoning laws, and to act as a legal officer in several other ways.

What is of greatest interest about these ordinances is the general principles of government they incorporate, the constitutional principles, if you will. There were two of these principles woven into these bodies of law that strike me as particularly revealing, for they reveal much of the fundamental nature of representative civic government not only in Geneva but also elsewhere. It is to these principles that I would now like to turn.

[9] For more on the origins of the Genevan diaconate, see R. M. Kingdon, 'Calvin's Ideas about the Diaconate: Social or Theological?' in C. Lindberg (ed.), *Piety, Politics, and Ethics: Reformation Studies in Honor of George Wolfgang Forell* (Kirksville, Mo., 1984), pp. 167–80, and E. A. McKee, *John Calvin on the Diaconate and Liturgical Almsgiving* (Geneva, 1984).

A first principle marking the Genevan constitution as Calvin drafted it is collegial rule. The Genevans had become thoroughly disenchanted with the monarchic rule of their prince-bishop and they were determined never again to let any one man gain such power, in either church or state. In this they were simply joining most other cities of the period in a settled distrust of one-man rule. The *Ecclesiastical Ordinances* make no provision at all for any one position of leadership in the church. The Company of Pastors is to meet weekly as a body and to make decisions of importance to the church as a whole, but there is no provision for its officers. In practice, of course, Calvin became the leader of the Company. He seems to have regularly convened its meetings and supervised its deliberations, and he was usually the member of the Company deputed to appear before the Small Council to negotiate on ecclesiastical matters. He was fairly often accompanied at these times by other pastors, however, and now and then replaced entirely by one or another of his colleagues. It is unfair to call him, as some have, 'the tyrant of Geneva.' While he usually won his way, it was by use of his considerable intellectual gifts or his forceful personality. He had no institutional position of preeminence.

The Geneva Company of Pastors did not actually face the problem of its own governance until after Calvin died. At that point it decided to elect as its moderator Theodore Beza, who had taken over many of Calvin's duties during the last months of his life. After some hesitation, Beza accepted this election, but for one year only. He was then reelected every year for the next sixteen years, until ill health finally drove him to refuse serving any longer. The city's Small Council was comfortable with this arrangement and obviously preferred to deal with Beza as the representative of the clergy. They were irritated when Beza decided to step down and doubly irritated when they were told that the Company had been secretly electing its own moderator every year, without consulting them. Beza finally persuaded the Council that he really did need to step down. The Company then turned to a weekly moderatorship, selecting a new one of its members every week to preside over its meetings and represent it before the government. The term of moderator did not stay that short for long. But no one person has ever again held it for as long a time as did Calvin and then Beza. There were uninformed outsiders who called Calvin, and after him Beza, the bishop of Geneva, and each did, of course, possess some of the supervisory powers of a bishop. But both indignantly refused to accept either the title or its real substance during their many years of leadership.[10]

---

[10] O. Labarthe, 'En marge de l'édition des Registres de la Compagnie des pasteurs de Genève: le changement du mode de présidence de la Compagnie, 1578–1580,' *Revue*

The *Ordinances on Offices and Officers* do provide for one-man leadership in the civil government, but only of a modest and ephemeral kind. One of the four syndics every year was to be designated First Syndic, and that position carried a ceremonial precedence and a few extra responsibilities. The choice of which syndic would be first, however, was determined entirely by seniority in service within the Small Council. And a man held the position for only one year. So a First Syndic of Geneva won very little lasting preeminence within the city. It is clear that actual control of the city government rested within the Small Council as a whole, not with any one individual. The sovereign of Geneva was always referred to in the plural, as 'Messieurs de Genève', even in correspondence with the representatives of the many resolutely monarchical governments with which Geneva had to deal.

This commitment to collegial rule still characterizes Swiss government, on the municipal, cantonal, and federal levels. It sets the Swiss apart from the many other types of modern government that still feel a need to personalize government by vesting the highest power, even if it be sharply limited and checked, in one single individual. And the contrast was surely even more striking in the sixteenth century, when one compares a government led by a king who led a highly public and even theatrical life supported by sweeping claims to absolute power with a government led by a council of relatively anonymous ordinary citizens with changes in its composition every year.

A second principle marking the Genevan constitution as Calvin drafted it is accountability. All public servants, both within the church and the state, were accountable to the general public. The fact that they were selected from among the general population for positions of leadership by their compatriots and only for as long as their leadership won the approval of those compatriots, underlines in an emphatic way the representative character of their positions. This principle of accountability was built into the very process of selection. Thus each candidate for the pastorate had to pass three hurdles: he had to demonstrate his orthodoxy and his competence to the Company of existing pastors; he had then to demonstrate his loyalty to the Small Council; he had finally to demonstrate his ability as a preacher to his parishioners. If he did not pass that final hurdle, the ordinance required the Company to proceed to the election of someone else. This prospect on occasion led the

d'histoire ecclésiastique suisse, LXVII (1972), pp. 160–86, provides an expert history of this institution. On the reputation of Calvin and Beza as leaders of the Genevan church, see R. M. Kingdon, *Geneva and the Consolidation of the French Protestant Movement* (Geneva and Madison, Wisc., 1967), p. 17, on Calvin as 'bishop'; p. 89 on Beza as 'Jupiter of the lake of Geneva,' and *passim*.

Company to pass over a candidate who seemed intellectually highly qualified because he had a 'too small voice',[11] no doubt incapable of filling an acoustically dead Gothic church building without the assistance of any modern method of amplification. And each pastor finally selected clearly served at the pleasure of the government. The Small Council could and did dismiss a pastor on very short notice and for reasons that seem minor, for example because its members were displeased with the content of a Sunday sermon. Calvin himself had been summarily dismissed, along with Farel, back in 1538, and he came close to being dismissed again several times after his return in 1541. A good number of his colleagues were thus dismissed, some of them with Calvin's consent, perhaps even with his connivance. Indeed it became somewhat unusual for a pastor to live out his life in the service of the Genevan church. Calvin and Beza were exceptional in that they died while still in office.

Pastors, at least, were appointed for indefinite periods of time. No such security was granted to most of the officers in the civil government. Most civil posts were filled for one year only. Some were open to renewal, others were not. Most of them, furthermore, were filled by election, often following a rather complex procedure. The most important of these elections, of course, was of the reigning syndics for the year, and it was particularly complicated. The process began when each member of the outgoing Small Council chose four nominees. The Council of Two Hundred then met and chose eight nominees, which could include the top eight suggested by members of the Small Council but did not have to. The General Council then met and was asked to make a final selection of four candidates from the slate of eight, but if a majority could not agree on four then it could ask for further nominations. This procedure guaranteed that each syndic had majority support of the bourgeoisie before he began his term of service. The candidates had to be citizens and the voters had to be either citizens or bourgeois, so this was not a truly democratic election. Women and men without property or an honorable profession had no share in the process. But the procedure did guarantee that each officer had solid support from at least one class – the propertied class. No one could win power solely because of birth or by appointment. All had to stand for election. There was, furthermore, an obligation to serve if elected. The ordinances spell out penalties enacted against any citizen who refused to accept public office, unless he could provide a persuasive excuse. Even the Lieutenant, the chief judicial officer in this government and clearly one of the busiest,

---

[11] *Registres de la Compagnie des Pasteurs de Genève au temps de Calvin*, R. M. Kingdon and J. -F. Bergier (eds.) (Geneva, 1962), II, pp. 66–7, gives this as the reason for assigning Claude Baduel to a rural church rather than a city parish.

had to be elected once a year. His four assistants, however, served for two-year terms, and their terms were staggered so that only two came up for reelection in any one year. That provision is one of the few recognitions one finds in this entire constitution of any need for continuity in office to provide some efficiency. All these civil servants, furthermore, like the pastors, served at the pleasure of the Small Council and could be dismissed with little notice. Taken together, these provisions made all the servants of the Genevan state, both clerical and lay, accountable to the ruling class.

These two principles of collegial rule and accountability made the government of Geneva somewhat different from many other types of government in the period. The role of inheritance was diminished, although not abolished, since only native-born citizens could hold the more important positions in the civil government. But no office was reserved to any one person by right of birth. The role of wealth was also diminished, although not abolished, since only men of property could vote. But no office was for sale. This de-emphasis on birth and wealth made the government of Geneva different from that of most of the secular principalities of the day in which the hereditary principle remained strong and in some of which, most notably the kingdom of France, more and more key offices were for sale. It also made Geneva different from many of the ecclesiastical principalities of the day, since nepotism, a version of the hereditary principle, and simony, the trade in church offices, were facts of life even though proscribed by church law.

Many of the free cities of Germany and Switzerland, to be sure, had governments similar to Geneva's in these respects. There was one key difference which sets Geneva apart even from them, however, and which may well have made the city's government virtually unique. This difference lay in the opening Geneva provided to immigrants. This is an opening not to be found in the texts of the constitutional laws Calvin drafted for Geneva, since those texts reserved most offices of significance to the natives. It is to be found rather in two loopholes in those laws, loopholes which proved to be of fateful significance.

The first loophole was provision for appointment by merit to certain offices. The most significant of these was the pastorate. The people of Geneva came to agree that every pastor had to have a certain type of advanced education, including some training in Greek and Hebrew, a type of training rare in the period. Since no native Genevan had had an opportunity to obtain this type of education, all the pastors had to be foreign. There seems to have been one holdover from the old Catholic days in the Genevan Company of Pastors, a man named Bernard, but he was certainly not one of the more prominent pastors.[12] Once Calvin was established, all the new pastors, without exception, were men foreign to Geneva. Almost all of them, furthermore, were from France, although there was an occasional pastor of Swiss origin.

The second loophole was provision for entry into the bourgeoisie by invitation or on payment of a large fee. The Small Council was free to vote a man into the bourgeoisie because of special services he was equipped to render to the city. Several lawyers and engineers were voted into the bourgeoisie for this reason. So were most of the pastors, eventually, although this was not the practice in the beginning, and Calvin himself was invited to join the bourgeoisie only after several of his colleagues in the pastorate had already won that distinction. More foreigners became bourgeois by payment of fee. The size of the fee varied considerably and would be accepted, in any event, only from a man whose background and business were regarded as honorable. The fees were large enough on average to constitute a useful source of supplementary income to the state, and that seems to have been one of the initial reasons for permitting the practice. Entrance into the bourgeoisie carried with it political rights, the key one of which was the right to participate in the General Council and to vote in those annual elections for most of the other officers of the state.[13]

I have now given you an account of Calvin's role in the drafting of the Genevan constitution and a sketch of that constitution's contents, both as he wrote them down and as they were modified in practice. Let me now turn to a consideration of the consequences of these developments. The most important initial consequence was that the experience gave Calvin an intimate acquaintance with the inner workings of the Genevan government, an acquaintance that he used to rise to a position of immense authority in the city and then to make of the city the headquarters of his brand of the Reformed Christian faith. Another important consequence, however, was that Calvin became closely identified in the contemporary mind with a certain type of government, an urban republic dominated in law by a representative institution although conceding an important indirect role in its leadership to the clergy. This identification may have won him support in some areas. But it also lost him support in other areas, including some of considerable importance.

[12] H. Heyer, *L'Eglise de Genève* (Geneva, 1909), p. 425, provides a biographical sketch of Bernard.
[13] For a list of these bourgeois and the fees most of them paid, see *Le Livre des bourgeois de l'ancienne république de Genève*, A. L. Covelle (ed.). For an account of the struggles over access to this status, see A. Roget, *Histoire du peuple de Genève...*, esp. vol. 4/2.

It is upon this final, somewhat negative, consequence that I now want to concentrate.

The first negative reaction to Calvin's role in the government of Geneva developed within Switzerland itself, specifically within the republic of Bern. Bern had originally inspired and promoted the growth of Protestantism in Geneva and Bernese military protection had made possible the survival of Geneva as an independent state in the face of armed threats from Savoy. Bernese troops occupied territory on every side of Geneva and effectively protected the city from invasion. But the triumph of Calvin and the constitution he had drafted mightily irritated the Bernese. They did not object, of course, to the power it granted to a representative council, since that was the very kind of government they possessed and treasured. But they did object to the role this constitution offered to the clergy in the control of morals, since the pastors joined the elders as members of the Consistory, and the Consistory succeeded in making good its claim to sole power to levy and to lift the feared sanction of excommunication. And they also objected to the role this government allowed to foreigners, specifically to immigrants from France, most notably Calvin. This loophole had been used so effectively by Calvin and his supporters that the city of Geneva was literally swamped with immigrants, actually doubling in size during the period of Calvin's ministry.[14] These changes had been engineered only over the opposition of a number of local Genevans, called Libertines by Calvin and his associates. When the Libertines were expelled from Geneva, Bern offered them asylum. The Bernese then proceeded to return to Savoy some of the territory they had occupied near Geneva. They made it clear that the Genevans could not expect as much military protection as in the past. This coolness of the Bernese towards the Genevans was slow to develop and did not have really important consequences until well after Calvin died, toward the end of the sixteenth century. But at that point it proved nearly fatal to independent Geneva. A revived and militant Savoy made serious efforts to capture the city, particularly between 1589 and 1602, and Geneva barely survived.[15] She came through the ordeal as a weaker and less illustrious state. She no longer served as the most important single center for the spread of Reformed Protestantism – as the Protestant Rome. That role she now had to share with other more protected university towns, notably Heidelberg and Leiden.

[14] A. Perrenoud, *La population de Genève, XVIᵉ-XIXᵉ siècles, Mèmoires et documents publiés par la société d'histoire et d'archéologie de Genève* (Geneva and Paris, 1979), p. 37.

[15] L. Cramer, 'La politique extérieure – la diplomatie et la guerre – 1536–1603,' in P. -E. Martin (ed.), *Histoire de Genève des origines à 1798* (Geneva, 1951), pp. 283–314, provides a useful narrative of these developments.

John Calvin

Even more instructive are the reactions within monarchies, however, for they rejected Calvinism not only for its clericalism but also for its association with government dominated by representative institutions. This reaction was pronounced in France, in the Empire, and in England. The negative reaction in France, to be sure, was closely connected to the French rejection of Protestant theology, for the majority of Frenchmen seem to have been persuaded by their own Catholic religious leaders that Calvinism really did contain a particularly dangerous heresy. But an important additional reason for the French rejection of Calvinism was its association with a certain kind of government. Calvinists were often accused within France of wanting to break the kingdom up into a set of relatively autonomous cantons, like Switzerland. This possibility surely generated some of the fear of Calvinism one finds at the royal court and in circles devoted to royal government.

An even purer reaction of this type can be found in England, particularly during the reigns of Elizabeth I and James I. For most Englishmen of this period, unlike the French, did adopt Calvin's theology, as the best way of defining the Protestant faith to which they were now committed. But they split sharply on whether to adopt Calvin's ecclesiology, into Puritan and Anglican factions. The Puritan faction tended to accept the claim of Calvin's followers that the only true way to organize the Christian church was the way Calvin had organized it in Geneva. The Anglican faction tended to resist this claim, arguing that Calvin's church was culture-bound, that it was designed solely for an urban republic like Geneva, that it could not be transplanted to a monarchy like England. This point of view was summed up in its most lapidary form by King James I, when he said: 'no bishop, no king!' It was summed up in a more extended and particularly revealing form by Richard Hooker, the most eloquent and erudite defender of the episcopalian government of the Church of England. In the preface to his master-work, *Of the Laws of Ecclesiastical Polity*, he considers the Genevan precedent.[16] Hooker makes clear his great admiration for Calvin as a theologian, calling him 'incomparably the wisest man that ever the French Church did enjoy,'[17] and he concedes that Calvin's publications, specifically his *Institutes of the Christian Religion* and his Biblical commentaries 'have deservedly procured him honour through-out the worlde.'[18] Hooker even concedes that the church structure created by Calvin fitted the needs of the Genevans. But it fitted their needs because 'the forme of their civill regiment was popular, as it

[16] Richard Hooker, *Of the Laws of Ecclesiastical Polity*, Georges Edelen (ed.) (Cambridge, Mass., 1977), I, pp. 3–12.
[17] *Ibid.*, p. 3.   [18] *Ibid.*, p. 10.

continueth at this day: neither King, nor Duke, nor noble man of any authoritie or power over them, but officers chosen by the people yerely out of themselves, to order all things with publique consent.'[19] A people this disorganized and unruly needed stern discipline, and this Calvin supplied with his consistorial system. But Hooker concluded that the Calvinist form of church organization had no value as a model for England, precisely because it was designed for an urban republic rather than for a unitary monarchy. He rejected flatly all arguments that this form of church organization was founded on Scripture alone, that it was the only form of church organization bequeathed to us by Christ and his apostles.

To Hooker, then, Calvin was the creator of a constitution, an ecclesiastical constitution closely fitted into the political context in which it was located. He did not know of Calvin's role in helping to shape that political context. But he expertly spotted the congruence between the ecclesiastical and political constitutions created in Geneva and he rejected both as a result. He wanted no part of either in England.

Let me now sum up: one of the greatest contributions of Reformation Geneva was the contribution of a special form of government, a government developed also in other cities, but dramatized and publicized to a special degree by Geneva. This contribution was not of an articulated body of political thought but of a political model. Geneva provided a living example of how church and state could be organized in ways radically different from most of the rest of contemporary society, in governments dominated by representative councils controlled by the principles of collegial leadership and accountability. These institutions and these principles seemed unnatural to many, a denial of the general assumption that ultimate power in any human institution, ranging from the family to the universal church, was best vested in one individual. But they provided an alternative of fateful importance to later generations.

[19] *Ibid.*, p. 3.

Luther and the humanists

A. G. DICKENS

It may at first sight appear that Luther's central doctrine of Justification by Faith Alone must divide him from the humanists, but this notion would seem entirely erroneous, for it depends upon a misreading of Luther's anthropology and upon an anachronistic misuse of the term 'humanist'. Let us clear the ground by a brief glance at each of these points.

Luther's rigorous interpretation of St Paul, which deprives man of all power to save himself, refers to the higher plane of human destiny: the plane of salvation. Luther does not make us automata on the worldly plane, where man does enjoy Free Will and cannot disclaim responsibility.[1] Considering the all-importance of salvation, Luther devoted a quite surprising amount of his writings and activities to the problems of fallen mankind in this terrestrial life, problems about which something could be done, and on which his own ceaseless counselling could be genuinely serviceable. Whatever we may think of his theology, his practical views – on everything from the structure of the Holy Roman Empire down to the organization of grammar schools – are in general marked by bold common sense and forthright expression. In the second place, let me restate what I regard as the proper use of the word humanist, the meaning with which it was normally invested from the late fifteenth century to the nineteenth. It did not mean what Auguste Comte meant by his emphasis upon the dignity of man and his refusal to find in the divine anything external or superior to mankind. Neither did it follow Burckhardt's association of humanism with the so-called Man of the Renaissance, the Borgia–Benevnuto Cellini type, full of self-will and ruthless individualism. It had not yet come to envisage H. G. Wells, or anybody else who discarded religion in favour of progress and redemption through science. Around 1500 a humanist was a teacher or student of

---

[1] For the complexities of Luther's 'Two Kingdoms' see W. D. J. Cargill Thompson, *Studies in the Reformation* (London, 1980), ch. 2.

the ancient classics: one who professed the *studia humanitatis*.[2] In this present essay I shall use the term 'humanism' in this uncomplicated sense, but shall extend it to 'Christian humanism' when I encounter the same 'new' critical methods applied to the biblical texts.

One might best envisage the humanist of that day as a poor scholar, still a Christian believer, somewhat on the periphery of university life, a pygmy hippopotamus among those mighty pachyderms, the theologians and the scholastic philosophers. True, several humanists gained appointments within the papal curia, where a few, notably Lorenzo Valla (1406–57) – a great influence upon both Erasmus and Luther – did their best to discredit the papal monarchy. As yet a sophisticated anticlerical might feel reasonably safe in the Vatican, where he might avoid fanatical Dominican friars and observe little reason to change his views. Yet in general the humanist officials and courtiers rarely enjoyed decisive political powers. Even those exceptional few who held office in High Renaissance Italy, such as Machiavelli and Guicciardini, exercised only limited influence – and for short periods – upon the actual decisions of princes and cities. Likewise Castiglione's *Book of the Courtier*, though in its way both charming and instructive, illustrates neither political power nor fundamental scholarship. Though it finishes with a Platonist rapture on Love, staged by Cardinal Bembo, it idealizes a group of real people in or near the papal service, who in real life consisted of ambitious careerists and downright thugs. Indeed, the subject matter itself, inspired by the fashionable ideal of *sprezzatura*, is too much concerned with courtly, even physical, accomplishments to have affected the course of high culture. Yet by now, in the first two decades of the sixteenth century, serious humanist studies had already crossed the Alps in force, and their devotees had begun more creative functions among the middle orders of society. They had attained importance at least as secretaries and administrators in the German and Swiss cities known to Luther and Zwingli early in the new century; but they also figured within the proliferating universities, among the lawyers, the lesser gentry, the secretaries of ministers and bishops, the civil servants, diplomats and propagandists of the rising monarchies in France and England. Moreover, some characteristically humanist opinions, especially those attacking popes, monks and scholastic thinkers, eventually seeped down to the masses through translations into the vernacular, and more directly through the immense surge of popular Lutheran pamphlet-literature during the early years of the Reformation.

Most amazingly of all, Erasmus, who never published a word in the

[2] The basic ideas are concisely stated by P. O. Kristeller, *Renaissance Thought II. Papers on Humanism and the Arts* (New York, 1965), pp. 1–19.

vernacular, managed to create an anticlerical atmosphere among literate men, which in course of time also affected public opinion as a whole, and in a manner denied to any other single writer before Voltaire. I need scarcely add that the multiplication of printer-publishers soon after 1500 provided another powerful impetus and was fully recognized by Luther and other intelligent observers as creating new dimensions for culture and religion. This diffusion owed much to business-acumen, since a printed book could not have become a profitable mass-seller, had it been limited to clerical uses or even had it remained in the specialized, academic world of *quattrocento* philologists and Platonists. Accordingly after 1500 the pot-bellied patrician folio yielded pride of place to the agile bourgeois octavo, which not only moved into the vernaculars, but also carried an increasing volume of social-religious comment into the lay world of gentry, merchants and even tradesmen. Of course this shift arose in some measure from the saleability among such laymen of revelations about clerical abuses and scandals, together with the desired proposals for reform. Both in Latin and German, Luther's early manifestos were huge sellers, but only less so were the more popular among the works of Erasmus, though these were not substantially translated into the vernaculars until the last decade (1526–36) of his life.

Perhaps the most superficial modern criticisms of humanism have arisen among observers over-impressed by its mere stylistic emphases. Humanism was never wholly dominated by the desire of the purists to write Latin exactly as Cicero had written it, and that ambition was laughed out of court by Erasmus himself. Even by 1500 such ambitions had not wholly died, yet the demand for substance, as distinct from form, had never been quenched, while the rising emphasis upon Greek was diversifying the narrow Ciceronian model. It has been argued that the Latin of Erasmus became more classical with his years in Italy (1506–9), yet at no time did he write Ciceronian Latin; rather did he create his own idiom, at once elegant, expressive, but often by purist standards unconventional. Furthermore in his dialogue *Ciceronianus* (1527) he ridiculed the pedants without mercy, so finally dismissing a dubious ideal which had already outlived its usefulness. In the event, Cicero acquired substance as the main vehicle of Stoicism, another of the pagan creeds which readily blended with Christianity.

If then humanism progressively shed much of its courtly, aristocratic, pagan and pedantic ambience, wherein remained that force which enabled it to continue altering the mental map of Europe? Did it not, through its observant scrutiny of texts, its rigorous demand for evidence, become essentially a historical study, the immediate forerunner of modern historical criticism? As the sixteenth century progressed, humanist training embraced the secondary school population and dominated the educational world. So commonly proceeding thereafter to legal studies, humanist writers applied the concepts of the ancient world to politics and society: they began to see historiography not merely as factual chronicling, but rather as the analysis of situations or as a critique of whole cultures. Inspired not only by Herodotus but also by the Book of Daniel (that humble forerunner of Arnold Toynbee!) some sixteenth-century scholars even began writing textbooks on the rise and fall of Empires.[3] Others, often inspired by distaste for the Papacy and the high Middle Ages, invested the annals of Christianity with a new chronology, showing how and when it had 'gone wrong,' even presuming to defend the medieval heresiarchs, and so giving the Protestant Reformation a dramatic pre-history.[4] Amid these various developments, educated men acquired as a result of their classical and historical knowledge a thirst for documentation, a period-sense, and above all the power of detecting anachronism, that well-nigh universal flaw in medieval thought. Even back in the days of *quattrocento* humanism Lorenzo Valla had already started applying these new critiques to polemical tasks, markedly with his exposure in 1440 of the Donation of Constantine, the forged document upon which papal claims to secular power had been partially based. More important still, Valla transferred the new insight from the pagan classics to the Scriptures, when he conducted a critical comparison between the Vulgate and the Greek New Testament in his *Collatio Novi Testamenti* (1440–2), one of the two versions of which was to be edited by Erasmus at Paris in 1505.[5] He constantly asks the question 'what does the Greek mean?' and of course gives the answers in Latin. Both as textual critic and as theologian, Valla exerted a direct influence upon both Erasmus and Luther. But above all Valla marks the transfer of humanist criticism to the Scriptures. Since Luther's theological foundations were to depend upon this shift, must we not begin the Luther story with Valla and humanism as well as with late medieval theology as comprising Nominalism, Biel, Staupitz and the *Devotio Moderna*?

[3] E.g., J. Sleidan, *De quatuor summis imperiis lib. iii* (Strasbourg, 1556), which became a standard educational text. Cf. A. G. Dickens, *Reformation Studies* (London, 1982), p. 545.

[4] Foxe's *Acts and Monuments* supplies a classic example of such a historiography, but the concepts go back to Luther, Melanchthon, Tyndale, and Foxe's immediate inspirer, John Bale.

[5] For the two versions and their manuscripts see A. Perosa (ed.), *Lorenzo Valla. Collatio Novi Testamenti*, Istituto Nazionale di Studi sal Rinascimento, Studi e Testi (n.d, c. 1970). On Valla's religion see M. Fois, *Il pensiero cristiano di Lorenzo Valla nel quadro storicoculturale del suo ambiente* (*Analecta Gregoriana*, CLXXIV, Rome, 1965); E. Muhlenberg, 'Laurentius Valla als Renaissancetheolog', *Zeitschrift für Theologie und Kirche*, LXVI (1969); G. Radetti, 'La Religione di Valla', *Mediaevo e Rinascimento, studi in onore di Bruno Vardi*, II (1955).

In 1496–7, forty years after Valla's death, John Colet returned from Italy and delivered his Oxford lectures on the Epistle to the Romans in the spirit of a historian as well as in that of a theologian. Having swept aside the concept of the Bible as a mere arsenal of texts, he scorns the schoolmen's failure to accept plain, literal interpretations, together with their servile respect for patristic and medieval exegetes. Despite his dry, puritanical restraint, Colet nevertheless displays a human interest in both the adventures and the mind of St Paul. He understands that he is dealing with a live man in a historical setting: he even reaches down his copy of Suetonius in order to discuss the social background of Paul's congregation in Rome.[6]

At this point Erasmus, becoming a figure of European renown, took the religious discussion still further ahead. As early as 1503–4 his *Enchiridion* pleaded for a scripturally orientated religion, freed from clerical monopoly, scholastic analysis and allegorical interpretations of the Bible. He called for a spiritual imitation of Christ upon this humanist basis. He demanded a church free of warlike popes, prelatical lordship and monkish hypocrisy, a religion cleansed also of that Latin complacency which had so long dismissed Origen and the Greek Fathers as heretics. However greatly his anthropology – his view of man and man's relationship with God – differed from that subsequently presented by Luther, this prince of humanists hence preceded Luther in a concept even more basic than that of Justification by Faith Alone. This ultimate concept was the superior authority of the Scriptures over all other sources: the Fathers, the doctrinal inventions of the ecclesiastical hierarchy, and the popular quasi-religious cults. Its strength lay in the demand of the humanists for solid textual evidence on Christ's teaching, and without this demand Luther could not have built a viable alternative theology to that accepted in Rome. Moreover in 1516, shortly before Luther erupted, Erasmus not only took additional steps to implement this claim, but sought to develop it into a biblical mission. He issued his own Latin translation taken direct from the best available Greek texts of the New Testament, thus delivering a public affront to the Vulgate, that hoary embodiment of Latin theocracy. Furthermore Erasmus accompanied this translation (1516) by an introduction, the *Paraclesis*, which adventurously called for free Bible-reading in vernacular translations for all Christians, lay and clerical, educated and uneducated, women as well as men. His powerful irony still rings in twentieth-century

---

[6] F. Seebohm, *The Oxford Reformers*, 2nd edn., (London, 1869), pp. 29–42, brought out the humanist aspects of Colet's work. Of the recent commentaries on Colet, see especially the articles by P. I. Kaufman in *Church History*, XLVI (1977), and in *The Journal of British Studies*, XXII (1982).

ears, foreshadowing Luther in his proclamation that the Bible – despite its complexities – spoke a lot of plain truth:

Indeed, I disagree very much with those who are unwilling that Holy Scripture, translated into the vulgar tongue, be read by the uneducated, as if Christ taught such intricate doctrines that they could scarcely be understood by very few theologians, or as if the strength of the Christian religion consisted in men's ignorance of it. The mysteries of kings, perhaps, are better concealed, but Christ wishes his mysteries published as openly as possible. I would that even the lowliest women read the Gospels and the Pauline Epistles. And I would that they were translated into all languages so that they could be read and understood not only by Scots and Irish but also by Turks and Saracens. Surely the first step is to understand in one way or another. It may be that many will ridicule, but some may be taken captive. Would that, as a result, the farmer should sing some portion of them at the plow, the weaver hum some parts of them to the movement of his shuttle, the traveller lighten the weariness of the journey with stories of this kind! Let all the conversations of every Christian be drawn from this source.[7]

Here indeed was the ready-made platform on which Luther the biblical theologian could build! No one familiar with the contemporary sources could doubt the explosive character of Bible-study and Bible-reading. Even modern liberals should sympathize somewhat with the restrictive attitudes of the Catholic hierarchy of that day, which continued to stress the need for authoritative interpretation, and then to denounce the divisions which did in fact soon occur on a far greater scale than either Erasmus or Luther had foreseen. As against this political wisdom, no doubt equally powerful arguments might be advanced, for here arose in one of its primary forms what has since proved the major debate over human freedom. This particular phase of the debate, arising originally from humanist scholarship, has by no means lost its significance. Amid the impressive rise of lay education and the huge spread of printing, how was it possible – let alone defensible – to stop the mass of Christians from reading (or hearing read) the foundation-documents of the Faith, the testimony which they now began to see as their very title to salvation? Though Christian humanists and Protestants were well aware of the arguments for the paramount authority of the New Testament, they were not technically equipped to use it so powerfully (or so perilously) as the scholars of our present century. Many still exaggerated the historical authority of the Fathers and the early Councils, though Luther himself, stubbornly but as it proved rightly, insisted on the altogether unique authority of the Bible texts.

The major issue should no longer be seen merely as a clash between

[7] J. C. Olin, *Desiderius Erasmus: Christian Humanism and the Reformation* (New York, 1965), pp. 96–7.

literalist bible-men and innovative fund-raisers. What specially offended the source-respecting, critical observers was the sub-Christian or even non-Christian character of so many cults and practices which had taken shelter in the penumbra of the Church: not only the dubious official theology which imaginatively extended the doctrine of Indulgences but the disproportionate devotions to minor saints, the boisterous materialism of the popular festivities and, lower still on the scale, that white magic of spells and incantations which had become the functional religion of peasants concerned to arrest crop-failures and cattle diseases rather than to define Justification.[8] Only during recent years have we come to see how widely medieval Christianity was accompanied and even pervaded by comforting superstitions. So, faced by the whole problem of authority and authentication, do we not come very near to the nexus between Christian Humanism and the Reformation? Here we observe a momentous encounter between a would-be Scriptural religion and a variegated host of cults, processed, mediated or merely tolerated by ecclesiastical authority, an authority which at that time paid too little regard to the prime sources and to the sane, purposeful, and unaffected atmosphere of Christ's earthly mission and of Apostolic Christianity. In this phraseology I fear I betray my own emotional sympathies, yet I am also well aware that, in the event, both the mediation and the interpretation of the Scriptures imposed problems more acute than the reformists could appreciate in that second decade of the sixteenth century. Yet with the application of humanist textual and historical methods a powerful new factor was entering the situation. Such activities soon went beyond the mere correction of erroneous passages of the Vulgate by reference to the Greek originals. As best they could, the Christian humanists entered upon the broader problems since known as the Higher Criticism. Guided by literary flair, by natural linguistic sense, Luther himself boldly trod parts of this minefield,[9] even though to us he may seem all too often a prey to literal acceptances, and even though in later years he became reluctant to allow his followers a similar liberty. Intelligent Christians of Luther's day were bound to start asking

---

[8] In England a major landmark on this level was the publication in 1971 of Keith Thomas, *Religion and the Decline of Magic*, though elsewhere studies of the folk-religion came earlier: e.g. M. Rumpf, *Das gemeine Volk, II, Religiöse Volkskunde* (Stuttgart, 1933); G. Le Bras, *Etudes de sociologie religieuse* (2 vols., Paris, 1955–6); J. Toussaert, *Le sentiment religieux en Flandre à la fin du Moyen Age* (Paris, 1963); J. Bossy, 'The Counter Reformation and the People of Catholic Europe', *Past and Present*, XLVII (1970). For some recent works see R. W. Scribner's reviews in *History Workshop*, XIV (1982) and in *European Studies Review*, XIII (1983). On the modern background: P. Burke, *Popular Culture in Early Modern Europe* (London and New York, 1978).

[9] On the broad principles of Luther's exegesis I follow J. Pelikan, *Luther the Expositor* (Companion volume to the American Edition of Luther's Works, St Louis, Mo., 1950).

who should be their guides in this brave new world. Surely not the *Schwärmer*, the 'mad saints' who believed in the Inner Light and who were desperately worrying Luther as early as 1521–3, when their antics brought him down from his Patmos, the Wartburg, in order to preach them out of Wittenberg itself. At the other extreme, surely not the German bishops and cathedral dignitaries of that day, so many of them innocent of religious motivation and theological learning alike, though doubtless qualified by high birth. If I remember rightly, it was Erasmus who said that if Christ himself returned to earth, he would never be appointed to a canonry at Strasbourg, since his coat of arms did not contain enough quarterings. By accident, when recently re-reading Philip Melanchthon's funeral speech over Luther, I came across his judgement on guidance and authority. We tend to think of Magister Philippus as a lieutenant, or in Luther's ambivalent phrase, as that 'scrawny little man' whose appearance so forcibly reminded him of St Paul. Yet I need scarcely add that Philip soon became known to all his countrymen as *Praeceptor Germaniae*, the man who not only filled the lecture halls of Wittenberg but who as reformer of schools and universities exercised a unique long-term influence on the history and the public life of Germany. What then does Melanchthon say about authority and leadership in the reform of the Church? He says that God 'calls to this (spiritual) warfare not only those who have ordinary power (i.e. 'ordinaries' or clerical office-holders), but often he (God) makes war against those same (office-holders), through Doctors chosen from other Orders. *Nec tantum illos vocat ad hanc militiam, qui tenent ordinariam potestatem, sed saepe illis ipsis bellum infert per Doctores ex aliis ordinibus delectos.*'[10] This is a none too tactful way of saying that the tasks of spiritual guidance belong to university professors rather than to bishops. While it was the acceptance of humanist methodology, now applied to the Bible, which produced this antithesis between scholarship and ecclesiastical governance, it would be fair criticism to add that, in the Europe of Erasmus and Luther, few Protestant humanists altogether lived up to such liberal ideals. As for Luther himself, he developed monumental convictions which, however arresting, were not all self-evident, and on some points failed to win a total consensus within Lutheranism itself. He provides the prime example of a scholar opposed to office-holders, yet he was by no means so tentative as to fit the normal pattern of a scholar. Yet most sincerely, most modestly, he felt himself nothing, unless he remained captive to the Word of God, which (as he put it) accomplished such mighty changes while he himself sat drinking

[10] C. G. Bretschneider (ed.), *Corpus Reformatorum, Philippi Melanchthonis Opera* (Halle, 1843), XI, col. 727.

beer with his friends Philip and Amsdorf. At this point we must clearly face the main question. In what senses was Martin Luther himself a humanist, and what exactly does he say on this issue? Some aspects of his case are obvious. If a humanist must behave like his unstable admirer Ulrich von Hutten – or somebody else out of the pages of Burckhardt – then Luther cannot be claimed as a member of the tribe. He did not proclaim secular individualism or regard man's true aspiration in terms of 'doing your own thing', which in Machiavelli's terminology appears as *il suo particolare*. Yet as I have already observed, the vast majority of those in his day whom we can rightly call humanists also failed to conform to these hectic nineteenth-century criteria. At the other extreme let us rid ourselves of the converse stereotype so popular among Luther's critics since the calumnies of Cochlaeus. Neither was Luther a professional simplifier, a bible-thumping, beer-swilling evangelist; nor was he a victim of some commonplace maladjustment drawn from a textbook of psychology. We observe in him a man highly educated in several exacting disciplines, one capable of thinking in high gear, of expressing complex ideas in concise and gripping terms, of prodigious energy in what he admitted to be the most wearisome of tasks: writing. He was neither a mystic nor a fundamentalist but a biblical theologian, widely criticized yet widely respected for his erudition, especially in the Old Testament. Yet in addition he had also enjoyed a good classical education, which in later life he constantly recalled, quoting a wide range of Latin classics from memory.[11] From the early years of the century he worked hard at both Greek and Hebrew. He was using Reuchlin's *Rudiments of Hebrew* soon after its publication in 1506, and he then hastened to obtain the most up-to-date Greek and Hebrew texts. How he followed his humanist predecessors has been clearly demonstrated. In his earlier days he had access to Valla's commentary in the edition by Erasmus and later he used Lefevre's edition of the Pauline Epistles (1512, 1515), which, having investigated the Greek, provided a revised version of the Vulgate in smaller type alongside the official version. Then from 1516 he used the Greek text by Erasmus, accompanied by its wholly new Latin translation. It was revised in 1519, which later edition Luther also used when preparing his first printed New Testament translation into German – the so-called *Septembertestament* of 1522. These relationships have been checked in detail by Professor Heinz Bluhm, who took as example Luther's translation of the Epistle to the Galatians.[12] Bluhm proved that whereas more than sixty divergences

[11] R. H. Fife, *The Revolt of Martin Luther* (New York, 1957), Index, s.v. Humanism.
[12] H. Bluhm, 'The Sources of Luther's *Septembertestament: Galatians*', in C. S. Meyer (ed.), *Luther for an Ecumenical Age* (St Louis, Mo., 1967), pp. 144–71.

occur between the Greek of Erasmus (1519) and the Vulgate text (Basel, 1509), in all but six of these sixty cases, Luther's translation agrees with Erasmus, not with the Vulgate. The six exceptions have no doctrinal importance, though Luther probably supposed that here the Vulgate made better sense. This exercise on Galatians shows him as a thoroughly up-to-date, yet by no means slavish representative of humanist scholarship. Had he not by this extended apprenticeship 'caught up' with a somewhat younger generation of specialists, he would have failed to dominate them in the decades to come. Obviously, at no stage did he become a *mere* humanist, a simple literary student. In his moving phrase, the Bible was for him the cradle in which Christ was laid. Yet the Bible also aroused some critical considerations, and as an expositor Luther was boldly selective, strongly discouraging the fanatics who believed the equal value of every text or book. He carried the rudimentary Higher Criticism of that day further than the rest. He dismissed the Epistle of St James as an 'epistle of straw', a deficient version of Apostolic teaching as based upon salvation through good works; and he picked out an inner core of the New Testament, though not necessarily the one most appealing to modern readers. Taking this Pauline – and also Johannine – core, he sought to structure the whole Word of God around the most exalted elements of Christian theology.

'In a word, St. John's Gospel and his first Epistle, St. Paul's Epistles, especially Romans, Galatians and Ephesians, and St. Peter's First Epistle are the books that show you Christ...'[13]

Whatever we may think of this selection and its cool attitude to the Synoptic Gospels,[14] Luther's actual expository methods in his voluminous sermons, commentaries and disputations are humanist as well as literalist: they often point the way toward modern biblical criticism and sometimes anticipate its conclusions, since he was not chained to outworn and subservient convention. Doubtless too absolute in his own convictions, he nevertheless believed in controversy as a necessary route to the meaning of the Bible. At the Leipzig Disputations of 4–14 July 1519, his able opponent John Eck appealed to the renowned doctors of the Latin tradition, and he was shocked when Luther openly ventured to differ on some point from a figure revered by both of them: St Bernard.[15]

[13] *Preface to the New Testament*, trans. E. G. Rupp and E. Drewery, *Martin Luther. Documents of Modern History*, (London, 1970), p. 94.
[14] According to Luther, the Synoptics 'do not describe much more than the history of the works and miracles of Christ' (G. Ebeling, *Luther. An Introduction to his Thought*, trans. R. A. Wilson), *Fontana* ed., p. 131 and citing *Weimarer Ausgabe (W.A.)*, vol. XII, p. 260.
[15] R. H. Fife, *op. cit.*, pp. 360–4. On the preponderance of Scripture over Councils and Fathers, see H. T. Kerr, *A Compend of Luther's Theology* (Philadelphia, c. 1945), pp. 13–15.

Luther on the other hand, instead of deferring to the early Fathers of the Church and to their prestigious medieval successors, insisted on confronting the biblical sources afresh in an independent re-examination. He interpreted the difficult passages in the light of the more straight-forward ones, Scripture being its own interpreter. Whether or not time has supported or refuted him in particular instances, his method is more humanist, more forward-looking than that of nearly all the contemporary theologians, who had less literary flair and sense of language. As a translator of the Bible – infinitely his greatest literary achievement – he had no doubts about the need for hard work on the linguistic discipline: 'Translating is not an art that everyone can practise, as the mad saints (i.e. the radical sectarians) think; it requires a right pious, faithful, diligent, God-fearing, experienced and practised spirit.'[16] He saw literary and linguistic studies not only as indispensable tools for the study of religion, but as in themselves a sacred discipline, providentially brought forth by God and prefiguring the attainment of a new and reformed Christianity. On a lower level he writes similarly of that other 'provi-dential' discovery: the craft of printing, which he calls 'God's highest and extremest act of grace, whereby the business of the Gospel is driven forward'. But in his tractate directed at the city-councils of Germany (*An die Ratherren aller Stadte*, 1524) he writes thus of humanism itself:

Formerly no one knew why God caused the languages to be revived, but now for the first time we see that it was done for the sake of the Gospel, which he intended to bring to light and use in exposing and destroying the Kingdom of Antichrist. To this end he gave over Greece to the Turk in order that the Greeks, driven out and scattered, might disseminate their language (i.e. in western Europe), and provide an incentive to the study of other languages as well.[17]

In a letter of 1523 to Eobanus Hessus he amplifies this statement.

I am persuaded that without a skilled training in literary studies, no true theology can establish and maintain itself, seeing that in times past it has invariably fallen miserably and lain prostrate with the decline and fall of learning. On the other hand, it is undoubtable that there has never been a signal revelation of divine truth unless first the way has been prepared for it, as by a John the Baptist, by the revival and pursuit of the study of languages and literature...My ardent desire is that there should be as many poets and rhetoricians as possible, because I see clearly that by no other methods is it possible to train men for the apt understanding, the right and felicitous treatment of sacred things.[18]

[16] *On Translating: An Open Letter* (1530), trans. Rupp and Drewery, *op. cit.*, p. 89.
[17] *W.A.*, xv, p. 37; *American Edition*, vol. 45, p. 359.
[18] *W.A., Briefwechsel*, III, pp. 49–50, tr. J. Mackinnon, *Luther and the Reformation*, 4 vols., (n.p., 1925–30), III, 216.

In the *Table Talk*, Luther is shown insisting upon the return to original sources, as opposed to glosses and commentaries. He exemplifies this first from legal studies and then from his personal experience as a bible-student.

I then read the commentators, but I soon threw them aside, for I found therein many things my conscience could not approve, as being contrary to the sacred text. It is always better to see with one's own eyes than with those of other people.[19]

Luther's thought thus shows a whole range of humanist components: he becomes highly conscious of this fact, and such lucid passages as these bear out my main contention. If his work and his statements do not make Luther some sort of a Christian humanist, I cannot attach any meaning to that term! More broadly still, he realized that he was living amid a great cultural revival, and he set out to Christianize what we call the Renaissance. Read attentively, Luther's plea to the city councillors to found municipal schools and libraries goes far beyond this immediate practical design. At many points it becomes in substance a glorification of Renaissance scholarship:

Almighty God has indeed graciously visited us Germans and proclaimed a truly golden year. We have today the finest and most learned group of men, adorned with languages and all the arts, who could also render real service if only we would make use of them as instructors of the young people. Now that God today so graciously bestowed upon us an abundance of arts, scholars and books it is time to reap and gather in the best as well as we can, and lay up treasure in order to preserve for the future something from these years of jubilee, and not lose this bountiful harvest.[20]

Short as it is, this pamphlet contains much else along this line: it proposes a framework for a study of Christian cultural history through the ages. Let us not be satisfied with a mere German-language culture, since the ancient languages are needed to promote both the Gospel and the secular commonwealth. Obviously, all Bible studies depend on Hebrew and Greek. Fortunately, continues Luther, the Apostles themselves put the Christian message into written Greek, foreseeing the wild interpretations and fancies which might otherwise disturb the Church. On the other hand the Fathers, and subsequently the Waldensians, ran into error largely because of their linguistic limitations. Even the pagan Greeks and Romans gave their young people a better education than that until recently available in Christian countries, especially in Germany,

---

[19] *Table Talk*, trans. W. Hazlitt, (edn. 1985), pp. 14–15, no. XXXIII.

[20] *W.A.*, XV, pp. 31, 52; *American Edition*, XLV, pp. 351, 377.

where university and monastic studies became unfruitful, since teachers and pupils 'failed to master either Latin or German'.

Of course when all these many striking passages have been taken into account, the mainstream of Luther's theology of salvation runs far closer to Paul and Augustine than to the more optimistic platonizing and stoicizing currents which largely pervaded Italy, and for that matter the *philosophia Christi* of Erasmus. Nevertheless, seen in full context, Luther's rigorous anthropology should not be allowed to dehumanize him or to indicate any remoteness, either as a person or as a thinker, from the struggles of men and women in their everyday lives. No religious leader has expressed a greater regard for people, as a tireless correspondent and personal counsellor, as an enthusiast for popular education, including that of women, as a commonsense propounder of social and political reform, above all as a genial advocate of those mental readjustments which could, without revolution, foster a caring community. As I remarked at the outset, a remarkably high proportion of Luther's writing is concerned with the worldly Kingdom or *Regiment*, where human beings enjoy Free Will, as opposed to the spiritual Kingdom, the higher plane upon which they are helpless and where Christ alone can bring salvation. Urging that God also created the worldly Kingdom, he exalts the role played in it by human reason, 'a kind of god' appointed (*Genesis*, i. 8) to control the rest of the Creation.[21] Again, introducing a translation of an Italian book on near-contemporary events, he praises historiography not merely for its human 'examples' but for the fact that it reveals something of God's ways. He takes the opportunity to denounce histories based on self-seeking political propaganda or upon nationalism.[22]

In regard to modern history, he certainly believed that the Reformation in which he was participating had long ago been prepared by God, down to the scattering of the Greek scholars, the provision of humanist techniques and the craft of printing. He never relegated either history or religion to stratospheres of their own. Like Rembrandt, he located spiritual truth amid the bustling human throng. By precept and by tireless example he taught religion also on the plane of the secular kingdom, where men still enjoyed a measure of free will, and there he bade them serve one another 'like little Christs'. Ceaselessly in his sermons he returns to the concept of *vocatio* or *Beruf*; he proclaims the

[21] *Disputatio de Homine* (1536), *W.A.*, xxxix (1), pp. 174–80; *American Edition*, xxxiv, pp. 135–44.
[22] *Vorrede zu Historia Galeatii Capellae* (1538), *W.A.*, L, pp. 381–5; *American Edition*, xxxiv, pp. 275–8.

sacredness of every calling, however lowly, when performed in a joyful, unforced spirit of love and goodwill. The ordained and sanctified duty of service is exemplified in the faithful maidservant, whose sweeping and dusting Luther places above the self-dramatizing and uncommanded austerities of monks and nuns.[23]

> A servant with this clause
> Makes drudgery divine,
> Who sweeps a room as for Thy laws
> Makes that and the action fine.

The words are those of George Herbert, but they are little more than a free translation of Luther's words. Luther ceaselessly thought in terms of paradoxes and antitheses, and this heartfelt emphasis upon service by mankind is the antithesis to his austere view of human depravity. Biblical humanism, as opposed to scholasticism or canon law, doubtless helped to enlarge his practical humanity. His scholarship, his literary experience, his sense of history, his return to the literal sense of the Bible, these were no sidelines but an integral aspect of his personality and his message. They still make him a communicator of the Word to many of us lesser people: they make him not a saint, but undoubtedly a prophet.

SELECT BIBLIOGRAPHY

Bernstein, E., *Die Literatur des deutschen Frühhumanismus* (Stuttgart, 1978).

Bornkamm, H., *Luther in Mid-Career* (trans. E. J. Bachmann, London, 1983).

Burger, H. O., *Renaissance, Humanismus, Reformation. Deutsche Literatur im Europäischen Kontext* (Bad Homburg, Berlin, Zurich, 1969).

Delius, H-U., 'Zu Luthers historischen Quellen', *Luther Jahrbuch*, XLII (1975).

Dickens, A. G., *The German Nation and Martin Luther* (London, 1974, 1976) (ch. 3).

Fife, R. H., *The Revolt of Martin Luther* (New York, 1957) (ch. 22).

Grossmann, Maria, *Humanism in Wittenberg, 1485–1517* (Niewkoop, 1975).

Harbison, E. H., *The Christian Scholar in the Age of the Reformation* (New York, 1956).

Joachimsen, P., 'Humanism and the Development of the German Mind', G. Strauss (ed.), *Pre-Reformation Germany* (London, 1972).

Junghans, H., 'Der Einfluss des Humanismus auf Luthers Entwicklung bis 1518', *Luther Jahrbuch*, XXXVII (1970).

Kalkoff, P., *Humanismus und Reformation in Erfurt, 1500–1530* (Halle, 1926).

Kleinhans, R. G., 'Luther and Erasmus, another Perspective', *Church History*, XXXIX (1970).

---

[23] *Hauspostille* (1544), *W.A.*, LII, pp. 470–1. References to vocation are numerous in Luther's sermons and occur elsewhere; e.g. in the *Treatise on Good Works* (1520); *On Monastic Vows* (1521); *Table Talk*.

McGrath, A. E., 'Humanist Elements in the Early Reformed Doctrine of Justification', *Archiv für Reformationsgeschichte*, LXXIII (1982).

Meyer, C. S., 'Christian Humanism and the Reformation: Erasmus and Melanchthon', *Concordia Theological Monthly*, XLI (1970).

Moeller, B., 'Religious Life in Germany on the Eve of the Reformation', G. Strauss (ed.), *Pre-Reformation Germany* (London, 1972).

Olin, J. C., *Desiderius Erasmus: Christian Humanism and the Reformation* (New York, 1965).

Ozment, S., 'Humanism, Scholasticism and the Intellectual Origins of the Reformation', F. F. Church & T. George (eds.), *Continuity and Discontinuity in Church History, Essays Presented to G. H. Williams* (London, 1979).

Pelikan, J., *Luther the Expositor* (Companion Volume to the American edition of Luther's Works, St Louis, 1950).

Ritter, G., 'Die geschichtliche Bedeutung des deutschen Humanismus', *Historische Zeitschrift*, CXXVII (1923).

Schmidt, O. G., *Luthers Bekanntschaft mit den alten Classikern* (Leipzig, 1883).

Spitz, L. W., *The Religious Renaissance of the German Humanists* (Cambridge, Mass., 1953) (ch. 10).

Spitz, L. W., 'Scholarship in the Renaissance: German Humanism', *Renaissance Quarterly*, XXI (1968).

Spitz, L. W., 'Humanism and the Reformation', R. M. Kingdon (ed.), *Transition and Revolution. Problems and Issues of European Renaissance and Reformation History* (Minneapolis, 1974).

Stange, C., 'Luther und der Geist der Renaissance', *Zeitschrift fur Systematische Theologie*, XVIII (1941).

Stupperich, R., 'Der Humanismus und die Wiedervereinigung der Konfessionen', *Schriften des Vereins für Reformationsgeschichte*, CLX (1936).

Wolf, E., 'Reformatorische Botschaft und Humanismus', L. Abramowaski and J. F. G. Goeters (eds.), *Studien zur Geschichte und Theologie der Reformation. Festschrift für Ernst Bizer* (Neukirchen, 1969).

Yule, G., 'Late Medieval Piety, Humanism and Luther's Theology', K. Robbins (ed.), *Religion and Humanism, Studies in Church History*, 17 (Oxford, 1981).

Zweynert, E., *Luthers Stellung zur humanistischen Schule und Wissenschaft* (Chemnitz, 1895).

Scholars and ecclesiastical history in the Early Modern period: the influence of Ferdinando Ughelli

DENYS HAY

The sixteenth and seventeenth centuries saw a remarkably rapid evolution in the aims and teachings of church history, both in Protestant and Catholic areas of Europe. That the early sixteenth century was obsessed with church history is hardly surprising. The history of the church was one of the most potent elements in controversial literature while the ideological struggle which we label 'Protestant' and 'Counter-Reformation' took shape.

In many ways, the interest in the history of the church was more vehement in Protestant areas than in Roman Catholic ones, and for compelling reasons. The Protestant had to investigate the history of the church he was criticising, had to defend his rebellion, so to speak. Put in other words, he was concerned to demonstrate that he was not really a rebel; that his church was the *true* church, near, very near, to the primitive church; and above all that his hierarchy was every bit as authentic as the Roman one (that is, orders in the Lutheran or Anglican Church were derived from the apostles). This was to remain an Anglican preoccupation down to the nineteenth century, when Bishop Stubbs produced massive evidence on the episcopal succession in his *Registrum sacrum Anglicanum*. It can indeed be traced back to some of the Tudor historians, and not least to the great collector and patron Matthew Parker, who compiled an account of the British church and its privileges together with a list of the seventy archbishops, a book which was privately printed in 1572.[1]

A version of this paper was delivered as the Annual David Murray Lecture for 1982 at the University of Glasgow. I have to thank the University authorities, including Professor A. A. M. Duncan, for kind hospitality.

[1] Only fifty copies of this were issued, and so it is a rare book. See May McKisack, *Medieval History in the Tudor Age* (Oxford, 1971), pp. 44, 114–15, 121, for other reflections regarding English interest in medieval church history in the later sixteenth century.

The pattern was not identical in all Protestant areas. In England, the Reformation was promoted by the Crown and in the end strengthened the monarchy. In Germany, the revolutions in religion were largely responsible for the destruction of such unity as had been possessed by the Empire; in sixteenth-century France, for some time it looked as though the state would be destroyed by a divided church. In both the Empire and France, a marked interest in the antiquities of the church in the Middle Ages is noticeable. In Germany, the emphasis was partly political, as in Carion's *Chronicle* (1531 and later editions), or theological (for instance, Melanchthon's revision and expansion of Carion of 1558). But the greatest scholarly monument to the new faith in Germany was, of course, the extraordinary volumes produced by the 'Magdeburg centuriators'.[2]

The team of scholars organised by Mathias Vlack or Flacius Illyricus planned and largely executed a remarkable survey of the history of the church as far back as the end of the twelfth century, which was published at Basel from 1559 to 1574. Their efforts were, of course, confessional in purpose, but there are several reasons for regarding this large work as seminal. It was a team effort and was so ambitiously conceived that no one man could have achieved it; among other reasons for collaboration were the *voyages litteraires* embarked on by some of the collaborators. A second reason for its influence was the sophisticated arrangement of the material; a third reason was the diffusion of this major work, which was printed and reprinted at Basel and other centres very rapidly. Finally, it was, despite its bias, a thoroughly scholarly work, one which Roman Catholics could not comfortably ignore.

The national effects on church history in both England and the Empire have been mentioned. One cannot deny that changes in church doctrine and organisation coincided with stronger princely government, or at any rate stronger government (princes must be omitted out of deference to the Swiss and the Low Countries, as well as to avoid the concept of the 'nation state' which many of us were brought up to believe was coincidental with the Reformation). There was obviously a patriotic element in the situation of the scholar which was in many ways congenial to him. After all, the Anglican Church had been so called for centuries, and so had the Gallican church. But this was of course not true of Germany and of many other areas, where political frontiers and church organisation did not coincide; after all, in 'Spain' we have a tripartite crown of Aragon, as well as Castile, Navarre, Portugal, and the pagan

---

[2] P. Polman, OFM, 'Flacius Illyricus, Historien de l'Église', *Revue de l'histoire ecclésiastique*, XXXVII (1931), pp. 27–73.

The influence of Ferdinando Ughelli

Moslem area in the south of the peninsula (until Moslems, and Jews were expelled at the end of the fifteenth century).

Clearly, Italy with its many towns and principalities was not like the monarchies who found the Reformation strengthening their grip on a community bound by common loyalties and, usually, by a common language. At any rate, we do not find an *ecclesia italica* in the Middle Ages, or at least I have seen no instance of the phrase. Hence, the heroes of church history found in France and England are not to be traced in a peninsula which, even when it had been dominated by Roman Catholic Germany, was still to await the 1860s and 1870s for unification. Of course, in Italy, as in France or Britain or in many other parts of Christendom, local antiquaries dealt with local church history. France was in many ways really in the lead in these developments (apart from Parker's list of archbishops). Some further evidence of French ecclesiastical scholarship will emerge in reviewing the work of the Italian scholar Ughelli.[3]

Before turning to him, however, it should be emphasised how much we need a comparative survey of European historical erudition in the late sixteenth and the seventeenth centuries, along the lines of some of David Knowles' studies.[4] One thinks not only of narrative histories, the more important of which are given a critical assessment, however schematic, in Fueter's history of modern historiography,[5] but of the men who published documents, prepared accurate catalogues and reference books, and who took advantage of the technical advances offered by the printing press.

The emphasis inevitably led to patriotism predominating. As soon as this had happened, it was inevitable that the history of the church should be rewritten in national terms, and would become the history of several national churches. This, I believe, happened first in France, perhaps because much had been written on individual French churches.[6] At all

---

[3] Below pp. 217–18.
[4] David Knowles, *Great Historical Enterprises* (Edinburgh, 1962), pp. 2, 34; there is a study of Mabillon by the same author in *The Historian and Character* (Cambridge, 1963), and a full but it seems unrevised life by Dom H. Leclercq, 2 volumes (Paris, 1953, 1957).
[5] Eduard Fueter, *Geschichte der neueren Historiographie* (Berlin, 1911); best consulted in the French edition revised by the author (Paris, 1914), where the reference to Ughelli is on p. 409.
[6] There have been several works on particular churches and provinces, such as C. Saussey, *Annales ecclesiae Aurelianensis* (1615); P. Louvet, *Nomenclatura et Chronologia Rerum Ecclesiasticorum Dioecesis Belvacencis* (1613), J. le Jau, *Series Episcoporum Ebroicensem;* J. Tavelli, *Vitae et Actus Senonensium Archiepiscoporum* (1608). An early example of such work was Jean Chenu's *Historia Brevis Reverendissimorum Ecclesiae Bituricensis Archiepisicoporum* (1603).

217

events, there appeared in 1621 Jean Chenu's *Archiepiscoporum et Episcoporum Galliae Chronologica Historia* and in 1620 the *Gallia Christiana* of Claude Robert. Chenu was a lawyer: it will be recalled how closely associated historical research was with the legal profession – mostly Gallican in sympathy – in sixteenth-century France.[7] Claude Robert was a priest from Langres who died in 1637. It was his work which the twin brothers, Scevole and Louis de Sainte-Marthe, revised and enlarged in their own *Gallia Christiana* (four volumes, 1656), a work which appeared after the authors were dead, seen through the press by yet another member of the astonishing Sainte-Marthe family. But by this time, however, Ughelli's work was well away.[8] That he owed something to the French writers Chenu and Robert there is no doubt – at least by way of inspiration or suggestion – but he owed nothing to the brothers Sainte-Marthe. His originality was all the greater in that, whereas Frenchmen had talked of the *Ecclesia Gallicana* for centuries, no one in Italy had employed in similar fashion the concept of *Ecclesia Italica*, which in effect was what Ughelli did.

A brief word is called for regarding Ughelli's relatively unexciting life. He was a Florentine, born in 1597. He entered the Cistercian Order, in which he was promoted through a series of abbacies to find himself, at the age of forty-one, abbot of the house of SS. Vincenzo and Anastasio. This convent is nowadays a rather shabby and dusty site between St. Paulo fuori le Mura and EUR, now occupied by Trappists who eke out their income by selling liqueurs made from eucalyptus – the tree having been planted at a time when the Roman *maremma* was infested with mosquitos and malaria. The fame of this convent derives from its being the scene of the martyrdom of St Paul. The little church of St Paul, which forms part of a complex, has a broken column which marks the spot where the saint was executed; his head bounced three times and led to the three fountains. When Abbot Ughelli died in 1670, his epitaph at the Tre Fontane was written by Cardinal Francesco Barberini. Ughelli was then recognised for what he was: a very great man. Cardinal Barberini was also responsible for gathering together in his own collections Ughelli's voluminous papers and in 1902 they became part of the Vatican library.[9] There at last some scholars are giving them attention.[10]

[7] Julian H. Franklin, *Jean Bodin and the Sixteenth Century Revolution in the Methodology of Law and History* (New York, 1963); Donald R. Kelley, *Foundations of Modern Historical Scholarship* (New York, 1970).

[8] For the date when the idea was formed in Ughelli's mind (about 1629 or a little earlier), see below pp. 220–21. The first reference in his correspondence to *Gallia Christiana* seems to be in a letter dated January 1646, Vat. Lib., MS., Barberini Lat. 3243, fos. 53–4.

[9] The main collections are Barb. Lat. 3239, 3240, 3242, 3244, 3245, 3246. Other Ughelli

Ughelli's *Italia Sacra* consists of a series of sections, each devoted to the history of a bishopric in Italy, beginning with a description of it and then dealing *seriatim* with the incumbents of the see. What were Ughelli's declared aims in embarking on his huge work, which in the first edition ran to nine folio volumes (1644–62)? He explains them in the preface to the first volume. The glory of Italy is revealed in its prelates, for the bishop is the pastor and supervisor of his flock. And prelates are more plentifully found there than elsewhere – a reflection of Italy's place in religion; it is 'the refuge of the Faith, the citadel of piety, the source of Catholic doctrine, home of the pope, origin of the emperors, nurse of civilisation, the most fruitful scene of holiness and honour, pregnant ever with men of genius and valour'. This multitude of bishops also reflects the proximity of the Holy See, whence holy examples can proceed to spread their warmth. He also intends to preserve the names of distinguished men, and in particular men from distinguished families, from oblivion and so inspire generations to come. After explaining how he has scrutinised sources of various kinds, he outlines his proposed work. It will be in six volumes, divided into twenty provinces, beginning with the bishops of Rome and the sees of the Roman province immediately subject to Rome (that is, without a metropolitan), and the origins of each see will be given. He will not brook fictions. The *nuda nomina* which are often in his lists bear witness to his desire to be truthful. (And in fact, there are not only bare names for early centuries but often no names at all.)

As was the case with the French authors, so with Ughelli: there was an immense amount of valuable material already in print. Ughelli's knowledge of this, due in part to his having helped with the revision of Ciaconius's lives of the popes and cardinals, is amply acknowledged in the early pages of the *Italia Sacra*, here referred to in the edition of Nicolo Coleti, the Venetian who procured a revised and updated version in ten volumes (Venice, 1717–33).[11] Quite apart from authors of the

material in Barb. Lat. 3238 (History of the Counts of Marsica); 3247 (Abbots of Cistercian Houses compiled by Dom G. Lauro for Ughelli); 3248 (Cistercian Chapter General, 1609); 3249 (papers of Cistercian Proctors at the Curia Romana, 1574 onwards). Material specifically collected for *Italia Sacra* (hereafter *I.S.*) in Barb. Lat. 3204, 3205, 3207, 3209, 2310, 5351. Ughelli's revisions of Ciacconius in Reg. Lat. 385, fos. 1–51; cf. A. Wilmart, *Codd. Reg. Latini*, II (Citta del Vaticano, 1945).

[10] Dr Giorgio Morelli has worked extensively on the *epistolario*; see his papers in *Strenna dei Romanisti* (1972), *Rivista Abruzzese*, XVI (1963); *Abruzzo*, XII (1974); he had been assisted by some of the Fathers at the Tre Fontane. Dr Morelli kindly looked at an early draft of these notes and pointed out that Ughelli was born in 1597, not as commonly stated 1596.

[11] J. D. Coleti, a scholarly printer at Venice, made extensive collections towards a revision of Ughelli. These were augmented and seen through the press by his nephew Nicolo (1680–1765). I am told by Professor Gaetano Cozzi, who kindly made enquiries

fifteenth century and of the Middle Ages to whom he pays tribute, he names a large number of scholars to whom scholars still occasionally turn: Panvinio, Baronio and Ciaconius (Alfonso Chacon) among many others, and especially writers on classical topography and physical antiquities, where the work of Renaissance scholars and seventeenth-century research has long been superseded. He was, moreover, fairly lucky in the time and place where he lived and worked; Rome in the mid seventeenth century was a notable centre of scholarly and in particular historical research. The revisions of Ciaconius, printed in 1630 at Rome, had been undertaken with Luke Wadding, the Irish Franciscan who wrote the history of his own Order, and with Andrea Vettorelli, author of a history of papal jubilees (Rome 1625) and other works. There were certain limitations placed on historical research in seventeenth-century Italy, but there were also compensations of an important character in the archives and libraries.

Printed materials were, however, only a part, a small part, of Ughelli's sources. His ten-year-long labours, he tells us, were due to searching published sources and private records, tombs and sepulchral inscriptions, charters and, of course, the historians of the past. (He apologises for sometimes reproducing the barbarous Latin of his sources.) He can thus hope to suppress the doubtful, cut away the ridiculous, and praise the true, basing himself on material which will yield names, surnames, coats of arms (frequently reproduced in poor wood-cuts) and deeds good and bad. When all else failed, he wrote away for information, which was not sometimes available or not forthcoming. So runs the preface.[12] Much of it verbally reproduces a letter from Ughelli's Florentine teacher, Abbot Niccolo Bacelli, which is quoted in the *Italia Sacra* apropos of an ancestor who had been a fourteenth-century Tuscan bishop; the letter is dated October 1641 and claims that the Florentine abbot had encouraged Ughelli to undertake the work.[13]

All of this is reflected in the Vatican Library manuscripts, where a large number of papers reflecting Ughelli's activities are collected, for the most part in eight volumes in the Barberini collection.[14] The earliest mention of the *Italia Sacra* I have come across is from a Jesuit father at Naples and is dated January 1629.[15] He has heard from one of Cardinal Borghese's gentlemen that Ughelli, then abbot of San Galgano (near

on my behalf, that there is no recent work on the family and its activities as regards *I.S.*. Despite its faults, the Coleti version is best and is used here. The Coleti edition has a tenth volume consisting mainly of 'Anecdota Ughelliani' (records collected by Ughelli), accounts of defunct sees, and a number of elaborate tables and indexes. The Coleti text has been conveniently reprinted in facsimile by A. Forni at Bologna, 1972–4.

[12] *I.S.*, I, p. 5.   [13] *I.S.*, 750–2.
[14] Above, n. 9.   [15] Barb. Lat. 3243, fo. 15.

Siena) was engaged on the preparation of a large-scale and impressive work (*un bellissma e degnissima opera*) on all the bishops of Italy; he offers his services. This probably marks about the beginning of the enterprise. Ughelli himself refers in the first volume (1644) to his ten years of work on the project.

From the early 1630s, the letters become more numerous and evidently the fame of the project secured Ughelli much help, frequently an important source of information – even the not infrequent information that there was *no* information.[16] The letters tend to be in groups in which the offerings of individual correspondents were kept together.[17] Some correspondents provided a good deal of matter: extracts from records, armorial drawings, copies of inscriptions. This ready response was naturally even more eager once the volumes began to appear in 1644. Then corrections came in for the expected revisions and appendices, and there were a few angry comments where local pride and local tradition had been flouted. Praise far outweighed irritation however and such praise increased[18] as the great folios steadily appeared – in the end extending from the original six to nine, with the promise of a tenth which would have dealt with the Islands.[19] There is evidence that Ughelli occasionally invited prior criticism, or solicited revision prior to publication, by sending out sheets at the proof stage and before publication.[20]

The work was issued at Rome by a series of printers,[21] but Rome was by no means an inevitable choice for publication. One of the most interesting of the letters kept by Ughelli is from Claude Dufour, a well-known printer of Lyons.[22] It is dated 15 August 1642 – that is, about a year and a half before volume I appeared in Rome. In his letter, the Lyons printer explains that he has heard from Dom Francois de St Robert of Chambery the title of a work which Ughelli wishes him to

[16] *Ibid.*, fo. 213 (1657, Archbishops of Rossano), but cf. Barb. lat. 3244 (a further letter regarding Rossano, dated 1660). Barb. Lat. 34 242, fo. 349 (nothing, because of the poverty of the place, 1649). And there are many similar reports.

[17] For example, Barb. Lat. 3242, fos. 335–7 (1649, Citta Nova); 3243, fos. 52–119 (1644, Pisa). For question and answer (regarding Ascoli Piceno), Barb. Lat. 3243, fo. 120, to be compared with *I.S.* I, 436–8.

[18] Some printed acclamation in the preliminary pages of the first edition of Vol. VI (1659). The letters praising the work in Ughelli's correspondence are too numerous to mention, but see Barb. Lat. 3239, fos. 43–110. For the effect of *I.S.* on local rivalries, see Barb. Lat. 3243, fos. 294–300vo (Matera *vs* Aceranza).

[19] Cf. Barb. Lat. 3240, fos. 83–7.

[20] A letter of 1643 refers to a *foglio stampato* being received by a correspondent; Barb. Lat. 3242, fo. 143.

[21] The first edition was published in Rome as follows:
I. B. Taunus, 1644; II. The same, 1647; III. The same, 1647; IV. B. Deversia and Z. Masott, 1642; V. The same, 1653; VI. Typographia rev. camerae apostolicae, 1659; VII. B. Deversin and V. Mascardus, 1659; VIII. The same, 1662. IX. The same, 1662.

[22] Barb. Lat. 3240, fos. 114–114vo.

print – the *Italia Sacra*. He understands that this will be in six volumes, of which the first two are ready for press. He had earlier told Maitre Naudé, when the latter passed through Lyons some time ago, that the printer must see the whole work; paper was expensive and workers were scarce; authors were expected to contribute towards advance expenses. He would like to oblige, he wrote, and would need all the copy he could print without a break (*sans discontinuation*); in order to cost the enterprise he must see volume I. Dufour ends by telling Ughelli that he has printed works by Wadding and other scholars, and at present has three large-scale works going through. In conclusion he protests his reliability.

The contents of this letter deserve some consideration because of the light it throws on Ughelli's desire for a wide market. (It also throws further light on printing at Lyons in the seventeenth century: the industry there was in full decline, it seems, and, while paper was expensive because of heavy customs dues, there was certainly no shortage of workers.)[23] Maitre Naudé and Luke Wadding are the names to stress. The former was the celebrated bibliographer: medical man by training, Gabriel Naudé had been in Rome for some years, latterly as librarian to Cardinal Barberini before becoming even more famous as Cardinal Masarin's librarian. Luke Wadding, with whom Ughelli had already collaborated as mentioned above, published volumes III through IV of his *Annales Ordinis Minorum* with Dufour at Lyons (1635–42). It is likely that the influential Irish friar suggested that Ughelli should print at Lyons. It is equally likely that he, in the end, advised against it, for the sixth volume of the *Annales* (1654) was printed at Rome.[24]

Rome was hardly celebrated typographically at this time, and the *Italia Sacra* is a plain and unattractive book both to look at and handle. If one compares it with the splendidly printed volumes of the *Gallia Christiana* of the Sainte-Marthes, which came out in Paris in 1656, one realises that all that Ughelli's volumes reflect of the beautiful baroque city in which they appeared was restricted to the Latin of the prefatory material, dedications and so on. The lives of the bishops seldom lent themselves to literary flights, although every conceivable change is rung on phrases meaning 'to be made a bishop'.[25] But technically Ughelli's work represents a remarkable exhibition of scholarship, especially in

[23] Jacqueline Roubert, 'La Situation de l'Imprimerie Lyonaise à la Fin du Dix-Septième Siècle', in H. J. Martin (ed.), *Cinq Études Lyonaises* (Geneva–Paris, 1966), pp. 77–111.

[24] Details in *Cat. genérale des livres imprimés à la Bibliothèque Nationale*. On Wadding's life, see Benignus Millet, in *Father Luke Wadding*, a commemorative volume ed. by the Franciscan Fathers, Dun Nhuire, Killeny (Dublin, 1957), pp. 229–62. For Naudé, see René Pintard, *Le Libertinage Érudit*, 2 volumes (Paris, 1943), *passim.*; for Naudé in Rome, pp. 245–68.

[25] *In sedem succedere, dignitatem suscipere, evectus, infulatus*, and many similar expressions.

view of the large number of bishoprics involved (over 320, including defunct sees but not including Sicily and Corsica). His correspondents and his own researches provided him with a vast amount of material, most of it accurate, which he digested and displayed in ways which rendered his book literally indispensable. His publication of much new charter material was extensive; his edition of several lengthy texts, narrative and otherwise, was a bonus which paid tribute to the activities currently being pursued by the early Maurists and soon to be emulated by Muratori, who admired the *Italia Sacra*. Indices were admirably complete. All in all, the work is a remarkable example of competence and sustained effort. Successive volumes carried corrections and amplifications (many supplied by his growing public) to earlier volumes; it was a work of what could be described as *continuing* scholarship. The gaps were there to be filled in, especially for the earlier centuries, and it was an invitation to activity which proved irresistible. The omission of the Islands is due presumably to the assumption that they were not part of Italy at the time; there are parallels to this in F. Biondo's *Italia Illustrata* in the mid fifteenth century, and, a century later, the same view is reflected in Leandro Alberti's *Descrittione di tutta Italia*. As already noted, Ughelli planned to include in a later volume the Sicilian and Corsican sees.

It must not be assumed from the foregoing that the Rome or even the Italy of the mid seventeenth century formed an especially enlightened background for scholarship. It was in some ways a dark world – the world that had tried to silence Galileo and Campanella, a world where monuments of antiquity were being spoiled to serve new taste in building and sculpture; 'what the barbarians did not destroy was destroyed by the Barberini'. For scholars working in sensitive areas, for scholars known to be, or suspected of being, of uncertain religious faith, librarians could be awkward and persecution could be a worrying reality.[26] Rome itself had in the Sapienza a fourth-rate university, and the Academy of the Lincei (founded in 1603), with an emphasis on the physical sciences, pursued a policy of secrecy. Despite the diplomatic importance of Rome, despite the consequent presence of the many influential foreigners, despite the patronage of cardinals interested in their own earthly immortality, there seems to have been much more lively intellectual activity in Florence and Venice, perhaps even in Naples. But for *church* history, Rome offered incomparable advantages and the main monuments of Roman erudition – apart from Ughelli – are the continuation of Baronio, the revisions of Ciaconius, Wadding's *Annales*, and

[26] A. Rotondò, 'La Censura Ecclesiastica e la Cultura', in *Einaudi storia d'Italia*, vol. v (Turin, 1973), pp. 1399–92.

223

so on. If one's credentials were in order, it was fairly easy to get prohibited literature and Rome had an impressive collection of libraries in addition to the Vatican.[27]

As for the influence exercised by Ughelli's work, this may be seen in the inspiration it exerted abroad. The earliest and most scholarly emulation came from France, where the *Gallia Christiana*, the work of the two Maurists, Scevole and Louis de Sainte-Marthe, was published in 1656. Besides being a monument of choice typography, the French work improved on its Italian predecessor in a number of ways. It added to the history of bishops lists of the principal dignitaries (whether provost or dean) in each cathedral. It also included in the final of its four volumes lists of abbots, generals of French orders, and congregations. A very fine engraved map of France made for easy reference. As with Ughelli, the work was superbly indexed – *nomina*, *cognomina*, vernacular names of dioceses and abbeys as well as Latin, chronological lists of popes and anti-popes.[28] The work differed from Ughelli's (a doubtful improvement) in placing all metropolitans apart in volume I, while all suffragans (in a single alphabet of Latin names of dioceses) are in volumes II and III, divided at the letter M. The Sainte-Marthes' book, which was seen through the press by Pierre Abel and Nicole de Sainte-Marthe (sons of Scevole and nephews of Louis) depended, like Ughelli, on many devoted helpers, as is generously acknowledged. Among those thanked is Abbot Ughelli, who had (say the editors) communicated information regarding many prelates taken from Roman archives, the consistorial records, the *Obligationes et solutiones*, and the Registers.

There are, however, some important differences in approach. Ughelli, papal favourite, client of the Medici Grand Duke (he was his offical theologian), and of the Barberini family, described an *Italia* which was not a political entity. And he most certainly did not deal with a country which pursued hostile policies towards the pope. There was in France, on the other hand, a tradition of Gallicanism almost as old as the tradition of Anglicanism on the other side of the Channel.[29] This is pointedly stressed in the preface to the Sainte-Marthes' work. Its purpose, we read, is to display (1) the origin and development of Christian faith among the French (or Gauls, as the authors persistently refer to the French); (2) the superiority of the French hierarchy to *all*

[27] See discussion in Pintard.
[28] In which, it may be noted, the Avignon popes during the Great Schism are now treated as anti-popes. For ecclesiastical geography at this time, see Carolus a Sancto Paulo (Paris, 1641), with fine maps engraved by N. Tavernia from drawings by A. de la Plaetfen.
[29] See my paper in *History*, LIII (1963), pp. 36–50.

others, save only the Roman; (3) the beginnings of French sees and monasteries (with their old documents, to be printed despite their rudimentary Latin); (4) the custom and usage of the Gallican Church; (5) decrees of Gallican councils; and (6) the geography of each city, its noble families, and so on. There is in Ughelli's preface little of all this (except the reference to bad Latin and geography). How could there be? There was no 'Italicanism', if the word be permitted, in the Italian church. (On the other hand, the *Italia Sacra* in its treatment of each see normally gives a general survey, for example of religious foundations.)

The 'national' form of church scholarship derived from strong central government or (relatively) unified states with a church subordinate to the prince. Such a state of affairs was to be found, outside France, in few parts of Europe, as I have indicated. We have to wait until 1747 for the beginning of an *Espana sagrada;* and in Germany, confessionally divided and subdivided, a similar project began in a faltering way only in 1929.[30] But in England, although a break with Rome had occurred in Henry VIII's reign (perhaps, indeed, it was because of that break), there was an insistence on continuity which became increasingly important to the hierarchy. Long before bishop Stubbs compiled his *Registrum Sacrum Anglicanum* (1858, reprinted in a revised form in 1897), Anglicanism had displayed itself in English church-historical scholarship. In some respects it antedates comparable French and Italian works if we begin, as perhaps we should, with Archbishop Parker and Francis Godwin's *Catalogue of the Bishops of England* (1601). There were several reprints of this and in 1616 a Latin version appeared which was also reprinted.[31] Bishop Godwin was, like Stubbs, preoccupied with the validity of the orders of the English hierarchy. Denying the Roman origin of the Anglican communion, he proudly proclaimed it 'the first begotten daughter of the Church of God'.[32] The *Monasticon* compiled by Dodsworth and Dugdale, which began to appear in 1655 (the year before the *Gallia Christiana*) also reflected Anglican sentiment and antedated Ughelli and the Sainte-Marthes in its inception, but was very different in its approach and execution from the fourth volume of the French work.[33] So too, despite its title, was Henry Wharton's *Anglica Sacra*

---

[30] *España Sagrada*, 52 volumes (Madrid, 1747–1879). Of *Germania Sacra*, only two volumes appeared (1929–33); Fueter complained that the absence of such a work hampered German medievalists.

[31] *Short Title Catalogue*, nos. 11937–42; cf. F. M. Powicke and E. B. Fryde (eds.), *A Handbook of British Chronology* (London, 1961), p. 202.

[32] *A Catalogue* (London. 1615), sig. A3. (The copy in Edinburgh University Library has copious annotations by Browne Willis.)

[33] David Douglas, *English Scholars* (London, 1939), pp. 34–47. I do not think that this work demonstrated the value of 'charter material' fifty years before Mabillon; many of the scholars mentioned above were well aware of the significance of such sources.

(1691), which is rather a collection of texts dealing with the lives of prelates which Wharton had assembled and edited; at any rate, it is the texts he assembled that proved more valuable than the lives he himself composed. The true heir of Ughelli and the Sainte-Marthes in England was rather John Le Neve. His *Fasti* were published in 1716, revised and expanded in the edition of Thomas Duffus Hardy in 1854; they are now currently being revised again to new and much more scholarly standards.[34] It is, on the other hand, important to stress that Le Neve did not write the lives of the bishops (or other Cathedral officers); his work was to assemble accurate lists and to that extent his work differs markedly from Ughelli's.

Of course, interest in ecclesiastical antiquities was not confined to large principalities. The seventeenth century saw the appearance of scores of works dealing with particular churches in the provinces of divided Germany and in the states of the Iberian peninsula and their constituent parts.[35] Other authors were concerned with the rest of Europe and some with parts of the Americas.

It would be foolish to attribute this widespread concern with church history only to Ughelli and the Sainte-Marthe twins. The Italia Sacra and the *Gallia Christiana* were simply the first elaborate and sophisticated treatments of their themes and were not to be superseded for centuries. In many ways, Ughelli's book is still essential for anyone working on Italian church history and it has never had the total revision which it merits. Muratori more than once urged the importance of such a task, envisaging it as the work of a co-operative team.[36] Certainly the worthy attempt of the Cistercian abbot Giulio Ambrogio Lucenti to abbreviate and correct Ughelli petered out after the first volume appeared in 1704.[37] Nor was Muratori satisfied with the revision and rearrangement of Ughelli completed by Nicolo Coleti in ten volumes at Venice, 1727–33.[38]

[34] The period 1300–1540 is now complete in 12 volumes ed. Joyce M. Horne, B. Jones, and H. P. F. King, under the auspices of the Institute for Historical Research; for details of Le Neve's work and subsequent revision, see the introduction to vol. 12, pp. 1–7.

[35] Richard Rawlinson's version of Langlet du Fresnoy, *A New Method of Studying History*, 2 volumes (London, 1728), II, pp. 146–52, 317–36, lists many of them.

[36] *Epistolario*, ed. M. Campori, 14 volumes (Modena, 1901–22), XII, pp. 5423–5.

[37] Lucenti proposed a three volume abbreviation; a subsequent fourth volume was to have dealt with origins of churches, situation of cities, etc. The main element of interest in the published vol. 1 is sig. c–c2, a brief account of Ughelli in an excerpt from a letter to Cardinal Francesco Maria Medici, written after Ughelli's death, when Lucenti participated in the burial service. In the same volume, cols. 454–1108, there is an account of the 'bishops' (which they were for a short time) and abbots of Monte Cassino, really a separate work, comprising nearly half the volume and with its own introductory letter *Ad Lectorem*.

[38] For Coleti's revision, see above p. 219 n. 11. Muratori's criticism is in *Epistolario*, x, 4383–4.

This is, however, the version which is still in use and no comparable surveys are of much value, with the exception of the 'Schedario' (unpublished but accessible in the Vatican Archives) of Cardinal Giuseppi Garampi (1728–92) intended to form the basis of a vast *Orbis Christianus*. Giuseppi Cappaletti's vernacular survey of Italian dioceses has, for the period covered by Ughelli–Coleti, no additional authority (21 volumes, Venice, 1844–79) and is much less scholarly than Gam's *Series Episcoporum* (1873–86) or Conrad Eubel's *Hierarchia Catholica* (1901 ff.), but of course these last two works merely list bishops, they do not attempt to describe their careers. Finally, there appeared in Rome in 1965 the first volume of a *Bibliotheca Ecclesiarum Italiae*, containing accounts of the bishops of Commacchio, Cesena, and the see of Brescello which existed in a fugitive way in the fourth and fifth centuries. The work was edited by P. Burchi and is presumably going no further. It is totally inconsistent; Commacchio is dealt with elaborately, Cesena on an entirely different plan, terser and with few references, and Brescello is given (and probably only needs) a page or two.

It would, of course, be wrong to suggest that no valuable recent work has been done on the bishoprics of Italy. But it would be true to say that this activity, which involves far too many scholarly publications to allude to here, has mainly been devoted to the early history of bishoprics, earlier than about AD 1000 and confined mainly to north and central Italy. For the fourteenth to the seventeenth century, Ughelli, in Coleti's revision, remains the basic study. Nor do I feel that all of the criticism levelled at Coleti is merited; doubtless fresh errors crept in as he was trying to correct the old ones. But he was a scholarly Venetian priest from a family of scholarly printers. His uncle had begun to accumulate materials for revision; Nicolo continued this and, in addition, extended entries down to his own day. Further, he amplified, sometimes considerably, entries on cathedral chapters, size of dioceses, numbers of conventual establishments, and so on. Lastly, he carefully distinguished typographically between his own *additiones* and Ughelli's original work, printing his own material in italics. Some interesting work could be done, one suspects, on the state of the Italian church in the fifty years between 1670 and 1720 merely by comparing the description of the dioceses as given by Ughelli and later corrected and amplified by Coleti. The Venetian scholar also took in Ughelli's *corrigenda* and supplementary material and several of the longer of Ughelli's *pièces justificatives* were placed in a final tenth volume, labelled *Anecdata Ughelliana*, together with details of 107 defunct bishoprics mainly derived from Philip Cluwer's *Italia Antiqua* (Leyden, 1616–24).

In this form, Ughelli–Coleti has proved extraordinarily tenacious. As noted, it lies behind the vernacular work of the nineteenth-century Venetian Cappaletti and behind many of the relevant entries in Moroni's vast *Dizionario*.[39] More deceptively, the chronology provided by Ughelli was often adopted (where no other Italian authority was available) by Gams in his *Series Episcoporum* and so (when Eubel could not find a name or a date in the records and had to rely on Gams), Ughelli in fact lies, albeit concealed, behind entries in the *Hierarchia Catholica*. Ughelli has also the further advantage of not (like Eubel and his later revisers) placing too much emphasis on papal provision, as recorded in the *Obligationes*. We frequently encounter in Ughelli's pages information that a bishop was prevented from obtaining possession of his see. In Eubel, it matters not a whit that a particular provision was never effective.

Ughelli must have known that he had a very considerable reputation among European scholars. His correspondents were scattered over the whole continent. One letter he kept was sent to him by favour of Cardinal Rossetti in March 1665. It was from 'Monsieur de Sainte-Marthe, councilor of the king in his councils and historiographer of his very Christian majesty, living on the rue de Sorbonne in Paris'. The writer thanks Ughelli for a genealogy he has sent, tells him of a proposed *Orbis Christianus* which will summarise Italy in one volume, and that Ughelli will be acknowledged in the preface.[40] What one can be sure of is that Ughelli cannot have known of the slow but steady effect of his labours in suggesting to his Italian helpers and correspondents that he was erecting a monument to a living Italy in his large work, much as Muratori was to do in his writings.

It must not be forgotten that beside Ughelli the scholar stood Ughelli the man of religion. His ideal was the Tridentine prelate, resident, active, learned and humble. His aim was, in a sense, to display such a good prelate. Had not one of Carlo Borromeo's injunctions been that all bishops should search out the documents and deeds of their predecessors and record them in a book? The Sainte-Marthe twins print this injunction prominently in *Gallia Christiana*. We must remember that the scholar at the Tre Fontane had rejected bishoprics for himself, and perhaps greater things, in order to play his quiet part in the reform of his church.

This last observation brings me back to the relationship of Christianity and scholarship at this time. Ughelli with his contemporaries was held

[39] Gaetano Moroni, *Dizionario di erudizione storico-ecclesiastica*, 103 volumes (Venice, 1840–61) and six volumes of index (Venice, 1878–9).

[40] Barb. Lat. 3240, fo. 15. Another French scholar involved in this, Noël Damy, corresponded with Ughelli in 1664 and solicited his help; Barb. Lat. 3239, fos. 23–4.

fast in a strait-jacket of conformity both doctrinal and stylistic, but not scholarly. A proper treatment of these matters would take several essays, which the recipient of this volume deserves, but from a more learned man than the author.

'By an Orphean charm': science and the two cultures in seventeenth-century England

JAMES R. JACOB

Recently historians have been tracing the emergence of two cultures, elite and popular, in early modern Europe and have come to some remarkably similar and startling conclusions.[1] The general outlines of the picture they have drawn apply to both England and the Continent. During the sixteenth century three things worked together to make the common people heard, particularly in the cities: the printing press, the Reformation, and the commercial revolution. Printing and the Reformation promoted literacy, and the commercial revolution gave hitherto obscure men (and a few women) access to the press and publication because what they had to say, whether about medicine or mechanics, would sell in a world of increasing literacy, prosperity, and economic opportunity. Finally, the Reformation gave ordinary people a vision, often millenarian in nature, of a better future order here on earth, while doctrines like predestination and the priesthood of all believers imparted a commitment to trying to achieve it.

During the seventeenth century, a dramatic change took place. The elite, having once patronized popular culture, became increasingly suspicious of and hostile to it. The price revolution had produced a widening gap between those who took advantage of it and those,

[1] For instance: M. Bakhtin, *Rabelais and His World* (Cambridge, Mass. 1968); R. Mandrou, *Magistrats et Sorciers en France au Dix-Septième Siècle* (Paris, 1968); John Bossy, 'The Counter-Reformation and the People of Catholic Europe', *Past and Present*, no. 47 (1970), pp. 51–70; Natalie Zemon Davis, *Society and Culture in Early Modern France* (Stanford, Cal., 1975); Peter Burke, *Popular Culture in Early Modern Europe* (New York, 1978); Carlo Ginzburg, *The Cheese and the Worms* (Harmondsworth, 1982); Brian Manning, *The English People and the English Revolution, 1640–1649* (London, 1976); Christopher Hill, *Society and Puritanism in Pre-revolutionary England* (London, 1966); *idem.*, 'Parliament and People in Seventeenth-Century England,' *Past and Present*, no. 92 (1981), pp. 100–24; Keith Wrightson and David Levine, *Poverty and Piety in an English Village: Terling, 1525–1700* (New York, 1979); Keith Wrightson, *English Society 1580–1680* (New Brunswick, N. J., 1982), and William Hunt, *The Puritan Moment: The Coming of Revolution in an English County* (Cambridge, Mass., 1983).

particularly at the bottom of society, who were victimized by it, and this was especially the case during the severe economic decline of the first half of the seventeenth century. Protestantism and spreading literacy, moreover, gave ordinary people the means to express their dissent and dissatisfaction as never before and thus to expose the fragility of the social fabric. From the point of view of the elite, the people and their culture had become dangerous. Clergy and magistrates, armed with their own versions of godly discipline and the powers of enforcement provided by the new bureaucratic state, sought to impose on the people one form or another of counter-reformation, whether Puritan or post-Tridentine Catholic. Throughout Western Europe, the elite, far from wishing any longer to foster popular culture, sought now to control and redirect it. The people must be weaned away from their errors and enthusiasms and taught to accept a regimen of work, worship, and taxes imposed from above.

Can the story of science, natural philosophy, the systematic study of nature in England during the sixteenth and seventeenth centuries, be assimilated to the pattern of the relations of elite and popular cultures sketched out here? To some extent the answer must be yes, thanks to some excellent ground-breaking work which, without being aware of its implications for the history of early modern science, suggests how this history can be fitted into the scheme provided by the historians of popular culture. We thus have available a new conceptual scheme for taking account of the social history of scientific ideas in the period of the so-called scientific revolution.

Let us begin with the work of B. S. Capp, modestly enough entitled *English Almanacs, 1500–1800*, which is really an exhaustive study of astrology in England, traced from its rise in the sixteenth century to its decline in the late seventeenth and eighteenth centuries. Capp's book illustrates the connection between scientific change and the relations of popular to elite culture in early modern Europe. Astrology developed to its fullest extent in the sixteenth and seventeenth centuries, the result, Capp argues, of several factors. Increasing literacy and the printing press made cheap almanacs available to a wide market, and this popular taste encouraged astrological practitioners to hang out their shingles and contribute further to the printed literature. Almanac sales passed a third of a million a year, which means that roughly one family in three bought an almanac each year.[2] Business was also brisk in the astrologers' private consulting rooms, and their patients embraced every level of society, sometimes including even the poorest who could not pay. The science appealed to the rich and those of very ordinary means, to the great and

[2] B. S. Capp, *English Almanacs 1500–1800* (Ithaca, N.Y., 1979), pp. 19–20, 283, 286.

the humble, to academic as well as popular taste.[3] John Dee, the Elizabethan court mathematician and Neoplatonist, gave it his stamp of approval, and practical mathematical problems arising from overseas navigation also promoted the serious study of the stars.[4] Finally, the doctrinal Reformation, in England as much as elsewhere, created a psychic vacuum which astrology rushed in to fill, a point made by Keith Thomas and Alan Macfarlane as well as by Capp. The Reformation stripped the priest of his magical spiritual power, thereby depriving ordinary people of their principal access route to the comforts and protections of the supernatural in a world fraught with danger and mystery. Thus 'it was natural for many laymen to seek substitutes' for sacerdotal magic, and among the chief of these was astrology.[5]

In this respect, however, astrology succeeded too well from the point of view of the elites in seventeenth-century England. Its appeal drew the masses away from church teachings which emphasized the sober and sobering disciplines of work and prayer.[6] This conflict grew particularly acute at mid-century when, during and after the Revolution, astrology came to be firmly associated with the radical religious and political views that flourished at the time. Ordinary people thought of astrology as one among several forms of knowledge giving them direct access to the supernatural and exempting them from obedience to ministers and magistrates. Even more extreme was the view that astrology offered a total explanation of the world of men and nature in which there was no place for God at all. All terrestrial phenomena, claimed the astrologer J.H. (probably John Heydon), could be explained by 'the motions of corpuscles...These have no first movers but stars.'[7] So for religious and ideological reasons, as Capp, Thomas, and Christopher Hill make clear, elite opinion gradually turned against astrology in the course of the seventeenth century, and by the next century the elite had ditched what had once been a universally popular science. In the eighteenth century, astrology survived in the shadows among the lower orders and 'cut off from the intellectual mainstream'.[8] The point is well taken: here we have an account of the rise and decline of a discrete science, explained in terms agreeable to the pattern worked out by early modern historians for

---

[3] *Ibid.*, pp. 21, 52–3, 392. See also Michael Macdonald, *Mystical Bedlam* (Cambridge, Eng., 1982).

[4] Capp, *English Almanacs 1500–1800*, pp. 19–20.

[5] *Ibid.*, p. 20; Keith Thomas, *Religion and the Decline of Magic* (New York, 1971); and Alan Macfarlane, *Witchcraft in Tudor and Stuart England* (London, 1970).

[6] Capp, *English Almanacs 1500–1800*, pp. 32, 71, 279.

[7] *Ibid.*, p. 184.

[8] *Ibid.*, pp. 69, 71–8, 186–7, 281, 283; and Christopher Hill, *The World Turned Upside Down* (New York, 1972).

understanding the changing relations between elite and popular cultures in early modern times.

But astrology is a special case; it was, as we have seen, one of the sciences that lost out in the competition for what would ultimately be deemed to be proper science. The victory in that race for establishing a monopoly of truth claims, the victory in England, went hands down to the experimental, corpuscular philosophy, to the Newtonian world-view rather than the astrologer's; indeed, his views were demoted to the status of pseudoscience. So the question must inevitably be whether the development of the science of the victors cannot also be assimilated to the same conceptual framework.

In what follows I shall argue, by drawing upon and extending considerable recent work, that the development of natural philosophy from Francis Bacon to the founding of the Royal Society conforms to the same pattern as astrology. Indeed, it would be impossible, I think, for it to have been otherwise, since the same social process that spelled astrology's demise made for the success of its chief adversary, the natural philosophy of Bacon, Boyle, and the early Royal Society. The story of this process is among the most carefully worked out in the history of science. Rather than summarizing the literature devoted to telling that story, what I wish to do here is to treat this process from a new angle of vision. In particular, I wish to show how the social foundations of modern science conform to a more fundamental pattern of change in early modern Europe which has been delineated by scholars who are not historians of science and who seem to have been unaware of the implications of their work for the history of science.

One of the key texts for understanding how the social relations of science are congruent with a more general historical pattern is Albert Hirschman's *The Passions and the Interests: The Argument for Capitalism before its Triumph*. Here is a work that illustrates the point I have just made. Written by a political economist whose area of expertise is the problems of underdevelopment in the twentieth century, it has tremendous bearing on the question of the social foundations of modern science, despite the fact that neither the author nor the historians of science have recognized its relevance.

What does Hirschman have to say that is so important? He sees that, throughout the seventeenth and eighteenth centuries, leading thinkers addressed themselves to the critical problem of maintaining social order. Hirschman provides further witness to the fragility of early modern polities in the face of repeated threats from below or to the perception of such fragility by thinkers at the time. He has detected an important thread running through the arguments for civil peace: every thinker built his argument around the key idea that the way to control unruly popular passions destructive of civil society was either to provide a safety valve for expressing them or to appeal to countervailing passions, the pursuit of which would curtail the destructive ones. In either case, thinkers looked to the pursuit of private gain, self-interest, as providing the solution to the problem of keeping order and maintaining authority. Men would become so caught up in their work and the opportunities for personal profit, so the argument ran, that they would both lack energy for and lose interest in fomenting rebellion. What was new in this argument was the revaluation of acquisitiveness that it entailed. The acquisitive urge was no longer seen in a negative light, as it had been in the Middle Ages. This revaluation, however, was only partial, because material self-interest was not regarded as an end unto itself but as a means to achieving the greater good of civil peace. The earliest arguments for capitalism, Hirschman maintains, pointed to its larger social benefits rather than to strictly economic ones.[9]

At the same time that the political philosophers whom Hirschman cites were building a social case for capitalism, the natural philosophers (whom he does not cite) were making a very similar case on behalf of science: the pursuit of natural philosophy should be encouraged and instilled because it captures the imagination, disciplines the mind, inspires awe before the wonders of Creation, creates jobs and increases prosperity; it harnesses destructive passions by diverting them into channels that generate both wealth and order. Science was seen to be valuable because *inter alia* it contributed to social stability in a world where that was often at a premium. Thus, the social argument for science fits very closely the picture of the relation of elite to popular culture drawn by the historians: science becomes another means, along with work discipline and the reformation of manners, by which European elites, having distanced themselves from the people, still seek to control and subject them to their authority. The natural philosopher joins the priest, minister and magistrate in the business of curbing potentially unruly popular passions.

It is time to look at the arguments of these natural philosophers. The evidence is drawn mainly from seventeenth-century English sources, although there will be occasion to see a connection between English and Italian patterns of argument.

The story begins with Bacon, who represents the way in which sixteenth-century elites, inspired by late Renaissance humanism, attempted to build bridges between the great and little traditions, that is

[9] Albert O. Hirschman, *The Passions and the Interests: The Argument for Capitalism Before Its Triumph* (Princeton, N. J., 1977), pp. 3–66.

to say, between courtly, academic and literate culture and the oral, folk traditions of the people. It is now widely known, largely thanks to Paolo Rossi's biography, that Bacon produced an idea of scientific enterprise that drew much of its strength from the techniques of mechanics and engineers and from the aims of practical alchemy. Bacon looked forward to the establishment of a court-centred science, sponsored, managed and instilled by the monarchical state, purged of the elite's addiction to Greek metaphysics, and informed by a devotion to utility and experiment drawn from popular craft traditions and artisanal practices.[10] The ideal was collaboration between the people and their traditional superiors, not for the sake of sharing power or rearranging society, but to increase knowledge, wealth and efficiency, reduce poverty, alleviate suffering – material benefit and the discovery of nature, not freedom and democracy. In this collaboration between the rulers and the ruled, the notables, the men on top, would have to pay a heavy price: it would be necessary for them to stoop to the level of the worker and be instructed by him in the lessons of experience before they would be able to shed their false and pretentious learning and read the language in which the book of nature is written.[11] According to Bacon, the elite, while maintaining their social superiority, would have literally to humble themselves, to be intellectually *déclassé* – never an easy thing for anyone to do, especially not for a traditional elite, and something that the stream of Baconian *virtuosi* in seventeenth-century England never, it seems to me, quite succeeded in pulling off, despite their insistence, following Bacon, that this is what had to be done.[12]

But what of their teachers, the lowly and humble themselves, what price would they be expected to pay? Here Bacon reveals himself to be a shrewd and subtle thinker, confronting the growing popular challenge to public order that many notables like him felt and remarked at the time. He had a deep faith in the capacity of the common people for rebellion or at least for producing disruption, with or without leadership from above. The social fabric was fragile and ever vulnerable to disturbances from below. While he proposed sweeping reforms in the realm of science and learning, he remained squarely opposed to fundamental alterations in established institutions, in part at least because such efforts might stir popular revolt and leave things worse than before.[13] 'Nothing is more

[10] Paolo Rossi, *Francis Bacon: From Magic to Science* (Chicago, 1968), pp. 7–11.
[11] *Ibid.*, pp. 25–32, 56–9.
[12] Francis Bacon, *Novum Organum*, in Hugh G. Dick (ed.), *Selected Writings of Francis Bacon* (New York, 1955), pp. 501, 531 (henceforth *Selected Writings*).
[13] Theodore K. Rabb, 'Francis Bacon and the Reform of Society,' in T. K. Rabb and E. Siegel (eds.), *Action and Conviction in Early Modern Europe* (Princeton, N.J., 1969), pp. 179–87; Henry E. I. Phillips, 'An Early Stuart Judaizing Sect,' *Transactions of the*

popular,' he said, than 'the supplanting or the opposing of authority established...'[14]

There is a paradox lying at the heart of Bacon's thought. On the one hand, he dreads the popular response to 'novelty' in thought or action. On the other, he offers a program for the total reform of the sciences. This is a major problem that deserves systematic treatment. I shall limit myself here to saying two things about it. First, Bacon made a distinction between the reform of knowledge and other kinds of reform. The advancement of learning was safe or at least could be made safe, while other reforms were fraught with peril. As he said, 'the reformation of a state in civil matters is seldom brought in without violence and confusion; but discoveries carry blessings with them, and confer benefits without causing harm or sorrow to any.'[15] In the second place, Bacon thought that the scientific enterprise itself, the very activity of doing science such as he envisaged it, would help to preserve the social order. Of course, in his scheme for the reform of learning, the artisan became tutor to the gentleman, and this could not help but raise his self-esteem, if not his actual status. In Bacon's fragile social world, there was an implicit danger in this lifting of popular sights. How then were the lowly tutors to be taught? What would serve to keep knowing artisans obedient?

Owing to the work of Rossi, James Stephens, and J. N. D. Bush among others, we know that crucial to Bacon's reform program was the invention of a new rhetoric.[16] Here we would perhaps do well to recall that, for the Renaissance humanists, rhetoric was a key discipline because they regarded it as furnishing the means by which knowledge could be communicated to achieve their civic goals.[17] For Bacon, an heir in some ways to the civic humanist tradition, the reform of rhetoric and its inculcation in the people were essential to the success of the scientific enterprise. Men, especially the common people, were led astray into 'anarchy and confusion' because the untrained or misguided imagination gave in to the senses rather than submitting to reason.[18] The

Jewish Historical Society of England, XV (1946), p. 65; David Cressy, *Literacy and the Social Order* (Cambridge, U.K., 1980), p. 187; J. C. Davis, *Utopia and the Ideal Society* (Cambridge, U.K., 1981) pp. 126–7 (henceforth Davis, *Utopia*); and Francis Bacon, *Essays*, in *Selected Writings*, p. 48.

[14] Bacon, *Essays*, in *Selected Writings*, p. 146.
[15] Bacon, *Novum Organum*, in *Selected Writings*, p. 538.
[16] Rossi, *Francis Bacon*, pp. 162–3, 180–5; James Stephens, *Francis Bacon and the Style of Science* (Chicago, 1975), pp. 17–18, 37–9, 57–8, 61–71; Katherine Park, 'Bacon's "Enchanted Glass",' *ISIS*, 75 (1984), pp. 290–302; and Davis, *Utopia*, pp. 131–2. Also, Robert P. Adams, 'The Social Responsibilities of Science in *Utopia*, *New Atlantis*, and After,' *Journal of the History of Ideas*, 10 (1949), pp. 387–92.
[17] Eugene Rice, *The Foundations of Early Modern Europe, 1460–1559* (New York, 1970), pp. 87–8.   [18] Davis, *Utopia*, p. 127.

new rhetoric would undo the damage by informing the imagination in such a way as to appeal to reason over the senses. The learned could then communicate their messages and findings to the people, and the people could participate in the scientific enterprise because they would be trained to forego the immediate gratification of their unruly passions for the sake of the material benefits of science and the prolonged and systematic inquiry required to obtain those benefits. Baconian rhetoric would teach the people to relinquish present indulgence in the hope of a greater future reward and to restrain sensual passion for the sake of intellectual passion, the pursuit of science itself. Thus, according to Bacon, the people, who taught intellectual humility to the great, would also be humbled, and kept humble, for service in the scientific state.[19] Baconian rhetoric would be both socially and intellectually beneficial. The reform of learning, so far from destabilizing society, as other kinds of reform tended to do, would have the reverse effect. The thinking of the notables would be enriched, the passions of common people chastened; science would advance, prosperity increase; and the delicate social fabric would be kept intact to every possible extent.

Even so, there was nothing foolproof about the process by which science might contribute to social stability, which in any case could never be automatically assured. 'The innate depravity and malignant disposition of the common people' would always have to be reckoned with, and Bacon's cyclical view of history did not bode well for the time when popular tumult might throw everything into disorder, despite the benefits of science and rhetoric.[20] Bacon, after all, consigned the fulfillment of his social and scientific ideal to a utopian paradise, New Atlantis; presumably beyond the corrupting reach of time.

Bacon's strategy for co-opting the people fits Hirschman's analysis and reflects the pattern of relations between the elite and the people in early modern Europe being charted by other historians. Hirschman's analysis is also borne out by other evidence that links the story which has so far been restricted to England to another part of Europe during the same period, namely, to Italy in the early seventeenth century. This linkage will suggest, I hope, the possibilities of discovering a more general pattern for Western Europe as a whole. Let us turn then to Galileo.

Galileo's views concerning the common man are representative of the more general attitude of seventeenth-century elites. In 1615, Galileo, while defending his own and Copernican ideas of the universe, insisted

[19] See references given in note 16 above; Davis, *Utopia*, p. 128; and Francis Bacon, *The Advancement of Learning*, in *Selected Writings*, pp. 309–11.

[20] Bacon, *De sapientia veterum*, in *Selected Writings*, pp. 408–13.

that 'the mobility of the earth' was 'a proposition far beyond the comprehension of the common people.'[21] He, moreover, castigated those clergy 'who would preach the damnability and heresy of the new doctrine from their very pulpits with unwonted confidence, thus doing impious and inconsiderate injury not only to that doctrine and its followers but to all mathematics and mathematicians in general.'[22] One of Galileo's friends, Giovanni Ciampoli, made clear in a letter to him the basis of his antagonism to such clerics: 'I have spoken to no one yet who did not judge it a great irrelevance for preachers to want to enter their pulpits and discuss such lofty and professional subjects among women and ordinary folk, where there exist such a small number of well-informed people.'[23]

Galileo went further than this. He displayed his attitude towards 'women and ordinary folk' in the defense he put forward on behalf of the new astronomy against the strictures of the Church. He constructed an argument that put himself on the side of clerical tradition against the common people. He made it seem, in other words, as if it were an issue of two professional elites, mathematicians and theologians, patronizing the masses. How did his argument run? The theologians, Galileo said, have long held that the Bible is full of passages 'set down... by the sacred scribes in order to accommodate them to the capacities of the common people who are rude and unlearned.'[24] These passages are capable of a deeper meaning, one which it has always been the responsibility of theologians to discover.[25] At this point, Galileo allied the new astronomy with this exegetical tradition. 'Hence even if the stability of heaven and the motion of earth should be more than certain in the minds of the wise, it would still be necessary to assert the contrary for the preservation of belief among the all-too-numerous vulgar.'[26] It was a clever argument, perhaps too clever: 'the shallow minds of the common people' must be protected from the truth about the universe lest they 'should become confused, obstinate, and contumacious in yielding assent to the principal articles that are absolutely matters of the faith.'[27] Clever or not, Galileo's argument in the long run, as we know, did not work. This however, was only the beginning of a longer story.

Five years later, in 1620, the Dominican Tommaso Campanella, having been imprisoned in 1599 for plotting revolt against Spain in Calabria, switched sides and became an apologist for the Spanish king.[28] In his

---

[21] Galileo Galilei, *Letter to the Grand Duchess Christina*, in *Discoveries and Opinions of Galileo* (Garden City, N.Y., 1957), p. 169.

[22] *Ibid.*, p. 177.   [23] *Ibid.*, p. 161.   [24] *Ibid.*, p. 181.

[25] *Ibid.*, pp. 181–2.   [26] *Ibid.*, p. 200.   [27] *Ibid.*, p. 200.

[28] Frances Yates, *Giordano Bruno and the Hermetic Tradition* (London, 1964), pp. 360–7, 385–9.

Monarchia di Spagna, he set forth another view of the connection between natural philosophy, political and religious authority and the common people, a view very different from Galileo's and remarkably Machiavellian. Campanella agreed with Galileo that ordinary men and women could be 'contumacious' towards authority. As a reformed revolutionary, Campanella would have known whereof he wrote. But here he departed from Galileo. The latter had said that natural philosophy should be kept from 'the vulgar' because it was likely to make them more contumacious. Campanella, on the other hand, argued that the study of nature should be encouraged among the people in order to promote obedience to authority. Campanella was convinced that natural philosophy, rather than causing people to question authority, would absorb their interest and hence turn their attention away from politics and religious dissent. Science would also channel human energies into productive enterprise, energies that might otherwise go to fuel popular disturbances. By means of scientific education, Campanella said, 'people's minds will be diverted from creating... any trouble, and will be incited to bend their studies that way which may be useful to the king.'[29] Popular science, in other words, served two purposes, technical and political.

Campanella may have been one of the first to put this striking argument, but he was by no means the last. As Carlo Ginzburg has recently shown, later in the century, after Galileo's trial, the Italian thinkers Sforza Pallavicino and Virgilio Malvezzi made a very similar case for the social utility of science. It was right, they argued, that ordinary people, artisans and peasants, should be kept out of politics, which are beyond their limited capacities to understand. Politics, they went on, presuppose a secret wisdom known only to princes. But science can be made available to everyone because nature is everywhere the same: its operations, unlike those of politics, are regular and predictable. Thus, scientific inquiry can safely be encouraged among the populace, and to the extent that ordinary people commit themselves to the study of nature, politics can become what it ought to be, a monopoly of the elite, with a consequent reduction of disorder produced by popular tumult.[30]

Here then is another argument for the conduct of science that derives from its putative social utility in maintaining traditional authority. The argument is enunciated in Counter-Reformation Italy partly in response to the Church's reaction to the new astronomy and particularly to

[29] Quoted in Henry Stubbe, *Campanella Revived* (London, 1670), p. 3.
[30] Carlo Ginzburg, 'High and Low: the Theme of Forbidden Knowledge in the Sixteenth and Seventeenth Centuries,' *Past and Present*, no. 73 (1976), pp. 28–41.

Galileo's defenses and demonstrations of it. Science, far from being dangerous, is politically valuable. The hallmark of this Italian argument is Machiavellism, the explicitness of its political calculation. Science becomes a repressive political tool, all the more effective because it is not punitive. It can be encouraged rather than imposed, inculcated rather than inflicted. Bacon's argument, as we have seen, was also politically calculated, but he looked forward, in addition, to a collective scientific enterprise in which the elite and the people would both participate and learn from each other. This Baconian argument surfaces again in England just before the civil wars and with a new millenarian thrust.

Bacon's strategy for accomplishing 'the advancement of learning' played an important role in the story of science in seventeenth-century England. Charles Webster has shown that Samuel Hartlib, John Dury and Gabriel Plattes, among others, took up Bacon's reform program in the three decades before 1660 and made it central to their own schemes for accomplishing the Protestant Reformation in England. Webster has persuasively argued that the Baconian projects of the Hartlib circle were also millenarian in inspiration, that is, 'the advancement of learning' was meant to contribute to a more general temporal and spiritual amelioration that would be tantamount to achieving a Protestant millennium, a long epoch of universal peace, piety, and prosperity in which England would take the lead.[31] The vision of these mid-century Baconians was certainly millenarian. They sought to build a holy commonwealth that would eliminate the abuses of the past, their motives were religious, specifically Puritan, and, in an effort to achieve their goals, they associated with the Puritan cause and the parliamentary party during the civil wars and interregnum.

What is interesting is the particular shape of their vision. When we look beneath the surface, we see that their picture of the millenarian future was remarkably rigid, static and hierarchical. True, they no longer put their trust in the king and a hereditary aristocracy, but in parliament and pious men of wealth and talent.[32] But there is an assumption in their thinking that if wealth often follows piety and talent, the reverse is equally the case. They see science, especially applied science, to be the key to prosperity, and so provision must be made for a program of scientific education. The structure of this program is revealing. There will be two types of school, 'mechanical schools' for the masses, teaching trades and technical subjects, and 'noble schools'

[31] Charles Webster, *The Great Instauration: Science, Medicine and Reform, 1626–1660* (London, 1975), pp. 1–31.
[32] Charles Webster (ed.), *Samuel Hartlib and the Advancement of Learning* (Cambridge, U.K., 1970), p. 112.

for the elite, teaching theory and advanced science. Nor is it ever spelled out that very few if any 'common people' will have the opportunity to attend the noble schools. The assumption is that the children of the poor will go to the mechanical schools and that the elite will pay to send their sons to the noble schools. The millennium will see the inauguration of a system of virtually universal education, and that is certainly new and radical. But the system itself is not egalitarian or even geared to promoting upward mobility.[33]

The assumptions behind this picture are illuminated by what Hartlib and Dury say elsewhere. The society they depict is one in which great numbers of people are poor, idle, and refractory. They represent so many obstacles in the way of achieving the millennium. Hartlib and his associates, like Bacon, see this population, the poor and the common people, as also constituting a menace to the social order. Like Bacon, too, they think of science as helping to provide the cure. From natural knowledge will come the industry and technology that will create jobs for the otherwise idle and dangerous poor. Science will foster both prosperity and a stable social order, and the two goals are equally important. In such a society, the poor not only know their place but obtain jobs and an education in 'mechanical schools' to keep them there.[34]

Nor does the argument for the social utility of science die out at the Restoration – far from it. The program of the Royal Society, founded in 1662, provides the richest, most complete evidence we have for the argument that modern science developed in part in response to popular disorder and elite perceptions of the threat from below. The leading spokesmen for the Society worked out in detail a social formula in which it was claimed that the scientific enterprise would play the key role in solving urgent political and religious problems and thus preserve the social hierarchy in church and state. Perhaps it is appropriate that the social argument for science should have reached its furthest development in England during the second half of the seventeenth century. There was the work and example of Bacon to draw on, and it has become a commonplace to say that the Royal Society was Baconian in inspiration. This usually is supposed to mean that the society was devoted to the experimental method and to the pursuit of useful knowledge. We now see that there was a third way in which the society could be characterized as following in Bacon's footsteps: science offered a formula for preserving

[33] *Ibid.*, pp. 165–92.
[34] *Ibid.*, pp. 112–13, 127–8. Valerie Pearl, 'Puritans and Poor Relief: the London Workhouse, 1649–1660,' in D. Pennington and K. Thomas, (eds.) *Puritans and Revolutionaries* (Oxford, 1978), pp. 217–22.

the existing hierarchical structure of society against subversion at the hands of the people. And, of course, this was a project that seemed particularly urgent to English magistrates and clergy after 1640 and especially after 1650. In no other nation-state in early modern Europe did the social order come so close to being turned upside down, and Baconian science was called in by the leaders of the Royal Society to help keep things right side up. Let us look at the social argument developed and put forward by the chief spokesmen of the Society – Robert Boyle, John Wilkins, Thomas Sprat, and Sir Christopher Wren.

According to these Anglican apologists, the cause of reformation is served by religious moderation, ecclesiastical comprehension, civil obedience, private enterprise, and profit. The prescription for the achievement of these mutually beneficial goals is experimental science. Its discipline tempers religious passion and helps men avoid two enemies of true religion, the enthusiasm of the sects and the wholesale submission of Catholics to papal authority and ecclesiastical tradition. If this is not sufficient incentive, there are the material advantages of science. Men will bury their religious differences in favor of the opportunities for profit that science creates. And with business investment comes employment for those who might otherwise make trouble for church and state. The new political economy which science can foster at home and abroad is tantamount to a fulfillment of the Reformation. To confirm this, one need only read the Bible. True religion is Scripture-based, and the Scriptures reveal a religion whose aims are exactly those of the Royal Society. The Society itself is a model for the nation as a whole: it invites to membership men of various religious persuasions, talents, and social backgrounds – lords, gentlemen, merchants, tradesmen, and mechanics – and submerges their religious differences, while drawing upon the variety of their skills, in the pursuit of experimental science for the common good, as the Society defines it.[35]

Encapsulating the ideology we have just been tracing and, in particular, the view that the science of the Royal Society is the foundation of both order and prosperity, Christopher Wren justifies the royal incorporation of the Society in these terms:

that obedience may be manifestly not only the publick but the private felicity of every subject...The way to so happy a government is in no manner more facilitate, than by promoting of useful arts and sciences, which, upon mature inspection, are found to be the basis of civil communities and free governments, and which gather multitudes by an Orphean charm into cities, and connect them in companies; that so, by laying in a stock as it were of several arts and methods

[35] J. R. Jacob, 'Restoration, Reformation, and the Origins of the Royal Society,' *History of Science*, 13 (1975), pp. 169–71.

of industry, the whole body may be supplied by a mutual commerce of each other's peculiar faculties, and, consequently, that the various miseries and toils of this frail life, may be, by as many various expedients ready at hand, remedied, or alleviated, and wealth and plenty diffused in just proportion to everyone's industry, that is, to everyone's desserts.[36]

Science, according to Wren, provides the means by which 'obedience' can be obtained and social order preserved, just as Bacon maintained. Indeed, the connection between Bacon and Wren is closer than this because the passage just quoted represents a gloss on the legend of Orpheus which makes much the same point that Bacon makes in a key passage in his own essay on Orpheus in *De sapientia veterum* (1609). There he argues that natural philosophy (science) works just like Wren's 'Orphean charm' to teach 'the peoples to assemble and unite and take upon them the yoke of laws and submit to authority, and forget their ungoverned appetites, in listening and conforming to precepts and discipline...'[37] During the Italian Renaissance Orpheus the musician had become a symbol of the eloquence that leads men out of barbarism into virtuous and civilized life.[38] For Bacon of course this was the function of science, and, drawing upon this Renaissance tradition of interpretation, he took for his key symbol of the civilizing power of natural philosophy the figure of Orpheus with his lyre.[39] Was Bacon saying that science represented a new and superior eloquence, a rhetoric equipped to tame the unruly multitude? I think he was, and I think Wren was probably drawing from Bacon's essay on this point. For both Bacon and the Baconian founders of the Royal Society, science did not represent a quiet retreat from religious and political turmoil, as has often been argued. Rather, for them, science constituted a formula for successful engagement with the world, a formula for damping popular tumult rather than retreating from it.

Wren and the Society, however, go beyond Bacon by specifying a new way in which science works to produce its social benefits. The 'Orphean charm' in Wren's science operates like an 'invisible hand' (to borrow Adam Smith's pregnant phrase), forging an identity between public

---

36 Christopher Wren, *Parentalia* (London, 1750), p. 196.
37 Bacon, *De sapientia veterum*, in *Selected Writings*, p. 412. For a similar reading of the legend of Orpheus in France in the reign of Henri III, see D. P. Walker, 'The Ancient Theology in Sixteenth-Century France,' in D. P. Walker, *The Ancient Theology* (London, 1972), p. 95.
38 John Warden, 'Orpheus and Ficino,' in *Orpheus: The Metamorphoses of a Myth*, John Warden (ed.) (Toronto, 1982), pp. 89–90.
39 For Bacon's debt to this Renaissance tradition of interpreting classical myths, including the legend of Orpheus: Charles W. Lemmi, *The Classical Deities in Bacon* (Baltimore, 1933), esp. pp. 1 and 129.

good and human selfishness. Science produces civil peace and private gain at the same time; in fact, the pursuit of gain leads to public order – and this in a particularly felicitous way, 'wealth and plenty,' as Wren says, being 'diffused in just proportion to everyone's industry, that is, to everyone's desserts.' Here is the industrial capitalist's dream more than a century before Adam Smith! We can see then that the founders of the Royal Society wedded Bacon's argument for science as an instrument of social control to an essentially capitalistic or market-oriented vision of society. In this regard, the thinking of the natural philosophers in the Royal Society constitutes important new evidence for the view, advanced recently by C. B. Macpherson, Joan Thirsk, Joyce Appleby and others, that it was in England during the seventeenth century and especially after 1650 that the idea of a market society took hold and the groundwork of capitalist theory was laid.[40] The argument put forward by the apologists for the Royal Society also neatly fits Hirschman's analysis. Science diverts destructive popular passions into socially harmless and economically productive channels by creating work and encouraging the pursuit of self-interest. Here, to use Hirschman's phrase, is a supreme example of 'the argument for capitalism before its triumph.'

The Royal Society's argument differs in another significant respect from Bacon's. For Bacon, as we have seen, the preservation of the social order, even with the help of science, was contingent upon fortune and the cyclical flow of history. All might be undone by 'perturbations and seditions and wars... ; and then a season of barbarism sets in...'.[41] In Bacon's view, an entirely stable polity in which science goes on flourishing *ad infinitum* is frankly utopian, represented by him in his portrait of New Atlantis. The Society's argument for the social utility of science is no longer bound by such conditions. Gone, too, is the utopianism. Or now, perhaps, utopia has become attainable. Wren's 'Orphean charm' operates in the here and now through an actual institution, the Royal Society, fledgling to be sure, but nonetheless real and not in the realm of fable like Bacon's Orpheus.

There is an even more fundamental distinction to be drawn between the two views. For Bacon the social order is a tender plant beset by the enemies, one of the nastiest of which is ambition, especially among the lowly. Private interest and public good make conflicting demands: 'And

[40] C. B. Macpherson, *The Political Theory of Possessive Individualism: Hobbes to Locke* (Oxford, 1962); Joyce Appleby, *Economic Thought and Ideology in Seventeenth-Century England* (Princeton, N. J., 1978); Joan Thirsk, *Economic Policy and Projects: The Development of a Consumer Society in Early Modern England* (Oxford, 1978); and G. N. Clark, *Science and Social Welfare in the Age of Newton*, 2nd edn (Oxford, 1970).
[41] Bacon, *De sapientia veterum*, in *Selected Writings*, pp. 412–13.

certainly men that are great lovers of themselves waste the public.'[42] In Wren's view, on the other hand, science works to keep individual striving and public order not only in balance but actually feeding on each other in symbiotic harmony. Once set in motion, the process becomes self-actualizing and exempt, it would seem, from the hazards (which Bacon stressed) of time and fortune. Bacon offered his readers a way of making the best of a bad situation, the fated conflict between the public and the private: 'Divide with reason between self-love and society...'[43] But for Wren there is never any question of having to lead such a double life, of dividing the self in this way. The pursuit of private gain, far from weakening society, contributes to it. And where Bacon admonished men to 'divide with reason,' for Wren a magical kind of rationality makes for the identity that exists between the public and the private: reason does not have to come from men; it is built into the very order of things. Private vice has not yet become public virtue, but we are on the way. Utopia is becoming realizable in the world via worldly means. As such, the arguments advanced by Wren and the Royal Society represent an important chapter in a long process, itself calling for systematic study, namely the domestication of English utopianism.

What, if anything, did the Royal Society's apologists know about the similar social arguments put forward in Italy? Campanella's works were known in England in the 1650s.[44] What is more, after the Restoration, the chief critic of the Royal Society, Henry Stubbe, accused the Society of falling for Campanella's strategy for re-Catholicizing Europe. Campanella argued that if the study of nature could divert Italians from popular revolt, it might also be deployed to win Protestants away from the Reformation. Stubbe insisted that the Royal Society was doing Campanella's dirty work for him, whether wittingly or no. Its natural philosophy, under the guise of true religion, undermined Protestantism and promoted popery and would eventually spell the ruin of the English church and state. All this lay at the surface of Stubbe's attack.

There was, however, a deeper layer of meaning beneath, which has eluded historians but that did not elude Stubbe's opponents at the time. He saw that the Royal Society was attempting to make the conduct of science serve the pursuit of conservative religious and political goals. In religion, he saw that the Society had tied the so-called experimental or corpuscular philosophy to latitudinarian Anglican Christianity in order to defend the providence of God, the immortality of the human soul, and a social ethic based on the notion of rewards and punishments to be meted out in the afterlife. This alliance between the Society and certain

[42] Bacon, *Essays*, in *Selected Writings*, p. 63.   [43] *Ibid.*, p. 63.
[44] William M. Lamont, *Richard Baxter and the Millennium* (London, 1979), pp. 186, 195.

segments of opinion in the restored Church put science and learning on the side of episcopal and clerical authority, ritual, dogma and persecution of dissent, all of which Stubbe the crypto-deist detested and equated with popery.[45]

In politics, the Royal Society would have an equally pernicious effect. As a defender of yeomen, artisans and the poor, Stubbe saw through the rhetoric of the Society to its covert elitism and diversionary strategy. Nor was the elitism always so covert. For example, one Fellow of the Royal Society, Edward Chamberlayne, had recently argued that because England was so rich in agriculture the yeomanry became prosperous without effort and hence lazy and disrespectful of 'nobility, gentry, and clergy.'[46] Chamberlayne's argument in this regard reflected an opinion, widely held at the time, that there could be such a thing as a 'surfeit of peace and plenty' a surfeit because prosperity beyond a point would spoil the lower orders, making them restive, discontented with their legitimate rulers and ready for insurrection.[47] Such a view only makes sense in a society, like that of seventeenth-century England, where many or most people live at or very close to subsistence. When such people have met their basic needs, they may stop working because there is little or no incentive to continue; and when they stop working, so the argument goes, they become idle and dangerous. Chamberlayne proposed to solve this problem by increasing taxes, which would 'necessitate the common people to be industrious in their callings, and so to mind their own, as not to disturb the state and church affairs.'[48] The burden of additional taxes would keep them too busy to sin. Other Fellows of the Royal Society, including Boyle, William Petty, and the Earl of Clarendon, expressed similar views.[49] Stubbe would have none of this: it was not, he said (*pace* Chamberlayne), 'the interest of our monarchy that all the commonalty be kept poor and in a complaining condition...'[50]

Stubbe's contemporary attack challenges the view which the Society chose to foster and which historians have continued to repeat, that

[45] James R. Jacob, *Henry Stubbe, Radical Protestantism and the Early Enlightenment* (Cambridge, U.K., 1983), chs. 3–5.
[46] Edward Chamberlayne, *Angliae Notitia*, 3rd edn (London, 1669), pp. 60–2.
[47] Royce Macgillivray, *Restoration Historians of the Civil War* (The Hague, 1974), pp. 237–42; Thomas More, *Utopia* (Harmondsworth, U.K., 1965), pp. 61–2; and D. C. Coleman, *The Economy of England 1450–1750* (Oxford, 1977), pp. 102–4.
[48] Chamberlayne, *Angliae Notitia*, pp. 60–2.
[49] J. R. Jacob, *Robert Boyle and the English Revolution* (New York, 1977), pp. 134–6; Jan De Vries, *The Economy of Europe in an Age of Crisis, 1600–1750* (Cambridge, U. K., 1976), p. 179; J. R. Hale (ed.), *The Evolution of British Historiography* (London, 1967), p. 20; and D. C. Coleman, 'Labour in the English Economy of the Seventeenth Century', *Economic History Review*, 2nd ser., VIII (1956), pp. 280–95.
[50] Stubbe, *Campanella Revived*, 'Preface to the Reader'.

science brought men from all estates together for their mutual advantage. To Stubbe's mind, in any case, the Society was doing just the opposite: it was pooling talents and interests in order to benefit the elite and not the people, in order indeed to contain and exploit the people by drawing upon their knowledge and skills, while at the same time deflecting them from political and religious courses that threatened constituted authority. In Stubbe's view, Wren's view of science in which 'wealth and plenty' are 'diffused in just proportion to everyone's industry' was less an example of the operation of an 'invisible hand' than it was a sleight of hand.

Stubbe's insight ties the organization of English science to a more general pattern that also emerged in Italy. Campanella and the others were voices of the Counter-Reformation. The Royal Society was staging a counter-reformation of its own, namely, a response to the social radicalism of the English Revolution. This is precisely what Stubbe saw and sought to point out. Long misread by historians of science, he saw three centuries ago what has until now been forgotten. As such, he must be reckoned an early historian of science of the first rank.

I have argued that the emergence of modern science in seventeenth-century England (and perhaps Italy) developed in part in response to the growing separation between the elite and the people that occurred during the same period. Thinkers argued that science might do two things. First, it might go some way towards pacifying the common people, reducing the level of popular violence and tumult, and shoring up the existing social hierarchy. Second, in England, men, with the exception of Stubbe, looked forward to a more positive result: the new order promoted by science might be such as to produce something like a common culture. Both high and low, rich and poor, might learn to submerge their differences in the joint pursuit of science and to share, if unequally, in its material benefits.

The story has been told from the point of view of the thinkers, themselves members of the elite, who produced the argument for the social utility of science, or, in Stubbe's case, exposed it. What of the common people for whom, or because of whom, the argument was designed, what did they think of it, how did they respond to it? The question is well worth asking but difficult if not impossible to answer. Margaret Spufford's recent portrait of the reading habits of common people during the Restoration offers a few clues. Popular taste in printed literature ran to chapbook versions of chivalric romances and especially to religious pulp of the fire-and-brimstone variety, in which sinners could do no more than repent and throw themselves on the mercy of an angry God.[51] He was depicted as a God of judgement rather than of reason, and life was a test of faith rather than a stage on which God could be worshipped through study of his works, as it was for the Royal Society. None of this suggests that science and social utility arguments made much impact on the popular mentality. In fact, it has often been assumed that science widened the gap between the two cultures rather than bridging it, and this may well have been the case. Even so, as we have seen, certain leading natural philosophers meant for science to have precisely the opposite effect, and in this matter results should not be allowed to stand for aims and intentions.

Nor did these philosophers seek to substitute science for religion in the lives of the common people. On the contrary, Boyle and John Locke, for example, urged men to study nature *and* Scripture. Boyle insisted that both sources revealed the same moral truths conducive at once to social peace and spiritual salvation.[52] Locke, who like Boyle was a Fellow of the Royal Society, believed that society should be arranged to permit all people, even the meanest, to devote at least three, and perhaps as many as six, hours a day to the study of natural and moral philosophy. The latter would afford an occasion for contemplating Christian doctrine, especially the doctrine of the divine retribution meted out to sinners in the afterlife. Locke, I think, would have approved of the religious pulp that flooded the chapbook market in his day. Natural philosophy for its part would yield material benefit. And both kinds of study would produce greater social stability.[53] In reference to the purely political payoff of such intellectual endeavor Locke wrote: 'The populace well instructed in their duty and removed from the implicit faith their ignorance submits them to in others would not be so easy to be blown into tumults and popular commotions by the breath and artifice of designing or discontented Grandees.'[54] Locke's words echo Bacon's and Boyle's. Throughout the seventeenth century natural and moral philosophers looked to science for a solution to 'tumults and popular commotions,' for a way of healing the breach between the two cultures.

[51] Margaret Spufford, *Small Books and Pleasant Histories: Popular Fiction and its Readership in Seventeenth-century England* (Athens, Ga., 1981), pp. 50–1, 75, 138, 145, 195–212.

[52] J. R. Jacob, 'Boyle's Circle in the Protectorate: Revelation, Politics and the Millennium,' *Journal of the History of Ideas*, xxxviii (1977), 131–40.

[53] John Dunn, *The Political Thought of John Locke*, (Cambridge, U.K., 1969), pp. 195, 197–8, 224–5, 231–2, 235–6, 251–2.

[54] Quoted in *Ibid.*, p. 236.

The crisis of the European mind: Hazard revisited

MARGARET C. JACOB

It is now fifty years since the brilliant French historian, Paul Hazard, published in 1935 his classic work, *La crise de la conscience européenne 1680–1715* (Paris, 1935). In it he propounded a thesis that has admirably withstood the passage of time and been capable of absorbing many, but by no means all, of the historical studies appearing since the Second World War. Briefly stated, Hazard and all subsequent historians have discerned at the end of the seventeenth and the beginning of the eighteenth centuries a crisis within the European mind, a moment of profound uncertainty, *une zone uncertaine, malaisée*. Out of that crisis emerged a new understanding of people and nature, of government, of religion in society which, as he saw it, prepared the way for the French Revolution. At that moment emerged a *mentalité* discernibly enlightened and modern, one with which Hazard and his generation of liberal French intellectuals could still identify.

Hazard identified one of those extraordinary cultural shifts – simultaneously the decline of traditional religious culture and the rise of a culture discernibly secular – which have so fascinated cultural historians. Helli Koenigsberger speculated about one such transformation within sixteenth-century Venetian culture.[1] Here I seek to explore the nature of Hazard's crisis, accepting his model of its being a critical turning point in European culture but offering a new reading of its origins and resolution.

In exploring *la crise* I shall return frequently to Hazard, to contrast his views with what contemporary historians would now describe as the sources of that crisis, its resolution, and its implications for eighteenth-century thought and society. There can be no higher tribute to an historian of any generation than to acknowledge that he or she set the

[1] H. G. Koenigsberger, 'Republics and Courts in Italian and European Culture in the Sixteenth and Seventeenth Centuries', *Past and Present*, No. 83 (May 1979), pp. 32–56.

251

terms of an historical discussion. We simply cannot understand the extraordinary transformation that occurred within European thought in those decades without invoking the concept of *la crise* as first identified by Hazard. We may assign different causes to it, and differ with him as to the nature of the culture it produced, but few deny the existence of a crisis which affected the educated classes in every European society with the possible exception of Russia and Spain, where it would seem the process out of which the Enlightenment was born was considerably delayed.

Central to Hazard's understanding of the crisis were the apparently contradictory impulses commonplace in the period. Within one mind of the late seventeenth-century it is possible to find both Calvinism and rationalism, both science and profound religiosity, both Christianity and heresy. The contradictions – more apparent than real – are present in the thought of Isaac Newton, scientist and alchemist, as they are manifest among many of his lesser-known followers. They can be found in the minds of Continental thinkers as diverse as the French refugee scholar and first encyclopedist, Pierre Bayle, or in the polemical writings of that Dutch opponent of magic and superstition, Balthazar Bekker. In all three their cultural postures were inextricably bound up with an understanding of what constituted safety and order in the polity. In diverse ways their lives had been touched by revolution or by the fear of the persecutions and injustices they associated with monarchical absolutism.

Hazard, of course, rightly saw that politics, or rather, given his resolutely idealist approach to history, political theory, was central to the crisis as he defined it. For him its central feature was the shift from a civilization founded upon *duty*, to one founded upon rights. In the realm of theory the formula works well enough. The retreat from any version of the theory of the divine right of kings was well underway by the 1690s. In its place we see an increasing emphasis upon natural law, contract theory, classical republicanism, even, although very rarely, utopian communism. Yet in characterizing the culture produced by this crisis, Hazard's formula tends to exaggerate the democratic implications of this transformation. Historians now see the crisis, in the first instance, as leading to the consolidation of a high European culture self-consciously distinct from popular culture and hostile to it.

This crisis occurred first among the literate classes, the readers and buyers of books, who in the course of the seventeenth-century increasingly distinguished their values from the superstitions (as they saw them) of the non-literate as well as from the hegemony in intellectual and religious matters enjoyed by the clergy, particularly in Catholic countries.[2] Of course, clergymen did also frequently play a major role in resolving this crisis. When they did, however, they addressed themselves to the interests and values of the literate and secular laity. Predictably the greatest clerical participation in this early stage of the Enlightenment occurred largely in an Erastian and Protestant context. Not least, the high culture that emerged from this crisis was, as we now know, fundamentally dependent upon the new science, both of Descartes and Newton, on a body of learning inaccessible to the uneducated.

Yet if the new science, when combined with the needs and interests of the educated laity, led to a resolution of the crisis – as well as also actually provoking it – we now see that the most fundamental cause of the crisis was directly political. Without the rise of French absolutism, coupled with the revolutionary upheaval in mid seventeenth-century England, and its important legacy for Continental opponents of absolutism, the crisis of the European mind would have been largely and simply a matter of shifting religious beliefs coupled with anti-clericalism. Its impact would never have been so general, encompassing every aspect of intellectual life, as to permit Hazard to relate it to the French Revolution. The crisis of the late seventeenth-century brought the intellectual legacy of the first of the great modern revolutions into the mainstream of Continental thought where it merged with indigenous traditions of anti-clericalism, philosophical heresy, and anti-absolutism.

To anchor the origins of *la crise* in the political experience of the English revolution and the European-wide fear of absolutism, to proclaim, therefore, the centrality of politics and ideology is to depart significantly from the vision of Hazard. His method, so rooted in idealism and *Ideengeschichte*, rendered mental processes into the essence of historical change, those things which, in his words 'commandent la vie' and take precedence over 'les forces materielles'.[3] Many contemporary historians no longer admit of such a discrete separation of human activities; the record of *la vie materielle* survives in the language of the past and language mediates between the material order, and the order of ideas. The origins, as well as the resolution of *la crise*, grew out of opposition to the power of kings and churches, courts and their bureaucracies, out of an earlier, political crisis of the mid seventeenth-century which manifested itself in revolutions and rebellions throughout the European state-system. Only the English Revolution of the mid-century, however,

---

[2] For a general discussion of this phenomenon see Peter Burke, *Popular Culture in Early Modern Europe* (New York; Harper and Row, 1978), pp. 245–81, and Natalie Davis, *Society and Culture in Early Modern France* (Stanford; University of California Press, 1975), pp. 189–267.

[3] Paul Hazard, *La crise de la conscience européenne, 1680–1715* (Paris; Boivin, 1935), preface.

produced a body of political, religious and scientific thought so rich and complex that once discovered by the European opponents of absolutism it laid the foundations for a new synthesis, for the phenomenon we describe as the Enlightenment. Yet in their voyage across the Channel the political philosophies and new science brought forth by the English Revolution were transformed, sometimes beyond all recognition, and the resulting Enlightenment was more truly European, or Scottish, or French, even Dutch and German, than it was English. The deeper *la crise* the greater the tendency to radicalize ideas that may have been revolutionary in their origin but which became strangely enervated or even forgotten in England, in their country of origin.[4]

Three traditions of political discourse emerged from the English Revolution, and by the late seventeenth-century all were antipathetic to Continental absolutism. The English Revolution, that social and political upheaval which began in 1640 and was only finally resolved in 1688–9, offered profoundly new and compelling justifications for the existence of the state just as it redefined who would have access to its power. In *Leviathan* (1651) Hobbes placed the origin of government among men grown weary of incessant internecine warfare, of endless competition 'that ceaseth only in the grave'. In their exhaustion they would seek peace by making a contract among themselves to accept a sovereign whose power would be absolute within the limits of certain natural laws. Although in fact seeking a new and *de facto* foundation for the absolute state, Hobbes appeared to the next generation of his interpreters, particularly on the Continent, not as a supporter of absolutism, but rather as a brilliant theorist of government by contract and as a materialist. Hobbes took his materialism, his characterization of human beings as solely pieces of matter in motion, creatures driven by passions and interests, directly from the new mechanical science. He had little use for an independent clergy, those 'bugbears', he called them, who prick the sides of their princes. Hobbes (d. 1679) wrote in response to revolutionary upheaval and he was a royalist. But where we find Hobbism in European thought after 1680 it will be used largely to mock the clergy or to lay the materialist foundations of government by contract, or simply to assert a more naturalistic definition of human needs and passions.

But the political legacy of the English Revolution was not confined to Hobbes. English republicans of the 1690s would look back to the

[4] On this question of the English Enlightenment see J. G. A. Pocock, 'Post-Puritan England and the Problem of the Enlightenment' in Perez Zagorin, *Politics and Culture in Early Modern Europe* (Berkeley; University of California Press, 1983), pp. 91–112. See also Roy Porter, 'The Enlightenment in England' in R. Porter and M. Teich, *The Enlightenment in National Context* (Cambridge; Cambridge University Press, 1981).

Commonwealth of the 1650s and the theories of James Harrington (*Oceana*, 1656) to argue for republican principles of government as the only alternative to court-centered and oligarchic government. In a Continental setting such republican arguments proved particularly appealing against the danger of French absolutism. In the early eighteenth-century the English freethinkers (as they called themselves) joined ideological forces in The Netherlands with the victims and opponents of French absolutism, the Huguenot refugees, as well as with the Dutch supporters of the English alliance.[5] These freethinking agents of the Whig party could trace their republican ideals back to a time when government in England had been established as the result of regicide (the parliamentary execution of Charles I in 1649). That kind of revolutionary heritage gave one a certain *cachet* in the republic of letters where millenarians as well as republicans dreamt about king-killing. The content of their fantasies were remarkably similar despite their profoundly different explanations of who ultimately justified the swinging of the axe.

The last of the three legacies drawn from the English Revolution is more difficult to trace on the European Continent. We may describe it as levelling, or democratic, and in the case of Winstanley, communistic. Its transmission to the New World, to the colonies in New England as well as to the Caribbean has now been documented,[6] but its Continental European impact is as yet difficult to establish. The communistic writings of Winstanley were in the library of the Quaker refugee, Benjamin Furly of Rotterdam, from at least the 1690s, if not earlier.[7] With some justification modern British socialists have invoked the legacy of the Levellers and Diggers; indeed in the 1790s Welsh radicals were reading Winstanley[8] while in the same decade the British supporters of the French Revolution were labelled 'levellers'. Yet despite the attempts of the original Levellers to find converts at Calais during the 1650s, and despite the occasionally levelling sentiments found a generation later in the writings of that Whig agent and pantheist, John Toland – an English radical with a vast Continental reputation if not a following – *la crise* and its resolution apparently owed little to English ideas we may now

[5] See Margaret C. Jacob, *The Radical Enlightenment: Pantheists, Freemasons and Republicans* (London and Boston; George Allen and Unwin, 1981); for a good survey of the literature on republicanism see J. G. A. Pocock, 'English Historical Thought in the Age of Harrington and Locke', *Topoi*, v. 2, 1983, pp. 149–62.
[6] On that transmission see Christopher Hill, 'Radical Pirates' in James R. Jacob and Margaret C. Jacob, *The Origins of Anglo-American Radicalism* (London and Boston; George Allen and Unwin, 1984), pp. 17–32.
[7] Margaret C. Jacob, *The Radical Enlightenment*, p. 161.
[8] Philip Jenkins, *The Making of a Ruling Class. The Glamorgan Gentry, 1640–1790* (Cambridge; Cambridge Universty Press, 1983), p. 18.

rightly describe as democratic and communistic. Continental spectatorial literature from this early period, for example, *Le Censeur* emanating from The Hague and quite possibly by Rousset de Missy, a follower of Toland, attacked private property, while the 1715 free translation into French of More's *Utopia* (by Gueudeville) preserved *in toto* the attack on private property.[9] Yet the radically democratic response to *la crise* is a mere whimper by comparison to the nearly universal attack upon the beliefs, values, and educability of *le peuple*. In that sense Hazard's assumption that there is an easily established link between the resolution of *la crise* and the origins of the French Revolution – in all but its earliest phase – requires considerable qualification.

To illustrate further the dangers awaiting the historian who assumes a direct link between *la crise* and the late eighteenth-century revolutions we need only investigate the career of John Locke (d. 1704) and his political writings. From any perspective Locke is central to the resolution of the constitutional crisis at the heart of the English Revolution. Yet his *Two Treatises of Government* published in 1689 was actually, as we now know, written before the Revolution of 1688, and therefore was never intended, at its origin, to justify it.[10] In that sense the post-1689 and largely Continental and American reading of Locke – in Europe almost always in French translation – missed his context and in some cases distorted his actual meaning. In 1935 Hazard saw Locke as having offered a resolution of *la crise*, and with regard to Lockean epistemology Hazard was undoubtedly correct. He could not have known that Locke's major political treatise was written in the early 1680s when he was deeply involved in Whig party circles, conspiratorial and therefore treasonable in their opposition to Stuart absolutism.[11]

Not only is Locke's treatise more a symptom of *la crise* than an attempt to offer a magisterial resolution of it, it also purposefully eschewed the republican tradition of the earlier revolution just as it repudiated Hobbist materialism with its democratic implications. In his 'appeal to heaven' for a 'dissolution of government' Locke sought a revolution led by magistrates – if the *Two Treatises* may be read as a call to action – and

[9] Aubrey Rosenberg, *Nicholas Gueudeville and his Work (1652–172?)* (The Hague; Nijhoff, 1982), pp. 102, 275.

[10] See Peter Laslett, ed., *Two Treatises of Government by John Locke* (Cambridge; Cambridge University Press, 1960); and for a sense of the way Locke was ignored by English apologists see J. P. Kenyon, *Revolution Principles: The Politics of Party, 1689–1720* (Cambridge; Cambridge University Press, 1977).

[11] Richard L. Ashcraft, 'The *Two Treatises* and the Exclusion Crisis: The Problem of Lockean Political Theory as Bourgeois Ideology' in J. G. A. Pocock and Richard L. Ashcraft, *John Locke* (Los Angeles; University of California Press, Clark Library series, 1980).

it was intended to bring about a change of government initiated by the landed and propertied classes to secure legally their privileges and interests. His political thought is probably much more closely related to the writings of civil law theorists than it is to that body of mid-century political theory that provided social and historical justifications for revolution.[12] Locke would have political transformations without social upheaval; a rearrangement of offices and responsibilities among the responsible opponents of tyranny, in a Continental sense among the propertied members of the second and third estates intent upon guaranteeing their right to engage in market transactions and to protect their property and liberty. The resolution of the English Revolution after 1660 depended upon political and intellectual leadership that feared above all else a 'turning of the world upside down' such as had nearly occurred in the 1650s when the lower classes threatened the very foundation of property rights and hierarchical control over the standing army.[13] In the first instance Locke belongs to that post-1660 reaction.

A reading of John Locke which could not take into account what we now know about his English context permitted Hazard to relate him too readily to the French Revolution. The revised account of Locke's influence on Continental radicalism is somewhat more complicated. The French Huguenots in the Dutch Republic seized upon Locke and in the process transformed him. David Mazel's French translation of the *Two Treatises* published in 1691, but reprinted in a multitude of editions, simply left out the first treatise, rearranged the second, and at every opportunity attempted to radicalize the text. The French Locke is more overtly anti-absolutist, given to forming opposition parties and interested in a wider system of representation than is the English Locke. Yet even after these adumbrations the French Huguenots and their friends would not leave the text alone, nor would they permit Locke's treatise to pass as a simple vindication of parliamentary government. In 1755 that now aged follower of Toland's pantheism, Jean Rousset de Missy (b. 1686), brought out in Amsterdam yet another edition of the French text of the *Two Treatises*, and in a new preface explained to his European audience that Locke had actually been a republican and an opponent of all forms of oligarchic corruption. Indeed Rousset asserted his relevance to the Dutch Republic, while painting him as a supporter of natural law theory similar to that argued in the 1740s by Burlamaqui. A fellow freemason and Amsterdam publisher, John Schreuder, published that 1755 edition

[12] Julian H. Franklin, *John Locke and the Theory of Sovereignty* (Cambridge; Cambridge University Press, 1979).
[13] Christopher Hill, *The World Turned Upside Down* (London, Temple Smith, 1972).

for Rousset, and it was the most widely circulated version of Mazel's translation on the Continent during the second half of the eighteenth-century.[14]

Yet the legacy of the English Revolution would have remained a largely British and American matter had it not been for the aggressive policies initiated in the 1680s by Louis XIV and his government. All the cultural factors Hazard identified as precipitating the crisis – the new familiarity with the religions and peoples of the world, the increasing movement of books as well as travellers within Europe, the new biblical criticism, both Catholic and Protestant in origin – came together to provoke a massive repudiation of long-cherished beliefs precisely because French absolutism threatened to destabilize the whole of Western Europe.

The revocation of the Edict of Nantes (1685) and the persecution of French Protestants revived in the minds of contemporaries the horrors of the late sixteenth-century wars of religion, while French territorial expansionism threatened the survival of the Low Countries, north and south, as well as the territorial integrity of various German principalities. The return of absolutist policies in England under James II (1685–8) made political crisis universal in Western Europe. By the late 1680s we can discern a steady stream of anti-absolutist propaganda coming from the French language presses in the Dutch Republic and various German cities, especially Cologne. These frequently anonymous tracts denounced the murderous tyranny of Louis XIV, proclaimed the virtues of the surviving European republics and darkly hinted at the right of subjects to overthrow their tyrants.[15] Some of this literature was in fact millenarian in origin and represented, particularly in the writings of the Huguenot refugee, Pierre Jurieu, a revival of Calvinist militancy of a late sixteenth-century variety. This religiosity determined the character of the earliest stage of the crisis: fearful of religious persecution, militantly Protestant with theocratic elements, internationally linked through the Huguenot coteries, with their Anglican sympathizers, and finding its outlet in the exiled French language press. In the first instance the republic of letters was born out of that older international, Dutch, Swiss, German, English, and French provincial Protestant culture; urban, literate, professional and clerical, ever hostile to the intolerance of absolutism in either its French or Spanish forms.[16] But the new literary

[14] Margaret C. Jacob, 'In the Aftermath of Revolution: Rousset de Missy, Freemasonry, and Locke's *Two Treatises of Government*' in *L'Eta dei Lumi. Studi storici sul settecento Europeo in onore di Franco Venturi* (Naples; Jovene, 1985), vol. I, pp. 487–521.
[15] Margaret C. Jacob, *The Radical Enlightenment*, p. 53.
[16] On that older, liberal tradition see Rosalie Colie, *Light and Enlightenment. A Study of the Cambridge Platonists and the Dutch Arminians* (Cambridge; Cambridge University Press, 1957).

republic quickly transcended the parochialism and the piety of that older religious concensus, and produced a cosmopolitan culture more enlightened than it was Protestant.

The transformation within international Protestant culture which began in the 1680s is dramatically depicted in the social gatherings at the Rotterdam home of the Quaker refugee, Benjamin Furly. His father had been a Quaker republican of the previous generation and lord mayor of Colchester in Cromwell's time. In the 1660s the family left England because of religious and political persecution. In the late 1680s John Locke, hounded by clerical spies and fearful of his own arrest after so many of his Whig associates had perished, crossed the Channel and took refuge in Furly's home. Together they freely discussed politics and philosophy amid Furly's superb library which contained the writings of almost every major early modern political theorist, including rare works by Giordano Bruno and various clandestine manuscripts about Spinoza. They were joined by itinerant visitors from Germany, medical reformers like the van Helmonts, and eventually by newly arrived Huguenot refugees.[17] With Furly's inner circle or his library we may rightly associate some of the most important works of the early Enlightenment: Locke's *Two Treatises*, his *Essay on Toleration* (1690), Toland's *Christianity not Mysterious* (1696), and not least, the infamous *Traité des trois imposteurs*. That impious clandestine manuscript labelled Jesus, Moses and Mohammed impostors, and it was extrapolated out of a manuscript text that the French Huguenot refugees, Charles Levier and Rousset de Missy, got in 1711 from Furly's library.[18]

How right Hazard was to see the Dutch Republic as the *entrepôt* wherein *la crise* first matured and found resolution. His Francophile characterization of The Netherlands was, however, based largely upon its geography and the strength of its French language press; it happened to be the place where the migration stopped and the English freethinkers first encountered the French Huguenot refugees. But the Republic was, as we now know, more than that. It was also the urban, commercial and diplomatic center of Western commercial capitalism in the late seventeenth-century. Its small but powerful elite commonly spoke and read French as well as Dutch, and the first stirrings of the Enlightenment on the Continent, the introduction of the new science, first in its Cartesian and then in its Newtonian forms; the violent pamphlet warfare against tyranny; the growth of spinozism and free thought; and the emergence of a periodical and spectatorial press were Dutch phenomena

---

[17] On Furly see William Hull, *Benjamin Furly and Quakerism in Rotterdam* (Philadelphia; Swarthmore College Monographs, 1941).

[18] Margaret C. Jacob, *The Radical Enlightenment*, pp. 218–27.

before they were European ones. We need to know more about the early Enlightenment in the Dutch Republic, but we now know enough to say that here we may find some of the first European intellectuals to come to terms with the moral and intellectual implications of commercial capitalism. That economic and social reality, more than any other factor, would seem to account for the particularly radical turn that the Enlightenment took there in its early years. The Huguenot refugees and their friends encountered what they came to see as republican decadence, and some of them, such as Rousset, privately responded by repudiating the Calvinism of the Dutch elite in all of its forms, and by using ideas developed during the English revolution to foment another within the Republic itself.[19]

Most Protestants affected by *la crise* did not adopt such a radical direction. The key to the nature of *la crise* as it affected the mainstream of the Protestant *internationale* seems to lie in what may be described as Calvinist rationalism. That paradoxical phrase captures the apparent contradictions, the ambiguities, common to such disparate seekers after new truths as the Anglican scientist, Isaac Newton, the Dutch Calvinist minister, Balthasar Bekker, and the Huguenot journalist, Pierre Bayle.

Calvinist rationalism permitted them to live in two worlds, to have their faith as well as their scientific enquiry, indeed to hold the tension of the crisis within their own minds without succumbing to intellectual madness, that is, to either atheism or enthusiasm. Their brand of Protestantism derived historically from Calvin, and at its core was an extreme monotheism, a God for whom the law of universal gravitation according to Newton is merely the divine will operating on the universe. Bekker described this Protestantism in his famous and brilliant treatise attacking magic as a true 'monotheism'.[20] Such a God could be worshipped anywhere, in one's alchemical laboratory in Cambridge, or in the workroom of your publisher where you strove, as did the refugee Pierre Bayle, to keep body and soul together by compiling a universal dictionary. Exposure to such a God literally made salvation possible especially if you were a defrocked Benedictine monk living in Amsterdam where prostitution, and other temptations of a more cerebral sort,

[19] *Ibid.*, pp. 88–9. See also William Montague, *The Delights of Holland* (London, 1696), pp. 162–4 on the republicanism of merchants as heard in the coffee houses. And J. J. V. M. de Vet, *Pieter Rabus* (1660–1702). *Een Wegbereider van de Noordnederlandse Verlichting. With Summary in English* (Amsterdam; Holland University Press, 1980). See also for the career of Jacob Campo Weyerman, *De Rotterdamsche Hermes*, ed. by A. Neuweboer (Amsterdam, 1980).
[20] Balthasar Bekker, *De Betoverde Weereld* (Leeuwarden, 1691), preface. On Newton's conception of universal gravity as the divine will see W. G. Hiscock, ed., *David Gregory, Isaac Newton and Their Circle* (Oxford, privately printed, 1937), p. 30.

were tolerated. The spectatorial journalist and former monk, Nicolas Gueudeville, was saved from *libertinage*, as he recalled, only by the intervention of a devout Calvinist.[21] You did not necessarily have to devote your life to such a God; in some cases it was sufficient just to know, as did Gueudeville, that he and his followers maintained an orderly existence.

With this God in your mind you could indulge your scepticism as did Bayle in his *Dictionnaire* (1697), or you could give assistance to younger, less pious, refugees. These young men's coffee-house flirtations with Spinozism – if Bayle knew about them – could not obscure their Protestantism and they, in turn, long after they had begun trafficking in the forbidden wares of atheism and clandestine manuscripts, would honor Bayle as their patriarch. And the possession of such a heady theism, when reconciled to Cartesianism, made a Calvinist minister like Bekker despise his fellow clerics who continued to use their God to obfuscate the power of reason. It is not accidental that he dedicated all his treatises either to the *burgermeesters* or *raden* of Amsterdam, or to professors of mathematics, lawyers, and doctors. Their common sense and learning, he believed, distinguished them from the masses and the clergy who court the lower orders out of a compatible and comparable ignorance. Bekker compiled a massive, documented assault on the paganism of the masses, at home and abroad. Using the evidence of religious practices from the travel literature, he denounced *tovery en spokery* – witchery and spookery. Bekker's purpose, as he put it in *De Betoverde Weereld* (*The World Bewitched*, 1691) was 'to banish the devil from the world and to bind him in hell so that the king Jesus may rule more freely on earth'.[22]

Such a ferocious monotheism was the only creed capable of destroying Catholicism, both its priests and its doctrines. Newton's anti-Catholicism permeated his life as well as his natural philosophy; among other factors it made possible his rejection of scholasticism. Bayle's made him into an anti-cleric with a particular dislike for the pretensions of his own credal overseers, and Bekker wrote against the intervention of devils because he knew that the papist church 'is the kingdom of the devil'.[23] Incidentally that overt anti-Catholicism was carefully removed by Bekker from his French translation, *Le monde enchanté* (1694). This may have led Hazard and subsequent commentators to overstate his rationalism at the expense of his extreme Calvinism. What is central to the Protestant crisis is the *mélange*, the interplay, indeed the fusion, of these only apparently contradictory impulses.

[21] Aubrey Rosenberg, *Nicolas Gueudeville*, p. 29.
[22] B. Bekker, *De Betoverde Weereld*, 1691, preface.   [23] *Ibid.*, p. 656.

Among these Calvinist rationalists only Bayle escaped the historical logic of his position; he alone eschewed millenarianism. In so doing he illustrates the wisdom to be extracted from a direct personal experience of persecution at the hands of absolutists and theocrats alike. Predictably, the absence of overt millenarianism in Bayle is linked to his anti-clericalism. Bayle was a Calvinist who took human history seriously because he feared that clergymen and state bureaucracies were to be the sole beneficiaries of the wars that must precede the apocalypse. Unknown in Hazard's time, Newton's millenarianism, so carefully buried in voluminous manuscript treatises, was his birthright as a true English Protestant who hated the Laudian pretension of the high church just as much as he feared the heresies of the vulgar.[24] Bekker's millenarianism was probably missed because it lay buried in a Dutch treatise on the prophecy of Daniel which he wrote in the spring of 1688 when the outfitting of the Dutch fleet (which was about to invade England) was plainly visible in the harbors. He knew at that moment that the French king would someday be smitten by the hand of God, just as he knew 'that natural science (*Natuurkunde*) permits us to know more the earth than the heaven...while the prophets teach us about the Messiah'.[25] Such a God permits his followers to know what they choose to know with an extraordinary certainty.

It is not wrong to emphasize the rationalism in these various intellectual postures provided we permit the fideism its rightful place. Just because Newton was an alchemist and a millenarian, Bekker also a millenarian, and Bayle, a fideist, does not justify our removing them from the early Enlightenment. Rather these facts – all the result of modern scholarship – require that we take the concept of *la crise* more seriously than ever; it also means that we must mold our definitions of the Enlightenment to fit the participants as we now see them. In the eighteenth-century reforming aristocrats could be pantheists, freemasons could be empiricists while worshipping at their secret rituals, and radical democrats and scientists like Priestley[26] could be millenarians because the categories in their minds had been inherited from the Protestant version of Christianity as transformed by the seventeenth-century revolutions, both political and intellectual, against absolutism.

[24] Walter Rex, *Pierre Bayle and Religious Controversy* (The Hague; Nijhoff, 1965), and Frank Manuel, *The Religion of Isaac Newton* (London; Oxford University Press, 1974).
[25] B. Bekker, *Uitlegginge van den Propheet Daniel* (Amsterdam, 1688), p. 715.
[26] Jack Fruchtman, *The Apocalyptic Politics of Richard Price and Joseph Priestley: A Study in Late 18th Century English Republican Millenarianism* (Philadelphia: American Philosophical Society, 1983).

Hazard revisited

The new element that coincided with those revolutions was science, in particular, the new mechanical philosophy. Hazard saw its importance yet even he understated the case. As we have found new ways of interpreting the language of science, of discerning its ideological content, we have now come to a richer understanding of its role, both in precipitating and resolving *la crise*. Indeed by the 1680s it could be said that the European elite had been badly served by the guardians of religious orthodoxy. In the sixteenth and early seventeenth-centuries both Catholic and Protestant theologians had based the metaphysical foundations of their doctrines, for example, the Trinity and transubstantiation, as well as consubstantiation, on scholasticism, that is, on the Aristotelianism of the schools and universities. But by the late 1630s after Galileo's confrontation with the Church, and the publication of Descartes' *Discourse on Method* (1637), it was clear that Aristotle and Ptolemy no longer adequately described the operations of the natural world, either celestial or terrestrial. The Scientific Revolution of the seventeenth-century was, in essence, a philosophical revolution that replaced Aristotle with the rival explanation of a mechanical universe verified by experiment and observation. In the 1680s one could still find Aristotelians in any school in almost any country, but in Western Europe they were now on the defensive. Yet no consensus had emerged to replace the old theology with a Christianity compatible with science. Of course Galileo had been a devout Catholic who had the misfortune to know more about the heavens than his clerical opponents, and Descartes had also been a devout Christian, and probably a Catholic. But neither had felt the need to offer solace to scholastic theologians desperately trying to maintain orthodoxy in the face of the destruction of Aristotelian natural philosophy. Neither could have imagined that eventually it would be necessary to construct a new Christian religiosity based in large measure upon mechanical assumptions. This was precisely the synthesis developed in the second half of the seventeenth-century by English Protestants forced under the impact of the English Revolution to rethink the relationship between the natural order, society and religion. Eventually all progressive Christians from Leibniz to *père* Malebranche would be forced to restructure the philosophical foundations of Christianity to conform to one or another version of the new science.

English scientists of the mid seventeenth-century like Robert Boyle (1632–91) attacked Aristotelianism because they believed that the religion it was used to support went hand-in-hand with absolutism. They also believed that scholasticism leads people to believe there is an *anima*

263

mundi which watches over the safety of the universe and that following from this they might believe that water, for example, has a tendency to move up in a hollow reed because such motion is natural to it. With ideas like that, Boyle believed, you could justify magic as well as transubstantiation; both were a threat from the 1640s to the 1680s for Protestant reformers who feared royal absolutism (and hence Catholicism) as much as they feared political agitation among the populace. As Christopher Hill has shown, popular beliefs, including materialism and the power they gave to lay preachers (or to the spirit within each individual), had indeed threatened to undermine the entire system of social order in revolutionary England.[27]

Out of the fears provoked by that experience Boyle and his friends in the Royal Society, coincidentally with Protestant theologians in Cambridge, worked out a synthesis between science and religion which was to have European-wide impact from the 1690s onward. It provided an alternative to the militant and purely Biblical Calvinism of the Puritan sectaries as well as to the doctrinal rigidity of Catholicism. Briefly stated, this new natural religion postulated a mechanical universe providentially controlled by God but operated according to laws, which were ordered, harmonious and comprehensible. In Restoration England, as well as in the republic of letters, this liberal Christianity was immensely appealing. Newton was taught it as a young Cambridge student. Locke and Furly embraced versions of it (it permitted Furly to retain certain of his mystical beliefs), the French refugee and important journalist of Amsterdam, Jean Le Clerc, used his journals in the 1690s to promote it, while in the 1720s a young French poet named Voltaire learned his first lessons in metaphysics from reading the liberal theologian, Samuel Clarke, who in his Boyle Lectures of 1704–5 offered a solution for the crisis which was based upon the science of Boyle and Newton.

What must be stressed about this liberal and Newtonian Christianity, whether it is found (in embryo) among the Cambridge Platonists of the 1670s, the Dutch Arminians of the 1690s, or liberal Italian Catholics of the 1720s is the *via media* it provided through a thicket of religious beliefs which had been of immense political significance throughout much of the seventeenth-century.[28] It was seen to undermine scholasticism, hence to attack the ultramontane clergy (the Jesuits, for example),

---

[27] For Boyle the classic study now is James R. Jacob, *Robert Boyle and the English Revolution* (New York; Burt Franklin, 1977); on this disorder see Christopher Hill, *The World Turned Upside Down* (London, 1972).

[28] See Margaret C. Jacob, *The Newtonians and the English Revolution, 1688–1720* (Ithaca, New York; Cornell University Press, 1976); Vincenzo Ferrone, *Scienza, Natura, Religione: Mondo Newtoniano and Cultura Italiana nel Primo Settecento* (Naples; Jovene, 1982).

as well as to challenge absolutism. It repudiated popular religiosity with its radical associations; and it offered a moderate Protestant alternative to that radical Calvinism whose millenarianism and emphasis upon the separate power of the clergy had proved so divisive. And not least, it permitted, indeed encouraged, scientific observation and experimentation. Hence it fostered a revival of both the Baconian dream and the Cartesian proclamation that science would provide mastery over nature.

After 1689 liberal Christianity became associated in the minds of Europeans with two extraordinary developments. The first was a successful and bloodless English revolution which removed an absolutist king, established parliamentary sovereignty, forced the Dutch stadholder, William of Orange, to accept the Bill of Rights as the condition for his kingship, and established a limited religious toleration for all English Protestants, although not for Catholics or anti-Trinitarians. The second innovation was Newtonian science. In the early 1690s liberal Anglican clergymen championed both the political settlement of 1689 and the Newtonian synthesis, and related one to the other. Suddenly a new consensus had been forged in England: a viable national church remained amid limited religious toleration, clergymen offered justifications for revolution and constitutional government, and experimental science had uncovered previously unknown and universal laws. The Newtonian system of the world could be championed as the model for the stable, harmonious, moderately Christian polity ruled by law, not by an arbitrary and capricious will. This was a scientific and political synthesis that repudiated the materialism of Hobbes, ignored the republicanism of Harrington, and labelled radical sectaries, Levellers, Diggers, Quakers, etc., as disorderly magicians. It justified political revolution without social upheaval. That new natural religion permitted Locke to argue for the reasonableness of Christianity against the deism of Toland, and it also permitted this guardian of respectable contract theory to lobby among his parliamentary friends for the abolition of the censorship laws. Partly as a result of Locke's efforts parliament permitted the Licensing Act to lapse in 1695, and the printing press in England acquired a freedom only rivalled by the French language press in the Dutch Republic.

With liberal, Newtonian Christianity as its centerpiece the English model of society and government captured the imagination of thousands of educated, largely urban, Europeans who frequently heard about it in the first instance from French language journals – or translations of English texts – undertaken by Huguenot refugees or Dutch scientists such as s'Gravesande. By the second decade of the eighteenth-century a new form of social gathering had been invented to celebrate this God of Newtonian science, the Grand Architect as he was called, to extend

265

informally the limits of toleration, and to celebrate English empiricism with its passion to classify and collect. In a formal sense Freemasonry began in London in 1717 and it was led by Newtonians and Whigs, but its roots stretch back to the 1690s, rather predictably to freethinking circles found within the Whig party. As early as 1710 Huguenot refugees in The Hague with the assistance of Toland had discovered a version of the masonic gathering; the earliest Continental lodge was probably in Rotterdam in 1720.[29] By the 1730s Freemasonry could be found in Paris, much to the distress of the authorities. Its official appearance in The Netherlands was not until 1734, and by then masons formed the core of the Anglo-Dutch lobby. Italian aristocrats in Naples set up lodges in the 1740s, and despite persecution in Catholic countries, Freemasonry flourished well into the age of democratic revolutions. Indeed in a social sense it became one of the most important links between the liberal and enlightened solution to *la crise* and the Continental breeding ground for the visionaries and the disillusioned of the later period.[30]

Yet just as the science of Newton wedded to liberal Protestantism – a new natural religion – offered one resolution of *la crise*, the new mechanical philosophy of the early seventeenth century had been one of its causes. The great intellectual revolutionary of that century had been René Descartes (d. 1650). In the *Discourse on Method* he argued that all enquiry begins within the mind of the individual and not in the prescriptions or dogmas offered by the clergy, so easily subjected as they had been to the mockery of the sceptics. According to Descartes science sprang from the individual's assumption that God would not deceive and systematically distort our perception of nature. The goal of science became the mathematical expression of mechanical laws that genuinely conform to physical reality. Descartes constructed a cosmic picture of the mechanical universe based upon logical formulations and hypotheses, and with that achievement he left problematic the exact role of continuing experimentation. Cartesianism offered no solace to the scholastics, and it separated matter from spirit so drastically as to render irrelevant that *anima mundi* also attacked by Boyle. Indeed this separation was the great danger in Cartesianism; it never adequately explained how to reunite matter and spirit in such a way as to guarantee the dominance of spirit over matter, of God over nature, of Christianity over pagan naturalism.

Many European Protestants in both England and The Netherlands during the 1640s and well beyond thought, however, that first and foremost Cartesianism refuted the scholastics while permitting a

[29] Margaret C. Jacob, 'The Knights of Jubilation: Masonic and Libertine', *Quaerendo*, XIV, 1 (1984), pp. 63–75.
[30] Margaret C. Jacob, 'In the Aftermath of Revolution', pp. 519–21.

Christian science to flourish. Indeed on the Continent that Protestant Cartesianism, of which Bekker is one of the most elegant representatives, flourished among the laity and their clerical allies in the universities. Biblicist Protestants like the Calvinist minister of Utrecht, Voet, attacked Cartesianism as atheism and enthusiasm, and tried to rally the populace against the lay magistrates who supported the teaching of Descartes within the university. Voet warned the people that their elders would desert their obligations to the Reformation in a world governed solely by impersonal mechanical laws.[31]

The controversies that erupted over the implications of Cartesianism from the 1650s onwards foreshadow *la crise*. These were particularly intense in the Dutch cities, but there by the late 1660s at the University of Leiden and elsewhere, Cartesianism had become accepted. Calvinist rationalists saw it as a more than adequate explanation for the laws that govern the material order, and the necessity for constant experimentation in a world made comfortable by the fruits of merchant capitalism seemed hardly a priority. When Leiden established a laboratory it was used solely to illustrate the laws of Cartesian science.

Only in England during the 1650s did the linkage between Cartesianism and atheism seem clearly apparent. The English flirtation with Descartes, led in the first instance by the Cambridge Platonists, turned sour for reasons that were local and unique to their experience of social revolution. When the English scientists and philosophers turned against Descartes they did so within the context of the materialist and mortalist heresies thrown up by Hobbes and the radical sectaries. Nowhere else in Protestant Europe at this time did such a complete repudiation occur within scientific circles. One of its not-incidental by-products came in the ease with which a young Cambridge undergraduate, like Newton, could turn his back on Descartes precisely in the late 1660s because as he put it, 'his philosophy leads directly to atheism'.[32] Newton was no more or less a devout Christian than Bekker or the natural philosophers at Leiden, but his social universe had been far less stable than the one governed by the *burgermeesters* and *regenten* of the Dutch Republic.

Above all else, the Cartesian material order is rigidly stable; indeed its God possesses many absolutist qualities, and the laws of nature hang largely upon his perceived honesty. Not surprisingly, Cartesianism made slow but steady inroads within the bastion of anti-Christ, the

---

31 Thomas Arthur McGahagan, 'Cartesianism in The Netherlands, 1639-76: The New Science and the Calvinist Counter Reformation', Ph.D., University of Pennsylvania, 1976.
32 Margaret C. Jacob, *The Cultural Meaning of the Scientific Revolution* (New York; Alfred Knopf, 1987) (forthcoming), chapter three.

kingdom of Louis XIV. While the schools and universities of France continued relentlessly to teach Aristotle, by the 1670s Parisian theorists brought Cartesianism to the society of the salons; it became both aristocratic and bourgeois, as well as polite. Cartesianism provided arguments for absolutism as well as for the domination over society by those same groups capable of mastering the new science. In *La Pluralité des Mondes* (1686) Fontenelle, an academician and Cartesian, presented his natural philosophy as the cosmic justification for the *status quo*; for absolutism and the rigid social system it supported.[33] The book went through dozens of French editions, as well as foreign translations. While Cartesianism may have shaken the foundations of scholasticism and hence provoked secular vs. clerical tensions within French intellectual life, in the first instance it offered an escape from doubt to its believers that rendered their crisis a mild affair by comparison to that experienced in the 1680s by French Huguenots, Dutch republicans, or English Whigs. But while Cartesianism was being used by the French scientific community to support absolutism, not surprisingly a French Protestant, Denis Vairasse, was one of the first to attack the solace offered by these new scientific mandarins to the pretensions of monarchy (in *Historie des Sevarambes*, 1677–8).[34]

Yet there was a dark side to Cartesianism that continued to disturb even its most enthusiastic and absolutist supporters. Were there not difficulties in reconciling spirit with matter when material vortices whirled through space in constant collision only with other material bodies?[35] The danger in the new mechanical philosophy had always been its potential for turning into materialism. In the first half of the century Hobbes had demonstrated the danger much to the horror of all his Christian opponents. By the 1680s it was clear that the greatest philosopher of the preceding generation had begun by reading Descartes and ended up with a new and extraordinary form of materialism. Benedictus Spinoza (1632–77) cut the gordian knot of the spirit–matter dichotomy by arguing that there is only one substance and it is both material and spiritual.

Out of the Jewish community in Amsterdam with its Cabalistic traditions of learning, Spinoza worked his way into metaphysical definitions that he himself labelled political (*Tractatus Theologico-Politicus,*

[33] Geoffrey Vincent Sutton, 'A Science for a Polite Society: Cartesian Natural Philosophy in Paris during the Reign of Louis XIII and Louis XIV', Ph.D. dissertation, Princeton University, 1982.

[34] Erica Harth, *Ideology and Culture in Seventeenth Century France* (Ithaca: Cornell University Press, 1983).

[35] See Aram Vartanian, *Diderot and Descartes: A Study of Scientific Naturalism in the Enlightenment* (Princeton: Princeton University Press, 1953).

1670). If our spirit and body are one, then necessity rules our fate, and to live out one's destiny requires freedom, not only to trade but also to believe and read, to participate in civic institutions, to worship as one pleases provided political tranquility is maintained. Contemporaries labelled this philosophy of freedom, atheism; Spinozism or pantheism were less pejorative contemporary descriptions, the latter term invented by John Toland in 1705.[36] Spinozism is central to *la crise*. It was what you might embrace after you had left scholasticism (if you had ever belonged), dabbled in the new scientific literature, discovered Descartes and found him compelling for a time, but then become disillusioned with the absolutist tendencies of the French Cartesians. You might have been prepared for it by Hobbes' materialism, although not by his politics, and you were probably a doctor, or a lawyer, or a journalist – a layman of professional status and some university training – who did not much like clergymen telling you what to think. Spinozism appealed to freethinkers, or created them, within every segment of the literate classes, first in The Netherlands, then in England and finally in France. By the 1680s Spinoza's ideas had been translated out of Latin into English or been made available in various clandestine manuscripts written in simple French in the Dutch Republic. We still have an imperfect understanding of the sources of this early Spinozism, of its actual believers and transmittors, but we now know it to have been widespread.

By the 1720s pantheism was everywhere,[37] its growth an unintended by-product of the new science. Without Descartes there would have been no Spinoza; without Spinoza, no pantheism; however many other intellectual traditions, including the writings of Giordano Bruno, we can legitimately point to as sources for this most virulent heresy of the early Enlightenment.

The new science in all its forms pried open minds that might otherwise have been content to explain nature by reference to its inherent properties, to what one sees on a daily basis. It also provided an alternative to seventeenth-century scepticism which was itself one civilized response to the endemic religious wars of the early modern period. Science also elevated God's work to the status of his word, and in the process made a literal reading of the Bible less necessary if not also, when it came to heliocentricity, simply impossible. To that extent it

[36] John Toland, *Socinianism Truly Stated: Being an example of fair dealing in all Theological Controversy. To which is prefixt Indifference in disputes. Recommended by a Pantheist to an Orthodox Friend* (London, 1705).
[37] Paul Vernière, *Spinoza et la pensée française de la Revolution* (Paris: Presses universitaire de France, 1954).

downgraded Biblical language and muted the message of sectarian groups with their special readings of the Bible.

The new science was the single most important source of arguments against witches, miracles, and special illuminations. One of the most visible symptoms of *la crise* in the 1680s was the European-wide assault on what contemporaries called enthusiasm. This was mysticism in one's religious piety; the appeal to the inner light in the hands of sectaries. When the French prophets, a group of Huguenots from the Savoy, rose in rebellion against Louis XIV during the early years of the War of Spanish Succession (1702–13), English and Dutch Protestants praised their heroism and the most millenarian among them took the uprising as a sign that the end of the world was near. When the prophets actually turned up on the streets of London assisted by Isaac Newton's close friend, Fatio de Duillier, the authorities arrested them, the doctors denounced them as mad, and the freethinkers labelled them as deluded by superstition. Liberal Anglicans argued that the new science provided the foundation for natural religion, for a social cement which rendered the disciplined public experience of divinity infinitely preferable to the private illuminations of the saint. The exiled French prophets took to wandering England, Scotland and finally, The Netherlands and Germany in a lonely search for converts. When Benjamin Furly saw them preach in Rotterdam he was appalled by their enthusiasm.[38]

It should be emphasized that the use of science to repudiate magic was frequently not the work of the scientists themselves. Both Boyle and Newton accepted some sort of apocalypse; Boyle believed in magical cures while denouncing the pretensions of the alchemists; Newton secretly practiced alchemy all his life. In Germany Leibniz dabbled in astrology. Their clerical friends worried that if one stopped prosecuting witches in the courts, religion might suffer. Yet by the late seventeenth-century English magistrates did stop prosecuting witches while in The Netherlands by the early 1730s the Calvinist clergy engaged in violent persecution of libertines and homosexuals, witches having all but disappeared from their list of concerns.[39]

It was the new science as interpreted by the educated laity of the late seventeenth and early eighteenth-centuries that forever banished the superstitions (as they saw them) of the people from polite discourse. It was what individuals made of the natural philosophies of Descartes, Spinoza, Boyle and Newton that provoked *la crise*; what resolved it was the creation of an elite and enlightened culture, one that might still in

[38] Margaret C. Jacob, *The Newtonians*, chapter seven.
[39] Theo van der Meer, *De wesentlijke sonde van Sodomie en andere vuyligheden. Sodomie-tenvervolging in Amsterdam 1730–1811* (Amsterdam, 1984) 11–12.

many cases be Christian but that recoiled from any form of personal illumination or magical power. In their place came liberal Christianity wedded to the new science. Excluded from that most cerebral form of religiosity were the vast majority of Europeans.

Throughout the eighteenth-century the religiosity of the European masses as well as of non-Westerners would continue to frighten both the godly and the enlightened. For those secularists such as Voltaire, who contrasted pagan societies with even the most enlightened European regimes, there was, however, an increasingly strong temptation to portray the former as utopias, to create Eldorado. Beneath the confidence bred by the new science there nevertheless lay powerful reservations about the virtue of the powerful and the entrenched within every Western society.

In the period from roughly 1680 to 1720 educated Europeans struggled through the Continental wars provoked by French absolutism, repudiated religious fanaticism and enthusiasm, discovered science and deism as respectable alternatives, and created a secular culture largely immune to the condemnations coming from orthodox clergy, both Protestant and Catholic. Yet by the middle of the eighteenth-century it was clear to liberal and secular thinkers that aspects of the *ancien régime* in every Continental country firmly resisted all efforts at enlightened reforms. At first the philosophes believed that a viable alternative lay across the Channel, in the social and political order created by the Revolution Settlement of 1689. That, at least, was what Voltaire preached, and the French language and Anglophile press in the Dutch Republic continued a massive propaganda effort to recommend the English system as the antithesis of tyranny and injustice. Given what we now know about the central role played by English science and revolutionary political theory in the origins of the European Enlightenment, the persistence of that idealization of the English system should hardly surprise us. What continued to surprise the Enlightenment was the intractability of the old order, the persistence of princes and priests long after the liberal reformers had mentally exorcized them.

Isaac Beeckman and music

D. P. WALKER

Isaac Beeckman (1588–1637) is chiefly known today because of his association with Descartes, whom he met by chance at Breda in November 1618.[1] In January 1619 Descartes, then aged twenty-two, sent him as a New Year's gift his earliest surviving work, the *Compendium musicae*. Theirs was a mutual interest in music and musical theory. Here I propose to deal only with Beeckman as a theoretician of music, although we should bear in mind that he had wide-ranging scientific interests. These grew out of his humanist education at the University of Leiden, his technical training in his father's business of candle- and tube-making, his highly individualistic Calvinism, and his own enquiring, independent mind. Except for a few pages in Koyré's *Études Galiléennes*[2] and a long note by Cornelis de Waard in the Mersenne *Correspondance*, Beeckman's scientific ideas have been little studied. There is now at least a most useful dissertation on Beeckman in Dutch,[3] but as little as is known about his science still less is his musical theory a subject for scholarly inquiry. This essay may serve as a remedy.

Beeckman was a qualified physician, but spent most of his life as a successful schoolteacher. He had been interested in music long before he met Descartes, but was presumably self-taught; for, in 1619, when teaching at Utrecht, he began, at the age of thirty-one, to take singing lessons from a colleague, Everard Verhaeren, a pupil of the great organist

This essay, written very shortly before the death of its author, was sent to me with the note that it might be altered as the editors saw fit. I have changed only the first paragraph to reflect the existence of K. van Berkel's thesis of which Perkin Walker had heard but which he had been unable to consult. MCJ

[1] For all biographical details see the *Vie de l'auteur* in front of *Journal tenu par Isaac Beeckman de 1604 à 1634*, ed. C. De Waard, 4 Vols. (La Haye, 1939–53) (hereafter: BJ.).

[2] A. Koyré, *Etudes Gal.*, Paris, 1966, pp. 107 seq.

[3] Marin Mersenne, *Correspondance*, ed. C. De Waard (Paris, 1932–), II, 118–24 (hereafter: MC.). See K. van Berkel, *Isaac Beeckman (1588–1637) en de Mechanisering van het Wereedbeeld* (Amsterdam, Rodopi), 1983.

and composer, Jan Sweelinck.[4] He was not naturally gifted for music; he writes, with engaging candour:[5]

My voice for singing is so bad that my master [i.e. Verhaeren] said he had never come across a worse one; however, I have studied so much that I can sing my part, though not very well; also I can't hear out-of-tuneness accurately (kan ook het discorderen niet wel hooren).

Our main sources for Beeckman's life and thought are: his *Journal*, in which during most of his life he noted, in Latin and Dutch, his musical and scientific speculations, and the Mersenne *Correspondance*. Both of these are easily available, competently edited by De Waard.[6] Beeckman himself published nothing except his theses on tertian fever for his degree of Doctor of Medicine at Caen in 1618.[7] At the end of these we find, rather to our surprise, after an assertion of the existence of a vacuum and a statement that comes near to the law of inertia, the thesis: 'the consonant third consists, not in the ratio 9:8 squared, but that of 5:4,' that is to say, just intonation rather than Pythagorean. After his death, his younger brother, Abraham, published in 1644 a *Centuria* of extracts from Isaac's *Journal*, which contains sixteen items on music; but it must have been a very small edition, since only one surviving copy is known, in the University of Leiden Library.[8]

Beeckman had decided by 1626 never to publish his *Journal*, but only to show it to friends, to at least three of them. The reasons he gives are his dislike of criticism, and the fear that his inventions might be misused, especially by enemies of The Netherlands.[9] The three friends to whom he did show his 'meditations,' as he called them, were: Descartes, in 1618 and 1628, Mersenne in 1630, and Martin Hortensius, professor of mathematics at Amsterdam, in 1634.[10] In spite of his *Journal* remaining unprinted, the diffusion and influence of Beeckman's ideas was considerable through his friendships with such scientists as Gassendi,[11] who visited him in 1629, and, above all, Mersenne, who

---

[4] BJ., II, 19.

[5] BJ., III, 221: 'Myn stemme om te synghen is so quaet dat myn meester seyde noyt geen slechter gesien te hebben; evenwel hebbe ik so veel geleert, dat ick mede partye singhen kan, maar niet seer wel; kan oock het discorderen niet wel hooren.'

[6] The manuscript of the *Journal* was badly damaged by water, at Middleburg in 1940 (see Post-scriptum at end of BJ., II).

[7] BJ., IV, 42–4.

[8] D. Isaaci Beeckmanni, Medici, & Rectoris apud Dordracenos, *Mathematico-physicarum meditationum, quaestionum, solutionum centuria* (Traiecti ad Rhenum, 1644). This copy has the *Ex libris* of Isaac Vossius. The musical items are: Nos. 58–69 (pp. 31–42) = BJ., I, 49–58; No. 85 (p. 53) = BJ., III, 26; No. 90 (p. 57) = BJ., III, 40; No. 99 (p. 62) = BJ., III, 79–80; No. 100 (p. 63) = BJ., III, 80–3.

[9] BJ., II, 377. [10] BJ., III, 354.

[11] BJ., III, 123.

stayed several days with him in 1630,[12] corresponded with him, and reproduced some of his theories in the *Harmonie universelle* and the *Harmonicorum libri*.[13] We must also remember that as a teacher he was active in encouraging an interest in natural science and mathematics. His inaugural address, when in 1627 he took up the post of Rector of the Latin School at Dordrecht, began with the wish to have inscribed over the door of his classroom the Platonic warning: οὐδεὶς ἀγεωμέτρητος εἰσίτω, continued with samples of the practical utility of knowing the different capacities of various isoperimetric figures, and ended with the hope that his pupils would by this kind of knowledge be led to the 'true, that is, the mathematico-physical philosophy' and thus introduce a new learned and 'truly golden age.'[14]

His friendship with Descartes certainly helped the diffusion of Beeckman's speculations, but was not conductive to his getting any credit for them at the time. Late in 1629 Descartes learnt from Mersenne and from Beeckman himself, that the latter had remarked, casually and quite truthfully, that Descartes had acquired some notions by reading the *Journal* and that some of these appeared in the *Compendium musicae*. He wrote furious letters to them both,[15] culminating in a long letter to Beeckman of October 1630, which is a shocking monument of spiteful ingratitude and megalomania.[16] To Mersenne Descartes wrote that, before their first meeting, at the time when 'ce personnage se vante d'avoir écrit de si belles choses sur la musique, il n'en scavoit que ce qu'il avoit appris dans Faber Stapulensis,' i.e. Lefevre d'Etaples's *Elementa musicalia* of 1496, 'et tenoit pour un grand secret de scavoir que la quinte estoit comme de 2 à 3 et la quarte [sic] de 4 à 5, et n'avoit jamais passé plus outre,' and was so proud of this that he ridiculously inserted it into his medical theses, as I have mentioned.[17] Although, owing to Beeckman's excessive capacity for forgiveness, they seem to have been reconciled in 1631 (at least they had dinner together in Amsterdam),[18] Descartes never retracted his mendacious sneers, and these make it difficult for the historian to assess accurately what the *Compendium* owes to Beeckman. One important debt that can be documented is Beeckman's law that frequency is in simple inverse ratio to string-length.[19]

In spite of his correct formulation of this fundamental law, already assumed but not stated by Benedetti in the 1580s,[20] Beeckman held an

[12] BJ., IV, 191.   [13] See MC., II, 525, III, 403–4, 406–8.
[14] BJ., IV, 122–6. In 1626 Beeckman founded a *Collegium Mechanicum* at Rotterdam (BJ., II, 429–45).   [15] See BJ., I, 269, IV, 163; MC., II, 380–1, 559, 564.
[16] BJ., IV, 194 *seq.*   [17] MC., II, 373.   [18] BJ., IV, 207.   [19] MC., II, 381.
[20] See D. P. Walker, *Studies in Musical Science in the Late Renaissance* (London, 1978), p. 31.

erroneous theory of the transmission of sound, according to which the
same particles of air struck by the sounding body were conveyed to the
hearer's ear. This was not a casual mistake, but a consequence of his
being a convinced atomist; for he discusses the wave-theory of the
propagation of sound, and firmly rejects it in favour of travelling
particles.[21] From a musical point of view, this error is of little importance.
Musical sound, on his theory, still consists of regular pulses that are
more frequent the higher the sound in the traditional ratios of just
intonation. He is thus able to formulate a theory of consonance based
on the coincidence of vibrations of two or more different pitches, again
preceded by Benedetti,[22] but independently of him, a theory communicated to Mersenne and Descartes, and accepted by them and later by
many other theorists, including Galilei,[23] though not in the elaborated
form devised by Beeckman.

Beeckman introduced the complication of dividing each pulse half
vibration into a point of rest (*pausa*, *media quies*), when the string is
changing its direction, and a point of maximum velocity, producing the
sound, when the string swings over its original starting point.[24] He later
used this in order to account for the supposed fact that sympathetic
vibration is stronger in strings tuned to a seventeenth or a tenth (5: 1, or
5:2) than to an octave (2:1).[25] His expositions are extremely difficult to
follow. Descartes said he found them unintelligible,[26] though this was
perhaps due to sheer ill-will – and I have not been able to make sense
of them. Mersenne, however, found them interesting enough to repro-
duce some of them, textually, in his *Harmonicorum libri* (1636), but
without committing himself to their validity.[27] Someone more clear-
headed than myself, and better disposed than Descartes, should try to
sort them out.

Of far greater interest are Beeckman's suggestions for dealing with the
problem of the fourth, that is, the problem, still unsolved today, arising
from the fact that since the beginning of the sixteenth century all
composers have treated a note making a fourth against the bass as dissonant, whereas by any theory of consonance, the fourth should be more
consonant than thirds and sixths, which are not so treated.[28] In a passage

[21] BJ., I, 92; cf. MC., II, 371, 379, III, 91, 593.
[22] See Walker, *ibid.*
[23] BJ., I, 52 (cf. MC., II, 126), 160–1, II, 15; MC., II, 350, 370, 464; cf. Walker, *ibid.*
[24] BJ., I, 52, 248, IV, 192; cf. MC., II, 566, IV, 144, V, 126.
[25] BJ., IV, 206; MC., III, 201.
[26] MC., II, 604–5, 608–10.
[27] BJ., I, 247–9.
[28] Cf. Walker, *op. cit.*, pp. 71 *seq.*

written soon after he had met Descartes, at the end of 1618, Beeckman states that in consonances such as the fifth (2:3) and the major third (4:5) the octave below the lower note is 'represented and slightly heard (*repraesentari et subaudiri*),' because, as the string vibrates more feebly, only every other pulse is audible; the fifth and third thus provide their own harmonious bass:

The fourth (3:4) cannot do this, since three is not divisible into two whole pulses.[29] Unfortunately, it is not clear whether Beeckman has consciously heard the low note. His physical explanation of it suggests that he has; but, on the other hand, he should also have heard the twelfth below the lower note of the fourth.[30] In any case, he is near to discovering difference tones nearly a century before Tartini did.[31] He explicitly denies that consonances produce any higher note.

Descartes's solution of the problem provides a neat contrast with Beeckman's. He begins by asserting what Beeckman denies: that 'the fifth is never heard without the fourth *above* being in some way perceived (*quin etiam quarta acutior quodammodo advertatur*).' The fourth is thus 'as it were the shadow of the fifth because it perpetually accompanies it (*quasi umbra quintae, quod illam perpetuo comitetur*).' Against the bass it does not, like other consonances (thirds and sixths), serve to vary the sweetness of the fifth, since the fourth (C–F) will produce the fifth above (C-f-c). In such $\frac{6}{4}$ chords the fourth seems to be moved from its proper place, and we feel that we are getting 'the shadow instead of the body, or the image instead of the thing itself (*umbra pro corpore, vel imago pro ipsa re*).'[32] Here, as with Beeckman and the difference tones, it is not clear that Descartes has actually heard the octave above the lower note, though in an earlier passage he comes near to asserting it: 'no sound is heard without the octave above seeming somehow to sound in one's ears (*quin auribus quodammodo videature resonare*).'[33] This statement, coupled with his other reason for the inferiority of the fourth: that sympathetic vibration occurs only in strings tuned to the octave, fifth and major third, but not to the fourth,[34] brings Descartes to the brink of discovering the

[29] BJ., I, 250–1. He had already read A. Papius, *De consonantiis, seu pro diatessaron libri duo* (Antwerp, 1581) (BJ., I, 56).
[30] The difference tone below the third should be an octave lower.
[31] See Walker, *op. cit.*, p. 137.
[32] Descartes, *Oeuvres*, ed. Adam and Tannery, x (Paris, 1908), pp. 107–8 (*Compendium musicae*).
[33] *Ibid.*, x, 99.
[34] *Ibid.*, x, 103.

series of overtones, which Mersenne and his correspondents, including Descartes and Beeckman, are trying to explain physically from 1633 onwards.[35]

Both Descartes's solutions, and Beeckman's in its more elaborate form, sent to Mersenne in 1629, which includes octaves being generated above as well as below consonances,[36] lead to the musically important theory of the inversion of intervals, i.e. that harmonically the fourth is considered to be the inversion of the fifth, the minor sixth of the major third, and the major sixth of the minor third. And this in turn leads to the theory of the inversion of triads, still current today, in which our unfortunate $^6_4$ chord appears as the second inversion of a root-position chord, and is still treated as dissonant.

Beeckman was interested not only in the mathematical and scientific aspects of music, but also in practical and aesthetic questions. He is aware of the cardinal importance of memory in musical understanding, noting that even monody has a harmonic dimension through the persistence of earlier sounds in the mind while later ones are being heard. He is also aware of the importance of expectation: singers, he claims, often adapt a melody to a foreseen note, e.g. instead of E a g f, will sing f a g f.[37] He is here thinking of the way in which, according to him, the common people (*plebs* or *rustici*) consistently and invariably alter the written version of psalm-tunes, always for the better, a subject that occupies a great deal of space in his *Journal*. For example, instead of

the plebs sings

This is because, if

D–G is a just fourth, then the minor thirds D–F, E–G cannot both be just; the plebs instinctively flatten the E, thus producing a melody in which no false consonances are implied.[38] Beeckman, writing to Mersenne, puts forward the general proposition, induced from many such examples, that 'all arts are taught and tested by the common people.' The people learn nothing from experts but what the latter have gathered from them, and later, often incompetently, systematized. The plebs may

---

[35] MC., III, 403–4, 449, 458–9, 542–8, 559.
[36] MC., II, 277, 524; BJ., III, 164.
[37] BJ., I, 95; MC., II, 276.
[38] MC., II, 231 (cf. 219–20).

sometimes adapt their ears and voices to the teaching of professional musicians, but left to themselves they will retain what is good in this teaching and correct its errors.[39]

This proposition entails the theory that just intonation, including a scale with major and minor tones, is natural; that is, what untaught people sing.[40] This is certainly what Beeckman believed, since all the good alterations in psalm-tunes made by the plebs are to obviate difficulties caused by the placing of major and minor tones in various modes. He knew of Simon Stevin's claim that equal temperament was natural; but, after examining it carefully, he rejected it. He admitted that equal temperament was in fact sometimes used in polyphony because it was easy and simple for many instruments, and its small errors were hidden by the multitude of parts. But in monodic song tempered consonances were not tolerated by the uncorrupted plebs, because the pulses of such consonances, owing to their irrational ratios, never coincided,[41] although of course in monody the pulse-coincidences of just consonances could occur only in the memory.

Beeckman's speculations on musical aesthetics are often interesting, but disappointingly fragmentary and undeveloped, as one would expect in stray notes not intended for publication.[42] He makes a comparison of music with architecture,[43] noting the obvious similarity that both arts are based on simple proportions; but he also points out the important dissimilarities arising from the difference between sight and hearing. Music, even if polyphonic, is experienced successively, in time; whereas the eye can perceive objects in a large field simultaneously. There is therefore nothing in architecture that corresponds to monodic melody. Moreover, with regard to proportions, what corresponds to the pulses in musical sound is visually the division of a line, and, according to Beeckman, the eye cannot divide a line equally into more than two parts. In consequence architectural proportions are based on simple dichotomies, corresponding to the octave; hence the importance of symmetry on each side of a vertical axis, which Beeckman, very acutely, connects with the symmetry of the human body.[44] I would not claim absolute validity for these distinctions; but I think Beeckman is on the

---

[39] MC., II, 276: 'artes omnes a rusticis doceri et per rusticos probari. Nihil igitur plebs à peritis discit quàm id quod periti in plebe se animadvertisse existimant, et dispersa in plebe, male interdum collegerunt. Aures quidem et vocem musicis plebs accomodat, et sibi relicta, tandem frequenti usu edocta, quod bonum est retinet, mala in bonum convertit.'

[40] Cf. Zarlino and Vincenzo Galilei on this (Walker, *op. cit.*, pp. 19–20).

[41] MC., II, 276, 452; BJ., II, 291–2. On Stevin, see Walker, *op. cit.*, pp. 120–2.

[42] On his hurried manner of writing down his notes, see BJ., III, 67.

[43] BJ., I, 285–6.

[44] BJ., I, 214.

right track. I very much doubt whether the musical ratios in the designs of Renaissance architects described by Wittkower[45] could be visually perceptible as such, still less an irrational proportion such as the notorious Golden Section.

Another comparison between sight and hearing sketched briefly by Beeckman concerns colours and music. The correspondences he suggests are not, as later were those of Isaac Newton, between degrees of the scale and colours of the spectrum, which has of course not yet been divided into seven for that very purpose, but between colours and consonances. His first shot at this[46] comes in an explanation of the opinion that the colour green, water and mirrors are good for vision, which he had found in Ficino's *De triplici Vita*,[47] odd reading for a scientific atomist; but he had also been put on to the subject by one of the Aphorisms in Bacon's *Novum organon*.[48] He suggests the following correspondences:

anything transparent (*perspicuum*) corresponds to unison, because it is like the eye;
white corresponds to the octave, because it is made of transparent and opaque particles in the ratio of $1:2$;
black corresponds to dissonance;
yellow corresponds to the fifth;
blue corresponds to the minor third;
red corresponds to the major third;
green corresponds to the fourth, because it is half-way between consonances, being made of yellow and blue.

In a later note[49] he pursued further the idea of mixtures of colours, starting from the obvious case of green, again assigned to the unfortunate fourth. If yellow corresponds to the fifth and blue (this time) to the major third, then, by the curious and arbitrary procedure of adding the terms of the ratios $3:2$, $5:4$, they produce $8:6 = 4:3$, the fourth, which is green. Since $4:3$ added to $6:5$, a minor third, produces $10:8 = 5:4$, a blue major third, the colour corresponding to the minor third when mixed with green should produce blue. By this method one should be able to discover all the correspondences. Apart from the oddity of adding instead of multiplying the ratios, I doubt whether this would have led very far, since there is, I think, no colour which mixed with green would produce blue.

[45] R. Wittkower, *Architectural Principles in the Age of Humanism* (London, 1949).
[46] BJ., II, 317–18.
[47] Ficino, *Opera omnia* (Basileae, 1576), I, 520 (*De tr. v.*, II, xiv).
[48] BJ., I, 251; Bacon, *Works*, ed. Spedding and Ellis, I (London, 1857), pp. 270–1 (*Novum organon*, Lib. II, Aph. xxiii).
[49] BJ., II, 329–30.

Like most of his contemporaries Beeckman was still interested in the central topic of Renaissance musical humanism: the marvellous effects of ancient music, and how they might be revived or surpassed. Like his younger compatriot, Jan Albert Ban, Beeckman did not believe in the reality of the effects of Greek music; but nevertheless he thought that music ought to produce striking emotional and moral reactions in the audience, and suggested ways it might do so, which also foreshadow Ban's.[50] Commenting on a proposition in Saloman de Caus's *Institution harmonique* (1615), namely, 'that the music of the ancients was less perfect than ours,' he writes, under the rubric 'why the music of the ancients seems to us miraculous (*Musica veterum cur nobis miraculosa*),' that, when the tall stories about Greek music originated, music was an unaccustomed novelty and it was therefore easy to get such exaggerations accepted. These tales were then believed in by later, otherwise reliable writers, who have passed them on to us. He then makes the very significant comparison with the accounts of demoniacs and exorcists, which, once they are printed, are believed and further embellished.[51] This was written in July 1633, when the terrible exorcisms at Loudun had already begun.

Beeckman's proposals for achieving musical effects are, in accordance with the tradition of musical humanism, centred on the importance of the verbal text of a song. He makes the observation, of doubtful truth, that whole periods of a speech (*oratio*) are of the same pitch, varying only in the loudness of certain words and syllables, whereas the variety of song consists mainly in differences of pitch, and then writes:

Since oratory can do so much to the souls of the hearers that it draws forth weeping, laughter, etc., what would happen if the powers of oratory were joined to song, by which people are said to be swept out of themselves? What emotions will this not arouse? Let us therefore strive that they may be so joined.[52]

In another note, headed 'Emotions aroused by voices and song,' he analyses the means of doing this into four: oratory, poetic metre, melody, harmony. 'He who wishes by sound to awake emotions in the human heart,' says Beeckman, should first, on a given subject, make up a speech, modelling himself on the slow or fast delivery of a good preacher (*predicant*), then put this into verse, then set the verse to a melody, and finally harmonize this tune, being careful in all three later stages to preserve the character of the original oration. Each of these four

[50] On Ban see Walker, *op. cit.*, Ch. VI.
[51] BJ., III, 287–8.
[52] BJ., II, 315: 'Cùm autem oratio tantum possit in animis auditorum ut fletum, risum etc. illiciat, quid si cantui, quo nonulli extra se dicuntur rapti, virtutes orationum adjungantur? Quos non affectûs ciet? Demus igitur operam ut conjungantur.'

means by itself produces powerful effects, 'What then,' he asks, 'would happen if all four were used together?'[53]

I shall end this paper with another group of Beeckman's reflections on music: his comments on other theorists. With regard to earlier writers, I have already mentioned his rejection of Stevin's theory of equal temperament. He had a copy of Zarlino (presumably the *Istitutioni*) in his library; but his knowledge of Italian was so defective that he could only understand the parts of it that dealt with what he knew already, and had therefore learnt nothing new from it.[54] Beeckman died too soon to comment on Mersenne's *Traité de l'harmonie universelle* of 1627, and picked out for approval the project of establishing a universal pitch by means of pipes of standard dimensions, although he considered this would be more easily achieved by using copper wire of given length, diameter and tension.[55] Commenting on Descartes's *Compendium* he pointed out the shortcomings of Descartes's method of showing the generation, not only of consonances, but also of melodic intervals, by successively bisecting a line, namely that, contrary to Descartes's claim, this would not produce diatonic and chromatic semitones (15:16, 24:25), but semitones 16:17 and 17:18, although it did give minor and major tones (8:9, 9:10). Beeckman therefore concluded, rightly, that the steps of any scale derive from the difference between consonances, and not from any mathematical principle of their own.[56]

In 1628 Beeckman read Kepler's *Harmonice mundi* (1619) and Bacon's *Sylva sylvarum* (1627). On the former he noted with satisfaction that Kepler agreed with him about the importance of memory in music, and also about the necessity of multiplicity of modes, owing to the different placings of the major and minor tones. Another point of agreement was Kepler's explanation of sympathetic vibration; but Beeckman was worried that Kepler wrote of sound as a *species immateriata* – how could something immaterial move a material object?[57] He returned to this criticism when discussing Kepler's doctrine of planetary aspects.[58] These act on the soul of the earth, producing meteorological changes, in a way analogous to the action of musical consonances on the soul of man. In both cases the soul recognizes certain simple proportions because God has imprinted on it the corresponding geometric archetypes. Beeckman, under the heading 'Whether the soul of the earth is moved at the

[53] BJ., II, 12: 'Wat soudt dan worden, waren dese vier soorten by een seffens gebruyckt!'
[54] BJ., III, 67.
[55] BJ., III, 132.
[56] BJ., III, 135–6.
[57] BJ., III, 67–9.
[58] Kepler, *Gesammelte Werke*, ed. M. Caspr, VI (Munich, 1940), pp. 264 *seq.* (*Harmonice mundi*, IV, vii).

command of the aspects (*Anima terrae an nutu aspetuum moveatur*),'
summarizes the doctrine thus:

Kepler considers that the influences of the stars can have no effect on us by their
own power, but in the same way that we frighten away boys by a look or
command, or dogs by only lifting a stick, so earthly things are moved by the
heavens; and, just as the command does not hurt the boys, nor the lifted stick
wound the dog, nor a consonance cause any local motion in the brain, so the rays
of the stars strike the sense of the earth and elements, which, thus touched, is
aroused and causes motion and agitation by its own power in accordance with
the emotion produced by the rays.

That boys and dogs do behave in this way is undeniable, says
Beeckman, and he has not yet succeeded in satisfactorily explaining the
phenomenon; but one must base any explanation on the principle that
both visual images and the sounds of commands and consonances do
cause local motion in the brain. This Kepler does not do; how then does
he think that the large bodies, not only of animals, but even of inanimate
things, can be moved by something immaterial?[59] Beeckman here is not
only an atomist, but seems to be something like an Epicurean materialist.

Bacon also is reproved by Beeckman for arguing that sound is
incorporeal. Bacon's argument, in Experiment 287 of the *Sylva*, is based
on the fact that an echo reproduces exactly the sounds of human speech,
which have been formed by the instruments of the throat, tongue and
mouth, whereas the surface producing the echo has no such
instruments.[60] Beeckman, on his atomist theory of the transmission of
sound, is able to reply: each particle of sound hitting the echoing surface
bounces off unchanged just as it arrived.[61] Beeckman is on firmer ground
in rejecting Bacon's vague 'sympathies and antipathies' of sounds, used
to account for why certain classes of musical instruments combine well
with each other or with voices, and others do not.[62] This shows, as

[59] BJ., III, 68–9: 'Kepleri autem philosophia hac in re consistere videtur, quod existimet
influxis stellarum apud nos nihil posse suâ vi, sed eo modo quo pueros solo visu aut
nutu, canes baculo tantùm elevato, fugamus, etiam ea, quae hîc sunt, moveri a
auperioribus; utque pueros nutus non laedit aut baculus elevatus canem non vulnerat,
aut consonantia in cerebro nihil loco movet, ita etiam radij stellarum sensum terrae et
elementorum feriunt, qui tactus se effert, movet et versat per propriam vim pro affectu
quo a radius afficitur.
    Hoc autem in animalibus verum esse nemo inficiabitur. Ac coepi ejus rei subinde
rationes inculcare etsi ne mihi ipsi satisfaciant ob rei difficultatem; posito tamen hoc
fundamento quòd species visibiles (quos radios solares ad baculum reflexos vocavi) ut
et nutuum et consonantiarum soni, aliquid reverâ in nobis loco moveant, quod
Keplerus non facit. Qui quomodo immateriatis rebus, non tantum in animalibus,
verùm (quod plane novum est) [etiam] in brutis, tam immensa corpora moveri possint
[orig. movere possit], ipse viderit.'
[60] Bacon, *Works*, ed. cit., II, 435 (cf. 436, on incorporeal sound).
[61] BJ., III, 55–6.   [62] Bacon, *Works*, II, 433 (Exp. 278).

Beeckman rightly remarks, that Bacon had no understanding of the nature of consonance, since the real reason is that instruments of fixed intonation are necessarily tempered, and tempered in different ways.[63] The same lack of understanding is shown in Bacon's extraordinary assertion, when dealing with the octave and its likeness to unison, that 'the cause is dark, and hath not been rendered by any.'[64] Beeckman says mildly that he thinks he has long ago discovered this cause, and then makes the shrewd judgment that 'Bacon was not sufficiently versed in combining physics with mathematics,' and contrasts him with Stevin, who he thinks was too addicted to mathematics and only seldom applied them to physical explanations (Bacon 'in mathesi non satis exercitatum fuisse'; Simon Stevin 'vero meo judicio nimis addictus fuit mathematicae, ac rarius physicam ei adjunxit').[65]

I have given you only a very sketchy account of Beeckman's speculations on music, and there is a lot I have left out; but I hope it may be enough to encourage someone else to make a more thorough study of his *Journal* and his correspondence with Mersenne.[66]

[63] BJ., III, 55.
[64] Bacon, *Works*, II, 386; cf. Walker, *op. cit.*, pp. 119–20.
[65] BJ., III, 51.
[66] There will be a chapter on Beeckman's musical theory in a forthcoming book, *The Qualification of Music*, by Dr. H. F. Cohen of The Hague.

Decadence, shift, cultural changes and the universality of Leonardo da Vinci

DOROTHY KOENIGSBERGER

...metamorphoses were popular among the Jews and the Pythagoreans.

Pico

Numerous tales of decline, fall and decadence have provided striking images for students of cultural history, images that have continued to be popular. The current emphasis on basic economic changes in Western society has not altered this perspective; the same images of decline and fall have simply reappeared in new contexts. However, H. G. Koenigsberger was not always convinced by them, especially when it came to the history of creative achievements. Instead, he suggested that historians might explore shifts in creative activities; shifts which were not necessarily tied to see-saw patterns.[1] For example, instead of focussing solely on decadence in literary and artistic achievement in Italy towards the end of the sixteenth century, historians should also include advances in the music and natural philosophy of the period. Descriptions would move from tracing a down-swing in certain fields to the more positive task of exploring the whole meaning of shifts in activity. Deterioration in some areas of creative endeavour and in certain cultural milieux might then be balanced by new emphases, albeit with significant differences in geographical, temporal, social, and political conditions.

Helli Koenigsberger's later pieces refined the concept of cultural shifts; music, religion, natural philosophy and the arts were all

In 1960, Helli Koenigsberger kindly sent me an off-print of his paper, 'Decadence or Shift? Changes in the Civilization of Italy and Europe in the Sixteenth and Seventeenth Centuries,' printed in *Transactions of the Royal Historical Society*, x (1960), pp. 1–18. It made a splendid impression on me then, and it also marked the beginning of a dialogue about issues in cultural history. Aspects of that continuing dialogue are presented in the following paper.

I would like to thank Dr Beverly Southgate for his helpful criticisms and suggestions for the improvement of a draft of this essay.

[1] H. G. Koenigsberger, 'Decadence or Shift? Changes in the Civilization of Italy and Europe in the Sixteenth and Seventeenth Centuries', *Transactions of the Royal Historical Society*, x (1960), pp. 1–18.

considered.[2] In dealing with music and religion, he moved from exploring shifts in achievement in western cultures, shifts that occurred both
in and between fields, to exploring changes in the public's perceptions.
The general idea of shift was both more sharply focussed and extended
from a different angle.

Historians were also asked to consider a shift of talent from theology
to natural philosophy in some parts of Europe. If in the early sixteenth
century the brightest minds were attracted to the established 'queen of
the sciences', theology, by the late sixteenth and early seventeenth
centuries many devout and equally gifted minds were drawn to the
politically more neutral field of natural philosophy. Thus Faust, a
contemporary archetype with creative anxieties, threw theology out
together with many of her handmaidens. Faust was looking for a more
potent discipline, magic:

What doctrine call you this? *Che sera sera.* What will it be, shall be? Divinity
adieu.[3]

Of course, the political neutrality of natural philosophy was more
characteristic of some places than of others.[4] Catholic lands in the grip
of counter-reformation, and very strictly Calvinist areas, were hardly
neutral. The executions of Gruet, Servetus and Bruno, the condemnation
of Galileo (recently exonerated), and Descarte's subsequent suppression
of *Le Monde* all illustrate this. But even then, the association of heretical
or dangerous ideas with the new philosophy was late and only partial;[5]
during the civil war in England it was often claimed as one of its virtues
that such philosophizing was politically neutral.[6]

These different reactions to the new natural philosophy seemed to me
to highlight another of H. G. Koenigsberger's central points. Many
shifts in the concentration of one or another kind of talent appear to have
depended on the political atmosphere and on the social reception of
specific talents. In the Renaissance, many creative activities seem to have

[2] H. G. Koenigsberger, 'Republics and Courts in Italian and European Culture in the
Sixteenth and Seventeenth Centuries', *Past and Present*, no. 83 (May 1979), pp. 32–56;
H. G. Koenigsberger, 'Music and Religion in Modern European History', in
J. H. Elliott and H. G. Koenigsberger (eds.), *The Diversity of History* (London, 1970),
III, pp. 35–78; H. G. Koenigsberger, 'Science and Religion in Early Modern Europe',
in S. Drescher, D. Sabean, A. Sharlin (eds.), *Political Symbolism in Modern Europe*
(London, 1982), VIII (henceforth H. G. Koenigsberger, 'Science and Religion'), pp.
168–93.
[3] Christopher Marlowe, 'Doctor Faustus', in J. B. Stean (ed.), *The Complete Plays*
(Harmondsworth, 1969), p. 267.
[4] H. G. Koenigsberger, 'Science and Religion', p. 173.
[5] Frances A. Yates, *Lull and Bruno*, I (London, 1982), p. 178; reprinted from, 'The
Religious Policy of Giordano Bruno', *Journal of the Warburg and Courtauld Institutes*,
III (1939, 1940).   [6] H. G. Koenigsberger, 'Science and Religion', pp. 185–6.

thrived in republican communities or, at the very least, in conditions of relatively free popular discourse. Later in the sixteenth century, gifted persons appear to have flocked to those capitals and courts which were also cosmopolitan, as opposed to provincial and poorer courts and to restricted authoritarian environments.[7]

Drawing from Helli Koenigsberger's suggestions, the point I want to emphasize here is that outstanding creative achievements, especially clusters of achievements in one or in a number of related fields, probably depended on political and cultural conditions as much as on either the particular state of development in a field or on individual genius. Genius, itself a concept that developed during the early modern period, was not simply an unusual quality of mind and/or talent; it appeared to originate from an intricate and subtle dialogue between gifted individuals and their cultural environment.[8] And that environment could account for the clustering of specific talents and also for the popularity of particular interdisciplinary associations.

Conditions could either attract or repel gifted persons in the mobile society of early modern Europe. This process ought not to be seen only in terms of material provision, of individual and/or institutional patronage. It was certainly social and political, but it was also psychological, intellectual, and spiritual.[9] The *uomo universale*, just like talented contemporaries with narrower gifts, was exposed to all variety of circumstances. However, it is likely that the fruition of such an intellect required exposure to a range of ideas, methods and attitudes within the cultural locus of the virtuoso's growing and working life. Personal motives were also important. For example, Leonardo da Vinci's return to and stay in Florence in the early 1500s was relatively uncomfortable. At that time he experienced both shifting personal motives and aims and conflicting claims from patrons. He had once been on rather more fertile ground there, in the studio tradition of his early years.[10] Thus, atmosphere can play an important part in the development

[7] H. G. Koenigsberger, 'Republics and Courts in Italian and European Culture in the Sixteenth and Seventeenth Centuries', pp. 54–9.
[8] For interesting points about the earlier history of the idea of genius, see M. A. Screech, *Montaigne and Melancholy: The Wisdom of the Essays* (London, 1983), pp. 9–21; for important points about sponsorship, censorship, and scientific talents, see Elizabeth L. Eisenstein, *The Printing Press As An Agent of Change* (Cambridge, 1979), II, pp. 636–82.
[9] Dorothy Koenigsberger, *Renaissance Man and Creative Thinking: A History of Concepts of Harmony, 1400–1700* (Sussex, 1979) (henceforth D. Koenigsberger, *Renaissance Man*), pp. 232–47.
[10] Martin Kemp, *Leonardo da Vinci: The Marvellous Works of Nature and Man*, (London, 1981) (henceforth Kemp, *Leonardo da Vinci*), pp. 42, 230–40.

of abilities, even of the abilities of a genius, and even of the multiple abilities that are called universal. Historians can view the mingling of skills, thoughts, attitudes, and beliefs, and their development in the minds of gifted persons as a fertile conceptual ground from which talents can begin to take shape and grow.

An historian might move in many directions in reaction to the diverse implications of the idea of shift. Among these I turned towards an historical appreciation of universality, particularly in the career of Leonardo da Vinci. This supreme *uomo universale*, whose individual gifts were rare and whose predictive sensitivities were unique in some fields, did not think or do anything that cannot be seen to have had real roots in his cultural experience. His diversity was not chaotic.[11] His mentality was a product of his time and culture.[12] Leonardo belongs to his era even though many of his artistic and purely conceptual pursuits represent unusual advances in the thinking of that time. Here, I am using the word 'advances' to indicate original thinking; for Leonardo had original ideas and presented some of these ideas in his work. I am not referring to the diffuse reception of Leonardo's thought or to that of his extant works.

In the generations surrounding Leonardo, patronage was certainly very important in the career development of outstanding artist-engineers of the Italian Renaissance, for example, Lorenzo Ghiberti, Filippo Brunelleschi, L. B. Alberti, Francesco di Giorgio Martini, Leonardo da Vinci, Luca Pacioli, Michelangelo and Palladio.[13] Equally important is the fact that contemporaries saw all of these individuals as having had either personal enthusiasm for the ideal of harmony or good friendships with others who were concerned about the order of reality and its universal harmony. So that in and above natural giftedness and patronage, a Renaissance genius's disposition towards personal universality also must have been supported by both the possibility of access to training to appropriate standards in multifarious arts and disciplines (including the possibility of self-education), and the adoption of a point of view. This view was expressed by a tendency or desire to reduce experiences, and the whole varied character of nature, to orderly and uniform principles. The stimuli for the inception of this tendency in any one person may have been conventional or deeper and more personal; but the adoption of such an attitude is so completely involved in the mentality of the *uomo universale*, in the intellectual and artistic develop-

[11] Kemp, *Leonardo da Vinci*, p. 349.
[12] V. P. Zubov, *Leonardo da Vinci*, tr. D. H. Kraus (Cambridge, Mass., 1968), pp. 41–88.
[13] Giorgio de Santillana, *Reflections on Men and Ideas* (Cambridge, Mass., 1968), pp. 137–66.

ment of this kind of person, that this development is really not fully appreciable without an appraisal of the individual's assimilation of that point of view. This will be made clearer from a consideration of Leonardo's universality.

Leonardo da Vinci was dramatically inspired by a number of related ideas. He was fascinated by metamorphoses, which he saw mainly but not exclusively as natural transformations. In the course of his career he also became increasingly interested in mathematical imagery and geometrical transmutations. He regarded both the natural and the mental processes as revealing harmony within change and unity as the basis of diversity in nature.

A critical demonstration of the full range and importance of these stimulating ideas for Leonardo's universality, and for the problem of universality in general, lies outside the scope of this essay. Nevertheless, observations about Leonardo's appreciation of these ideas can distinguish his own particular type of universality and relate an important representative of the personal style of the Renaissance to shifts in the long-term expression of the ideal.

Leonardo da Vinci enacted the role of personal universality. To debate whether the desire to do so was kindled in him, or if he wrung it from his surroundings, is to begin a chicken-or-egg type discussion. It looks as if the social and intellectual environs allowed for the portrayal of this exceptional and rather spectacular role by him and by a few other highly gifted individuals. The popularity of contemporary ideals which acclaimed the harmony of nature and praised the powers of the artist to master many disciplines has been noted repeatedly. To this picture I want to add that, although Leonardo was not primarily involved with humanism, specific works and some humanists' viewpoints did significantly influence him. But does this have anything to do with his universality? Now I am not trying, as it were, to scoop up humanistic studies in order to add them to the long list of Leonardo's attainments. However, some points can be made about the matter of how Renaissance humanism affected Leonardo. These can clarify his extreme cultural stance and his whole intellectual position. For instance, there is the *Metamorphoses* of Ovid, a favoured author who was reproduced in many editions by humanist scholars in the Renaissance. Leonardo was inspired by the *Metamorphoses* in more ways than one, and he possessed a copy of this work as well as a translation of Ovid's letters.[14] The condition of metamorphosis, or unity within change, fascinated him; and violent changes and even more gradual changes seem to have charged him with definite emotional ambivalences. Death, dissolution, and decay caused

[14] Kemp, *Leonardo da Vinci*, pp. 104, 159, 319–22.

Leonardo to accuse nature of fearful indifference; the natural order was persistent but wholly impersonal.[15] Leonardo felt great sympathy with men and even with animals who all suffered lacerating changes. Ovid's metaphors for these relentless processes moved him; he noted that the god had wept when the desired nymph was transformed into a tree, a tree with her heart still beating. Nevertheless, Leonardo also coined the analogy of the tree of veins, and he superimposed that tree in and on the human body while in search of an explanation for blood flow.

Thus transformations could have positive aspects. The artist's understanding of them might allow him to aspire to a kind of divinity, and his insight into the reasons underlying changes amounted to his attaining an overview of the orderly variability of reality itself. Not only this, but even though everything, including man, was subject to natural change, and even though the human mind could, to some degree, overcome this passive condition by the cultivation of an understanding of nature's metamorphoses, by discovering the reasons for changes, the artist's mind could aspire to something greater still. It could employ its understanding in the making of new combinations and different things. Beyond the imitation of nature, but really also because of it, and by using the understanding that was required to produce such an imitation, Leonardo da Vinci was attempting the enactment of creation itself, creation on the human level. He did not envisage the artist's models as fixed archetypes. On the contrary, Leonardo tried to acquire understanding by using the powers of the mind to examine the actual fluxes in nature, the harmonies of design, and to perform some purely mental exercises. These exercises often took the form of trying to work out geometrical transformations, for instance, the squaring of the circle. The prize that Leonardo sought was always the rationale behind change. Seeming monsters and miracles could be made by men when the designer understood the underlying reason for the variant but truly related forms of things.

Historians have remarked about the extreme improbability of some of Leonardo's ponderings and projects, for example, the proposal for the canalization of the Arno and the seemingly overambitious designs for the Sforza monument.[16] His curious sense of humour, his delight in *chimaerae* and in observing grotesques also relates to this evaluation of some of his thoughts. But those who think about him in this way have not fully appreciated the manner of Leonardo's universality. He realized that artists could design and invent things that were overtly, but not essentially, different from existing things. These inventions could cert-

---

[15] D. Koenigsberger, *Renaissance Man*, p. 151.
[16] This is even after the clarification of *Codex Madrid II*, see M. V. Brugnoli, 'The sculptor', *Leonardo The Artist* (London, 1981), pp. 96–135, especially pp. 104–10.

ainly seem as natural as anything else, but only in so far as their artificiality was conceived according to true rules or axioms. Thus, when Vasari wrote about Leonardo's tricks with a live lizard cum mini dragon and with a bellows and a bull's gut, he was reporting the playful side of Leonardo's transformations. Leonardo's witnesses (or victims) did not know that what they were seeing or experiencing was perfectly natural, natural but rearranged.[17] The artist both selected from and superimposed on natural things. And the spirit of his light-hearted metamorphoses is completely related to another more serious project, to the artist's desire to make natural-looking images on two-dimensional surfaces. These activities are similar because the maker has observed and knows all of the possible conditions of his materials, and he has altered these conditions according to a design or plan that expresses both his technique and his insight into the true states and causes of real things.

Examples of this point of view are found in Leonardo's riddles and *profetie*. These often show the riddler's delight in his own secret comprehension of transformations. The joke is directed at those who will be astounded at the metamorphosis of one thing or another. Wits are strained when things appear in unexpected forms. Seasonal variations in plants and the different natural conditions of water were particularly interesting to Leonardo in some prophecies and riddles that have been decoded by Professor Carlo Pedretti. The crux of the guess-work set by Leonardo hinges on an unseen and unrealized transformation. Thus, Leonardo set a puzzle in which he described the falling of summer snow off mountain peaks during festivals held in piazzas. This is answered most plausibly by explaining that the warmth melted the snow that flowed into the rivers; and that river water was normally used in piazza fountains.[18] Thus, sun transforms the snows and men put them to diverse uses, possibly for irrigation, but in this instance for pure pleasure. Other very similar puzzles are based on the change of sea water into clouds, and again, of rainwater into snow on top of mountains.[19] These riddle-transformations were entirely natural; but men had to know something about nature in order to be able to guess the answers.

Other transformations were performed by artists in imitation of nature, by their creation of both natural-looking and apparently artificial things. All things that were created by design could only be natural in so far as the rules in the mind of the designer were real and true. The design, the law, the axiom, and the rule or principle was the universal

---

[17] Leonardo's fantasy was related to the processes of invention that he used in his sciences; see Kemp, *Leonardo da Vinci*, p. 161–2.

[18] Carlo Pedretti, 'Three Leonardo riddles', *Renaissance Quarterly*, vol. XXX, no. 2 (summer, 1977), pp. 153–4.

[19] *Ibid.*, p. 155.

element. Leonardo's own universality eventually came to depend on his belief in this idea far more than it did on his range of talents. Nevertheless, the acquisition of that range opened him to many thought processes that indicated and confirmed the universal orderliness of nature and experience. He remarked: 'You who speculate on the nature of things, I praise you not for knowing the processes which nature ordinarily effects of herself, but rejoice if you know the issue of such things as your mind conceives.'[20] So Leonardo does not entirely praise the passive understanding of what is normally executed naturally. What excites him far more is the human mind's ability to endow or embody its rationale within its own issue, in its own work; man is *massimo strumento di natura*, but he is hardly nature's best instrument as he is acted upon but primarily as he acts. Leonardo has a comprehensive view of the imitation of nature; not only does the artist copy nature in works, he designs in the way that nature generates.

Still, how do the *Metamorphoses* relate to this view? From a basic arrangement, nature creates an extraordinarily infinite panorama.[21] For instance, when men do battle their features are amazingly transformed, as Leonardo depicted and as scholars know from studies and reports of his *Battle of Anghiari*. His word paintings of a fish turned fossil, and of the living and physical changes that are evident when ascending Mount Taurus, and his observations of the skeleton remains of a very large ship in Candia in Lombardy, all such imagery suggests the imaginative potency of the *Metamorphoses*. And when nature's simplicity in the variety of its operations is understood, designers can work their own transformations and create innumerable combinations of forms, forms that are not actually wholly present in the natural world.

In 1450, a somewhat older universalist, a mathematician, theologian and philosopher, Nicholas of Cusa, created a character called the Simpleton or Idiot. This was an unlearned man who had become wise through a keen observation of everything that went on in the Roman market place. His sagacity was of the Petrarchian stamp, very like that of the Simpleton in Petrarch's dialogues of true wisdom.[22] The ultimate model was, of course, Socratic. Renaissance thinkers who were attracted to Augustinian platonist and neoplatonic views tended to admire the unlearned wise man. Expressing this spirit, Cusa's Idiot similarly did not rely on authorities for knowledge but on his own astute analyses of mundane experience; and he suggested that this kind of experience could provide a basis for human knowledge.[23] The Idiot made his points

[20] G. 47r; Mac Curdy 70, quoted in Zubov, *Leonardo da Vinci*, p. 99.   [21] *Ibid.*, p. 98.
[22] Francesco Petrarcha, *Opera*, '*De vera sapientia*', dialogi II (Basileae, 1554), pp. 364–72.
[23] N. de Cusa, *Opera*, '*Idiotae*', Vol I, book III, chapter vii, (Basileae, 1565), pp. 157–60.

in conversations with educated people, a philosopher and an orator. At the beginning of the first conversation in Book III of Cusa's dialogues, the Simpleton was in the process of making spoons, and he observed that the forms of the spoons were not actually natural. The transformation of a hunk of wood into a spoon required an idea; but, while thoughts about wood carving and about suitable kinds of wood were clear adaptations of experience, the original notion of the spoon was not. The spoon was somehow a creature of the human maker's mind. Later Cusa's Idiot also taught that that concept could not really have been drawn from a fixed and eternal archetypal spoon. Thus, the human notion of the spoon was conceived from the natural powers of the mind, conceived by means of an inborn ability to organize in flux and to rearrange, synthesize and unify in the face of variety, sequence and change.

I am not about to suggest any direct link from Cusa to Leonardo; even though I have argued for specific kinds of conceptual influence in another place.[24] Others too have noted connections.[25] However, the only work by Cusa that historians verify that Leonardo actually knew was *De transformationibus geometricus* (Corte Maggiore, 1502).[26] Knowing this alone cannot account for the variety of Cusan-type ideas that were expressed by Leonardo. The type is distinctive because of its basis in paradox and also because, though platonist, Cusa's model completely excludes the *Ideas* and replaces them with an innate power of knowing.[27] So, if Leonardo did adopt a Cusan view of knowledge, it looks as if his exposure to it must have come from intermediaries. There are a number of possible candidates, and it is likely that more than one person contributed to its advertisement; Luca Pacioli may have been especially instrumental in expanding Leonardo's view of Cusan epistemology. At this point, I simply want to call the reader's attention to the absence of any guiding eternal *Ideas* in Nicholas of Cusa's epistemology and to his spokesmen's reliance on an alternative natural capacity of the mind.[28]

Leonardo shows a similar reliance on the mind's power to both understand and invent through its own knowledge. He believed that artists could fashion transformations and create synthetic but seemingly

[24] D. Koenigsberger, *Renaissance Man*, pp. 62–90, 114–32, 138–9.
[25] Notably, Pierre Duhem, *Études sur Léonard De Vinci*, 3 vols. (Paris, 1906–13), 1955 edition, vol II, pp. 99–279; R. Klibansky, 'Copernic et Nicolas de Cues', *Leonard De Vinci et L'Expérience Scientifique au Seizième Siècle* (Paris, 1952), pp. 225–35; Zubov, *Leonardo da Vinci*, pp. 149–50.
[26] Kemp, *Leonardo da Vinci*, p. 251.
[27] For paradoxical aspects of Leonardo's thinking, see D. Koenigsberger, *Renaissance Man*, pp. 68–84; Rosalie Colie, *Paradoxia epidemica* (Princeton, N. J., 1966), pp. 293–4.
[28] P. M. Watts, *Nicolaus Cusanus: A Fifteenth Century Vision of Man* (Leiden, 1982), pp. 67–74, 227–32; D. Koenigsberger, *Renaissance Man*, pp. 114–19.

real objects through their arts. In addition, his education was not of the standard academic type for the time. Although Leonardo studied all that he could, and this was a great deal, he did not regard himself as a *litterato* but as one who sought knowledge through experience:

> I well know that, not being a literary man, certain presumptuous persons will think that they may reasonably deride me with the allegation that I am a man without letters. Stupid fellows!...But do they not know that my subjects are to be better illustrated from experience than by yet more words? – Experience which has been the mistress of all those who wrote well, and, thus as mistress, I will cite her in all cases.[29]

Perhaps the influence of Petrarchian humanism and revised Augustinian platonism enabled Leonardo to cast himself in the role of a wise simpleton, of the unlearned sage who saw that experience taught the causes of things; such a one could make spoons and much more too in the way of human inventions. In the light of this, for example, straight wooden beams could actually be converted into arches. They were bent for the design of a bridge by a method of notching that Leonardo demonstrated in a drawing.[30] The technique worked, as is shown by bridges built in this way in the nineteenth century. This particular conception and transformation by the artist was part of an exercise in thinking about civil engineering. It is distinct in all of its details, but it is certainly not different in kind from any of Leonardo's other ideas for the transformation of something or other. In his thoughts, all natural sequences, the times, the seasons, and all possible movements, from those of the elements, to bodies, to sound waves, to light, – they were all paradoxically totally unified in nature itself, and gradually united in the notional life of the artist's mind.

Leonardo da Vinci was primarily an *uomo universale* because he sought to mentally encompass the pattern or order of all the things that actually existed. Almost all of the analogies he makes illustrates this single point. One very nice example is cited by Martin Kemp from a letter that was probably sent to the Cathedral authorities in Milan when Leonardo submitted his *tiburio* (crossing tower) model in 1488. Leonardo explains how medicine and architecture are alike:

> Doctors, teachers and those who nurse the sick should be aware what sort of thing is man, what is life, what is health and in what manner a parity and concordance of the elements maintains it; while a discordance of these elements ruins and destroys it; and one with a good knowledge of the nature of the things mentioned above will be better also to repair it than one who lacks knowledge

---

[29] Quoted from C.A. 119va, in Kemp, *Leonardo da Vinci*, p. 102.
[30] Ladislao Reti, 'The Engineer', *Leonardo The Inventor* (London, 1981), pp. 130–1.

of them...the same is necessary for the ailing cathedral, in that a doctor–architect understands what kind of thing is a building and from what rules a correct building derives and whence these rules originate and into how many parts they may be divided and what are the causes which hold the building together and make it permanent, and what is the nature of weight and what is the potential of force, and in what manner they may be conjoined and interrelated, and what effect they will produce combined. He who has true knowledge of the things listed above will present the work satisfactorily to your understanding.[31]

Here Leonardo emphasized the concept. He saw priority in the idea. This is why doctors need to be aware and architects should understand; for, the one who has knowledge can both create and nurture.

Thoughts like these look less like unadulterated aristotelianism than they do like Cusan platonism. The Cusan emphasis is confirmed by the energetic and truly vitalizing character that Leonardo generally attached to nature. By contrast, the traditional unmoved–mover makes the figure of a remote impulse, a very distant trigger; but Leonardo's order of nature was implicit in all phases of its activity. Its rationale somehow had to be prior to individuals, and real, in order to be expressed in all things. In a similar way, Leonardo taught that the mental picture first had to be both true and clear, if the designer was to execute the work properly. Leonardo's nature was totally invisible as an entity; it was a hidden God. While natural operations were impersonal, nature was definitely intimate in all of the developments and activites of existing things.[32]

This whole figure of a formless identity outside of nature's specific operations in all things, of nature's unifying and generative powers, of the unquestionable investment of those powers in the development of each individual and in all of the phases of their operations, and finally, of the developing imitation of this whole order in the mind of the artist: this complete pattern looks very like a Cusan over-view of knowledge and reality. Itself eclectic, that view began with the absolute unity of an invisible and formless generator. The unity emerged as lawfulness when it was enunciated in (limited in) sequences. Thus, an absolute order somehow expressed itself in the moving actuality of nature, both in the whole and in each part. It accounted for natural harmony. Finally, a piece-meal but infinitely perfectible model of this order could be developed in the mind of an unbiased sage, in the mind of the kind of idiot who consulted experience first, and who even subjected authority to experience. Much later, Galileo's *Simplicio* changed this picture because he was made to represent a traditionalist. However, I think that

---

[31] Quoted from C.A. 270rc, in Kemp, *Leonardo da Vinci*, p. 107.

[32] *Ibid.*, pp. 91, 151; and God holds the whole universe in his thoughts, (*la mente de Dio nella quale s'include l'universo*), Leonardo da Vinci, *Literary Works*, ed. J. P. Richter, vol. II (Oxford, 1939), (1210).

it is not too far fetched to suggest that, for whatever reason, Leonardo played the Renaissance Petrarchian and Cusan sage. His quest for universality rested more in his desire to understand the order of reality from experience, and in his belief in the mysterious divine endowment of that order, than it did in his rainbow display of talents.

The compendium of knowledge was lodged in mind, in understanding, not in a myriad of unconnected conditions. And this was precisely the view that many of Leonardo's contemporaries had of Ovid's *Metamorphoses*. They saw it as an encyclopaedia of ancient knowledge, and envisaged its use as the basis of a sound liberal education; geography, astrology, music, rhetoric, and moral and natural philosophy were all seen to be encompassed.[33] The work held codified knowledge. Thus, it represented far more than a mere dictionary of fables.[34] Leonardo certainly appreciated it in this way. If anything, he took its basis of identity-in-change to heart and tried to interpret all changes, gradual or rapid, pacific or violent, as expressing competely natural and logical transformations. Historians have thought that they could see the prediction of evolution in this; but Leonardo's image is even more universal than all that is implied in such a prediction.[35] Microcosm and macrocosm both conformed to the laws of reality; and Leonardo cast both conception and death in the totally natural drama of metamorphoses. In this way, '...animals are a type of life of the world'.[36] And, '...man is the image of the world'.[37]

A final point about Leonardo's role of personal universality pertains to a degree of scholarly puzzlement about his geometrical exercises. Leonardo developed mathematical knowledge and skills relatively late in his career. Historians of mathematics and of the sciences have often been bewildered either by the fragmentary and rather arbitrary character of Leonardo's knowledge of sections of this subject or by his extraordinary zeal in the performance of seemingly almost pointless exercises involving geometrical transmutations.[38] These exercises can look obsessional.[39] And this raises the question of why they should have been so. But, when

[33] Ann Moss, *Ovid in Renaissance France*, Warburg Institute Surveys VIII (London, 1982), pp. 28–36, 59, 61.   [34] *Ibid.*, p. 29.

[35] André Chastel, 'Léonard et la culture', *Leonard De Vinci et L'Expérience Scientifique au Seizième Siècle* (Paris, 1952), pp. 251–63, especially p. 255; and, by the same author, 'The Arts during the Renaissance', *The Renaissance: Essays in Interpretation* (London, 1982), pp. 227–71, especially p. 262.

[36] Leonardo da Vinci, *Literary Works*, II, (1219).   [37] *Ibid.*, (1162).

[38] Marshall Clagett, *Archimedes in the Middle Ages*, III, part 3 (Philadelphia, 1978), pp. 478–81; Edward Grant, *Physical Science in the Middle Ages* (Cambridge, 1977), first edn., 1971, p. 54; Morris Kline, *Mathematical Thought from Ancient to Modern Times* (New York, 1972), pp. 234–5.

[39] Kemp, *Leonardo da Vinci*, pp. 150, 215–16, 248, 296–302, 348.

viewed in another light, Leonardo's fixation with problems such as the squaring of the circle and the exploration of the capacities of spiral lines, can uncover important aspects of both his methodological concerns and his metaphysical imagination. This is in and above the search for practical solutions to specific problems. Among other things, when dealing with spiral lines, Leonardo was captivated by the image of the physical unwinding of a curved length to produce a straight one (that is, the tracing of a straight line by rolling out a curved one on a plane).[40] This exercise in the resolution of apparent opposites by the physical rectification of a curved line, taken together with Leonardo's emotional and exultant claims to have discovered the quadrature of the circle may, in fact, show historians that he was in the process of being diversely influenced by sources in mathematical thinking, sources that also presented him with appealing methodological and spiritual ideas.

Both Nicole Oresme and Nicholas of Cusa seem to have influenced Leonardo in this way. Oresme first, because he defined the spiral in a way that was actually copied by Leonardo; and Cusa, because he employed conceptual transformations to highlight a spiritual vision that appealed to Leonardo.[41] Cusa worked out the resolution of shapes, such as a line into a triangle and a circle into a line, in order to strain the human intellect and imagination, to force it to visualize beyond the normal appearances of things, to stretch towards an invisible, non-spatial and infinite field.[42] In this spiritual territory, all existing forms were reduced to a point and that point was equal to nothing. Cusa's aim in developing these exercises was to show how things that are normally perceived as opposites can be made to coincide in the human mind. Such imaginative mental resolutions were signs of the ultimate reduction of everything in God; or indeed, of the expansion of everything in God; in whom smallest and greatest, minimum and maximum coincided. After c. 1496 Leonardo grew close to Luca Pacioli. Pacioli enlivened Leonardo's interest in mathematics, while he himself was thinking along Cusan lines. Thus, this friendship reinforces the suggestion that Leonardo's energetic exercises may represent a spiritual style of reductionism, one that confirmed and shaped his universality. Leonardo tried to transform shapes and also to reduce the many to one single point. That one point became a symbol of true unity behind the diversity of the world.[43]

The influence of Nicole Oresme was probably not limited to mathe-

[40] Clagett, *Archimedes in the Middle Ages*, p. 484.
[41] *Ibid.*, pp. 484–5; Duhem, *Études sur Léonard De Vinci*, III, pp. 481–92.
[42] N. de Cusa, *Opera*, '*De Docta Ignorantia*', vol. I, book I, chs. xii, xiii, xv, xvi, pp. 9–13.
[43] D. Koenigsberger, *Renaissance Man*, pp. 68–84.

matical problem-solving and definitions of spirals. A whole approach to
metaphysical questions that had been invented by Oresme may have
influenced Leonardo directly or indirectly. Oresme had taken an original
position with respect to both theology and science. Although he placed
the supreme ground of truth in faith alone, he also devised philosophical
exercises wherein he placed reasoned demonstrations up against equally
reasonable alternatives, superimposing points of view about various
matters in natural philosophy.[44] His motives were mixed. He wanted
both to explore unconventional solutions to scientific problems and to
expose the limitations of human reason as against faith. If conflicting
solutions could be seen to be equally reasonable, then reason itself was
unmasked as a fragile mentor. His methods are interesting in their own
right. Oresme juxtaposed and superimposed arguments to show both the
logical consequences of human reason and the uncertainties that must
arise from its use. His *modus operandi* and his general motives are here
more interesting than the content of his arguments. For, in a later era,
superimposition, overlay, underpinning and juxtapositioning were the
mental and diagrammatic tools employed by Leonardo da Vinci in his
studies of nature and of geometrical form.[45] By these tools Leonardo
attempted to imitate the many-sided vision of *la natura* herself.

One important point, then, is that similar methods had been and
continued to be developed in many different areas of cultural activity in
the period between the fourteenth and the sixteenth centuries. For
example, simultaneous composition and polyphonic music are inter-
textured techniques and styles of composition that gradually matured
from the era of Guillaume de Machaut (d. 1377). They reached a
culminating point in the generation of Josquin Desprez (d. 1521), the
same generation as Leonardo. Parallel and comparable literary techniques
were also introduced by Dante and by Machaut. These involved the
overlapping of points of view and the contrast and conjunction of witness
and protagonist narrators.[46] In Dante's early work, *La Vita Nuova*
(c. 1290), the reader is made to simultaneously appreciate the Dante who
lives in the experience, the Dante who reflects on the experience, and the
poet, the Dante who represents the experience in specific poems. Such
many-textured ventures may lead cultural historians to mark a very
general tendency of artists and thinkers, a tendency to employ combined
perspectives, the weaving of vistas, and various modes of superimposition

[44] Edward Grant, 'Scientific Thought in Fourteenth-Century Paris: Jean Buridan and
Nicole Oresme', in M. P. Cosman, B. Chandler (eds.), *Machaut's World*, Annals of the
New York Academy of Sciences, vol. 314. (New York, 1978), pp. 105–24.
[45] For some examples, see Kemp, *Leonardo da Vinci*, pp. 228, 261, 286, 329, 334.
[46] William Calin, 'The Poet at the Fountain: Machaut as Narrative Poet', in Cosman and
Chandler (eds.), *Machaut's World*, pp. 177–87, especially pp. 183–4.

in order to create concurrent impressions and to achieve representational diversity and depth. This happened in accounting, in sound, in space and form, and in both the imaginative and the logical assessment of experience. The development of pictorial perspective in the early 1400s can be seen in relation to these other techniques – for artists using perspective knew that any alteration in the position of the eye from which the perspective was planned, would alter the reality in the presented scene. The development of all these methods implied universality; for, in one way or another, the desires of these artists were *omnipercipient*.

In this spirit, Leonardo da Vinci used related techniques in anatomy, physiology, drawing, painting, discovering and planning and, perhaps, even in his unusual geometrical exercises. Such modes of seeing and of presenting experience helped him to achieve a more universal concept of any specific problem. Leonardo lodged apparent differences, conflicts, and opposites in the ground of his own mind. If, in the past, influential philosophers such as Oresme and Cusa had suggested that these mental resolutions intimated the ultimate reduction of differences in God, can we honestly believe that Leonardo was completely indifferent to this established image? So my discussion ends with the suggestion that Leonardo was probably seeking mental and metaphysical perspectives and assurances when he energetically pursued some of his seemingly pointless geometrical exercises.

The essence of Renaissance universality seems to have been conceptual and historians can appreciate the metamorphoses of that essence. Changes in patronage from personal and princely to royal and institutional corresponded with major changes in civilization. The centralization of kingdoms, the growth of a commercial and capitalistic economy and society, the invention of printing and engraving, the development of modern communications, the increase of travel, all of these things occurred at about the same time as an awakening of interest in projects that expressed the desire to regularize; for instance, to agree to uniform standards of measurement, to invent a universal language. Thus, all of these affairs are of fundamental importance for historians who are trying to refine their own understanding of the shifts in emphasis from Renaissance universality to later styles. However, even with these things in mind, there are still important points to be made about notional bases of universality. All such bases thrive within very specific cultural environments and so all such assemblies of concepts, thoughts, and beliefs participate in the more general historical phenomena of the shift of human talents and abilities.

In the centuries after Leonardo, the occurrence of universal personalities gradually diminished. Certainly individual examples of it extend to that period when amateurs could still make original contributions to the sciences, to the generations of Goethe (d. 1832) and Alexander von Humboldt (d. 1859). But, in the long view, it looks as if personal universality was comparatively fragile. The search for universal axioms, however, and/or for the bonds of a corpus of knowledge, or for common methods of discovery, came to be widely expressed in the learned world in the early modern period; and, in this sense, these expressions of universality tended to endure.

In either adopting or growing into the role of *uomo universale*, Leonardo da Vinci may have partly heralded and certainly came to personify a long-term preoccupation in Western civilization with universality in one or another style. One such style combined strong methodological and theoretical syntheses; for example, Nicholas of Cusa, Paolo Toscanelli, and Luca Pacioli. Others employed rather more eclectic methods of analysis, invention, and creation, while they also sought the universal bases of knowledge. These are men such as: Leon Battista Alberti, Leonardo, Marsilio Ficino, Cosimo Bartoli, Girolamo Fracastoro, Girolamo Cardano, and Giordano Bruno.[47] The evolution in styles of universality is certainly not a matter of historical necessity; it is something that stems from the extensive character of the personal style. And so historians may find it useful to view the styles of universality of the late Renaissance and of the seventeenth and eighteenth centuries as having developed from the earlier classic style. Further, a fragmentation of the Renaissance ideal also appears to have occurred. This fragmentation admits the expression of entirely new ideas and fashions in thinking. But, as far as universality is concerned, most of these newer fashions tended to emphasize and/or intensify and develop one or another feature of the personal type of universality.

For example, while Renaissance universalists tended to see God as a transcendent and formless being, prior to the world, and as the real ground of a less perfect unity that was also expressed within the sequential and extended world, pantheists of the early eighteenth century saw that expanded world of nature as the true deity.[48] As nature, the deity was actually extended. God composed and filled the infinite universe. This whole world was unified by means of His rare and total vivifying materiality. This curious spiritualized materialism certainly looks very different from a Renaissance view; still, there are notional similarities and historical links affiliating these variant images of the

[47] D. Koenigsberger, *Renaissance Man*, pp. 213–60.
[48] M. C. Jacob, *The Radical Enlightenment*, pp. 115, 221, 223–4.

ultimate basis of unity in the world. These may account for the accusation of pantheism that was wrongly aimed at Nicholas of Cusa. Leonardo was also frequently seen as one who worshipped nature as the deity. In a very special sense he did this; but this was really not in the manner of the later pantheist–universalists. Giordano Bruno also fits into this picture; for, although he first saw himself as a reforming and believing Catholic, later pantheists saw some of their own antecedents in Bruno's religion of the world. It seems that, in one way or another, personal universality contained the seeds of later styles.

This manner of thinking intimates a transformation of the goals of universalists after the Italian Renaissance. From the conscious or unconscious enactment of the role of the *uomo universale*, the expression of universality tended to shift from individuals to groups. Public, private, and, sometimes, secret organizations sustained forms of the ideal. Also, distinguished philosophers of knowledge, among them, Francis Bacon, Leibniz, d'Alembert, and Immanuel Kant assumed and/or taught universality in one or another form. Later, the romantics, Goethe, William Blake, and Samuel Taylor Coleridge revived interests in the classic personal style. The dual representation of universality, universality-in-act, together with the complementary search for a satisfactory theory to explain and unify the diversity of experience, had already been abundantly expressed by Leonardo da Vinci.

In the course of the seventeenth century, aspects of the Renaissance ideal were expressed in the vision of a community of effort. Group efforts were made to discover axioms of nature and to associate branches of learning. The origin of this emphasis on the community was in the idealistic reforming movements of the sixteenth century, especially Christian Humanism and the Protestant Reformation. The Renaissance community of effort had been envisaged in terms of philosophical, educational, social, ethical and religious reforms. However, by the late sixteenth and seventeenth centuries, the reforming mood frequently appeared in works about the discovery of nature and of the wider world, and in the continuing revision of methods of learning and knowing.[49] Timely preoccupations with the usefulness of knowledge and with the natural world tended to incorporate and intensify older desires for the conceptual bases of universality.

Thus the quest for a universal corpus became very popular in the seventeenth century, especially in France. Universalists of the generation

[49] Frances A. Yates, *The Occult Philosophy in the Elizabethan Age* (London, 1979), pp. 174–5; Anthony Quinton, *Francis Bacon* (Oxford, 1980), pp. 39–54, 66–9; Bacon's *The New Atlantis* makes a good synthesis; humanist, religious, mystical, methodological, and scientific ideals are all expressed in a utopian community.

of Marin Mersenne (d. 1648) frequently acted as intermediaries between the humanism of the Renaissance and the development of the sciences.[50] In this vein they often used music both as a basis of association between the disciplines and as an image of the universal encyclopaedia. The natural philosophers who wrote about music were legion; among them in France, René Descartes, Pierre Gassendi, Gérard Desargues, Claude Hardy, Ismaël Boulliau, Jean de Beugrand, Pierre de Fermat, Claude Bredeau, Gabriel de La Charlonye, Etienne Pascal, Gilles Personne de Roberval, and La Voye-Mignot.[51] Outside France distinguished philosophers, including Constantijn Huygens, Galileo Galilei, Isaac Beeckman, J. B. van Helmont, John Wallis and Theodore Haack participated in this tradition.[52]

Earlier on, universalist ideals had already been expressed in the objectives of Baïf's *Académie de Poésie et de Musique* (1571–3). The aims of this association foreshadowed those of Adrian Auzot, who proposed a *Compagnie des Sciences et des Arts* to Louis XIV. In some measure, similar unifying ideals were enunciated in 1666, in the formation of the French *Académie des Sciences*. They were also evident, strangely in an even more comprehensive way, in many of the activities and motives of early members of the Royal Society of London. These communal and overt efforts to discover and assemble knowledge, and, hopefully, to unite it in valid methods of discovery, together with the prevalent assumption of an essential relatedness between branches of knowledge, all of these rather official activities and beliefs, eventually culminated in the proposed system of cross references of the encyclopaedia edited by Diderot and d'Alembert.[53]

In whatever way it began, Leonardo's universality came to be expressed in a manner that was almost wholly conceptual. After 1510 he even moved away from his reliance on the platonic analogy between the earth and man; he shifted to a more sophisticated version of it wherein everything was seen to have been perfectly created to perform an infinite

[50] Albert Cohen, *Music in the French Royal Academy of Sciences* (Princeton, 1981), pp. 5–16.

[51] *Ibid.*, p. 5.

[52] *Ibid.*, p. 5; D. P. Walker, *Studies in Musical Science in the Late Renaissance* (London, 1978), pp. 81–122.

[53] R. McRae, *The Problem of the Unity of the Sciences: Bacon to Kant* (Toronto, 1961) pp. 107–22; Peter France, *Diderot* (Oxford, 1983) pp. 50–2, 60–2, 102, 103; M. C. Jacob, *The Radical Enlightenment: Pantheists, Freemasons and Republicans* (London, 1981), pp. 166–8, 256–61; J. N. Shklar, 'Jean d'Alembert and the Rehabilitation of History', *Journal of the History of Ideas*, XLII, no. 4 (Oct.–Dec., 1981), pp. 643, 649–50, 656, 660–1.

variety of actions that were all unified in nature.⁵⁴ As noted above, the popularity of this particular expression of universality extended beyond the period of the Italian Renaissance. While it is true that not all subsequent generations of universalists hoped to hold a conception of the whole world in their own minds, the notional vitality of this ideal certainly overextended the heyday of personal universality. Changing conditions in Western European cultural climes effected dramatic changes in the expression of this ideal. No detailed mapping is possible here; but the decline of the *uomo universale* certainly does not describe the dissolution of the ideal. This is despite acute distractions from the sceptics in the late sixteenth and seventeenth centuries.⁵⁵ In the telling of this story historians can expect to discover many shifts in the concentration of human talents, just as Helli Koenigsberger first suggested, and these were frequently accompanied by related but similarly important shifts in the expression of the fundamental ideal of universality.

⁵⁴ Kemp, *Leonardo da Vinci*, pp. 261, 317; D. Koenigsberger, *Renaissance Man*, pp. 58–9, 119.
⁵⁵ *Ibid.*, p. 236.

BIBLIOGRAPHY
OF THE WRITINGS OF
HELMUT GEORG KOENIGSBERGER

BOOKS

Co-editor with Brigitta Oestreich of *Neostoicism and the early modern state* by Gerhard Oestreich, trans. David McLintock (Cambridge, 1982) (Cambridge Studies in Early Modern History.)

Luther: A Profile, Introduction and edition (New York and London, 1973) (World Profiles)

The Diversity of History: Essays in Honour of Sir Herbert Butterfield, co-editor with J. H. Elliott (London and Ithaca, 1970)

The Habsburgs and Europe 1516–1660 (Ithaca, 1971). Chapters originally written for *New Cambridge Modern History*, vols. II and III, and for *The Age of Expansion*, ed. H. R. Trevor-Roper (London and New York, 1968). This latter also in French and German translations.

Estates and Revolutions: Essays in Early Modern European History (Ithaca, 1971) (Studies presented to the International Commission for the History of Representative and Parliamentary Institutions XL)

Europe in the Sixteenth Century, co-author with George L. Mosse (London and New York, 1968). Italian translation (Bari, 1969); French translation (Paris, 1970); Spanish translation (Madrid, 1974).

The Practice of Empire (Ithaca, 1969), emended edition of *The Government of Sicily under Philip II of Spain* (London, 1951). Spanish translation published in 1975; Italian translation forthcoming.

Politicians and Virtuosi: Essays in Early Modern History (London and Ronceverte, W. Va.: Hambledon Press, 1986)

ARTICLES

'Formen und Tendenzen des europäischen Ständewesens im 16. und 17. Jahrhundert,' in *Ständetum und Staatsbildung im Brandenburg-Preussen*, eds. O. Büsch and P. Baumgart. Historische Kommission zu Berlin Bd. 55. 1983

'Orange, Granvelle and Philip II, BMGN, 99 (1984) no. 4, pp. 573–95

305

Bibliography

'Warum wurden di Generalstaaten der Niederlande im 16. Jahrhundert revolutionär?' *Das römisch–deutsche Reich im impolitischen System Karls V*, Heinrich Lutz, Schriften des Historischen Kollegs, Kolloquien (Munich and Vienna, 1982), pp. 239–52

'Charles V' with G. Parker, Sussex Tapes, Wiltshire, 1982.

'Diskussionsbericht: Die bedingten Erbreiche,' in *Der dynastische Fürstenstaat*, ed. J. Kunisch and H. Neuhaus (Berlin, 1982)

'I parlamenti in Europa e in Italia nell'età moderna,' in *La rappresentanza nelle istituzioni e nelle dottrine moderne*, ed. C. Carini, Florence 1986

'Die Krise des 17. Jahrhunderts,' *Zeitschrift für Historische Forschung* IX, no. 2 (1982)

'Science and Religion in Early Modern European History,' in S. Drescher et al, eds. *Political Symbolism in Modern Europe* (New Brunswick and London, 1982)

'Wissenschaft und Religion in der frühmodernen europäischen Geschichte,' in *Wissenschaft als historisches Problem*, ed. K.–G. Faber (Stuttgart, 1977)

'Why did the States General of the Netherlands become revolutionary?' in *Parliaments, Estates and Representation*, II, no. 2, 1982

'Republics and Courts in Italian and European Culture in the Sixteenth and Seventeenth Centuries,' *Past and Present*, no, 83, May 1979

'The Italian Parliaments from their Origins to the End of the 18th Century,' *The Journal of Italian History*, I, no. 1, Spring 1978

'Monarchies and Parliaments in Early Modern Europe – Dominium Regale or Dominium Politicum et Regale,' *Theory and Society*, v, no. 2 (1978)

Dominium regale or dominium politicum et regale. Monarchies and Parliaments in Early Modern Europe. Inaugural Lecture in the Chair of History at University of London King's College 1975 and in *Der moderne Parlamentarismus und seine Grundlagen in der ständischen Repräsentation*, ed. K. Bosl and K. Möckl (Berlin, 1977)

'National Consciousness in Early Modern Spain,' O. Ranum, ed. *National Consciousness, History and Political Culture in Early Modern Europe* (Baltimore and London, 1975)

'Introduction,' *The Massacres of Saint Bartholomew*, ed. A. Soman (The Hague, 1975)

'The History of Spain 1479–1700,' greatly expanded and completely rewritten article for the *Encyclopaedia Britannica*, 1974

Twelve articles on Spanish history and biography in the *Encyclopaedia Britannica*, 1960s

'Revolutionary Conclusions,' Review article in *History*, LVII, October 1971

'Great Britain and the Thirty Years' War,' in *History of the English-Speaking Peoples*, no. 45 (London, 1970)

'The Unity of the Church and the Reformation,' *Journal of Interdisciplinary History*, I, no. 3, 1971

'The Statecraft of Philip II of Spain,' *European Studies Review*, I, no. 1, 1971. Spanish version in *Revista d'Occidente*, no. 197, 1972

Bibliography

'Music and Religion in Modern European History,' in *The Diversity of History* (1970). Partly in German translation in *Wiener Beiträge zur Geschichte der Neuzeit*, 8, 1981

'The Student of History in School and University,' *University of Nottingham Bulletin*, no. 37, 1961

SOME RECENT REVIEWS

Y. Bercé, *Revolts and Revolutions in Modern Europe*, *Journal of Modern History*, LV, no. 1, 1983

A. Hess, *The Forgotten Frontier – A History of the 16th Century Ibero-African Frontier*, *International Journal of Middle East Studies*, XII, no. 1, 1980

R. Vierhaus, *Treaties, Elections, Fundamental Laws*, History, LXIV, no. 210, 1979

H. Trevor-Roper, *Princes and Artists. Patronage and Ideology at Four Habsburg Courts, 1517–1633* History, LXIII, no. 207, 1978

P. Pierson, *Philip II of Spain*, *American Historical Review*, LXXXII, no. 4, 1977

W. Hubatsch, *Frederick the Great of Prussia. Absolutism and Administration*, *American Historical Review*, LXXXII, no. 4, 1977

M. Alvarez, *Charles V. Elected Emperor and Hereditary Ruler*, *American Historical Review*, LXXXII, no. 4, 1977

M. Biskup, *State Documents of Royal Prussia*, *Slavonic and East European Review*, LV, no. 1, 1977

A. Myers, *Parliaments and Estates in Europe to 1789*, History, LXI, no. 203, 1976

H. J. Hillerbrand, *World of Reformation*, History, LXI, no. 202, 1976

G. Catalano, *Legazia-Apostolica of Silicy*, *Journal of Modern History*, XLVIII, no. 1, 1976

D. L. Jensen, *Confrontation at Worms*, History, LX, no. 200, 1975

N. M. Sutherland, *The Massacre of St. Bartholomew and the European Conflict, 1559–1572*, *Catholic Historical Review*, LXI, no. 1, 1975

A. Ryder, *The Kingdom of Naples under Alfonso the Magnanimous. The Making of a Modern State*, *Journal of Modern History*, L, no. 4, 1978

Lawrence Stone, *The Causes of the English Revolution, 1529–1642*, *Journal of Modern History*, XLVI, 1. 1974 (Early Modern Revolutions: An Exchange)

FORTHCOMING

History of Europe, 400–1789 (Longmans and Open Court, 1986), vol. I, *Medieval Europe*, vol. II, *Early Modern Europe*, 1986 (vol III, 1789–present, by Asa Briggs).

Republiken und Republikanismus in der frühen Neuzeit; Republics and Republicanism in early modern Europe, Eds H. G. Koenigsberger & Elisabeth Müller-Luckner (Munich: Oldenbourg, 1986/7).

INDEX

Absolutism 113, 154, 254–58, 262–63,
    265, 268;
  fear of 252
  French 253, 255, 271
  anti-absolutism 268
Académie des Sciences 302
Accolti, Benedetto 143–44
aesthetics 279
Affaire des Placcards 77
Africa 145
aggression 142
Aitzema, Foppe van 171
Aitzema, Lieuwe van 169–82
Åkerhielm, Samuel 107
Alamanni, Piero 45, 50
Alba, Duke of 14–15, 92
Alberti, Leandro 223, 288
Alcázar 7, 11, 16
Alchemy 236, 260, 270
Alençon, Duke of 94
Alexander 38
allegory 64, 70–72, 80–83; *see* myth
almanacs 232
Alva, Duke of *see* Alba
ancients 281; *see also* paganism
American Revolution 25
Amsterdam 179, 268, 275
Ancien Régime 95
Andorre 98
Anglican church 63, 197, 215–16, 225,
    243
  Latitudinarian 246
Anna of Saxony 89
Anne, Queen of England 104
Antichrist 209
anticlerical 200–01, 253
Antoine of Burgundy 95–96
Antwerp 91–92, 96–99
Apocalypse 56, 262, 270; *see* millenarian
Apology, Orange's 85–87

Apostles 124–25
Appleby, Joyce 245
Aragona, Alfonso d', duca di Calabria 48
Aragona, Eleanora d' 52
Aragona, Ferrante d', King of Naples 32,
    52, 55
Aranjuez 17–18
architecture 279–80, 294
Arezzo 120
Aristocracy 63, 67, 72, 89, 91, 247, 262
  of Spain 14, 17–19, 33, 52
  of France 163–65
  of the Netherlands 175
  of Brabant 95–99
Aristotle 123–30, 138, 143
armies 35, 75, 91
Arminians 178–79, 264
artisans 175, 237, 247, 273
art and the arts 1, 3, 34, 47–49, 210, 288,
    297, 300
d'Asfeld, Abbé 115
d'Asfeld, Bidal 115, 116
Asia 145
assassination 32, 89
Assemblies 165, 176; *see* Estates
astrology 232–33, 270
astronomy 239
atheism 67, 260, 267, 269
atomism 276, 280, 283
Augustine, Saint 124
Augustus, Roman Emperor 40
Austria 95
auto de fé 10
d'Avaux, Jean Antoine de Mesme, Conte
    105–06

Bacon, Francis 234–37, 241, 265, 280–84,
    301
balance of power 30, 45, 110
Ban, Jan Albert 281

Index

banking 31, 47, 49
Barbadoro, Donato 133, 135
Barbaro, Ermolao 50
Barbaro, Francesco 126
Barberini (family) 224
Barcelona 10
Bartolomeo da Montepulciano 126
Basel, city of 190, 216
Bassompierre 14
baths 50, 150
  bathing (Protestant) 123
Bayle, Pierre 182, 252, 260
beauty 69, 70, 72, 78–83
Becchi, Gentile 41
beds 9, 74
Beeckman, Isaac 3, 273–84, 302
Bekker, Balthazar 252, 260–61, 267
Bembo, Cardinal 200
Beggars, the 90–92, 99
Bellay, Joachim de 70
Benedetti 275
Benedictines 99
Bensimon, Marc 65
Bern 196
Bertaut, François 13
Beza, Theodore 191, 193
Bible *see* Scriptures
Bielke, Count Nils 101–17
Bielke, Count Sten 110
Blathwayt, William 107
Bois-le-Duc 96–99
Bluhm, Heinz 207
Bodin, Jean 162
Boniface IX, Pope 121
Bonne Espérance, monastery in Brabant
  97
books 51, 64, 77, 103, 170, 200–01, 208,
  210, 252, 258
Borromeo, Carlo 228
Botticelli, Sandro 49
Bourbons, dynasty 11
bourgeoisie 62, 99, 175, 189, 192–93,
  195, 201, 256 n. 11, 268
  middle orders of society 200
Boyle, Robert 234, 243, 249, 264, 266
Brabant 2
  Estates of 95–100
Brandenburg 112, 115
  Elector of 114
Brandolini, Lippo 40
Braun, Christian 115
Breda, town of 97
Brederode 92
Bremen 113
bribery 101, 105, 171; and extortion 161;
  see corruption

Brill, capture of 93
Brownists 180
Brunel, Antoine de 13
Brunelleschi, Filippo 288
Bruni, Leonardo 119–20, 122, 131,
  135–36
Bruno, Giordano 259, 269, 286, 300
Brussels, city 15, 90–91, 97–99
Bucer, Martin 184
Buen Retiro, palace of 20, 22–23
bugbears *see* clergy
Burckard, Johannis 55–56
Burgundy 9, 15–16, 123
Burlamaqui 257
Bush, J. N. D. 237

Caen 274
Caesar 38, 73–74, 78, 80, 136, 139
Calabria, Duke of 48
Calais 60, 255
calling 190, 247
  Beruf 211
Calvin, John 3, 178, 184, 186, 193
Calvinism 89, 91–92, 170, 178, 197, 252,
  265, 273; *see also* Protestantism
  consistory in 187
  organization of 198
  and rationalism 260–61
Cambrai, Bishop of 98
Cambridge 260, 264, 267
Cambron, monastery in Brabant 97
Campanella, Tommaso 223, 239–40, 246,
  248
Canons of St. Augustine, in Brabant 99
capitalism 234–35, 245, 259, 260, 299
Capp, Bernard 232–33
Cappel, Jacques 161
Carafa, Oliviero, Cardinal 49
Cardano, G. 300
Caribbean 255
Carlos II, of Spain 13, 23, 92
Carolingian 99
Carrillo, Alonso 20
Carthusians, in Brabant 99
Castiglione 64, 68, 200
Castile 9–10, 15–17, 19, 21
  Council of 12
Cateau-Cambrésis, treaty of 86
Catholic League 2, 77
Cats, Jacob 179
de Caus, Saloman 281
censorship 77, 170, 265, 287 n.
ceremony, at court 5, 17–18, 19, 24, 161
Chamberlayne, Edward 247
Chancellor of Brabant 97
chapters, diocesan (in Brabant) 99

Index

Charles I, of England 5, 9, 12, 22, 176–77, 255
Charles II, of England 177
Charles II, of Spain see Carlos
Charles V, Emperor and Duke of Brabant 9, 14, 16, 23, 60, 61, 77, 89, 95–96, 155, 158, 160, 161
Charles VIII, of France 35–36, 56
Charles X, of Sweden 111
Charles XI, of Sweden 106–07, 110–15, 117
Charles XII, of Sweden 104–05, 113–14, 116
Charles the Bold, Duke of Burgundy and Brabant 95
Chenu, Jean 218
Chièvres, Councillor 61
children 116, 129, 134, 159, 171
  catechism of 188
chivalry 59, 61, 110
Choppin, René 162
Christian, King of Denmark and Sweden 49, 177
Christina of Lorraine 89
Church, Roman Catholic 10, 51, 91, 124, 133, 169, 178, 180, 239
  bishops of 98
  convent of 99
  Jesuits and 264; see clergy
Ciampoli, Giovanni 239
Cibo, Franceschetto 46
ciphers 105–09, 171
Cistercians in Brabant 99
cities 18, 92, 127, 140, 145, 158, 183, 190, 194, 231
  in city-state 141, 185
  and urban republic 195, 197–98
  of Brabant 95–98
citizenship 189, 194
Clarendon, Earl of 147
Clemente, Claudio 11
clergy 99, 158, 178, 180, 203, 206, 212, 232, 239, 243, 247, 252–54, 264–65, 271;
  see Church, Roman Catholic
  in Geneva 186, 194–96
  bishops 98–99, 188, 191, 197, 200, 206
  defrocked 260
  Benedictines 99
  secular, in Brabant 99
Clouet, Jean 60
Cochlaeus 207
Colegio Imperial 20
Colet, Jean 203
Coleti, Nicolo 219
Coligny, Count of 92–93

Cologne 258
collecting 21, 37, 49
commerce 46, 243
Comte, Auguste 199
Condé, Prince of 92
Congress of Ryswick 113
Constantinople 49
Constitutions 184, 198, 265
  in French 153–68
  and Public Law 155, 157–65
  and Law of Inalienability 157–62
constitutionalism 154, 157–63, 183, 190
contract theory 254
Copernicus 238–39
Cornwallis, Sir Charles 18
corporations, in Brabant 97–98
corruption 101, 129, 177–78, 201, 257, 260
  and decadence 285–89, 299–303
Council of Constance 123
Council of Ten 44, 48
Counter-Reformation 23, 232, 240, 248, 286
coup see revolution
Court 62, 67, 71, 74, 77–78, 287
  of Spain 5–24
  in early modern Europe 6, 9, 23
  see festivals
courtiers 66–68, 81, 103, 200
crisis 163;
  of European consciousness 3, 251 et seq.
  of Italy 36, 42, 58
Cromwell, Oliver 169, 176, 259
cults 126, 203, 205
culture 62, 65, 78; popular 3, 252; high 231 et seq.
custom (France) 155

Danckelmann 114
Dante 298
death 54–57, 89, 124, 289–90
decadence see corruption
Dee, John 233
Dei, Bartolomeo 54
deism 247, 271
democracy 252, 255–56
Denmark 112, 115
Descartes, René 253, 259, 261, 265–66, 269, 270, 273–74, 276–77, 282, 286, 302
Deschamps, Eustaches 80
desires see passions
Desprez, Josquin 298
discourse, constitutional (French) 154–55, 157–68

Index

Devotio Moderna 202
Diepolz 108
diplomacy 37, 42, 44, 44–46, 49, 104, 109, 200
  ambassadors 43–44, 61, 74, 107
dissonance 280
Divine intervention 134, 173, 255, 260
doctors 50
Dominicans 99; *see* church
Donation of Constantine 202
Dordrecht 275
drinking (beer) 206–07
Duillier, Fatio de 270
Dury, John 241
dynastic crests, in Brabant 96
dynasticism 73, 95–96

eating 171
Eck, John 208
Edict of Nantes, revocation of 258
education 20, 21, 43, 110–11, 179, 187, 194, 199, 202, 204, 206–07, 210–11, 240, 241–42, 275, 279
Edward IV, of England 9
Egmont, Count of 91, 93
election in Geneva 190, 191
Elias, Norbert 6, 14, 62, 66 n.22, 67 n.22
elites 238, 248
Elizabeth I, of England 197
eloquence 122, 124–25, 138; *see* rhetoric
Empire, Holy Roman 15, 136
  Emperor, Holy Roman 133
encyclopaedia 296, 302
engineers 195, 236, 288, 297, 300
England 3, 69, 71, 76, 198, 248; *see* constitution; revolution; monarchs; Reformation
  parliament 257
English revolution 176–77, 181, 233, 253–55, 258, 263, 265, 271
  restoration 246
Enlightenment 27, 252 *et seq.*
epicureanism 121; *see* materialism
epistemology 292–95, 301
Erasmus 170, 200, 201, 203, 211
Ernst August, Duke of Calenberg 108
Escurial, palace 17, 74
Estates of France 158–59
Estates of Holland 92
Etruscans 134
exorcism *see* witchcraft

Faille, Jean-Charles della 21
Farel, William 184
Faust 286
Febvre, Lucien 62

Ferdinand II, Roman Emperor 9, 12
Ferrara, city 44
festivals 31, 51–54, 62, 71, 76–77, 291; *see* courts
Ficino, Marsilio 37, 39–41, 50, 55, 280, 300
Field of Cloth of Gold 59–83
Fisher, John, Anglican bishop 63
Flemish styles 16
Floreffe, monastery in Brabant 97
Florence 25–58, 85, 119–21, 131, 132, 134, 135, 140, 143, 287; and Council of Ten 44–45, 48; Great Council of 33–34, 36; *reggimento* 53; Signoria 44–45, 47, 55
Foix, Françoise de 76
Fontenelle 268
food 63
force *see* power
foreigners 196
fortification 21
fortune 88, 89, 92, 93, 134, 245, 246
France 2, 10, 69, 71, 75, 89, 110, 153–68, 187, 197; *see* revolution; historiography; monarchs; culture; absolutism; *and* wars of religion
Francis I, of France 2, 59, 69, 70, 73, 74, 77, 157, 160
Francis II, of France 92
Franciscans 99; *see* church
freedom 130, 204; *see* liberty
freemasonry 257–58, 262, 266
freethinkers 255, 259
friendship 60, 69, 120, 140, 274–75, 288
Friesland 170
Fubini, Riccardo 121
Fundamental Law, French *see* constitutions, French
Furly, Benjamin 255, 259

Galilei 238–40, 263, 276, 279, 286, 295, 302
Gallican church 216, 217–18, 224–25
Garampi, Guiseppi 227
Garden of Delights 123
Gassendi, Pierre 274
Gembloux, in Brabant 94, 99
Geneva 184, 187, 192, 196, 197
genius 287–88
Genoa 54
gentry 200, 247
George I, of England 102
Georg Wilhelm, Duke of Celle 108
Germany 1, 92, 123, 171, 180, 216
  and German bishops, innocence of 206

Index

Ghiberti, Lorenzo 288
Ghirlandaio, Domenico 49
Gilbert, Felix 33
Ginzburg, Carlo 240
geometry 3, 289–90, 293, 296–99
gifts 101, 103
God 99, 172, 180, 282, 295, 296–97, 299, 300–01
   and monarchs and politics 41, 47
   and sinners 249
   unmoved Mover 295
   gods 147, 290
   see divine intervention
Godwin, Francis 225
Goethe 300
Golden Age 29, 31, 40, 51, 275
Gomarians 178
Gombrich, Ernst 29
Gramont, Maréchal de 11, 13
de Grassaille, Charles 162
s'Gravesande, William 265
Greece, ancient 49
greed 126
Greek 194, 207, 210
Grégoire, Pierre 162
Gueudeville, N. 256, 261
Guicciardini, Francesco 2, 27, 35–36, 41, 50, 55, 200; his *History of Italy* 36, 39; his *Storie fiorentine* 36, 39
guilds 120
Guise, Duke of 90
Guzmán, family of 19
Guzzone, Boccolino of Osimo 46
Gyldenstolpe, Baron Nils 107
Gyllenstierna, Nils 114

Hague, The 171, 256
Hanover 109, 112, 115
Hapsburgs, dynasty 5, 96
harmony 281, 289–90, 292, 294–95
Haro, Don Luis de 19, 21
Harrington, James 265
Hartlib, Samuel 241
Hastfer, Count John 107
hats 13, 15
Hazard, Paul 3, 251 *et seq.*
Hebrew 123, 179, 194, 207, 210 (includes Hebrews), 268, 285
Heidelberg 196
Henrietta Maria, of England 12
Henry II, of France 86, 92, 162, 163
Henry IV, of France 162
Henry VIII, of England 59, 60, 69, 70, 74
Herbert, George 212
Herbert of Cherbury, Lord 5

heresy 90, 125–26, 150, 239, 252, 253
Heyden, John 233
Hill, Christopher 233, 264
Hirschman, Albert 234, 238
historiography, French 153–57, 163–65, 168; *see also* Jean du Tillet
history (the discipline) 22, 25, 27, 36, 38, 41, 42, 57, 58, 61, 66, 87, 106, 121, 125, 132, 134, 136–38, 140, 150, 155, 163, 167, 172, 182, 201, 205, 211, 226, 234, 251, 253, 262, 288, 290, 296; *see* Poggio
Hobbes, Thomas 182, 254
Holbein 59
Holland, Estates of 92
Holstein-Gottorp, Duke of 112
holy pretence 174
homosexuality 67, 270
honor 46
Hooker, Richard 197
Horn, Count of 91, 93
Horn, Eva 111
horses 37–38
Hortensius, Martin 274
Hotman, François 162
House of Burgundy 96
Huguenots 93, 255–58, 265
humanism 28, 39, 41, 43, 44, 50, 52, 64, 68, 121, 123, 138, 151, 199, 200, 201, 205, 207, 208, 210, 235, 237, 281, 289, 292–96, 301–02
Hundred Years' War 76
Hus, Jan 124, 172

iconoclasm 91, 92
idiot (wise fool) 292–96
impostors 26, 259
individual, the 127, 128, 134, 151
   individualism 199, 207
   see Renaissance
indulgence 205; *see* corruption
inheritance 194
innate powers (of mind) 293–96
inner light 206
Innocent VIII 46–47
Inquisition, the 86, 89, 181
interests, *see* passions
International Commission for the History of Representative and Parliamentary Institutions 1, 183
intonation (music) 284
Islam 10
Italy 28, 30, 36, 42, 45, 51, 129, 136, 145, 200, 238, 285
   and wars 33–36
   invasion of 35

Italy (*cont.*)
  liberal Catholics in 264
  see Renaissance

James I, of England 197
James II, of England 258
Jansen, Cornelius 11
Jaquéray 94
Jean II, of France 163
Jean IV, of Burgundy, Duke of Brabant 95–96
Jeanne, Duchess of Brabant 95
Jerome of Prague 123–25, 150; *see* nudity
Jessée, Jean de la 67
Jesuits 75 n.43
Jesus 259, 261
Jews *see* Hebrews
Joanna, of Spain 16
Joseph, George 69
Joyous Entrance, in Brabant 95–96
Juan of Austria, Don 94
Judaism 10
Jurieu, Pierre 258
justice 137, 138, 144, 147, 185
justification by faith 199, 203

Kant, Emmanuel 301
Kepler, Johannes 282–83
kings 71; *see* monarchs
Knowles, David 217
Koenigsberger, H. G. 6, 18, 67 n.23, 71, 90 n.12, 183, 251, 285–87, 303; and civilizing graduate students 4

Lanciola 120
Landino, Cristoforo 50
Landucci, Luca 52, 55–56
Lanfredini, Giovanni 45–46
Latin (language) 21, 139, 201, 207, 273
law courts 70, 136, 137
  laws 120, 121, 128, 138, 139, 140, 141, 143, 144, 146, 147, 148, 161, 172, 184, 185, 194; *see* Roman law; French public law 155
lawyers 195, 200
Le Clerc, Jean 264
Lefevre d'Etaples 275
Leganés, Count of 21
Leibniz, G. 263
Leiden (city) 196, 227, 267, 273–74
Leipzig disputations 208
Lerma, Duke of 8, 9, 18, 19
Leo X 37–39
Leonardo da Vinci 285, 287–301, 303
Leopold I, Roman Emperor 108, 111, 112

Le Paige, Louis-Adrien 153
Lescaille, Jean 70
lèse-majesté 161
Levellers 255
Levier, Charles 259
Libertines, sect of 196
libertines 261, 270
liberty 57, 94, 133–35, 143, 174, 205, 236, 269
Liège, bishopric 98
Lierre 96
Lillieroot, Nils 107; *see* ambassadors
Limbourg, duchy 98
Lippi, Filippino 49
Lit de Justice, assembly (France) 3, 153–68
literacy 232, 253
lizard *cum* mini dragon 291
Lizet, Pierre 163, 165
Lobbes (in Brabant) 97
Locke, John 182, 249, 256, 257, 259
Lodi, Peace of (1454) 45
London 10, 270
Loudun 281
Louis IX, of France 163
Louis XIII, of France 19
Louis XIV, of France 2, 6, 13, 23, 53, 74, 102, 105, 110–13, 115, 117, 258, 270, 302; as Anti-Christ 267–68
Louis of Orange 90
Louvain 95, 96, 98
love 48, 60, 61, 69, 70, 72–74, 78, 79, 80, 81, 86, 176, 200, 245, 246
Lucca 135, 141
Luther, Martin 3, 181, 199–213
Lutheranism 89, 180; *see* Protestantism
luxury 31, 51, 63, 80
Lyons 221–22

Maastricht 98
Macfarlane, Alan 233
Machaut, Guillaume de 298
Machiavelli, Niccolò 1, 27, 35, 39, 41, 44, 50, 85, 86, 93–94, 136, 137, 151, 173, 200, 207; *History of Florence* 35, 39; *The Prince* 44
Machiavellism 85–94, 142, 149, 241
Macpherson, C. B. 245
Madrid 5, 7, 8, 10, 13, 17, 18, 23
  treaty of 157, 158, 160
magic 233, 264; *see* astrology; alchemy
magistrates 139, 189, 232, 235, 243, 256, 270
Malebranche 263
des Marez, Guillaume, Belgian historian 96

Index

Margaret of Parma 90–92
Marguerite of Angoulême 68, 83
Marguerite de Valois 70
Marie Antoinette, of France 14
Marignano, battle of 77
maritime powers 112, 115
Marlborough, Duke of 104
Maramaldo, Cardinal 121
Marot, Clément 2, 59–83
Marot, Jean 65, 79
marriage 46, 51, 89, 111, 124, 171, 176, 180, 188
  marriage metaphor 159, 160–62
Marsuppini, Carlo 143
Martini, Francesco 288
martyrs 125
Mary of Burgundy, Duchess of Brabant 16, 95
Mary Tudor, of England 92
Mary, of England (d. 1695) 112
Masi, Bartolomeo 52
materialism 254, 256, 264, 267–69, 300–01
  and pantheism 257
mathematics 233, 239, 275, 282, 284, 289, 296, 297–98, 299
  mathematical instruments 116
Maurice of Nassau, Prince 170
Maximilian, of Austria 16, 95
maxims of the Kingdom, French 158–60, 165
  quod omnes tangit 158
  the King's two bodies 158–59, 162
Mayer, C. A. 66
Mazel, David 257
Mazzuoli, Giovanni di Domenico 38
medicine 103, 121, 144, 259, 274, 294
Medici
  Cosimo di Giovanni de' 39–41, 44
  Codimo I de' 30
  Giovanni di Lorenzo, Cardinal 51
  Giuliano di Piero de' 32, 51
  Lorenzo di Piero 25–58
    L'Altercazione 41
    death of 54–56, 58
    his cultural politics 48–54
    his statecraft 30, 32, 35, 42–51, 53–54
    his patronage 26, 29–30, 34, 40, 48–49
    portents about 37, 41, 55–56
  Maddalena de' 46
  Piero di Cosimo de' 40, 44
  Piero di Lorenzo de' 35–36, 46, 50, 56
medieval 21, 61, 65, 66, 139, 156, 157, 163, 235
Medina de Las Torres, Duke of 8
Melanchthon, Philip 206, 216

memory 278–79
Mennonites 178, 181
mentalités 61
merchants 201
Mersenne, Marin 273, 274, 278, 282, 301, 302
metamorphoses 289–96, 299
Michelangelo 288
middle class see bourgeoisie
Milan 45, 50, 120, 133, 135, 294
millenarian 241, 255, 258, 262, 265
Milton, John 177
miracles 37, 53, 55, 134, 270, 290
Moeller, Bernd 183
Mohammed 259
monarchs 7–8, 20, 74, 79, 112, 128, 159, 163, 165–66, 176, 192, 197, 200;
  being pricked 254; and God 23;
  divine right of 252; king-killing 255; king's touch 74; king's two bodies 158, 162; see also beds
money 22, 67, 75, 81, 102, 107, 109, 114, 116, 120, 125, 127, 129, 130, 158, 178, 188, 194, 245, 248
Monterrey, Count of 21
Monteverdi 1
Montmorency, Duke of 90
More, Sir Thomas 75, 256
Moses 124, 125, 147, 175; an imposter 259
Motley, John L. 86, 87 n.6
Mühlber, victory at 15
Muratori 223, 228
music 1, 76, 273–84, 285–86, 298, 302–03; singing 274
mutability 140
mysticism 270
myth 25–32, 41, 44, 55, 56–58, 71–74, 76, 78, 81–83, 124, 149, 244–45

Naples 32, 37, 45, 48, 120, 132, 133
  Ferrante, King of 32, 55
Nassau, William of see Orange
natural law 252
natural philosophy, see science
naturalism 150, 254; nature 288, 290–95, 301, 303
Naudé, Gabriel 222
Neoplatonism 31, 37, 40, 42, 55, 64, 73, 76, 83, 233, 264, 267, 292–95, 302;
  Augustinian 294
nepotism 194
Netherlands, The 2, 15, 85, 90, 92, 107, 112, 170, 255, 257, 258, 267; see States General
New England 255, 258

Newton, Isaac 252, 253, 260, 261, 264, 267, 270, 280
Newtonian 234
Niccoli, Niccolò 123, 128
Nicholas of Cusa 292–93, 295–97, 300–01
Nienberg 108
Nine Years' War 104–06, 109, 112
Nivelles, convent and city 99
nobility (the virtue of) 128, 130, 144, 151, 158; *see* aristocracy
nominalism 122, 202
Norbertins, in Brabant 99
nudity 123
Nuñez de Castro, Alonso 7, 24

oligarchy 13, 194, 255, 257, 271
Olivares, Count-Duke of 8, 9, 14, 19, 20–23
Olivekrans, Johan 107
Olivier, François 163
Oosterweel 92
Orange, William of Nassau, Prince of 2, 85–94, 173
orators *see* rhetoric, art of
order and stability 33, 179, 235, 237, 244, 245, 249; of all things 294
Oresme, Nichole 297–98
Orgel, Stephen 65
Orsini, Roberto 46–47
Orti Oricellari 33, 35, 50
Osuna, Duke of 19
Outre-Meuse 98
Ovid 289
Oxenstierna, Bengt, Count of 107, 110
Oxford 203

Pacioli, Luca 297
paganism 75, 122, 125, 128, 147, 202, 261, 266, 271; and oracles 38; and stoics 124; *see* myth
Palatinate, war of 112
Palazzo Vecchio 34, 36
Palladio 288
pantheism *see* materialism
Papacy 16, 32, 47, 128, 134, 136, 140, 141, 148, 180–81, 200, 202, 203
    Eugene IV 136
    Gregory XI 134, 135
    Innocent VIII 46
    Leo X 37, 38
    Sixtus IV 37, 45, 56
    papal curia 119, 133, 200
    papal states 42, 46
Pardo, the 17
Paris 10, 13, 228
Parker, Matthew 215

Parlement (France) 153, 155, 164
parliamentarians 100
passions 127, 171–74, 179; and interests 234, 238, 245, 254, 257
patriarchy 94
patronage 21, 22, 28, 29, 34, 37, 48, 61, 62, 67, 68, 75, 78, 90, 287–88, 299
Pavia, battle of 77
Pazzi conspiracy 32, 37, 41, 45, 53–54, 57, 58
peace 244
Peace of Lodi 45
Pedretti, Carlo 291
pensions 102, 104, 109, 110, 116, 117
people, the 52–53, 63, 81, 147, 159, 175, 180–81, 192, 197, 203–05, 231–33, 236–39, 240, 246, 247–48, 256–57, 261, 270–71, 278; as peasants 67; superstitions of 252
persecution 124, 247
perspective 298–99
Petrarch, Francesco 31, 40, 48, 79, 122, 125, 150, 292, 294
Petty, William 247
Pico della Mirandola, Giovanni 50
Pierleone of Spoleto 50
Plato 123, 124, 130; Platonism 200–01, 211; *see also* Neo-platonism
Plattes, Gabriel 241
pleasures *see* passions
Philip II, of Spain 5, 14, 17, 19, 23, 71, 74, 86, 89–90, 92, 173
Philip III, of France 163
Philip III, of Spain 11, 13, 17, 19
Philip IV, of France 163
Philip IV, of Spain 5, 7, 8, 10, 11, 13, 19, 20–23
Philip the Fair, Archduke of Austria, Duke of Brabant 16, 95
Philip the Good, Duke of Burgundy and Brabant 95–96
Philippe de Saint-Pol of Brabant 95–96
Pico della Mirandola 50
Pierleone of Spoleto 50
piety 61
Piper, Count Karl 104, 107
Pisa 54
Pitti palace 34, 36
pleasure 123
Pléiade 65
poetry 48, 52, 59, 65–66, 78, 82–83
Poggio Bracciolini 63, 119–52
politeness 103
political discourse 61
political model 198
Poliziano, Angelo 39–40, 50, 52, 55

Index

Pollaiuolo, Antonio da 48
Polus, Thomas 107
polyphony 279
Pomerania 107, 111, 114
popery 246, 247
Popkin, R. H. 182
Povar, Marquis of 14
poverty 99, 188, 232, 236, 242, 247
power 43, 81, 143, 148–52, 172, 174, 192,
    253; and force 133; and separation
    of 163, 167
preference see privilege
Prescott, William 86
price revolution 231–32
Priestley, Joseph 262
priests 71, 123
printer-publishers 200, 211, 231, 299
printing 204, 209, 216–17, 219–22, 258,
    265; printing press 232
privilege 15, 89, 94, 163, 174, 177, 257
propaganda 44, 52, 75, 211, 258
prophecy 56, 262, 291
prosperity 238
prostitution 260–61
Protestantism 10, 67, 86, 89, 90, 183,
    184, 202; see Calvinism; Lutheranism
prudence 24, 82
public behavior 128
public law, French see constitutions,
    French
Public Record Office, State Papers,
    Sweden 106
Puritans 62, 180–81, 197
Pythagoreans 285

Quakers 178, 181, 255, 259, 265
Quarters, of Brabant 99; see corporations
Quevedo, Francisco de 23

Rachfahl, Felix 87
radical sectaries 209, 233, 243, 265, 270
    Diggers 255
    Levellers 255
    Waldensians 210
reading 204
reason 237, 246, 252
reason of state 61, 172
rebellions 175, 235, 236, 239, 246, 249,
    253
reform (of state and institutions) 16, 53,
    201, 228; of learning 238
reformation of manners 235
Reformation, Protestant 180, 185, 211,
    215, 231, 241, 243, 246, 267, 301; see
    also Luther; Calvin; Calvinism
Regency in Brabant 96

reggimento 53
republic of letters 255, 258
religion 1, 23, 179–80; and ceremonies
    10–11
Rembrandt 211
Renaissance 25–61, 65, 67 n.22, 77, 200,
    210, 280–81, 288, 303
    individualism 31, 244
    see humanism
representative government 158, 183–85,
    188, 190, 192–93 (in Geneva), 197
republicanism 33, 34, 45, 131, 132, 135,
    136, 138, 142–45, 174, 176, 252, 255
reputation 43
Requesens 93
revolution 36, 62, 87, 90, 92, 96, 211,
    246, 252
    revolution of 1688–89 112
    in France 154, 251, 253, 256, 257
    in Geneva 185
    in the Netherlands 173
    see English revolution
rhetoric, art of 39, 52, 55, 59, 65, 130,
    155, 165, 167, 172, 192, 193, 209,
    237, 238, 244, 281, 293
rhetoric, epideictic 28, 39–42
Riario, Raffaele, Cardinal 53
Richelieu 19
riddles 291–92
Rinaldo degli Albizzi 135
ritual, ceremonial 13, 153–68, 161–62
Rome 46, 49, 55, 140, 221–2; emperors
    of 25, 136, 145; republic of 132, 134
    and n.63, 147; law of 137, 139,
    144–46, 148, 149
Ronsard 67
Roscoe, William 28
Rossi, Paolo 236
Rotterdam 255, 266
Rousset de Missy, Jean 257, 259
royal séance (France) 153–68
Royal Society 234, 242, 243, 245, 247–49,
    264, 302
Rubini, Riccardo 121
Rucellai, Bernardo 33, 35–36, 50

Sacramori, Sacramoro 43–44
saints 179; see mad saints 206
St. Bartholomew's Day massacre 93
St. Bernard 208
St. Giovanni 52
St. Michael 59
St. Paul 199, 200, 203, 206
Saint-Simon 6, 11, 13
St. Trond, city and monastery 97–98
Salmasius 177

Index

Salutati 119–22, 137, 144, 149, 150
salvation 32, 199, 246, 249, 260
San Bernardino of Siena 126
San Marco 30
Sandoval, family of 19
Santiago, Archbishop of 7
Sarzana 54
Sauch, de la 61
Savonarola, Girolamo 31, 33, 56–57
Savoy 196
Saxony 112, 115
Scala, Bartolomeo 41
Scanian War 111
scepticism 121, 182, 261, 266, 303
Scève, Maurice 65
Schiller, F. 86
scholasticism 200, 203, 212, 263, 266,
    268, 295
science 3, 121, 139, 199, 233–34, 235,
    238, 245, 248, 259, 262–63, 268–69,
    274, 278, 284–86, 288, 292, 296, 298,
    300, 302–03; *see* astronomy
scriptures 179, 187, 198, 202–03, 206–07,
    208–09, 243, 258, 270; and
    fund-raisers 205; and science 269
séance, royal, French 155–56
secrecy 19, 101, 105, 108, 114, 116, 163,
    170, 191, 261
sects *see* radical sectaries
Segovia letters 90
self-interest 235, 244
servants 8, 171, 177, 188, 212
Sessa, Duke of 19
Seville 19
sexuality 77
Sforza, family of 45, 48, 49
Shakespeare 59
Sicily 1
Siena 46
Sigismund, Emperor 136
Signoria 120
signs from Heaven (portents) 38, 283; *see*
    miracles
Sigonney, Jean 16
Silvestri, Domenico 133
simony 194; *see* corruption
sin 248–49; *see* Geneva; ambition 245
Sixtus IV 37, 45, 47, 54, 56
Socrates 124, 125, 130, 292
Soderini, Francesco, Cardinal 50
sovereignty 176
Sozzini, Bartolomeo 50
Spain 5–24, 71, 85, 91, 93, 252; *see* court,
    Escorial; revolt against in Calabria 239
Sparta 76
Spinola 170

Spinoza 259, 261, 268–69, 270
sports 17–21, 71, 74, 112
Sprat, Thomas 243
sprezzatura 200
Spufford, Margaret 248
spying 61, 101, 104, 171, 259
Stanhope, James 102
stadholderate 171, 174–76
Staupitz 202
States General 2, 176; *see* Netherlands,
    The
Stenbock, Count 107
Stephens, James 237
Stevin, Simon 279, 282, 284
Stockholm 107, 109, 112
Stoicism 201
Stoics 130
Strasbourg 184, 190
Stuarts 171
Stubbe, Henry 246
Stubbs, Bishop 225
Studio fiorentino 50
Suetonius 37
superimposition 290–91, 293, 298–99
Sweden 2, 105, 112, 115
Sweelinck, Jan 274
Swiss, the 124, 150, 192; *see* baths
symbols 26, 64, 65, 69

Tartini 277
taxation 75, 138, 232, 247; taxes 95–96
technology 242
theatre 7, 19, 22, 23, 172
theologians (and theology) 239, 285–86,
    298
Thirsk, Joan 245
Thirty Years' War 111
Thomson, Mark A. 105, 108 n.20
Thurloe, John 170–71
Tignosi da Foligno, Niccolò 143, 144
du Tillet, Jean 155, 163
Toland, John 255–56, 259, 265, 269
toleration 265
Tott, Klaus 110
Tournai 92
traditions 144
transubstantiation 263–64
treason 114–16, 171
treaties 102, 104, 157–58, 160
Trinkaus, Charles 121, 151
tyranny 33, 56, 57, 94, 96, 135, 141, 143,
    181, 191, 257, 258, 271

Uceda, Duke of 14
Ughelli, Ferdinando 3, 215–30
uniformity 288, 291–97, 299, 301–03

universal man 30, 31, 287–88, 292, 294, 300–03
universities 50, 100, 206, 211, 267–68; in Geneva 187
utopian 238, 245–46, 252, 256, 271
Utrecht 267, 273
Uzzano, Niccolò da 135

Vairasse, Denis 268
Valenciennes 92
Valla, Lorenzo 200, 202
Valladolid 18
Valori, Niccolò 27, 37–39, 41, 55
van Roosbroeck, Robert 87
Vasa, Sigismund, of Poland 110
Vasari, Giorgio 27, 30, 34, 39
Vatican Library 220
Velázquez 22
Venice 45, 49, 120, 131–33, 138, 139
Verhaeren, Everard 273
vernacular 201
Verrocchio, Andrea 49
Versailles 6, 12, 23, 53, 74
Vettorelli, Andrea 220
Vienna 9, 12, 15, 23, 115
Villon, François 81
Vilorde, city in Brabant 96
Viret, Pierre 184
virtù 88, 93–94
virtue 127, 128, 130, 138
Visconti, Giangaleazzo 131–32
Visconti, Giovanni 120, 132
Voetius 267
Voltaire 27, 201, 264, 271
von Hutten, Ulrich 207
voting 195

de Waard, Cornelius 273
Wallenstedt, Count 104, 107
war and war-making 54, 59, 60, 71, 76, 77, 80, 89, 111, 112, 120, 133–35, 148, 203

wars of religion, French 67, 77, 89, 258
Washington, George 25–26
Watson, Robert 22
wealth *see* money
Wedgwood, C. V. 87
Weems, Parson 25–26
Wells, H. G. 199
Whitehall 110
Whigs 256, 259
Wilkins, John 243
William III, of England 105, 108, 112–14, 265
William of Orange *see* Orange
Winstanley, Gerrard 255
wisdom 30
witchcraft 261, 270, 281
Witt, John de 171
Wittenberg 206
Wittrock, Georg 114
Wolsey, Cardinal 75
women 8, 55, 62, 71, 73, 77, 81, 97, 99, 103, 124, 134, 147, 171, 175, 189, 192, 204, 211, 231, 239
debauching 178
in convents 99
work 233; *see* artisans
Wrede, Count Fabian 107
Wren, Sir Christopher 243–46, 248

Yates, Frances 64, 239 n.28, 301 n.
Year of Wonders (1566–7) 89–91

Zarlino 282
Zeeland 92, 174
Zeno 124
Zúñiga, family of 19
Zurich 123, 184
Zweibrücken (Deux-Ponts) 113
Zwingli, Ulrich 184, 200